THE SCHWEICH LECTURES ON
BIBLICAL ARCHAEOLOGY, 1925

THE RELIGION OF ANCIENT PALESTINE IN THE LIGHT OF ARCHAEOLOGY

THE GOD OF BETH-SHAN

THE RELIGION OF ANCIENT PALESTINE IN THE LIGHT OF ARCHAEOLOGY

BY

STANLEY A. COOK, M.A., Litt.D.

FELLOW OF GONVILLE AND CAIUS COLLEGE, CAMBRIDGE
UNIVERSITY LECTURER IN HEBREW AND ARAMAIC

THE SCHWEICH LECTURES
OF THE BRITISH ACADEMY

1925

LONDON
PUBLISHED FOR THE BRITISH ACADEMY
BY HUMPHREY MILFORD, OXFORD UNIVERSITY PRESS
AMEN HOUSE, E.C.
1930

OXFORD UNIVERSITY PRESS

AMEN HOUSE, E.C. 4

LONDON EDINBURGH GLASGOW
LEIPZIG NEW YORK TORONTO
MELBOURNE CAPETOWN BOMBAY
CALCUTTA MADRAS SHANGHAI

HUMPHREY MILFORD

PUBLISHER TO THE
UNIVERSITY

Printed in Great Britain

PREFACE

THE title and subject of this book will recall the inauguration of the *Schweich Lectures* more than twenty years ago, when the late Samuel Rolles Driver gave an account of the contribution of archaeology and the monuments to Biblical study. *Modern Research as illustrating the Bible*, the title of his lectures, was a subject to which that great and many-sided scholar felt himself closely drawn; and neither that book nor any of his other writings on the subject can be ignored to-day in spite of the time that has elapsed. For although much has been done, especially since the War, in adding to our knowledge of Oriental archaeology and in the discussion of problems arising therefrom, Dr. Driver performed lasting service, not only in opening up what to many readers was a new world, but also in setting forth, with his usual completeness and clearness, both the real significance of the new discoveries and the principles to be employed when the Biblical records and the 'external' evidence are inter-related.[1]

When, therefore, I was asked, in 1925, to deliver the *Schweich Lectures*, the suggestion that some account might be given of the work subsequent to 1908 encouraged the wish I had long entertained: to reconsider the religion of Palestine primarily and mainly from the point of view of archaeology. Dr. Driver's *Schweich Lectures* was still one of the most helpful books on the subject; but while it was unnecessary to traverse the ground which he had already covered, I could not take it for granted that my audience would necessarily have any special knowledge of his or any other similar work. Accordingly, I did not hesitate to repeat well-known facts and even to use familiar illus-

---

[1] See the important remarks in his *Introduction to the Literature of the Old Testament*, 8th ed., Preface, pp. xviii sqq.; and *Genesis* (in the Westminster Commentary Series), *Introduction*, pp. xlviii sqq.; also the essay cited below, p. 2, n. 2.

trations which could already be found in his book or elsewhere. I aimed at furnishing a fresh and general survey of
what archaeology was contributing to our knowledge of
Palestinian religion, and, making a fairly extensive survey,
I attempted to show that here was a fascinating field, the
importance of which was hardly realized as it deserved.

For the prolonged delay in the publication of the Lectures I can only offer the sincerest apologies. Their pre-
paration had taken me away from other tasks which had
first claim, and a much more formal treatment proved
necessary if the book was to be worthy of the series. Consequently, although I have adhered to the scheme and
scope of the original Lectures, they have been rewritten,
considerably expanded, and illustrated afresh. The delay
has, however, enabled me to use much new and valuable
material. I need only mention the discoveries at Byblus
and Beisan (Beth-Shan) since 1925, the brilliant articles by
Father Hugues Vincent in the *Revue Biblique* on these and
other excavations, the encyclopaedic volumes on Zeus
(i and ii. 1, 2) by my colleague, Dr. A. B. Cook, which
have so much that appeals to the Orientalist; and, not
least of all, the new edition of Gressmann's admirable
Altorientalische Texte und Bilder zum Alten Testament.

By means of references to these and other works I have
tried to minimize overlapping with standard works and
the repetition of better known illustrations, especially those
contained in other volumes of the *Schweich Lectures.* A
handbook naturally lay far outside my scope, but the
endeavour has been made to provide an introductory
account with notes and references for interested readers.
The mass of material is steadily increasing, and it has not
always been easy to steer between the extremes of a sketch
lacking the references which students need, and the fullness
of detail which ordinary readers find wearisome.[1] As it is,

[1] I attempted the former in *The Religion of Ancient Palestine in the
Second Millennium B.C. in the Light of Archaeology and the Inscriptions* (Con-
stable's *Religions Ancient and Modern,* 1908).

while the latter may freely ignore the innumerable foot-
notes, students, it is hoped, will quickly grasp the method
adopted to facilitate reference to the most frequently cited
works (see Bibliography, p. 231).

The reader will soon discover that in order to illustrate
Biblical beliefs and customs it is frequently necessary to go
outside the land of Israel. After all, the Israelites were only
a small part of a much larger group of closely inter-related
peoples. At the same time, it constantly happens that the
archaeological material from the land itself cannot be
readily interpreted from Biblical or Palestinian sources
alone. Consequently a narrow treatment of the subject is
impossible. But an adequate discussion of the many points
that arise would involve difficult questions of Biblical
Criticism and Comparative Religion, and however essential
they may be for the understanding of the Bible, this was
not the place for them. Hence I have deliberately left on
one side questions of the literary and historical criticism of
the Biblical records, and all theories of the development of
religion, whether within the Bible or in the lands amid
which the Bible grew up. I have allowed the archaeological
evidence—fairly and honestly interpreted, as I believe—to
speak for itself.

To what extent a compilation of this kind is indebted to
others will be evident from the references, and it is a pleasant
duty to make grateful acknowledgement of the courtesy I
have met with on all sides. In particular I would express
my indebtedness to the University of Pennsylvania Museum
and Mr. Alan Rowe for allowing me to make free use of
their remarkably interesting discoveries at Beth-Shan; to
the Louvre, to M. Cumont and M. Dussaud and the
publishers of *Syria* for photographs and permission to use
their articles; to Père Dhorme and Père Vincent of the
École Biblique, Jerusalem, for photographs, and to the
latter especially for information on the mosaic at Ain Duk
(p. 207); to the late Father Orfali for the photograph of
the wheeled coffer at Capernaum; to the American

colony, Jerusalem, for the interesting photograph of the 'Rock'; to the Egyptian Department of the Berlin Museum, to Prof. Dalman, and, above all, to the late Hugo Gressmann, for photographs and kindly help; to Dr. A. B. Cook and the Syndics of the Cambridge University Press for the photographs and blocks specified in their proper place; to Dr. H. R. Hall, Keeper of Egyptian and Assyrian Departments, British Museum, for permission to have photographs of various seals; to Dr. G. F. Hill, Keeper of Coins at the British Museum, and also to the Keeper of Coins at the Fitzwilliam Museum, Cambridge, for casts of coins. I have especially to thank the Palestine Exploration Fund for the loan of numerous blocks without which this book could not have been so fully illustrated. I am also indebted to the British Academy for kindly permitting me to expand the original lectures and publish them in their present form; and here I would like to record my deep appreciation of the friendly interest which the late Secretary, Sir Israel Gollancz, throughout took in the work: to his guidance and suggestions I owed much at every stage. Finally, in the course of passing the sheets and illustrations through the press I have been indebted for much practical advice and help to Mr. John Johnson, Printer to the University, Oxford, and his staff.[1]

STANLEY A. COOK.

July, 1930.

[1] It may be added that a chronological scheme more precise than that on pp. 242–4 divides each of the chief periods into two, and dates the second respectively: Middle Bronze ii, 1800 B.C.; Late Bronze ii, 1400 B.C., and Early Iron ii, 900 B.C.

As English measures are used in this book it may be useful to state that 1 yard = 0·91438 metre, and 1 metre = 39·37079 inches, or roughly 11 yards = 10 metres.

CONTENTS

b

maritime deities, 171. Europa and the bull, 175. Gods of Ammon and Moab, 177. Phanebal of Askalon, 178. Marnas of Gaza, 180. Coins of Samaria, 187. Antiochus IV, Epiphanes, 188. Coins of Jerusalem and the Jews, 190. Greek inscriptions of Kadesh-Naphtali and Hermon, 196. Magical inscriptions at Tell Sandaḥannah, 200. Painted tombs of Marissa; the god Kos, 202. Mosaics, zodiacal and other, 205. Mosaic map of Medeba, 208. Galilean synagogues, 209. Eagle, seal of David, Torah shrine, &c., 212. The great Baals of Syria: Palmyra, 215. Baal-Shamin, Bel, &c., 217. Baal of Heliopolis, 218. Baal of Doliche, 222. Cults at Dura-Europos, 223. Emperor cults; monotheism, &c., 224. Christianity, early archaeological characteristics, 225. Orpheus, 227. Conclusions, individuality of Palestinian archaeology, 229.

MAPS

LIST OF PLATES

THE RELIGION OF ANCIENT PALESTINE IN THE LIGHT OF ARCHAEOLOGY

CHAPTER I

MISCELLANEOUS EXAMPLES

MODERN research has profoundly changed old ideas of the distant past, and has brought many new problems touching the development of ancient history and religion. In these the Bible naturally holds—and will always hold—the first place, and the task of Biblical study is essentially that of placing the Book in the light of the continuously increasing store of knowledge which exploration and excavation have accumulated. Indeed, there is to-day a certain tendency to ascribe greater value to the 'external' evidence, that is, to the results of excavations, and to the monuments, and to topographical survey, than to the Biblical narratives themselves. For this two reasons can be found. In the first place, there are some radical differences of opinion regarding the Biblical records of the history and religion of the Hebrews or Israelites ; and further, the conviction prevails that the last word must always lie with the ancient and contemporary data from the Bible-lands themselves.

Accordingly, besides the more 'internal' and intensive study of the Bible, attention is now directed, and in increasing degree, to the 'external' evidence of the lands wherein the Bible arose; and in these pages we shall leave on one side 'Biblical criticism', and the problems arising out of the written documents, in order that the external data, the importance of which cannot be over-estimated, may be approached and interpreted without reference to any presupposition or prejudice.

By 'archaeology' is here meant 'the science of the treatment of the material remains of the human past'—of all, in fact, that belongs to 'unwritten history'. There is an obvious contrast between written records, compiled and preserved intentionally, and the more disjointed and miscellaneous fragments of archaeology, which are without the continuity that is the essence of history.[1] On the other hand, the contrast between the apparently plain testimony of the unwritten remains and the methods adopted by fallible and apparently 'tendentious' scholars in the study of the records of ancient writers who were no less open to error, has been unduly exaggerated. 'An inch of potsherd is worth all Herodotus'—it has been said. But the contrast that is often drawn between 'archaeology' and 'criticism' is a misleading one; and it is a mistake to suppose that archaeology is the purely objective study of 'facts' and the literary and historical 'criticism' of written records some purely subjective exercise in theoretical reasoning.[2] When experts are seen to differ, as they do, as to whether archaeology 'proves' or 'disproves' certain views, or supports or refutes certain methods, the first important fact which has to be grasped is that archaeology has placed the study of ancient history and religion in an entirely new light, and has raised questions the answers to which often cannot be easily found.

In these pages we can do little more than touch upon a number of points in order to suggest what archaeology has to contribute to our knowledge of the religion of Palestine. Thus, it is well known that Palestinian archaeology throws direct light upon the use of magic, the prevalence of false weights, human sacrifice, and so on. But often enough it is outside Palestine that we have to look for illustrations to the Bible, e. g. the overshadowing wings of the god, the meal 'before the god', the enemy as one's 'footstool'. Again, the archaeology of Palestine and of its immediate neighbours often leads us outside Biblical evi-

[1] See especially A. A. Bevan, *Cambridge Biblical Essays* (ed. Swete, 1909), p. 3 sq.

[2] See D. G. Hogarth in *Authority and Archaeology, Sacred and Profane* (p. ix, on the nature of archaeology).

dence, notably as regards the beliefs concerning life and death; and frequently we have to determine how our archaeological evidence is to be interpreted, whether, for example, the Egyptian 'sign of life (*ankh*)' found upon Palestinian objects had any meaning for the people, and if so what ideas were associated with it.

Unfortunately, from the archaeological point of view, Palestine is relatively poor; but, as we shall see, the land cannot be severed, archaeologically speaking, from its environment. Moreover, there have been fewer of the 'spectacular' discoveries that from time to time are made in Egypt or in Babylonia. But it has to be remembered that the innumerable minor objects, even the less imposing discoveries of walls or tombs, all have their meaning, and lead in due course to important results. Best known is the fact that archaeological research was set upon a scientific basis in 1890 through the discovery by Sir Flinders Petrie at Tell el-Ḥesy, or Lachish, in South Palestine that the apparently valueless pottery sherds were the surest criteria for determining the relative age of strata: 'a knowledge of pottery is really the essential key to all archaeological research'.[1] But nothing is negligible. Whether it be the frequency and distribution of some very ordinary type of pottery, or the patterns on dresses or on lamps, the spokes of wheels, men's beards and the rest of their toilet, humped cattle—all of these tell their own story. The discovery in Susa of fragments of alabaster vases with Hebrew writing, among debris of the seventh century B. C., arouses speculation as to the cause of their presence at so early a date and in so distant a land.[2] Again, in Syria have been found

[1] Petrie, *Q.S.* (*Quarterly Statements*) *of the Palestine Exploration Fund*, 1891, p. 68. See his statement, *Q.S.*, 1890, p. 143 (and, in the first instance, his *Tell el-Hesy*, p. 40), and cf. the remarks by Father Vincent, *Canaan d'après l'Exploration Récente* (1907), p. 301. For a criticism of pottery criteria, see especially H. Frankfort, *Studies in Early Pottery of the Near East*, i (1924), ch. i. It should be mentioned that the identification of the *site* Tell el-Ḥesy with Lachish is disputed (Albright).

[2] Clermont-Ganneau, *Recueil d'Archéologie Orientale*, vii, § 37.

specimens (1) of Greek written from right to left, presumably
under the influence of Semites, and (2) of Syriac letters
written from left to right, presumably under Greek influence;
and though such evidence might seem to be merely curious,
it enables us to realize some of the results when Semites
and Greeks were living together.[1] The data of archaeology
always have *some* meaning—though precisely what may
safely be inferred from each object is often disputable.

Palestine cannot be treated as an isolated land; and by
the religion of Palestine we do not mean precisely the
religion of the Israelites or Jews. Israel (Jacob) and
Edom (Esau) were brother-peoples, and both could claim
close relationship with Moab and Ammon, and more
especially with the Aramaeans of the north, whence the
tribes of Israel derived their 'mothers'.[2] With Phoenicia
and the Levant, with Syria, Mesopotamia, and Asia Minor,
and finally with the tribes of the desert, Palestine was in
close contact. It is true that the more carefully the Bible
is compared with the thought and literature of the lands
in which it grew up, the more impressive are its characteristic religious contents. None the less, it is necessary to
recognize what Palestine as a whole shared with its neigh-

[1] See Bliss-Macalister, *Excavations in Palestine*, 1898–1900, p. 178,
no. 38 (a Rhodian jar-handle, the Greek runs right to left); Lidzbarski,
Ephemeris für Semitische Epigraphik, iii. 182 sq. (a Greek inscription
written boustrophēdon through Arab influence); see also Rendel
Harris, *Z.N.T.W.*, 1914, p. 99 (Greek dates reversed); Littmann, *Z.A.*,
xxxii. 101 n., *Semitic Inscriptions*, p. 7. On a cross with Ω and A in the
reverse order, see Macalister, *A Century of Excavation in Palestine*, p. 252.
The coin which G. Hoffmann read as Phoenician in Greek letters read
in the reverse order (*Zeit. f. Numismat.* ix. 96), is, as Dr. G. F. Hill
informs me, explained to be Armenian in Greek letters (Babelon, *Rois
de Syrie*, p. cxcviii).

[2] The term 'Hebrew' is properly wider than 'Israel' which, in the
time of the divided monarchy, denotes the northern tribes as against
Judah. In these pages the term 'Israel' will be used with special
reference to the Biblical records of the history and religion of the
Israelite tribes, while 'Hebrew' is less exclusive and is not confined to
the Israelite area.

bours if we are to understand what gives it its distinctiveness; and indeed we gain a more accurate and more
impressive conception of the history of Palestinian religion
only when we regard the land, as we must, as an integral
part of the larger area with whose history and religion (or
religions) it was always and intimately bound up.

Viewed physically, Palestine seems small and insignifi-
cant in comparison with the Syrian states of the north. Its
prominent cities (Jerusalem, Jericho, Samaria, &c.) are few
indeed when we consider the Phoenician Tyre, Sidon, and
Byblus, or the Syrian Damascus, Baalbek, Hamath, Aleppo,
Palmyra, Kadesh (on the Orontes), and the many evidently
once important cities which survive only as mounds or
tells. There is nothing more striking, perhaps, than the
contrast between the apparently inconspicuous territory of
the tribes of Israel from Dan to Beersheba, and the
Mediterranean coastlands from Carchemish in the north
to Petra in the south. With Egypt, South Palestine was
always in close touch; and relations between Egypt,
Palestine, and Phoenicia go back at least to the third
millennium B.C. Levantine influence (Aegean or Cretan,
Mycenaean, Cypriote) is especially marked in the second
millennium. What may be called the 'Amarna' age (in
and about the 14th cent. B.C.) was one of internationalism,
when the use of the Akkadian (Babylonian) script and
language, as the vehicle of diplomatic intercourse in
south-west Asia and Egypt, points to the depth—earlier—
of the cultural influence of Babylonia.[1] While Babylonia,
after centuries of relative quiescence, came to the front
again in the sixth century B.C. (properly 612–539 B.C.) at
the downfall of Assyria, the influence of Assyria on the
west during the Hebrew monarchies belongs to the third

---

[1] The 'Amarna age' is that illustrated by the cuneiform tablets
from el-Amarna in Egypt, the city founded by Amenhotep IV (Ikhnaton), and by the art, history, and cultural connexions of *c.* 1450–1350;
broadly speaking this period may be extended to *c.* 1550–1250. See
especially James Baikie, *The Amarna Age* (1926).

and last period of Assyrian history; and it is not yet clear
what influence it was able to exert during the 'Middle
Assyrian' period (i.e. 13th–11th cent. B.C.), or in the more
remote and obscure days of its rise.[1]

The Achaemenid or Persian period, which followed the
Neo-Babylonian, and was brought to an end by the conquests of Alexander the Great, 332–331 B.C., was not pre-
cisely the only one of its kind, for, later, the influence of
Parthians and Sasanians can be at least indirectly traced,
and centuries earlier, in the Amarna period, when the
North Syrian state of Mitanni was related by marriage
with the court of Egypt, names of Mitannian, Iranian, and
cognate affinity are to be found as far south as Jerusalem.
And finally, when Jerusalem itself is said by the prophet
Ezekiel (xvi. 3, 45) to be of partly Amorite and partly
Hittite origin, the tradition recognizes the debt both to
the Semitic Amorites of Syria and Mesopotamia and to the
Hittite and related peoples, whether of the ancient empire
of the second millennium B.C. whose centre was at Boghaz-
keui, or of the later sub-Hittite states in North Syria.[2]
Trade-routes in all directions linked Palestine with the
neighbouring lands, and even the great invasion of
Israelite tribes at the Exodus was not the only conspicuous
occasion when the desert did or could leave its mark upon
the settled inhabitants of the ancient land.

With all these diverse influences there are certain periods
when one or other was stronger than the rest, or when
one or other of the great powers succeeded in giving a
certain homogeneity to the lands over which it ruled. At
the same time, there is, in any case, a certain similarity
of religion throughout Egypt and South-west Asia, not-
withstanding ethnical, linguistic, economic, and other
differences. Even on archaeological grounds alone it is

[1] For the term 'Middle Assyrian', see Sidney Smith, *Early History of
Assyria*, p. 317.

[2] See Hogarth, Schweich Lectures, *Kings of the Hittites*, 1924; and
C.A.H., ii, ch. vi sq.

more convenient to regard the area as a whole, as a single canvas, as it were, upon which to place the different peoples and states, and their different cultures, than to treat these as separate units which sometimes happen to be politically or culturally united. In the same way, it is more convenient to view the history of the area throughout as a single stream, consisting of a series of interconnected periods, for only in this way are we able to recognize the real continuity in the religious development as a whole amid the historical vicissitudes of one or other of the several religions.

Frequently it is helpful to compare, with all due caution, the Palestine of ancient Israelite times with the Palestine of the Roman, or Christian, or even medieval periods. Indeed, the modern tombs, shrines, and other centres of local cults, the sacred trees, wells, or stones, and the customs at birth, marriage, or death, will throw light upon the general features of ancient religious life and thought; and they enable us, at one time to interpret some ancient piece of written or unwritten evidence, and at another, to grasp the nature of the historical development at successive periods. 'The Permanence of Religion at Holy Places in the East'[1] is a fact that constantly impresses itself upon the observer, for the local and popular beliefs and customs will survive political changes and the rise and fall of national cults and sects. The cults of the modern saints and *welis*, and the interrelations between them and the national or orthodox religion have much to suggest, when one has to consider the local deities of the past, and their place in the great religions; and although these pages are concerned primarily with the archaeological evidence, a correct estimate of the ancient religion depends upon

---

[1] The title of a valuable and suggestive paper by Sir William Ramsay (*The Expositor*, Nov. 1906, pp. 454–75), dealing with Anatolia (now printed in *Pauline and other Studies*, pp. 163 sqq.). For Palestine, see especially the series of articles by T. Canaan in the *Journal of the Palestine Oriental Society*.

some knowledge of the characteristic features of the general history and development of religion.

Indeed, we may go further and observe that, since we are constantly obliged to rely upon the evidence of Hebrew and classical writers, and the traditions they report, even the characteristics of modern and medieval Palestinian traditions repay study.[1] Thus, traditions tend to collect around places already famous (e. g. Jerusalem, Hebron, Damascus). They readily spread from one place to another; and where similar traditions are found in several places, it may prove difficult to decide that any given tradition is in its only form, or in its oldest form, or attached to its original locality.[2] Traditions are very often centred upon well-known Christian or Mohammedan figures or incidents; but these are not necessarily their original form: often they represent a typical attempt to give them and the cults to which they belong an appearance of orthodoxy. Traditions often become complicated by the confusion of names, e. g. Joshua and Hosea (the prophet), Lazarus and Eleazar (and also Ezra), Job and Joab, Amittai (the father of Jonah) and Matthew. Traditions will arise around new cults; and even within recent years fresh traditions have come into existence.[3] In some cases, where old Biblical or classical traditions persist, it is by no means improbable that they have been revived by medieval pilgrims and travellers; so, e. g. the trace of the myth of Astarte and Adonis at Aphaca.[4] In general, Palestinian traditions must

---

[1] See e. g. C. C. McCown, *Annual of the American Schools*, ii. 47 sqq. (literature on p. 49 n.); Herzberg, *Pal. Jahrbuch*, xxii. 84–104.

[2] The story of Melchizedek is attached to Jerusalem (the Temple, and later, Golgotha), Shechem and Tabor. A flood-story was found at Gezer. Mt. Gerizim has naturally attracted many Biblical traditions.

[3] For examples of the rise of new (and even false) traditions, see *Rev. Biblique*, 1904, pp. 425 sqq.; 1907, pp. 113 sqq., 607 sqq.; 1908, pp. 152, note 2, 635; 1914, p. 379, n. 2. Cf. also Zev Vilnay, 'The New Folk-lore of Palestine' in *The New Judaea*, May 1929, p. 145.

[4] See *Rel. Sem.* p. 536. Traditional sites owe much to the labours of the monk Quaresmius of the seventeenth century (*Q.S.*, 1914, p. 183).

always be used with caution; and since we often have to depend upon the antiquarianism of Greek and Roman writers for the interpretation of archaeological objects (images, coins, &c.), it is necessary to bear in mind the characteristic vicissitudes of traditions and the human weakness of their collectors all the world over.

Out of the many examples of modern cults it may suffice to cite that of Nebi Yehudah, 'the prophet Judah', a sacred tree, south of Banias, near the source of the Jordan. A hereditary priesthood receives the first-fruits of the harvest and the first milk of the flock; there are spring and autumn pilgrim feasts, and sacred dances are held in the court of the sacred place.[1] Again, in the upper valley of the Jordan are graves, popularly believed to be those of the 'daughters of Jacob'. The name may point to some belief in dryads or nymphs of the oak.[2] But we do not know how old is the association with Judah and Jacob respectively, and there is no reason to suppose that the names are original. A circle (?) of stones at Gilgal commemorated the passage of the Jordan by the Israelites; but if this, like many other stone monuments, was older than Joshua's day, the question will arise whether the narratives (Joshua iv) are preserving merely the tradition current in Israelite days, the original explanation having been lost beyond recall.[3] The Israelites themselves spoke of the earlier Zuzim, Rephaim, &c.; and it is a safe assumption that the ancient stone monuments which they found, then as always excited curiosity.

[1] L. B. Paton, *Annual of the American Schools*, i. 60.

[2] Frazer, *Folk-lore in the Old Testament*, iii. 37, 46. On the famous group of monuments known as the 'graves of the children of Israel', at Hizmah near er-Rām, see R. A. S. Macalister, *Q.S.*, 1912, p. 82; Vincent, *Canaan*, pp. 96, 256 sq., 412. The so-called 'tomb of Hiram' near Tyre, it may be mentioned, is not old Phoenician, but of the Roman period.

[3] Cf. the pillar of salt which for long continued to be known as Lot's wife (Gen. xix. 26, Wisd. of Sol. x. 7; Josephus, *Antiq.* i. xi. 4). It is not certain that a *gilgāl* was necessarily a circle of stones, though circles are to be found (Thomsen, *Reallex. Vorg.*, 'Gilgal', § 2 sq.).

Stones are still erected and venerated; offerings are made
to them, and there will be invocations to the local spirit
or deity.[1] So inveterate are stone-cults that they may form
the starting-point of our rapid summary. Simple upright
stones (Menhirs) are found singly, or arranged in an alinement, or in a circle (Cromlech); or stones are laid roof-wise
across two upright stones (Dolmen), or rest upon layers of
stones ('false dolmen'). With the dolmen as the 'unit',
structures of varying complexity (double rooms, &c.) are
found.[2] Stone monuments and dolmens (Pl. i) are particularly common in Transjordania; and in spite of earlier
opinion to the contrary, they are by no means rare west of
the Jordan.[3] Their relative infrequency in the west has
been ascribed to Israelite iconoclasm and antipathy to
stone-cults. But it is not improbable that the settled life
and the natural caves on the western side of the Jordan did
not favour the construction and preservation of megalithic
monuments; and that if the dolmens served as burial-
places, other types of burial were more often utilized.
None the less, some of the megalithic groups east of the
Jordan are distinctly remarkable, one group consisting of
about a thousand dolmens.[4]

The origin, cause of distribution, and the purpose of

[1] Cf. the dolmen called 'the Ghoul's house', noted by Conder (*Q.S.*,
1882, pp. 10 sqq.). For ancient stone-cults, see *Rel. Sem.* (Index, *s. v.*
'Stones'); G. F. Moore, *Ency. Bib.*, 'Massebah'; G. B. Gray, *Sacrifice in
the O. T.*, pp. 102 sqq.; Thomsen, *Reallex. Vorg.*, 'Megalith-Grab',
'Menhir'.

[2] See the study of the megalithic remains at Rabbath Ammon at
Ammān, by Duncan Mackenzie (*P.E.F. Annual*, i). The group at
Ḥizmah (see p. 9, n. 2 above) illustrates the more advanced type (loc.
cit., pp. 12, 38). Pl. i illustrates the dolmen at el-Mareighāt, Wady
Zerka Ma'in (*Q.S.* 1905, p. 220).

[3] Mader, *J.P.O.S.*, vii. 95 sqq., estimates nearly 300 in Judah,
Samaria, and Galilee; and about 5,000 in Transjordania.

[4] See further Vincent, *Canaan*, pp. 394 sq., 408 sqq.; Abel, *Rev. Bib.*,
1922, pp. 590–602; 1928, pp. 420 sqq.; P. Thomsen, *Pal. Altertumskunde*,
p. 22 sq., and *Reallex. Vorg.*, 'Giab' (§ 7); Gressmann, *Z.A.T.W.*, 1909,
pp. 113–28; cf. also Ed. Meyer, *Gesch. d. Alt.* i. 535 sq.

megalithic monuments, in general, have been keenly discussed. They date back from well before the Iron Age; they do not appear to be necessarily due to any one single historical factor, viz. some decisive migration, whether from east to west, or the reverse; nor do they seem to be peculiar to some single stage in the history of religion or culture. Not all dolmens were altars: some are too high, others too crowded together. More probable is the view that they were sepulchral, and associated with the cult of the dead; and in so far as they were therefore 'sacred', it is reasonable to suppose that some could often be used as altars, the horizontal stone serving as a table. They are commonly oriented towards the west; and hollows or cup-marks are often found associated with them.[1]

'Cup-marks' are found on or by the side of the stones, upon bare patches of rock ('rock-altars'), and in caves. They date from Neolithic times, and many conjectures have been made as to their meaning. When cut out upon the rock-surface, it has even been suggested that they represent the relative position of certain planets and constellations at the time of some important festival! In one case, where the cups are arranged in five parallel rows of five each, the suggestion has been made that they were used for playing a game not unlike Reversi.[2] The hollows on the front and back of a menhir at el-Mererat are supposed to be tribal marks.[3] Again, it has been urged that the hollows were entirely utilitarian: they collected rain-water, or the pointed bottom jars, often found in excavation,

---

[1] The practice of erecting a dolmen at a grave has persisted (Conder, *Heth and Moab*, p. 327 sq.), and altars with Greek and Palmyrene inscriptions are even used by Mohammedans for the head-stones on graves (Littmann, *Sem. Inscr.*, p. 82). The so-called 'throne or bedstead (*sarīr*)' of the Nebi Shema, near Safed, is between a dolmen and a rock-tomb (Macalister, *Q.S.*, 1909, pp. 195 sqq.), see Pl. i. 2.

[2] Petrie, cited by D. P. Blair, *Q.S.*, 1919, p. 171.

[3] Dalman, *Pal. Jahrb.*, 1908, p. 51 (see further ibid., pp. 23 sqq.).

were placed in them, or the rock-surfaces were not altars, but wine- or olive-presses.[1]

Indeed, it has sometimes been asserted that archaeologists —and not the amateurs alone—have been too ready to see some sacral purpose everywhere. Every standing-stone becomes a sacred pillar, every wine or olive-press an altar, and the holes and channels for carrying off the liquid are imaginatively seen overflowing with the blood of sacrificial victims. Yet there is no doubt that such hollows are used when the modern Bedouin sacrifices a sheep or goat.[2] Moreover, the wine that gladdened gods and men was no ordinary drink; and the Talmud restricts the Jews in their dealings with the wine-presses of pagans on account of the religious beliefs and practices connected with viticulture.[3] In fact, corn and wine and the means of life were intimately bound up with cults—as we gather from Hosea—and what may be called the 'economic' stage or phase of religion usually makes all that upon which life depends the centre of popular and practical religion.

Again, it has been suggested that the cup-marks on rocks were for the purpose of collecting drinking water for the innumerable pigeons and doves of Palestine, and that they were therefore of purely humanitarian origin. But the birds were sacred to the great goddesses of the Astarte type, as has been recently illustrated at the Astarte temple at Beth-Shan; and there are some traces of the belief that the souls of the dead might take the form of a

---

[1] See the careful study by R. A. S. Macalister, *Gezer*, i. 153 sqq., who was less and less inclined to discern any religious or symbolical use in them (p. 156). The view that they have any sexual meaning may— apart from some exceptional cases—be dismissed (see Kittel, *Studien*, p. 127 sq.).

[2] Gray, p. 123 (citing Schumacher).

[3] W. A. L. Elmslie, *Abodah Zarah*, pp. 69 sqq., 87 sq.; see *Rel. Sem.*, p. 575; also Judges ix. 27 (Abimelech at Shechem; cf. Jer. xxv. 30, Isa. xvi. 10). In the ruins of Arḍ Khaldi ('Abeih) near Beirut, a wine-press (?) seems to have been the scene of sacred rites (Macalister, *Q.S.*, 1910, pp. 99 sqq.).

bird, if not of the bird sacred to the mother-goddess.[1] The evidence itself is slight, but it was commonly understood that the dead were thirsty, and water may have been poured into the cup-holes or allowed to collect, the question *how* the dead were supposed to enjoy it being unanswered— if it was ever raised. In every case, it is necessary to bear in mind that archaeological data are not to be confused with the particular *interpretation* put upon them. The data stand in need of interpretation; and this must be in accordance with known beliefs and practices.

Cup-marks or hollows on standing-stones obviously cannot be for holding liquids; but since blood or fat or oil is wont to be applied to sacred stones devoid of hollows, it is not improbable that the lateral cup-marks served the same purpose, though whether gods or the dead were being venerated is another question. In like manner the cup-markings on the roofing stones of dolmens may be either for offerings or symbolic of food-offerings.[2] At Serabiṭ el-Khādim in the Sinaitic peninsula Petrie found in an enclosure a stele at the base of which was a stone with squared hollows, evidently for offerings on behalf of those to whom the stele was erected. Simpler blocks with shallow saucers were found there in the 'Shrine of the Kings', and 'might well be for the meal offerings or cakes of flour and oil, a kind of pastry'.[3] Also at Dougga, in Punic North

---

[1] On the sanctity of birds, see Frazer, *F.O.T.*, iii. 19 sq.; and for the hunting or snaring of souls, op. cit. ii. 510 sqq. (on Ezek. xiii. 17–21). Apart from this, and metaphors (flying, Ps. xc. 10; the chirping of the dead, Isa. viii. 19, xxix. 4), cf. the Arab belief that the dead take the form of a bird, especially an owl (Doughty, *Arabia Deserta*, ed. 1921, p. 168, Wellhausen, *Heid.*, p. 185), the Egyptian soul-bird (Klebs, *Aeg. Z.*, lxi. 104 sqq.): cf. Gressmann, no. 246, and his article on the dove as the bird of the mother-goddess, giver of life (*A.f.R.*, xx. 328 sq.). In the Assyrian myth of Ishtar's descent into the Lower World the dead have wings like birds, but they are unable to escape.

[2] See G. Elliot Smith in *Essays and Studies presented to William Ridgeway* (1913), p. 537 (with Egyptian analogies).

[3] Petrie, *Sinai*, pp. 66 sqq. (fig. 80), 134 (fig. 142, nos. 8 sq.); Num

Africa, slabs with hollows and channels were laid before
stelae; and with these relatively late examples may be compared the so-called 'tables of offerings' which Macalister
found at Gezer from about the beginning of the Second
Semitic period down to and including the Hellenistic.[1]
Here, their resemblance to wine- and olive-presses led him
to suggest that they were miniature models designed for
the offering of the *primitiae* of the fruit-harvest.

At all events, it is noteworthy that the practice of offering
food and drink to the dead persists as late as the Book of
Tobit (iv. 17), that is, to about the third or second century
B.C., though 'it would appear to have been a subject of
considerable dispute as to whether such offerings were
right and proper and a matter of duty, or whether they
were definitely to be excluded by Judaism and its ad-
herents'.[2] It was one thing to provide for the needs of the
dead, but it was an easy step to the belief that the dead
would show their gratitude; and since it would happen that,
the more powerful the dead the more likely were they to
be venerated and feared, the line between care for the dead,
cults of the dead (and especially ancestors), and cults of
gods (who also were often regarded as ancestors) was not
clearly drawn. Hence the precise interpretation of the old
cup-marks must often be entirely a matter of conjecture.

Several interesting examples of rock-altars, rock-surfaces

---

xxviii. 5, xxix. 3; cf. the ritual in the story of Gideon (Judges vi. 20; cf.
Manoah, xiii. 19).

[1] Vincent, p. 129 sq. (at Dougga); Macalister, *Gezer*, ii. 425 and
Plate ccxxiv; cf. Tell Judeideh, Graeco-Roman period (Bliss and
Macalister, *Excavations in Palestine*, p. 145). For Cretan tables of offerings with saucers, see *C.A.H.*, Plates i. 198 c. (also Chapouthier on such
a table at the Palace of Mallia, *Bull. de Correspond. Hellen.*, July–Dec.
1928). In Jerusalem Weill found a little limestone table for offerings
with four cup-holes (one at each corner) and a fifth in the centre; this
was in a burial of the Middle Canaanite Period (FitzGerald, *Q.S.*,
1922, p. 18).

[2] D. C. Simpson in Charles's *Aprocrypha*, p. 198; cf. the latter's *Eschato-
logy*, pp. 24 sqq.

with cup-marks, &c., are known.[1] At Taanach excavation revealed a rock-surface about one metre high with a step, it had hollows, and near by were infant burials.[2] At Zorah, west of Jerusalem, the 'altar' is hewn out of the rock; it is five to six feet high and has steps, which well illustrate the prohibition in Exod. xx. 26 guarding against exposure of the person.[3] The rock-surface at Megiddo lay below the mound itself and on a terrace; beneath were chambers with niches where lamps had been placed, with some human remains.[4]

Fine examples of the use of the rock-altar in Nabataean and Graeco-Roman times are to be found at Petra; and at Baalbek the original rock-altar, with steps, became part of a great altar of sacrifice in the centre of the large court, lying to the east of the temple of Jupiter Heliopolitanus.[5] But the most famous of all is that at Jerusalem: the ancient *sakhra* in the Ḥaram esh-Sherīf, the Dome of the Rock, the so-called Mosque of 'Omar (Pl. ii).[6] The rock stands 4–6½ ft.

[1] See more fully the works cited in the following notes, together with Vincent, ch. ii; Kittel, *Studien*, also in the *Hilprecht Anniversary Volume* (1909), pp. 243–55.

[2] Already described and illustrated by Driver, *Schweich Lectures*, p. 81 sq. (see Sellin, *Tell el-Taannek*, pp. 34, 103 sq.).

[3] Driver, p. 65 sq.; Kittel, *Studien*, pp. 105 sqq.; Galling (*Altar*, p. 63) rejects, but Thomsen (*Reallex. Vorg.*, 'Altar', § 3) accepts the identification with the rock in Judges xiii. 19.

[4] Steuernagel, *Tell el-Mutesellim*, pp. 154 sqq. (and Tafel xlix); Driver, p. 67.

[5] For Petra, see Gressmann, nos. 446–9; Driver, p. 61 sq.; also S. I. Curtiss, *Q.S.*, 1900, pp. 350 sqq.; Galling, p. 62 sq., and the works of Dalman (see Bibliography). On Baalbek, see Bliss, *Q.S.*, 1902, pp. 168 sqq. (on the German excavations, by Schültz, Kreucker, and Puchstein); and Theirsch, *Gött. Nachr.* 1925, pp. 1 sqq. The Baalbek altar is sunk in the floor of the Christian basilica (A. B. Cook, *Zeus*, i. 559). There is an interesting parallel to the steps to the Petra 'high place' at Byblus (Dunand, *Syria*, x. 211).

[6] Kittel, *Studien*, pp. 13 sqq.; Gressmann, no. 405; Dalman, *Neue Petra Forschungen*, pp. 111 sqq.; R. Hartmann, *Der Felsendom in Jerusalem* (1909); cf. also E. Richmond, *Dome of the Rock* (1924), figs. 6 and 7.

above the ground; the measurements vary: 55 (58) × 40 (44) ft. There are the usual cup-marks and channels, and, at the southern end, a hole leads to a cavern the nature and contents of which remain unknown. As the surface in the middle of the rock sounds hollow the cavern is not improbably extensive, and it is tempting to suppose that it was here that the Jebusite and his four sons 'hid themselves' (1 Chron. xxi. 20). Against the old tradition that the Rock was the site of the Holy of Holies it is objected that the latter was too small to contain the whole rock; while the alternative view, that it represents the Altar of Burnt-offering which lay to the east of the Temple, has against it the objection that, owing to the configuration of the ground, an enormous mass of masonry would be needed to support the heavy walls of the temple.[1] The threshing-floor of Araunah the Jebusite which David bought for the altar (2 Sam. xxiv) was presumably exposed and fairly level, whereas the Rock itself is too irregular to serve the purpose.   But the threshing-floor may have been *near* the Rock; and, certainly, the old cults which the prophets condemned were at or by the threshing-floors (Hos. ix. 1 sq.).

Be that as it may, the Rock became famous in tradition. It was the 'foundation stone' upon which the world was established; it sealed the mouth of the great deep, and beneath it could be heard the waters of the flood.[2] Jerusalem was the navel, the omphalos, the centre of the world;[3] and the belief in the supremacy of the Holy City, and the

[1] See Benzinger, *E. Bi.*, col. 4928; Sir Charles Watson, *Q.S.*, 1910, pp. 15 sqq. (in favour of the former view), and the recent discussion by G. B. Gray, *Sacrifice*, pp. 130 sqq.

[2] See the Targum Jerushalmi on Exod. xxviii. 30. Elsewhere there are traditions of the flood, e.g. at Hieropolis (Lucian, § 1 3), and near Gezer (Macalister, i. 264); see Frazer, *F.O.T.*, i. 152 sq.; *Rel. Sem.*, p. 567; and Feuchtwang, *Das Wasseropfer*, with W. Schultz's review, *O.L.Z.*, 1913, col. 127 (on the connexion between 'water-pouring ceremonies' and the belief in subterranean waters).

[3] Ez. xxxviii. 12 (*ṭabbūr*; Sept. *omphalos*, cf. v. 5), also Jos. *B.J.*, III. iii. 5; *Jubilees*, viii. 12, 19, and Enoch, xxvi. 1.   A central position

nature of the religious importance of the whole neighbourhood (Tophet, Valley of Rephaim, Anathoth, &c.), point to ideas which, so far from being due to the influence of the Israelites from the desert, doubtless go back to a far earlier period. Indeed, in the Amarna Letters (*c.* 1400 B.C.), Jerusalem is already a prominent city; and to an earlier date we may ascribe what is perhaps its oldest place of cult. Inside the old city-limits, and at the highest point, was found a rock three feet square, with pigeon-holes beneath it suitable for receiving offerings, and to the south a smooth area of rock about twenty-eight by twenty feet with a group of cup-marks and large basins, one of which seemed to show traces of fire (see Pl. iii).[1]

The Hebrew 'altar' (*mizbēᵃh*) is primarily a place of sacrificial *slaughter*. But the term comes to be used more loosely; and, conversely, sacred places, the centres of cult, do not necessarily owe their origin to sacrificial rites, and the 'pillar' (*maṣṣebah*) may have been used as an altar.[2] The cippus or *masgĕdā*, often mentioned in Nabataean inscriptions (1st cent. A.D.), was primarily the *object* of worship, rather than the sacred *place* or 'mosque' (Arabic *masjid*) where one prostrates oneself.[3] It takes various pillar shapes: a square pillar, a hexagonal column like a Greek altar, a pillar six feet high. One forms the abacus of a

was similarly claimed for Delphi and for Mecca. On the omphalos, see A. B. Cook, *Zeus*, ii. 166 sqq. Golgotha (in the Church of the Holy Sepulchre in Jerusalem) also has its cleft, which is supposed to reach to the centre of the earth; and in the 'Catholicon' is a cup containing a stone covered with network, and regarded as the earth's centre (Baedeker, pp. 42, 44). On the transference of traditions from the Jewish Temple to Golgotha, see J. Jeremias, *Golgotha* (Leipzig, 1926).

[1] Macalister and Garrow Duncan, *P.E.F. Annual*, iv. 35 sq.; cf. *Q.S.*, 1924, p. 59 sq. The history of Jerusalem can be carried back to *c.* 2000 B.C.; so Sethe, Dussaud, and Albright, who agree that it is mentioned among the enemies of Egypt at about that date (see Albright, *J.P.O.S.*, viii. 247 sq.; and cf. *Q.S.*, 1928, p. 216 sq.; 1929, p. 121).

[2] See Gray's discussion, op. cit., pp. 96 sqq.

[3] See G. A. Cooke, *North Semitic Inscriptions*, p. 238; Lagrange, *Études des Rel. Sem.*, p. 210; and Lammens in *Mélanges Beirut*, xi (1926), 37 sqq.

pillar in a church and is still venerated locally, and another bears an altar-like device carved in relief.[1] The cippus may be explicitly made for a single deity (e.g. Dushara), or even for two.[2] Sometimes a deity will be associated with the 'place'. Thus, the goddess Allath is called 'mistress (*rabbath*) of the place'; and the title 'lord (*mār*) of the house' appears to be applied to Dushara.[3] The 'lady of the house' is mentioned on a Palmyrene fragment from Baalbek. 'Place' is specifically a holy place, like the modern *maḳām* and the corresponding use of *māḳōm* in the Old Testament (Gen. xxviii. 11, &c.).[4] Whether the Baal-ḥamman so frequently mentioned upon Carthaginian votive tablets was the lord of the pillar dedicated to the sun-god is uncertain. At all events, it was possible to speak both of the god of a specified place or object, and also, as the word 'Beth-el' testifies, of the place or embodiment of the god.

If a stone represents or even embodies a deity it does not follow that there were as many stones as gods.[5] But there

---

[1] Euting, *Nabat. Inschr.*, p. 61 sq. (Doughty, *Arabia Deserta*, plate xlv, no. 35) = *C.I.S.*, ii. 218. Near Beirut an altar is carved out in front of a pillar; *Q.S.*, 1910, facing p. 99 (Gressmann, no. 450; Galling, 68).

[2] Cooke, no. 101; here, however Dushara (Dusares) and A'ra perhaps represent one god, see Lidzbarski, *Ephem.* ii. 262. For the interpretation of A'ra see *Rel. Sem.*, p. 603 sq., and note that, if it means 'pillar' (so Littmann, comparing the Ar. *ghariy*), Dushara is the god of the pillar, or the god-pillar; cf. Beth-el and El-Shaddai, pp. 145, 159 sq.

[3] For the former (רבת אלאתר), see Littmann, *Nab. Inscr.*, no. 24; and for the latter, *Eph.* iii. 87 sq.; cf. the 'lord of the house' in the Koran, Sura cvi (Nöldeke, *Z.A.*, xxiii. 184); see also *Eph.* ii. 301.

[4] The Aramaic *athrā* is similarly used in Jewish inscriptions (*Q.S.*, 1920, p. 84 sq.). In a Nabataean inscription from Khalasa 'this place' is made for the 'life' of king Aretas (*P.E.F. Annual*, iii. 145). The word can even be applied to a large rock (Moritz, in *Abhand. Götting. Gesell.* xvi. 31). The meaning of the name אתרקדשו, *C.I.S.*, ii. 312 ('holy place'?) is quite obscure.

[5] See *Rel. Sem.*, p. 210 sq. (Herod. iii. 8), and Moore, *Ency. Bib.*, 2980, n. 7 (the thirty stones at Pharai each with the name of a god; Pausanias, vii. 22); cf. the three *skēnai* in Mark ix. 5.

was a tendency in this direction. Similarly there was a tendency to have separate memorials for the deceased.[1] Such a memorial (Aramaic *naphshā*) was set up over a grave, and represented the soul, or the personality, of the deceased. The practice is illustrated by the carving of a pyramid standing upon a cube.[2] In a Palmyrene inscription the words 'this *naphshā*' is engraved on the side of a bust (*R.E.S.*, 158). But the term is also applied to a building.[3] By a curious refinement, although it is a feminine word, it is sometimes treated as masculine when the reference is to a male (*C.I.S.*, ii. 159, &c.), even as, conversely, the Aramaic terms for image (*ṣalmā*) and idol (*pethakrā*) assume a feminine termination when they refer to females.[4] This desire for greater precision is in harmony with the iconographic tendency, well illustrated by Ronzevalle, to give a more anthropomorphic form to symbols and memorials of the dead by depicting a head, or even the whole human body; and it is important to observe that rude drawings, which by their very poverty were at first taken to be of very considerable antiquity, were subse-

[1] The three 'pyramids' erected by Helena of Adiabene for Izates, Monobazus and herself; the seven pyramids at Modin for the parents and the five sons (1 Macc. xiii. 28; Syr. *naphshāthā*); the two *naphshāthā* for the father and son of 'Abd-'obdath at Medeba (*C.I.S.*, ii. 196; Cooke, no. 96; cf. *Eph.* iii. 88 sq.); at Nīḥa four brothers are represented by four cones; see Jalabert, *Mélanges Beirut*, ii. 284 sq., Ronzevalle, ib., iv. 189 sqq., 195 sqq. (seventeen stelae carved outside a sepulchral chamber of the Roman period). See *Rec.* ii. 190 sq., and, on Jewish usage, Levy, *s.v.*

[2] Cooke, p. 214 (see Vogüé, *Syr. Centr.* 90), cf. Galling, p. 67 sq. and Tafel 13; for the idea of the 'soul' (Heb. *néphesh*), see H. Wheeler Robinson in *The People and the Book* (ed. Peake), pp. 354 sqq.

[3] So, especially, *C.I.S.*, ii. 162 (cf. *Eph.* iii. 292). *naphshā*=μνημεῖον on a Nabataean bilingual (Littmann in *Florilegium Vogüé*, p. 378). 'Shrines (*naoi*) of (? and) *naphshāthā*' are built over sacred relics, in the Syriac Romance of Julian the Apostate (ed. Hoffmann), p. 222, l. 27.

[4] For the latter see 1 Kings xv. 13 (Peshitta), and cf. the fem. use of *ḳabrā*, Chwolson, *Grabinschr.* 122, 162; for a Phoenician analogy, see Cooke, no. 13, l. 2. See further Duval, *Rev. Semit.*, 1894, p. 259; D. H. Müller, *Vienna Or. Journal*, vi. 321.

quently recognized to be of Roman date.[1] Neither the crudeness of an object nor the tendency to anthropomorphize a symbol is in itself the indication of any one particular age.

The *cippus* or other object served to commemorate the dead. The formula 'remembered be X' occurs frequently in Nabataean, Palmyrene, and Sinaitic inscriptions of the first Christian centuries, and in one case we read that those who say 'remembered be all these for good' shall themselves be remembered (Cooke, no. 140 b). Sometimes the god is specifically mentioned: e.g. a man is to be remembered 'before Dushara'; and once an enemy has prefixed a negative.[2] It was an old custom (notably in Egypt) to build or repair temples, synagogues, &c., in order to be remembered; and on a Phoenician inscription near Tyre a man who has dedicated a gate and doors hopes for 'a memorial and a good name under the foot' of his lord, the Sky Baal (Baal-Shamim).[3] Older usage is illustrated by the eighth-century inscriptions from Sam'āl in North Syria. One of these, on a huge statue of the god Hadad, speaks in the name of king Panammu and calls down blessings upon a faithful successor and a curse upon him who fails to pray to Hadad on his behalf; while another is a memorial set up by a son to his father whose achieve-

[1] Ronzevalle, op. cit., p. 207. A well-known Sardinian menhir has female breasts (Mackenzie, *P.E.F. Annual*, i. 36).

[2] See *C.I.S.*, ii. 338 and *Eph.* iii. 87 (on *C.I.S.*, ii. 235). For the ceremonial commemoration, see below, p. 38 n. 4.

[3] Cooke, no. 9; cf. Lam ii. 1. To be 'under the feet' is a sign of humility and of defeat. Such phrases as 'the footstool of the king's feet' and 'the ground upon which he treads', are found in the Amarna Letters (nos. 185, 195, &c.), and Josh. x. 24, Ps. cx. 1 are illustrated by a representation of Amenhotep II with his feet on the neck of his enemies (Gressmann, in *The Psalmists*, ed. Simpson, p. 17 sq.). More recently Tutankhamen's footstool or hassock has been found with a representation of foreign captives, prostrate, and with their hands tied behind them; and similarly his sandals depict the prisoners upon which he walked (*Illustrated London News*, 1929, July 20, and August 3).

ments he narrates. In general, stelae are erected to the
dead by their descendants; but men like Absalom can set
up pillars for themselves or for others during their lifetime.[1] In fact, the pillar can represent the dead who
speaks, e.g., 'I am X which Y set up to me,' or it can also
at the same time commemorate the donor, 'I am X . . .
which I, Y, set up.'[2]

Steps could also be taken to provide for the presence
of a deity. At Tēma a man dedicates a 'seat to the god
Ṣalm for the life of his soul'; or a man will make a niche
for a statue and a bed, or a couch.[3] The Babylonian
custom of providing couches for gods was well known elsewhere.[4] A stone seat found near Tyre (2nd cent. B.C.),
with sphinxes cut on the sides, was carved on its front with
two stelae; on one is a female figure lifting her hand as
though to bless the bearded figure who faces her on the
other. The inscription is, 'To my lady Astarte, who is within
the Sanctuary which is mine'.[5] A seat could in itself be a
sufficient symbol of the presence of a god; and M. Cumont
has quoted from the account of the physician Thessalus, how
he stood alone before the throne of Asklepios at Thebes;
at first it was merely an empty throne, but, moved by the
power of the ineffable names (ἀπόρρητα ὀνόματα) pronounced
by the priest, the god appeared, seated, a radiant vision.[6]

Much has been written on the cult of the empty throne,

[1] 2 Sam. xviii. 18; cf. C.I.S., i. 46 (Cooke, no. 16; of 4th–3rd cent.).
On North Semitic tomb inscriptions in general, see Lidzbarski, *Handbuch*, pp. 137–48.

[2] Cooke, nos. 35 (*C.I.S.*, i. 119) and 32 (i. 115). A South Arabian
altar and stela combined is illustrated in Nielsen, *Handbuch*, i. 170,
fig. 65 (=Grohmann, p. 38, fig. 84).

[3] See (a) *C.I.S.*, ii. 114 (Cooke, no. 70; מותבא); (b) Cooke, p. 296 *note*
(כפתא וערשא, καμάρα κ. κλίνη); (c) ib., p. 255 n. (ארכתא).

[4] See Herod. i. 181 sq., Lagrange, *Ét.* 509, Frazer on Pausanias, ii. 17, 3.
The רבעתא made for Dushara (*C.I.S.*, ii. 160) was perhaps a cube.

[5] Ronzevalle, *Mélanges*, iii. 755 sqq. (*Eph.* iii. 52 sq.).

[6] 'Le culte Égyptien et le Mysticisme de Plotin', *Monuments et
Mémoires Piot*, xxv (1921–2), 77 sqq. (esp. p. 83).

and the mountain (with or without a throne) as the seat of the god.[1] The throne or seat itself becomes a sacred object of worship, apart from the god.[2] Similarly the altar and image are one at Duma in Arabia (*Rel. Sem.*, p. 205) and in the 'god-altar', Zeus Madbakhos.[3] Although the view that the ark of the Israelites was an empty throne cannot be proved, models of empty seats have actually been discovered in the course of excavation. At Gezer there was a limestone chair of the Fourth Semitic period; it was about four inches in height, with a device which has been thought to be derived from the 'double axe' (Macalister, *Gezer*, ii. 423). At Beth-Shan was a basalt model of a seat resembling those on the Cretan hieroglyphs, and Egyptian in decoration.[4] The date is round about 1400 B.C. Rather later are the terra-cotta thrones found at Ain Shemesh (Beth-Shemesh) which have a fracture in the seat, suggesting that originally there was a seated figure.[5]

[1] A. B. Cook, *Zeus*, i. 138 sqq., Herter, *Rhein. Mus.*, 1925, pp. 164–73. The empty throne at Lycaonia, a high and broad seat, has a seated figure cut on the back (Ramsay, *The MI. Churches*, p. 507).

[2] Cf. Plutarch's account of the tent with the golden throne and regalia of Alexander the Great to which Eumenes offered sacrifice; also the festival of Mani's chair. In Nabataean Dushara and his 'seat' (מותב) are virtually two (*C.I.S.*, ii. 198; Cooke, no. 80). A Palmyrene dedication (?) to 'the (*or* a) throne of the holy god' is doubtful (Clermont-Ganneau, *Rec.* vii. 36 sq., Lidz. *Eph.* ii. 310, and Littmann, *Sem. Inscr.*, pp. 50, 83). For *thrones* as denoting Christian altars, see Clermont-Ganneau, *Rec.* iv. 247–50. See further *Rel. Sem.*, p. 562.

[3] *Rel. Sem.*, pp. 205, 562; A. B. Cook, *Zeus*, i. 519 sqq. An 'altar statue' (בומס צלם) for Philip the son of Herod, is cited by Littmann, *Nab. Inscr.*, no. 101 (*Eph.* iii. 293).

[4] A vulture with extended wings holds the emblem of eternity (*shen*); beneath is the *ded* emblem of stability, with arms from which hang *ankh* signs; Rowe, *Q.S.*, 1927, p. 148 (illustrated in *Pennsyl. Museum Journal*, 1927, p. 19; cf. *Rev. Bibl.*, 1927, p. 98 and pl. iii, no. 4). Rowe compares the thrones on the Kassite kudurru-stones (cf. below, p. 103 n. 1). At Phalasarna in West Crete a seat is cut out of the solid rock and a pillar carved on the inner surface of its back.

[5] *PE.F. Annual*, iii. 55. For a Phoenician example of *c.* 6th–5th cent. from Sidon, see Gressmann, no. 520.

The 'empty throne' is not a thing of the past, for near Blūdān is the famous *kursi* or chair, the untenanted seat of a weli, or even, of Mohammed himself, whither the peasants bring offerings.[1] It is a huge rock-pinnacle on the very edge of a precipice, 2,000 feet or more above the village of Medaya. The *kursi* itself is some four metres high and resembles a huge armchair; it is known in the neighbourhood as 'chair of the king', or of the 'prophet'. A grove of sacred oaks and a cave, wherein a lamp burns all night, add to the religious significance of the place. In fact the whole district is rich in ancient remains, in survivals of primitive custom and interesting snatches of folklore. Specially noteworthy is the *makām* ('sacred place'), south of Blūdān, known as 'the little lame mother of potsherds'. The platform with its grove of oaks, hereditary ministrants, and an annual spring festival, is remarkable for the innumerable fragments of broken pottery, it being the custom for women (Moslem and Christian) to break *new* jars in fulfilment of vows, and, in particular, when granted offspring. There is a tradition that a girl, the patroness of the holy place, lies buried there; and Hanauer suspects that 'the breaking of unused earthern vessels by females may be the survival of some ancient form of gross nature worship, such as that of Mylitta or Astarte, and the jars shattered symbols of the nameless sacrifices connected with the impure ritual'.[2] When, however, in tombs or in sacred areas, figurines, pottery, &c., are found broken, and apparently with intention, it is possible that the object was to ensure that they were given over wholly to the god,

[1] Hanauer, 'Notes from Damascus and the Anti-Libanus', *Q.S.*, 1909, pp. 119–38 (esp. p. 134 sq.).

[2] Hanauer, p. 134; cf. S. I. Curtiss, *Primitive Semitic Religion To-day*, pp. 44, 46, 82, 259; and S. A. Cook, *Rel. of Anc. Pal.*, p. 45 sq. In itself the smashing of pottery may sometimes be prophylactic; cf. R. Campbell Thompson, *Devils and Evil Spirits*, i. 153, 'Like the sherd that is cast aside by the potter may they (i. e. the evil demons) be broken in the broad places': the breaking either symbolizing or magically effecting the destruction of the demon of sickness.

or that by destroying or 'killing' them, they (i. e. their 'spirit' or 'soul') would accompany the deceased.[1]

One well-known type of stone cult-object consists of representations of a triad of pillars. Sometimes these stand upon a platform, or they have a common base; they are contiguous, or they stand apart. They are not necessarily of the same height; and in Petra, where they stand in niches, the largest stands in the middle (so elsewhere), but the one on its left may be smaller than that on its right (Pl. vi. 2).[2] The triads do not necessarily symbolize *three* deities; and in Carthage they are associated with symbols of the moon, or with the caduceus and 'Tanit' symbol (see below, p. 47).[3] In the old water-passage at Gezer a block is left carved in a niche—a sort of baetyl; and in the late Jewish lamps a common ornament consists of an upright object under an arch.[4] The lamp-decorations not infrequently testify to the persistence, though often in a highly conventional form, of older cult and other motifs, and the one specified illustrates the sort of composite cult objects that had once been familiar.

Upon Neo-Babylonian seals from about the sixth century B. C. downwards, a base (? altar) is surmounted by sacred animals, dog, cock, goat-fish, or by an oval block of stone, upon which is a symbol (Adad's thunderbolt, the star of Ishtar, or the crescent of Sin); see Pl. v. 1–3.[5] We may compare the *ḥammānīm* above the altars of the Baals which

[1] Cf. Vincent, p. 293.

[2] Dalman, *Petra u. s. Forsch.*, no. 606, fig. 263; cf. further ib. *Neue Petra Forschungen*, p. 49, fig. 47, no. 179 (2), and fig. 48, no. 298, 1. In a Cretan example each is surmounted by a dove (J. Harrison, *Themis*, p. 193). On a rock-carving near Dahariyeh at least four (funereal?) pillars are marked (*Q.S.*, 1919, p. 17); see Pl. iv. 1.

[3] Cf. Gressmann, no. 437, Jane Harrison, *Themis*, p. 192.

[4] See (1) *Gezer*, i. fig. 135 (cf. also ii, fig. 527), and (2) ib., i. 317, Pl. ci *a*. 16.

[5] See Ward, nos. 545, 549, 553 sq., 557. See also Weber, 461 sqq. For the block bearing a symbol, cf. perhaps Petrie, *Gerar*, Pl. xix. 27 (a stone with a crescent and ribbons?).

Josiah destroyed (2 Chron. xxxiv. 4; wanting in the parallel 2 Kings). Later, a Nabataean temple at el-Umta'iyyeh, south-west of Bostra, bears on the ornamentation of the lintel altars (?) with three or four stelae, the middle altar having steps.[1] More curious are some devices found on Transjordanian coins. Thus, from Adraa (Der'a) comes a coin of 174 A. D. depicting a semi-spherical stone or baetyl on an altar, with some unintelligible ornaments on either side.[2] But still more strange is the Bostra coin where, on a platform approached by steps, stand three stones, the outside ones surmounted by a single object, while above the middle one are seven flat objects, sometimes taken to be offerings of bread, similar to those on Egyptian monuments.[3] On the alternative view (de Saulcy, Morey) we have here the wine-press, the symbol of Dushara. See Pl. xxxiii. 3, 4.

Altar-steps are not merely utilitarian. The deity is seated above on high, and Egyptian scenes will depict the god or the king at the top of a flight of steps.[4] Steps led up to temples, shrines and sacred places.[5] Besides the difficult 'chimney' to the rock-cut throne on Mt. Sipylos in Lydia (*Zeus*, i. 137), and the 'ladder of Tyre' at Rās en-Nāḳūra, there is something of the nature of a series of steps at Bethel.[6] The idea of a ladder reaching to the sky, the abode of

[1] Gressmann, no. 452 (*Princeton Expedition to Syria*, ii. A, fig. 68).

[2] Hill, *Coins of Arabia*, p. xxiii (a baetyl between the 'horns' of an altar); Dussaud, *Mythol. Syr.*, pp. 167 sqq.

[3] Hill, *Coins of Arabia*, p. xxvii sq.; Dussaud, op. cit., p. 169 sq. See Morey's discussion of the Bostra coins in the *Revue Numismatique*, 1911, pp. 69–85. Cf. *Rev. Bib.*, 1913, p. 151, and, for a discussion of Nabataean altars, baetyls, &c., ib., pp. 150–4.

[4] See Rowe, *Q.S.*, 1929, p. 84 sq., apropos of the fine stepped altar discovered by him in one of the Beth-Shan temples; below, p. 100.

[5] Cf. the steps to the temples of Byblus, Baalbek, &c.; 300 steps led to the top of Mt. Gerizim (cf. the coins; see e. g. Montgomery, *The Samaritans*, facing p. 88); for Armenia, see Lehmann-Haupt, *Armenien*, ii. 120 sq., 144, 154, 163 (sanctuaries difficult of access; see also *Rev. Bib.*, 1927, p. 587 n.).

[6] J. P. Peters, *Presentation Volume to Prof. Toy*, p. 235 (see p. 237, for a 'ladder' in the Taurus mountains); cf. Skinner, *Gen.*, p. 378.

the gods, is a very familiar one, for the way by which men ascend is that by which the gods come down to earth. It is an ancient notion, met with as early as the 'Pyramid Texts' of Egypt, where there is a ladder for the king to reach the abode of the gods.[1] A ladder-like design is often found upon late Palestinian lamps;[2] and on Neo-Babylonian seals of the type referred to above, a worshipper stands before bases upon which are sacred objects, and the stone or baetyl sometimes has a vertical ladder decoration, perhaps symbolical of the ascent to the divine symbol (crescent, star, or the thunderbolt of Adad) placed above it.[3]

The Babylonian ziggurat was a pyramid-like tower with a shrine at the top. Its shape has been the subject of much discussion; and it is interesting to see on the ruins of that at Ur the steps leading to the summit.[4] The tower was the approach to heaven. Similarly, a 'ladder' (*sullām*) at Bethel joins heaven and earth; the 'place' is the gateway to heaven, and the sacred stone which Jacob anoints with oil and sets up as a *maṣṣēbah* is a 'Beth-el', the abode of a spirit or *numen*. The association of 'Bethel' with a 'ladder' is therefore noteworthy, the more especially as the 'baetyls' of the Graeco-Roman period can hardly be separated from the Semitic 'Beth-el'. These 'animated stones' (λίθοι

---

[1] Breasted, *Rel. and Thought in Ancient Egypt* (Index, s.v. Ladder). Cf. Frazer, *F.O.T.*, ii. 52 sq.; A. B. Cook, *Zeus*, ii. 114–40.

[2] Galling, *Z.D.P.V.*, xlvi. *taf.* iv, nos. 13 and 14 (*Gezer*, iii, pls. cx–cxii); also on Gezer pottery of the Fourth Semitic period (pl. lxxiv. 3; clxxiii. 16).

[3] See Ward, nos. 550 (Weber 461), 552 and 550*a* (our Pl. v. 1–3); in 555 the deity is the moon-god Sin; related to these is no. 554, where the lunar crescent is on top of a ziggurat-like object. See also Sidney Smith, *Bab. Historical Texts*, p. 65 sq.; where the earliest example is the British Museum cone seal, no. 89902, of about 650–600 B.C. (cf. Andrae, *M.D.O.G.*, no. 62, 49).

[4] Gressmann, no. 662. On the *ziggurat* as a stepped tower, see Dombart, *Hommel Festschrift*, i. 1 sqq.; Andrae, *M.D.O.G.*, no. 64; Moberg, *Torn Babels* (Lund, 1918); cf. Dombart, *Arch. f. Orient.*, v. 223 sq.

ἔμψυχοι), as Philo of Byblus calls them, were the seat or embodiment of some *numen*. Further, just as a mountain may be not merely the seat of a god, but divine in itself, so the sacred stone tends to be not only the place where the god may be found, but the very god: 'The distinction might indeed be overlooked by the vulgar, but it was vital to the progress of religion.'[1]

Besides the baetyls on altars, or the like, which are found on Neo-Babylonian seals, sometimes (on N. Syrian seals) a bull stands on a base or platform (Pl. v. 9, 12, 14). The bull was the animal of the West Semitic god Hadad, it entered conspicuously into Palestinian cult, and it is even possible that the 'horns of the altars' were originally bulls' horns.[2] The bellowing of the bull, its strength and its virility, made it a fitting animal of the god of thunder, storm and rain, by whatever name that god was known (Teshub, Addu, Hadad, Ramman), and on early plaques from Ur (*c.* 3000 B.C.) the animal bears a thunderbolt on its back.

The cult of the animal is spread through the Aegean, Egyptian and Semitic area; and the Mitannian name Teshub probably reappears in the god Teisbas of Urarṭu (Armenia), and very possibly also in Sisyphos 'the faded sun-god of Corinth'.[3] The persistence of the cult to the Christian era is in striking contrast to the main current of Israelite religion. Small models of the bull are sometimes found.[4] It is represented on the Israelite seal of Shemaiah, and it was part of the Temple furniture (1 Kings vii. 25, 29), the 'Brazen

[1] A. B. Cook, *Zeus*, i. 521 (apropos of the sky-god and his stone embodiment). Against the tendency to explain away all sacred stones as merely 'commemorative', see *Rel. Sem.*, p. 569.

[2] See in general *Zeus*, i. 633 sq.

[3] *Zeus*, i. 639. The association of bull and sun persists to late times, cf. the ox-head and sun-disk at Kefr Kenna (*Eph.* iii. 162; for the second example from Ḥoms cf. also Ronzevalle, *Mélanges Beirut*, vii. 155 sqq.). A Palmyrene tessera calls both 'Aglibol and Malakbel (the moon- and the sun-god) 'ox', see *Eph.* iii. 153 sq.

[4] Handcock, *Archaeology of the Holy Land*, p. 285.

Sea' being probably a symbol of the cosmic ocean.[1] Bulls' heads are common at all ages. They are represented on early vases sent from Syria to Egypt;[2] they reappear on the sides of an altar found at Samaria,[3] and are widely distributed.[4]

Sometimes a bull's head is placed on the altar.[5] More noteworthy are the Syro-Hittite or North Syrian seals (Pl. v. 9–12, 14 sq.). In one case the bull stands upon some altar or table underneath a shelter (perhaps the roof of the shrine), while a figure seated before it is engaged in the characteristic act of drinking up liquid from a vessel on the ground by means of a pipe.[6] Sometimes the bull has on its back a bird, or something taken to be a cone or perhaps a flame; or it has two projecting arms, or a child is beneath it.[7]

[1] There is a good example of a bull on the inscription of Ḳaṣyu from es-Suweida (below p. 158, n. 5); another from er-Rummān has on its back a fish (Gressmann, no. 353, who observes that while the place er-Rummān recalls Ramman [Rimmon], i.e. Hadad, the fish was sacred to the goddess Atargatis or Derketo).

[2] See W. M. Müller, *Asien u. Europa*, p. 308 sq., *Liv. A.A.A.*, vi. 58, and Knudtzon, *Amarna Tafeln*, p. 1029 (on no. x. 29).

[3] *Samaria*, i, fig. 123 (three bulls' heads connected by garlands); cf. later, the base of the altar from Sīʿ (Gressmann, no. 465), and the sarcophagus of the Christian era (*Syria*, v. 127, pl. xxxv).

[4] Cf. Vincent, *Canaan*, p. 169 sq.; Mrs. Alice Grenfell, *P.S.B.A.*, xxiv. 26 sqq. (for Egyptian, Cretan and Cypriote examples); the rhytons, *C.A.H.*, pl. i. 168(*b*) (possibly for libations in some bull cult).

[5] Carthage (*C.I.S.*, i. 283, see Vassel, *Rev. Hist. Rel.*, xci. 7 sqq.), also Tēma (Galling, *Altar*, Taf., xiii. 36), where Lagrange (*Études*, p. 502) interprets the bull as the local god Ṣalm, whom he identifies with Saturn—Baal Ḳarnaim.

[6] Contenau, *Glyptique Syro-Hittite*, p. 110, and no. 193; similarly at Eyuk, north of Boghaz-keui, the bull stands on a pedestal (Garstang, *The Hittite Empire*, p. 134; cf. *Zeus*, i. fig. 495).

[7] See Ward, pp. 307 sqq., *Zeus*, i. 784 sq. (with illustrations); and Legrain, *The Culture of the Babylonians*, no. 510. A seal, said to come from the Hauran district, includes *inter alia*, a man kneeling before a bull (not a 'bull-altar') and an undraped female. With the latter we may compare the seals where she stands over or by the bull. Hadad and Astarte (or their equivalents) are no doubt represented (Ward, 914 [cf. 930 and 915], *Zeus*, i. 644, figs. 503 sq.).

The bird (a dove) will be the symbol of a goddess; and on one remarkable seal (Pl. v. 9) besides the bull and the dove there is a quadriga driven by a goddess. The square body of the bull, with its gridiron-like pattern, looks more like some mechanical construction than an animal, and it is generally supposed that it is not a bull, but a bull-altar that is represented.[1] The shape, the flames, the projecting arms, and even the child, combine to suggest that we have an illustration of the bronze bulls in which victims were burnt to death.[2] On the other hand, it is perhaps unsafe to regard these as illustrations of the Molech cult of Palestine; for not only are the 'bull altars' found outside Palestine itself, but it is by no means certain that the human victims to Molech were burnt in some image; the Tophet was rather a fire-place or a pit.[3]

Horns were a symbol of strength, superhuman power, and deity. As emblems of divine rank they are found on gods, genii and great kings, as many as four pairs of horns indicating special pre-eminence.[4] Amulets in crescent shape (boar's tusks, silver, &c.) were common in Gezer,

[1] But the similarly squared body of the animal (? gazelle) on a Gezer votive altar of the Greek age may be noticed (*Gezer*, ii. 441). The 'hatching' of animal bodies is a North Syrian feature (Hogarth, *J.E.A.*, viii. 213).

[2] See *Zeus*, i. 643, ii. 924, for reminiscences of such human sacrifice (of adults). It should be observed, however, that the familiar Jewish descriptions of the Molech-image (cited, e. g. *Zeus*, i. 723 n.) are based upon Greek accounts of the Carthaginian image of Kronos (G. F. Moore, *J.B.L.*, xvi. 161 sqq., *E.Bi.*, 'Molech', col. 3186; Lagrange, *Ét. Sem.*, p. 104).

[3] Moore, *E. Bi.*, 'Molech', § 3; cf. *Rel. Sem.*, p. 377.

[4] Cf. the helmets with horns worn by the spearmen on the Warrior Vase of Mycenae (*C.A.H.*, pl. i. 180*b*); and the bull similes of the kings of Egypt and Babylonia (S. A. Cook, *Rel. of Anc. Pal.*, p. 91). On the 'horns' of Moses (Exod. xxxiv. 29), see Elworthy, *Horns of Honour*, pp. 21 sqq. (ib., p. 76 sq. on the 'horn' symbolism of the bishop's mitre, cf. *Ency. Brit.*, 11th ed., xviii. 625). On Alexander 'of the horns', see Abrahams, *Schweich Lect.*, p. 21; and for the horns of Gabriel and other Jewish angels, see Gaster, *P.S.B.A.*, xxx. 340, 343.

especially in the Second Semitic period; and the practice of making amulets of the tusks or claws of powerful or savage animals fuses with lunary ideas, so that both the material and the shape are significant.[1] Among the Dinkas of the White Nile shrines are made of mud roughly shaped as a bull, and the horns of the animal are fixed at one end.[2] This evidence, which is of the greatest value, in that it suggests how 'bull-altars' and 'horned altars' could originate, can be supplemented when we go back from modern custom to the ancient world, for bronze horns were placed on top of the famous ziggurat of Bel at Babylon, and there were similar horns on the ziggurat at Susa and on that at Nineveh.[3] How readily horns attached to sacred places or objects become stylized can be seen by a comparison of the multifarious forms of the Minoan altar horns.[4] The high conical type is especially noteworthy, because the altars in Palestine have merely depressions on the top; or show protuberances or knobs, and were thus capable of holding liquids (Pl. iv. 2).[5] But at Tēma (*C.I.S.*,

[1] *Gezer*, ii. 450; cf. Ridgeway on the origin of the Turkish crescent (*J. Royal Anthrop. Inst.*, xxxviii. 241 sqq.); for a S. Arabian ox-head with crescent-shaped horns (? and a thunderbolt between), used as an amulet, see Gressmann, no. 402. The moon-god Sin has four pairs of horns surmounted by a crescent (*Pennsylv. Museum*, 1927, p. 82), and in S. Arabia the moon-god is called 'bull' and represented as one (Nielsen, *Handbuch*, i. 214).

[2] See A. B. Cook, *Zeus*, i. 508 sqq.

[3] (*a*) Gressmann, no. 473 (see *Texte*, p. 123, l. 49, [from *Enuma Eliš*]); (*b*) S. Smith, *J.R.A.S.*, 1928, p. 858; (*c*) Gressmann, no. 474 (cf. Dombart, *Arch. f. Orientforsch.*, iii. 177 sq.).

[4] *Zeus*, i. 512; cf. *C.A.H.*, pl. i. 194(*b*), 198(*e*). For other explanations of the 'horns', see Newbury, *Liv. A.A.A.*, i. 27 sqq.; Sjövall, *Arch. f. Rel.*, xxiii. 185 sqq.

[5] See J. de Groot, *Die Altäre des Salomonischen Tempelhofes* (1924), pp. 76 sqq. Cf. the representation of the Elamite sanctuary, Vincent, *Canaan*, p. 144 (Gressmann, no. 468): the tower with the four knobs at the top (dated *c*. 1100 B.C.). For examples, see Beth-Shan, temple of Thutmose III (*Q.S.*, 1928, p. 77, pl. iii, no. 1), described as a portable Cretan altar-stand; Shechem (*Q.S.*, 1926, p. 206), dated *c*. 8th–7th cent.;

ii. 113, *c.* 500 B.C.) the knobs are much more prominent; similarly in the Graeco-Roman period the corner pieces are sharper, note especially the Byblus altar represented on coins.[1] The 'horns' were the most sacred part of the altar, upon them was put the blood of the sin-offering. They are not described; but in the vision of Ezekiel they are a cubit in height. They could be seized by the fugitive who sought asylum; to them the sacrificial victim was bound; and they could be hewn off.[2] Accordingly they would seem to have been much more prominent than those discovered in excavation. The latter hardly admit of being called 'horned'; and it is conceivable that the more important altars (Jerusalem, Bethel, &c.) differed from the commoner variety with mere bosses or knobs.

A fine cylinder (probably Syrian or Cappadocian), to which reference has already been made, represents two 'bull-altars' surmounted by birds, facing an altar with cakes, kneeling figures of Gilgamesh and Enkidu, bulls and lions crossed heraldically, and in particular a goddess on a four-wheeled car, drawn by four horses (?) with four attendants by the side (Pl. v. 9).[3] The deities had their chariots: on a bas-relief (from Ur) an empty chariot is drawn by four lions; on another it is drawn by two man-headed bulls; the goddess of Innana of Uruk, according to an inscription

Gezer (Macalister, ii. 424, Gressmann, no. 444), built into a building of about the 6th cent. (our Pl. iv. 2). See also discussion by Wiener, *Altars* (1927).

[1] Galling, p. 65 sq. (taf. 12 sq.), finds fifty-three examples of 'horned' altars; they are characteristic of the Syro-Phoenician area; cf. Vincent, p. 124 n., Gressmann, nos. 426, 458 sqq., and for the coin, ib., no. 521 (and below, p. 160). At 'Abdeh (Oboda) was an altar with a depression in the middle and nine radiating channels (*Rev. Bib.*, 1904, p. 403 sq., 1905, pp. 74 sq., 235).

[2] Ez. xliii. 15 (LXX); 1 Kings, i. 50, ii. 28; Ps. cxviii. 27; Amos, iii. 14 (as symbols of strength, cf. Lam. ii. 3, Jer. xlviii. 25).

[3] Ward, no. 978 (Du Clercq, *Catalogue*, 284), cf. no. 976 (bull altar, &c.), and for the goddess in the wagon, nos. 977, 979, also no. 983 (Astarte).

of Nabonidus, had a team of seven lions.[1] The sun-god of
Sippar had his chariot; and in a procession of gods at
Malatia he stands on a horse. The temple of Jerusalem had
horses and chariots of the sun (2 Kings xxiii. 11, *cf.* xi. 16).
But although Israelite reformers destroyed these indications of sun-worship, a quadriga is represented on coins of
Aelia Capitolina and Neapolis, and outside Israel deities
continue to be conveyed on cars in the Graeco-Roman
period (see p. 165).[2] Instead of a deity the car might contain a symbol (a baetyl or omphalos), and in Israel the
ark itself was so sacred that its loss spelt disaster.[3] Finally,
the author of the book of Enoch seems to have found it
natural that sun, moon and stars should move in chariots,
and his age was accustomed to the notion that the sun
should ride on horseback.[4]

But the deities also had boats; though it is sometimes
difficult to distinguish between a boat and a crescent, and
it was naturally easy to compare the crescent to a bark
in which the moon-deity sailed along the sky.[5] The symbol

---

[1] See (*a*) *Pennsylv. Mus.*, 1927, p. 151; (*b*) Meyer, *Sumerier u. Semiten*,
i. taf. viii; (*c*) Thureau-Dangin, *Rev. d. Ass.*, xxiv. 203 sq.

[2] Cf. the late fragment of a votive bronze chariot found at Nāblus
(*Q.S.*, 1908, p. 340; 1909, p. 73); and the Jerusalem seal mentioned
below (p. 140 n. 3). White horses were specially valued (Sidney Smith,
Ass., p. 254); eight of them drew the car of Ahura-mazda (Herod.,
vii. 40) and four the chariot of Anaïtis (*Sacred Books of the East*,
xxiii. 57).

[3] It is drawn by oxen (1 Sam. vi. 7). Cf. also the chariot with the
Assyrian standards before whom priests offer a sacrifice (Gr., no. 538),
and see *Rel. Sem.*, p. 37.

[4] See Enoch, lxxii. 5, lxxiii. 2, lxxv. 8 sq., *Syria*, v. 120, and Dussaud,
Mythol. Syr, pp. 53 sq., 57; for a Syrian god on a camel, see Cumont,
Syria, x. 30 sqq., and iv. 172, n. 2; v. pl. xxxi. 4. For gods on horse-
back, see also Mouterde, *Beirut Mélanges*, xi. 311; Dussaud, *Syria*, v. 120;
Lammens, *Bull. de l'Inst. Franç. d'arch. orient.*, xvii. 51 sq.

[5] See Jastrow, *Rel. Belief in Bab. and Ass.*, pp. 114, 336 sq.; *C.I.S.*, ii.
104, the seal of אחת; and that from Marathus (Amrit) with חב (Levy,
Phoen., no. 11, Vogüé, no. 12). In Ward no. 553 the moon-god Sin
stands on a crescent which looks very much like a boat. On the ritual

of Zeus Ammon (image, baetyl or omphalos) was carried
in a huge golden boat by eighty priests.[1] Like the ark of
Israel it was believed to choose its own path (Num. x. 33,
cf. 1 Sam. vi. 12). More realistic was the boat in the old
Pyramid Texts which served to carry the deceased
Pharaoh to the land across the lake: '*all* was alive, whether
it was the seat into which the king dropped, or the steering-
oar to which he reached out his hand, or the bark into
which he stepped. . . .'[2] We may recall the animal heads
on the stem and stern of Egyptian barks of the gods; and
the semi-human boats of Babylonia (Pl. v. 4–8).[3] One, on a
seal assigned to the third Dynasty of Ur, has a prow in the
shape of a bearded human figure, with a conical hat, and
the stem seems to end in a serpent's head.[4] With this
compare the human busts at the ends of the boat (Pl.
v. 8): Shamash sits with his ring and rod on a seat
flanked by animals. In this case there is no oar or
punting-pole. Sometimes the boat is represented as a
snake with up-turned extremities (Ward, no. 108). Finally
it is a quadruped with long neck and tail, and upon it sits
a goddess (Bau ?) with her bird (Pl. v. 6). Archaic
though these are, the state barges of Marduk and Nebo in

for constructing a boat as the symbol of the crescent moon, see Sidney
Smith, *Bab. Hist. Texts*, p. 72 sq. For boats on seals, see in general
Ward, ch. vi, Weber, 406 sqq., 428.

[1] *Zeus*, i. 355 sq. Note the quadriga of Helios and Selene, rising out
of a boat, op. cit., i. 358, n. 3. Boat festivals still survive in Egypt
(Seligmann, *Ridgeway Volume*, p. 453). Another survival is the model
of a boat in the tombs of sheikhs (Miss W. S. Blackman, *Fellahin of
Upper Egypt*, p. 243).

[2] Breasted, *Rel. and Thought*, pp. 105, 107.

[3] Gressmann, nos. 494, 497; cf. L. W. King, *Babylon*, figs. 56 sq.

[4] S. Smith, op. cit., p. 73 sq. (Frontispiece, nos. 4, 5). He identifies
the seated figure with the oar with Adapa who daily journeys in a
crescent or boat over the celestial waters (p. 71). Note the horned
cap and the wavy lines, as in Pl. v. 4, where Ea or Shamash with
streamers from his shoulders (? ears of corn) stands in a boat; also
Pl. v. 5, where Shamash, with streamers, sits in a boat. Here and elsewhere the interpretation is at the best only probable.

F

the time of Nebuchadrezzar II (*c.* 600 B.C.) were still adorned with lions and serpent-headed animals.[1]

It would be precarious to see a survival of the old usage in the images fixed to the ends of ships (see *Ency. Bib.*, *s.v.* Castor and Pollux). On the other hand, mention must certainly be made of the remarkable seal of 'Elishama son of Gedaliah', which was obtained in Jerusalem (Pl. ix. 1).[2] On a boat with bird-like ends, and between two objects resembling palms on stands, sits a figure, holding something in his right hand.[3] The names are of good Hebrew type, and are written in a well-known script, perhaps of about the seventh century. While Sayce sees an Egyptianizing scene, a goddess between two altars (*Q.S.*, 1909, p. 156), the suggestion has been made that we possibly have here a representation of Yahweh, the god of Israel. The genuineness of the object has been questioned by no less an authority than Father Vincent; but although it is certainly unique as regards Palestine, its *motifs* are not isolated, and it would be interesting to know whence the forger derived his inspiration.[4] No doubt boats are not to be expected in a land that had no Nile or Euphrates; yet there were mystical streams and celestial waters,[5] and Jerusalem was the centre of antique ideas more akin to those of Egypt and Babylonia than to the characteristic spiritual teaching of the prophets. Hence, although Yahweh rode in the clouds or moved in his chariot drawn by cherubim (1 Chron.

---

[1] Legrain, *University of Pennsylvania, Babylonian Section*, vol. xv.

[2] Dalman, *Paläst. Jahrbuch*, 1906, pp. 48 sqq.; Vincent, *Rev. Bib.*, 1909, pp. 121 sqq.; cf. Weber, no. 411; Gressmann, no. 598.

[3] The palm is familiar also in the late period; cf. Orfali, *Capharnaüm*, p. 40, fig. 60, and fig. 122; cf. also p. 212, n. 4 below.

[4] For Palestinian forgeries, see A. Reifenberg, *Paläst. Kleinkunst*, pp. 114 sqq., with illustrations.

[5] Cf. Ezek. xlvii. 1–12 (and Hermann's commentary), Ps. civ. 3, cxlviii. 4, and the still surviving belief that beneath the Dome of the Rock at Jerusalem flow the four rivers of Paradise (Canaan, *J.P.O.S.*, ix. 64 sqq.). See Volz, *Das Neujahrsfest Jahwes*, pp. 31, 56 sq., and below, p. 174 sq.

xxviii. 18), this does not exclude the idea of a sacred boat.[1]

The belief in a *boat* to convey the dead is not one that we should expect to find in Palestine; it is Egyptian and Babylonian, and can perhaps be traced in Anatolia.[2] As regards the dead some interesting seals are worth noticing.[3] One (Pl. v. 17), an example of the frequent blending of Egyptian and Babylonian or Mesopotamian elements, seems to represent genii and other figures bringing animals to the dead for food. Very similar is the scene on a seal from the Hauran district (Ward, no. 859). On another, from the same locality (Pl. v. 13), besides the animals (for the dead) there is a human head between two lions, and an eagle, perhaps the bird which carried the dead up to the sky (see p. 212).

Of the first importance is the recently discovered sarcophagus of Aḥiram king of Byblus, *c.* 1200 B.C.[4] Here the king sits with a lotus in his hand upon a throne flanked by winged sphinxes. Before him is a typically Assyrian table of offerings, and attendants approach with food. Two of the panels depict lines of dancing and weeping women, two of whom have their hands on their head (Pl. vi. 1; cf. 2 Sam. xiii. 19; Jer. ii. 37).

[1] Cf. also the boat-shaped *ḍollah* of the Arabs (*Rel. Sem.*, p. 508).

[2] Viz. Ward, no. 857. A Babylonian seal (Pl. v. 7), dated to the fourth millennium, may represent the passage of the dead and a funeral feast in which two participate (Weber, no. 410, cf. Ward, no. 103 ?). In Ward, no. 857, the dead lies on a bier (see now Ronzevalle's discussion, *Mélanges Beirut*, xii. 177 sqq.). The old tablet, Ward, no. 856, Gressmann, no. 387, is no longer interpreted as a scene from the underworld (cf. Jastrow, *Bildermappe z. Rel. Bab. u. Ass.*, no. 100).

[3] Ward, pp. 280 sqq. No. 854, which may represent the dead brought for judgement, may, in view of the guilloche-pattern, be of North Syrian origin. On the scene, see, however, Contenau, p. 113 sq.

[4] Vincent, 'Les Fouilles de Byblos', *Rev. Bib.*, 1925, pp. 161 sqq., pl. vi; Gressmann, nos. 665 sq. Approximately contemporary is the tomb-painting of a dead Egyptian official and his wife enjoying a feast and music (Gressmann, no. 667). Both reflect a mingling of Egyptian and Syrian or Phoenician art. See p. 94, n. 1.

Egyptians living and dying in Palestine would familiarize people with Egyptian beliefs concerning the life after death. Thus at Beth-Shan, the stele of Amen-em-Apt of the XIXth Dynasty illustrates Egyptian prayers for the man's soul in the other world, where he will see the gods adoring the sun-god as his solar bark traverses the heavens.[1] Here, too, certain graves, supposed to be those of Levantine mercenaries of the same period, contained the typical Egyptian Ushabti figures which were expected to work for the deceased in the next life.[2] Yet, on the whole, it is unnecessary to suppose, either that Palestine and Syria lacked beliefs concerning the state after death, or that such beliefs were mechanically imported from Egypt. It is possible that there was an Israelite reaction against them, because of their Egyptian associations, or because they were bound up with beliefs and practices which the re-forming prophets repudiated; and it is by no means improbable that even where there were no positive beliefs of this sort, there was no explicit belief that death brought any very radical change.[3]

The painted tombs of a Sidonian colony at Mareshah of the Graeco-Roman period illustrate how the dead could be entertained by musicians (see p. 202). Going back to an

[1] *Pennsylv. Museum Journal*, 1925, p. 309.

[2] *Q.S.*, 1927, p. 75. The Aramaic 'Carpentras' inscription (*C.I.S.*, ii. 141; Cooke, no. 75), and others, show how readily foreigners in Egypt would assimilate native ideas; cf. I. Lévy, *Journ. Asiat.*, ccxi (1927), 287 sqq., 308 sqq.

[3] For the former, see e. g. Ward, p. 283; and for the latter, Alan Gardiner, *J.E.A.*, iv. 205. In any case, there is a certain gloom, morbidity, and absence of 'other-worldliness' among the Semites; see *C.A.H.*, i. 202; S. Smith, *Ass.*, p. 338. Although provision is made for the needs of the dead in Palestine and Syria, no care is taken (as in Egypt) to preserve the body (cf. Barrois, *Syria*, ix. 206); but ideas of 'mother earth' were not unknown (*Rel. Sem.*, p. 517), and man's body returns to the 'dust' whence it came. What we should call his 'spirit' or 'soul' would—probably normally—be supposed to be bound up with the family (tribe, &c.) or the god (cf. 1 Sam. xxv. 29).

earlier period, we have, in an important Aramaic inscription of the eighth century from Zenjirli (Sinjerli), in North Syria, valuable testimony to the belief that the dead would eat and drink in the presence of the god (below, p. 39). A somewhat later monument from Nerab, also in North Syria, depicts Agbar, the priest of the moon-god Sahr, sitting before an altar or table, holding a cup to his lips, while behind him is an attendant with a fan or lotus.[1] The scene is of additional interest for the fact that his inscriptions contain no reference to a life after death. The priest rejoices that he dies with a good reputation; he leaves children of the fourth generation, and, as on other inscriptions, a curse is uttered against men who shall disturb his image (ṣalmā) and couch.

Excavation in Palestine itself has brought to light abundant evidence for the belief in the efficacy of figurines, scarabs, amulets, 'Horus eyes' (p. 42), and for the care taken to supply the needs of the dead in their new existence.[2] Sometimes a large number of dead are buried together, and in two caves of the Early Bronze Age at en-Nasbeh were the bones of seventy or more persons, who seem to have been literally 'gathered unto their fathers' (W. F. Badé, Q.S., 1927, pp. 10–12). Among the contents of Palestinian tombs are plates, knives, and vessels, with ashes, remains of animals—in one case a whole sheep for one man (Gezer, i. 292)—and drink. Lamps abound, and those in a tomb at Ain Shemesh had apparently been lit

---

[1] See for the former, p. 38, n. 4 below; and for the latter, Cooke, nos. 64, 65, Lagrange, pp. 499 sqq., also Clermont-Ganneau, Études d'Archéol. Orient., ii. 182 sqq., and Album, pls. i, ii, and Sayce, P.S.B.A., xxxii. 253 sq. (a funeral feast based upon the communion ceremony, see below, p. 39, n. 1).

[2] Vincent, ch. iv, and especially pp. 284 sqq.; Handcock, ch. viii. It is interesting to notice that blue (pearls, &c.) is a favourite colour (Taannek, p. 79, cf. Folk-lore, xxxiii. 141 sqq., Westermarck, Morocco, i. 440), and that cornelian is now supposed to be a charm against ophthalmia (Beth-Shemesh, Annual, ii. 63). See in general Thomsen, Reallex. Vorg., 'Amulett', 'Siegel'.

on the occasion of funerary feasts.[1] Holes have been found for communicating with the dead. Among the small objects are figurines of deities (the mother-goddess and others), jewellery, hair-pins, &c., models of a donkey water-carrier, and of a horse and rider (Ain Shemesh, pp. 49, 88); also rattles and clay animal toys, along with remains of the skeletons of children.[2] Speaking of Ain Shemesh, Dr. Duncan Mackenzie says (p. 83): 'the chamber tomb is modelled on the abode of the living, and the images put there to keep company with the spirit of the dead person are the same images of domestic deities that have played so prominent a part in early Semitic religion.' Of special interest is the so-called 'Philistine' grave, no. 4 (*Gezer*, i. 292 sq., our Pl. vii), which contains the skeleton of a woman with (besides a few sheep-bones near her head) a rich assortment of mirrors, vases, bracelets, &c. Mr. E. J. Pilcher (*Q.S.*, 1912, pp. 30 sqq.) compares the Aramaic marriage-contract of Mibṭaḥiah, a Jewish woman at Elephantine in the fifth century (Cowley's edition, no. 15); and, although it is not easy to interpret the complete list of her bridal gifts and dowry, he points out that if she 'had been buried with her bridal gifts and dowry, her tomb would have yielded to the modern explorer a series of objects almost identical with those found in the "Philistine" graves of Gezer'.[3]

Besides ceremonial mourning festivals (cf. Jer. xvi. 7 sq.), there were meals before or with the god. The best evidence is the inscription of king Panammu on the statue of the god Hadad from North Syria.[4] The Hebrew kings evidently

[1] Mackenzie, *Annual*, ii. 58, 67; cf. Steuernagel, *Mutesellim*, pp. 19, 21. Gressmann, no. 194: the dead Egyptian gives a feast.

[2] Mackenzie, p. 89; Macalister, *Gezer* (Index, s.v. 'Rattles'); Badé, *Q.S.*, 1927, p. 12 sq. (en-Nasbeh).

[3] Gressmann, no. 218, gives 'Philistine' tomb no. 5 (*Gezer*, i. 296). As Pilcher argues, it is difficult to believe that the tombs are as old as the 'Philistine' period; cf. below, p. 95. Cf. the elaborate provision for the toilet of the dead woman in a Nerab tomb (*Syria*, ix. 201 sq.).

[4] *c.* 750 B.C. Cooke, no. 61; Lagrange, *Études*, pp. 492 sqq., cf. pp.

used to eat 'bread before Yahweh' at the eastern gate of the
Temple (Ezek. xliv. 3); though it would not always be
easy to say how Yahweh was believed to manifest his
presence (Ex. xviii. 12; Deut. xii. 7, &c., see *Rel. Sem.*,
p. 596). The references, together with the remarkable
allusion to the meal before the God of Israel on the top of
the mountain (Ex. xxiv), point unambiguously to definite
ideas of communal feasts; but for illustrations we have
once more to look to North Syria (Carchemish, Mar'ash,
&c.), of the period round about 1000 B.C. Here are found
a series of so-called 'communion scenes', though to be sure
it is not certain that they all have a religious significance
and that the meal is invariably shared with a deity.[1]

On North Syrian seals a man sometimes sits and drinks
before an altar upon which stands a bull; or two seated
figures are in the presence of a bull upon which stands an
undraped goddess.[2] On one from Memphis, North Syrian
in type, a figure is seated before a well-laden table; facing

319, 335. The dead king desires that his successor shall sacrifice to
Hadad, and make mention of the name of Hadad and of Panammu,
and make mention of the soul of Panammu along with Hadad, and
say, 'May the soul of Panammu eat with Hadad, and may the soul of
Panammu drink with Hadad.'

[1] See Sayce, *P.S.B.A.*, xxviii. 95, xxxii. 177 sqq., 253 sq. (cf. A.
Grenfell, pp. 268 sqq.), xxxiii. 259; Hogarth, *Hittite Seals*, p. 51, *Schweich
Lectures*, p. 44; Woolley and Lawrence, *Carchemish*, ii, pl. xxx; Messer-
schmidt, *M.V.A.G.*, 1900, v, taf. 16*b*, 22, 26.1; Garstang, *Hittite Empire*,
p. 149 and Index, s.v. Ceremonial Feasts; Lidzbarski, *Eph.*, iii. 195
(the stele of Ördek-burnu). For some criticisms, see Przeworski, *Arch. f.
Orientforschung*, iii. 172 sqq. E. Burrows (*J.R.A.S.*, 1925, p. 284), who
compares the meeting of Melchizedek and Abraham (Gen. xiv. 18),
observes that in one representation the cup is apparently blessed. He
notes that in the ritual of Boghaz-keui there was something like a blessing of bread and wine (*Z.D.M.G.*, 1922, p. 190).

[2] Contenau, *Glyptique*, pp. 109 sqq. and no. 193 (=Ward, no. 732;
the long pipe out of which the man drinks is characteristic, see Gressmann, no. 79); ib., no. 140 (an undraped goddess on a bull). See also
nos. 138, 157. On the seal of אחתמלך wife of ישע (Lévy, no. 6; Vogüé,
no. 6), a female on a raised seat is served by a figure with a jug—the
dead are thirsty (cf. Cooke, no. 75).

him is a figure with uplifted hands, while behind, another (? a priest) cuts up the body of a stag which lies upon a similar sort of table (? altar).[1] It may be noticed that the Hebrew king (Ezekiel's 'prince') took part in sacrificial offerings, and would be present when the priests prepared the sacrifices (Ezek. xlvi. 2, 12).

For the Egyptian, to 'see the god Amon' was to receive length of life (cf. Ps. xvi. 11); and to come 'before' a god or to 'see his face' was a typical old Oriental ceremony.[2] Men danced before the god, and David's dance before the Ark, i.e., before Yahweh (2 Sam. vi. 14, 16, 21), and the dance before the Golden Bull (Exod. xxxii) can be illustrated by the archaic ritual dance of the Pharaoh before Osiris.[3] When Hezekiah lays a letter 'before Yahweh' (2 Kings xix. 14), or it is forbidden to 'see' the god with empty hands (Exod. xxiii. 15), the words imply that primarily there was some visible embodiment or symbol. In the old religions a god might be visibly represented, not by an image, but by the king. The 'breath' (or 'spirit') of both the god and the king was life-giving; and both would show favour to a man by 'lifting up' his face.[4] The representations on seals and monuments of the introduction of the worshipper (sometimes the king) to the god are analogous to those where the officer or servant comes before his lord. The inferior is led before the superior, though it is sometimes doubtful whether the latter is a god, or a divine or deified king. On Babylonian seals the god sits with notched sword (or saw ?); or he holds out a hand, half-raised, with friendly gesture.[5] At Beth-Shan and else-

---

[1] Sayce, *P.S.B.A.*, xxxiii. 259.

[2] On 'seeing' the god, see Baudissin, *Arch. f. Rel.*, xviii. 173 sqq. (p. 218, Egyptian evidence); Nötscher, *Das Angesicht Gottes schauen* (Würzburg, 1924).

[3] Legrain, *Culture of the Babylonians*, i. 72; see Kees, *Aeg. Z.*, lii. 61; Thutmose dancing before Hathor, Haas, *Bilderatlas : Aegypt*, no. 94; see in general, Oesterley, *The Sacred Dance* (1923).

[4] The phrase is also Akkadian, see Dhorme, *Rev. Bib.*, xxx. 379 sq.

[5] Cf. the N. Syrian king Bar-rekub and his official (*C.A.H.*, pl. i,

where have been found small models of seated figures with the arms slightly raised 'comme en un geste d'accueil ou de protection'.[1] In the inner chamber of Tomb II at Marissa (Mareshah) is painted a tall candelabrum surmounted by a lamp; by the side, a figure, with his right hand raised towards it, advances leading a smaller figure, almost nude—it is apparently an introduction scene, the candelabrum having a religious significance.[2] In one of the best-known examples (in the British Museum), the priest introduces the worshipper to the sun-god of Sippar; he touches the altar with his left hand, and holds the worshipper with his right, behind stands the goddess Aa, wife of Shamash.[3] In another, the goddess with raised hands implores the deity or deified king on behalf of the worshipper, to whom the god or king holds out a cup.[4] The worshipper or the intermediary is sometimes made to resemble the god.[5] The intermediary is often bifrons or janifrons,

240b). A goddess is said to 'bless with her right hand' (Dhorme, *Rev. Bib.*, xxxv. 333). The worshipper also raises his hand as a request to be blessed. On the gesture, see Lidz., *Eph.* iii. 167, *O.L.Z.*, 1928, p. 236 n., Cumont, *Doura-Europos*, p. 70 sq., and especially Langdon, *J.R.A.S.*, 1919, pp. 531–55.

[1] Vincent, *Rev. Bib.*, 1929, p. 101 sq.

[2] Peters and Thiersch, *Painted Tombs in the Necropolis of Marissa*, p. 32. Cf. the strange seal (with the name Gehazi?) bearing an Egyptianizing scene of a king slaying an enemy, and the familiar Mesopotamian introduction of a man to the god (Pilcher, *P.S.B.A.*, 1901, p. 362; cf. *Eph.* i. 275 sq.); also the coin where Gordian III, seated, receives the new king of Edessa whom he has installed (Hill, *Arab. Coins*, p. cvi).

[3] *C.A.H.*, pl. i. 74 (Gressmann, no. 322). Cf. ib., 58c (Gressmann, no. 323), where the goddess introduces a man to the moon-god and the moon-goddess stands behind; cf. also 54c, 56b. On the seal of Gudea the king is introduced by his god to Ea who gives him the running water of life (Gressmann, no. 45).

[4] Langdon, *J.R.A.S.*, 1927, p. 43.

[5] The intermediary may be a priest clad in imitation of the presiding god (Mercer, *J.S.O.R.*, v. 14); cf. the Oriental medallion where the priest resembles his deity (*Zeus*, ii. 630). For the *imitatio dei*, see *Rel. Sem.*, p. 674, and on intermediary deities, see Dhorme, *Rel. Ass.-Bab.*, pp. 261 sqq., and *Rev. Bib.*, 1926, pp. 335, 348, n. 2.

bicephalic; it is an artistic convention, in order to make him face both the god and the worshipper, and to represent him as a true intermediary, partly human, partly divine.[1]

The god 'sees' the worshipper, hence the 'eye' is a symbol of his watchfulness (Ps. xxxiii. 18; Ezra v. 5). Egyptian eye-beads ('Horus eyes') are often found in Palestine,[2] and the 'eye' and the winged disk appear on the Hebrew or Israelite seal of Kanayau.[3] A rhomboid or eye is found on some seals (Ward, nos. 526, 531); sometimes it is unusually large, like the large ears p. 142 below. A fine Babylonian seal of about the time of the Hebrew monarchy has two eyes, and invocations to two gods: 'Marduk, look on me, have mercy'; 'Shamesh, look on me, have mercy' (C.A.H., pl. i, 226 b). With the many-eyed wheels of the cherubim in Ezekiel's vision (x. 12, cf. also i. 18), and the six-winged and many-eyed cherubim and seraphim in Enoch's vision (Secrets of Enoch, xxi. 1), we may compare the many-eyed Bes, with four arms, four wings, and a fish tail, from the Serapeum at Memphis (Gressmann, no. 567). To the Egyptian, the 'eye' symbolized the Sun-god's providence, and the filial piety of Horus who lost his eye in his struggle

[1] The intermediary is thus most closely associated with the god and the man (see O. Weber, Altor. Siegelbilder, i, p. 115; Dhorme, Rev. Bib., 1926, p. 349 sq.). Another view is that the device represents male and female in one; for other explanations, see Zeus, ii. 189. There is a similar convention on Philisto-Arabian coins. Marduk is the intermediary god par excellence, his father Ea gave him all his knowledge: 'what dost thou not know, what can I add unto thy knowledge? what I know, thou knowest also.' Marduk is represented in double with four ears and four eyes (J.E.A., viii. 84; cf. also Gressmann, no. 368); for an example of triplication, see Haas, Bilderatlas, Urchristentum, p. xvi, and fig. 121 (Zeus Dolichenus).

[2] Gezer, i. 296, 342, ii. 331; some fine examples from Megiddo (Gressmann, no. 555); cf. also Samaria (i. 380); Ain Shemesh (pp. 60 [18 in a tomb], 62 [eye-like marks on club-shaped amulets]), Nerab (Syria, ix. 205), Beth-Shan, &c.

[3] For the seal of קני (cf. the Biblical name Mikneiah), see Clermont-Ganneau, Rec., iii. 189, and Lidzbarski, Handbuch, p. 486. There are two eyes on the seal of Baal-nathan (Gressmann, no. 584).

with Set, and offered it to his dead father Osiris, and thus restored him to life, or rather made of him a soul.[1] Precisely what the 'Horus eye' meant to the Palestinian it would be difficult to say; but we meet with the god himself on later Hebrew seals, and in view of the close connexions between Palestine and Egypt there would certainly be some who knew that the 'eye' was a symbol of the god's care, or that it would turn the dead into a living 'soul', or that it had some sacrificial value.

The gods stood in a closer relationship to kings or priests than to ordinary folk. Consequently the intermediary is not always necessary, and, as at Ivriz in Anatolia, it is the king himself who stands before the great god (see p. 137). At Iasily Kaya the beardless god with typical conical hat has his left arm round the neck of his protégé.[2] Not very dissimilar was the scene on the occasion of the treaty between Ramses II and the Hittites (1272 B.C.), when the god, the lord of heavens, and the corresponding goddess, embraced respectively the Hittite king Ḥattushil and his wife.[3] This is a fine distinction, for the great gods were sometimes thought of as indifferently male or female.[4] Realistic language was often used of the intimate relations between kings and their deities: and while Babylonian texts refer to kings as children of the mother of the gods and nourished by her milk (Boissier, *O.L.Z.*, 1908, col. 234 sqq.) —and especially Ashurbanipal (*K.A.T.*, 379)—at Abydos we can see Seti I suckled by a goddess (Gressmann, no. 88).

Yahweh taught Israel to walk (Hos. xi. 3); and the god who teaches men to war (Ps. xviii. 34; cxliv. 1) is seen when Setekh assists Thutmose III to hold the bow—cf. Elisha and

[1] Breasted, *Rel. and Thought*, pp. 12 sqq., 59 sqq.; Mercer, *J.S.O.R.*, iv. 29 sqq., 55 sqq.

[2] Gressmann, no. 342 (Garstang, *Land of Hittites*, p. 232, pl. lxxi, *Hitt. Empire*, fig. 7, p. 111); cf. Frazer, *Adonis*, i. 131, 139 sq.

[3] Breasted, *Anc. Records of Eg.*, iii, § 391; Frazer, *Adonis*, i. 136.

[4] Cf. Deut. xxxii. 18, *Rel. Sem.*, p. 517, and *Rev. Bib.*, 1926, pp. 350 sqq. (see 351, n. 1, 354 n., 357).

Joash (2 Kings xiii. 16)—or when Horus instructs the Pharaoh in the use of the spear; or when hands reach down from the sun-disk and hold out a bow and arrows to the Assyrian king Adad-nirari II.[1] The part taken by the gods in war is also illustrated on a seal from Beth-Shan, where Ramses II shoots an arrow at a shield, a symbol of a fortress, set up on a post to which two captives (a Syrian and a Hittite) are tied. Above and behind the king is a figure whose wings overshadow him; and facing him is the god Setekh holding a scimitar (Pl. xxv. 3).[2] The symbol of the imageless Asshur is represented over the Assyrian army marching against the foe; and on the hunting-scene at Sakje-geuzi the winged sun is above the head of the king (Garstang, The Hittite Empire, pl. xlvi).

To the god who holds people with his hand correspond the designs on the coins of Aelia Capitolina, Neapolis, Tiberias, &c., where the city-goddess or Tyche holds the bust of the reigning emperor (p. 191). Divine power was imparted to the kneeling Pharaoh by the god laying his hand on his back (Ancient Egypt, 1920, p. 58). To take hold of the hand was a sign of help as well as of friendship, and in the Amarna Letters the men of Tunip in Syria lament that there is none to take hold of their hand. On the summit of Nemrūd Dagh Antiochos I of Commagene (1st cent. B.C.) is seen having his hand grasped by Zeus (Ahura-mazda): the two are dressed alike, and the king is adorned with the symbols of the god.[3] Especially significant is the characteristic symbolism of the reforming king Amenhotep IV or Ikhnaton: rays issuing from the sun-disk, each holding out either a hand or the sign of life (ankh).[4] The cult of the

[1] Gressmann, no. 53; W. Max Müller, Egypt. Mythol., fig. 99; Gressm., no. 332 (S. Smith, Ass., p. 333 sq., pl. xvii).

[2] See Vincent, Rev. Bib., 1928, p. 529 sq., and p. 111 sq. below.

[3] A. B. Cook, Zeus, i. 748 sqq.

[4] Gressmann, no. 539, C.A.H., pl. i. 128, 142a; see C.A.H., ii. 111 sq., 399. The hand from heaven (with or without rays) was also a natural symbol in the Middle Ages (Elworthy, Horns of Honour, pp. 156 sqq.).

beneficent life-giving sun-disk Aton would be known in south-west Asia (*C.A.H.*, ii. 399); but the symbol does not seem to have spread, although traces of it have been suspected here and there, e.g. in the above-mentioned monument of Adad-nirari II.

The symbol of the hand frequently recurs in the old oriental area.[1] It is painted on walls as a charm, and is now often popularly supposed to be the hand of Fatima, or of the Virgin, or of God. In Carthaginian inscriptions it is the hand of the god that bestows blessings; while the pair of hands on Palmyrene altars is taken to be a symbol of prayer.[2] Again, it seems to have been a sign of adoration, an appeal for justice, or the hand is 'a part for the whole', a token of the presence of the worshipper or the god.[3] Sometimes, on Mesopotamian seals, a hand is set up on an altar.[4]

Like the lotus, the Egyptian emblem of life, the *ankh* or 'sign of life' (☥), spread through south-west Asia. It is the gods' gift to the Pharaoh, as when the goddess Anukit holds it to the nostrils of Usertesen III (XIIth Dynasty), saying,

[1] *J.P.O.S.*, iv. 12; Canney, *Givers of Life* (1923), ch. iv; Trumbull, *Threshold Covenant* (1896), pp. 67 sqq.; Eerdmans, *Z.A.*, ix. 295.

[2] Chabot, *Inscr. Palm.*, pp. 19, 79–86, pl. xxiv. There are clasped hands on the Aramaic seal of תסמר ('she [Aṭargatis?] preserves', see Lidz., *Eph.* iii. 298), and upon Alexandrian coins (Poole, *Coins of Alexandria*, pl. xxx. 1279). As a symbol of friendship, see *A.J.S.L.*, 1928, p. 229. Two hands joined within a wreath, on coins of Herod Agrippa I (Madden, p. 136). For votive hands (symbolical) of the helping hand of the god in the cult of Sabazios, see Perdrizet, *Arch. f. Rel.*, xiv. 118 sqq., Haas, *Bilderatlas . . . Urchristentum*, no. 162. Hands with more than five fingers symbolize increased power (*P.S.B.A.*, xxiv. 38).

[3] Hogarth, *Hittite Seals*, p. 65.

[4] Contenau, *Glypt.*, no. 129 (*Kerkouk*, no. 34). Hands in no obvious relation to the scene, Contenau, *Glypt.*, nos. 166, 211 (*Kerkouk*, no. 48 and p. 59), Hogarth, op. cit., p. 56 (no. 154). Fusion of hand with palm or cypress, Contenau, *Glypt.*, p. 83; *Brit. Museum, Coins of Galatia*, p. 292, pl. xxxvi. 6. On the Carthaginian inscription, *C.I.S.*, i. 536 (t. ii, tab. iv), the palm of the hand is marked with 'X' (cf. Ezek. ix. 4, 6).

'I give thee life, stability, purity, like Re [the sun-god], eternally'.[1] On the old seal of 'Atanaḥil, the servant of Nergal', found at Taanach, the sign (which is repeated), the use of the Akkadian script, and the scene representing a female figure with raised hand blessing a man, make up a mixture of elements characteristic of Palestine of about 1500 B.C. (Gressmann, no. 577). The sign is painted upon (*a*) the fine Israelite lion-seal of 'Shama, the servant of Jeroboam' found at Megiddo (see p. 60); and, together with a basilisk, it can be traced upon (*b*) the rather later seal of 'Yoram (son of) Zimriyyahu'. Upon (*c*) that of 'Yehoshua son of Asayahu', besides a six-rayed star and a 'shield of David' at the end of the text, the lines are divided, as often in Israelite seals, by a double line which, in this case, is made up of two *ankhs*.[2] A symbol somewhat resembling an *ankh* (but with an inverted triangle at the head) is found upon a Gezer contract seal, but may be a rough representation of an altar (p. 64). It does not follow that the sign was always intelligently used; and a scarab found at Ophel—itself of *c*. 1900 B.C.—contains an arrangement of *ankhs* and other ideographs which 'may be regarded with some plausibility as signifying a wish that life, protection, and peace may be "behind" or surround the owner'.[3]

The origin of the *ankh* is disputed.[4] It undergoes some remarkable developments, characteristic being the Hittite

---

[1] It was often painted green, hence the (modern) view that it was a knot made of some plant, and, as such, a symbol of life.

[2] Throughout, the actual pronunciation of the names upon the unvocalized North Semitic seals is quite conjectural, and the spelling is approximated to biblical analogies. The references are: (*a*) Gressm., no. 578, cf. Steuernagel, *Tell el-Mutesellim*, i. 99 (fig. 147), dated to the eighth century; (*b*) *Eph.*, i. 11; (*c*) Torrey, *J.A.O.S.*, 1908, p. 193 sq.

[3] H. R. Hall, see *Q.S.*, 1924, p. 183; *P.E.F. Annual*, iv. 178.

[4] Among the explanations are: (*a*) a degenerate form of the winged sun (but see below, p. 51); (*b*) a jar on an altar; (*c*) a cravat-shaped ornament worn round neck, head or waist (Montet, *Rev. Arch.*, xxi. 101); (*d*) a knot (Gressm., on no. 568; but knots are represented otherwise, see M. A. Murray, *Anc. Eg.*, 1922, pp. 14–19).

form which broadens out the arms and base.[1] The late
Carthaginian symbol of the goddess Tanit (⚲) is interpreted as an attempt to give it anthropomorphic form.[2]
Of special interest is the form at Petra (△) which, as
seen by Prof. Burkitt in 1926, had horizontal arms, and
traces of ΖѠΗ within the triangle, a significant fact if
indeed the Egyptian 'sign of life' was the ancestor of the
sign of Tanit.[3] Symbols frequently contaminate each
other and the lines of development interlock; the *ankh* was
taken over by the Egyptian Christians and the *crux ansata*
finally became the Christian monogram (☧, etc.).[4]

More familiar than the 'sign of life', and more complex
in its development, is the 'winged solar disk'. Horus, as the
sun flying as a falcon, with the two uraei, goddesses of
Upper and Lower Egypt, overcame the enemies of his
father Re, who gave command that this symbol should be

[1] Hogarth, *Hittite Seals*, p. 74, nos. 164, 181; *J.E.A.*, viii. 214 (pl. no.
15, two vultures each with a sign); Contenau, *Kerkouk*, pp. 44 (no. 25,
three on one seal), 56 (no. 56, a figure holds the Egyptian *ankh*). The
Hittite form recurs on the Syrian or Palestinian seal in S. Smith, *Ass.*,
pl. xiv. The Kassite form resembles a Maltese cross (ib., p. 329, fig. 21).

[2] Cf. Ed. Meyer, *Ency. Bib.*, 'Phoenicia', § 8. For Carthage, see
Gauckler, *Bull. Arch.*, 1894, pp. 295 sqq. W. R. Smith suggested that
the arms represent the horns of sheep and symbolize a male or female
deity (*Rel. Sem.*, p. 478). Many varying forms are found, e.g. in con-
junction with a caduceus in front of a tomb, near the 'Tomb of Hiram'
(*Syria*, v. 45). The 'mistresses Astarte and Tanit in Lebanon' are
named in a Carthaginian inscription (Cooke, no. 45); but it is not certain that Lebanon in Phoenicia is meant. If Tanit occurs in the old
inscriptions of Serabit (Gardiner, *Q.S.*, 1929, p. 53 sq.) there is an
enormous gulf between Sinai of *c*. XIIth Dynasty and the Hellenistic
age. See, in general, D'Alviella, *Migration of Symbols* (Index), and *Ency.
Rel. Ethics*, iv. 326; Montet (see p. 46, n. 4); Gaerte, *Arch. f. Rel.*, xxi. 92.

[3] The form to which Prof. Burkitt refers (in a private communication)
is given rather differently by Brünnow and Domaszewski, *Provincia
Arabia*, i. 407, fig. 460, no. 825.

[4] For transitional forms, see Mrs. E. L. Butcher and Sir Flinders
Petrie, *Anc. Eg.*, 1916, pp. 97 sqq.; Scott-Moncrieff, *Paganism and
Christianity in Egypt*, p. 108; De Zwaan, *J.T.S.*, xxi. 332.

erected in sacred places in order to ward off evil.[1] It spread at an early date; and at Beth-Shan it appears on the stelae of Seti I and Ramses II (very rough workmanship).[2] In its Asiatic forms emphasis is laid, now upon its solar form and its rays, and now upon its bird form, and it coalesces with the common symbol of the eagle (Pl. viii. 1).[3] On the seal of Sirpad it is over a candelabrum (Pl. xiii. 3).[4] It recurs on the splendid seal of Mar-barak (ib. no. 4), 'Mar (the lord) blesses', where the name is divided by the *ankh*. The symbol has the characteristic Assyrian triad of heads.[5] It stands above a small shrine, and, in harmony with a familiar idea, is supported by genii; cf. the posts held by protecting genii.[6] The figure with sacrificial animals is a familiar *motif*.[7] Characteristic also is the single figure of the usually imageless Asshur, the sun-disk with rays or wings 'material-

---

[1] See, in general, D'Alviella, *Migration of Symbols*, pp. 204–26; A. B. Cook, *Zeus*, i. 205 sqq.; Gressmann, nos. 307–11, and, for the myth, Roeder, *Urkunden zur Rel. der alten Ägypter* (1923), pp. 120 sqq.

[2] Gressmann, no. 97 sq. Cf. the similar form on the Amrit stela (Gr., no. 307), and on the seal of 'Shebanyau son of Uzziyau' (Gr., no. 588).

[3] We give a combination of the winged sun and the eagle (itself a solar bird) from a Phoenician holy place, 'Ain el-Hayat (Cook, *Zeus*, i. 206 sq., fig. 150). In Anatolia the rosette (in the place of the disk), with the crescent under it, is perhaps the prototype of the Turkish star and crescent (Garstang, *Hittite Empire*, p. 269).

[4] *C.I.S.*, ii. 81. Among other forms, cf. the seal of Yish'a (ישעא), with two stars and a crescent (*Eph.*, i. 11, 277); the fragment from the Shephelah (Bliss-Macalister, fig. 45, our Pl. vi. 3); the seal of סראל (*C.I.S.*, ii. 82); and the evidently Moabite seal of Chemosh-yeḥi (Gressm., no. 581, *Eph.*, i. 140). Closely akin are (*a*) the seal from Nerab (*Syria*, 1928, p. 200, fig. 6*b*), and (*b*) Legrain, no. 756 (said to come from Gezer): three parallel lines with a crescent above and rays below.

[5] *C.I.S.*, ii. 85. For the triad, cf. *Eph.*, ii. 146, with the man kneeling beneath it, and cult objects behind.

[6] *C.A.H.*, pl. i. 226 *d*; S. Smith, *Ass.*, pl. xxi. *c*; similarly the seal Pl. xiii. 5 (*C.I.S.*, ii. 80).

[7] Cf. 1 Sam. x. 3; Zenjirli, O. Weber, *Hethit. Kunst*, pl. 33 (Haas, *Bilderatlas: Rel. d. Hethiter*, pl. 12); Carchemish (Hogarth, *Schweich Lectures*, p. 36, fig. 43). For one of the Graeco-Roman period at Ḳaryatein, see *Rev. Bib.*, 1920, p. 364, fig. 1.

ized', so to speak, by the addition of a warrior with bow and arrow within the disk.[1] On a fine enamel of the time of Tukulti-Ninurta II (*c.* 890 B.C.), the god, presumably Asshur, is surrounded by flames (cf. Ezek. i. 27), and draws his bow, fighting on behalf of his king and country.[2] The scene is in the rain-clouds, and the rain-drops are seen stored up in skins (cf. Job xxvi. 8, xxxviii. 37; Ps. xxxiii. 7). Later, the god is the Persian Ahura-mazda, distinguished by his mitre and by the ring he holds in his hand.[3] He is found on the seal with the Persian name of Mithras (*C.I.S.*, ii. 101), and on that of Yaḥaṣ, from Beirut (Levy, no. 15; Vogüé, no. 42). Specially noteworthy is the seal of 'Menaḥemeth wife of Gad-melek'.[4] Here, two men worship the god beneath whom are sun and moon; the seal has the double dividing-line, often found on Israelite seals, and the name of the man does not necessarily point outside Israel—cf. the name Gaddayau (?) on the ostraka discovered in Samaria (p. 97).

Streamers sometimes hang down from the symbol, and touch or are held by the worshippers (Pl. v. 19). This is a realistic expression of the god's help and favour; and it finds a parallel in court-usage when Esther must touch the sceptre which the Persian monarch graciously extends to her (Esther iv. 11; v. 2; viii. 4). On the seal of 'Irpeel son of Hor'eder(?)' the god Asshur is approached by a man who is accompanied by two giant winged figures. Beneath the symbol is possibly a fountain.[5] And on another (Legrain, no. 596), said to come from Gezer, a tree stands beneath the solar-disk, and a kneeling figure touches both. We

---

[1] Jastrow, *Rel. Beliefs in Bab. and Ass.*, pp. 51, 122.

[2] Gressmann, no. 333. For the conventional types, see *Zeus*, i. 207, fig. 152 (and ib., n. 6, on Asshur as a nature-god). Yahweh, like Asshur, fights in the storm (Judg. v. 20; 1 Sam. vii. 10).

[3] Cf. the cylinder seal of Darius I, *C.A.H.*, pl. i. 324 (*a*); ib. 312 (*a*), the Behistun relief; Gressmann, no. 311, *Zeus*, l.c., fig. 153. Ahura-mazda begins to appear also on coins of Tarsus and Issus of the fourth cent. B.C.   [4] Gressmann, no. 594, Levy, no. 14, Vogüé 40.

[5] Pl. ix. 2. *C.I.S.*, ii. 77; Cooke, p. 150, n. 3.

give further illustrations after Ward.[1] The duplication of the worshipper is often merely for the sake of symmetry. The stylized tree is familiar enough in both the Mesopotamian and the Cretan areas; and the ceremony of fertilization (Ward, 1154) recurs also in North Syria at Sakje-geuzi.[2] This is perhaps not fortuitous. Asshur, the national god, was not merely in some respects a nature god; there is reason to believe that he was once also a tree-god. Whether the name of the Asherah or sacred tree trunk is to be connected with his is purely conjectural; but at all events there was an Assyrian rite centred upon a tree trunk ornamented with branches and bound with metal bands.[3] Cult-objects of this character may be recognized upon Syro-Palestinian seals; and there is no *a priori* objection to the view that very similar rites prevailed over Egypt and south-west Asia. Moreover, throughout the development of early religion the practical needs of man as regards food and vegetation are never lost sight of, and nature-gods of sun and rain, and food-gods continue to persist.

The seal of 'Nehemiah son of Micaiah' (Pl. xiii. 6), to judge from the personal names and the script, is typically Israelite. Instead of the double lines it has what may be

[1] Pl. v. 16, Ward, 667; ib. no. 18, Ward, 668; note the object beneath the symbol; cf. the seal of Elishama (Pl. ix, no. 1). No. 20 is from the embroidery on Ashurbanipal's robe. No. 21, Ward, 1154 (from the British Museum); note the triad, the 'sign of life', wedge, crescent, dog and ape. In one case, worshippers are touched by the streamers coming from a gate-like object, with wings, resting upon a bull (Ward, *Amer. J. of Arch.*, iii, p. 25).

[2] Garstang, *Hittite Empire*, p. 269, *Land of Hittites*, p. 303 and pl. lxxx; Weber, *Hethit. Kunst*, no. 17; see also *C.A.H.*, pl. i. 226*f*, 228*d* (cf. 72*c*). On the evolution of the date-palm type, see Evans, *Palace of Minos*, ii. 496.

[3] See S. Smith, *Ass.*, pp. 123 sqq. and fig. 10, for Asshur as a tree-god (after Contenau, *Kerkouk*, pl. x); id. *C.A.H.*, iii. 92, and *Ass.*, p. 377, for further references. He conjectures that there was a New Year festival of the revival of nature, and compares the Egyptian *ṭeṭ* or *ded* column connected with the worship of Osiris, the dead god who came to life again (an Assyrian parallel on the seal, pl. vii *c*, facing p. 34). The *ded* amulet is common in Palestine, e.g. *Gezer*, ii. 333.

interpreted as a degraded or intentionally altered form of the winged sun.[1] There is no reason to doubt that this widespread symbol was familiar in Palestine—it has been found at Beth-Shan—and when the prophet speaks of 'the Sun of Righteousness arising with healing in his wings', it is a reasonable assumption that this is one of those 'isolated allusions' which 'suggest how little we really know of the social and aesthetic background of Hebrew literature'.[2] The individuality of the Hebrews or Israelites repeatedly shows itself in the way they reshaped or adjusted what they received from outside (e.g. myths and legends); and various intermediate and divergent forms of the symbol can be suspected. So (a) where the double line is divided by a circle, or two parallel rays spring from either side of the circle, and (b) where, instead of parallel lines, the ends are expanded into a floral ornamentation.[3] Finally, it may be remarked that although the plain double line is found on the plain seals of men with such 'Biblical' names as Maaseiah son of Meshullam, Haggai son of Shebanyau (Shebaniah), and Jeḳamiah son of Ishmael, this device recurs on seals by no means plain and with names that are not distinctively Israelite.[4]

[1] Brit. Mus. 1049, Clermont-Ganneau, no. 42. Closely related to it are the seals of 'Nethaniah son of Buzi' (Torrey, *Annual of the American Schools*, 1923, p. 105, no. 2), 'Ḥonen son of Jaazaniah' (חנן בן יאזניה, ib. no. 3, ascribed to the fifth century B.C.), and 'Uzziyahu son of Ḥereph' (חרף, *Rev. d'Études Juives*, xli. 174, n. 1). Somewhat similar is the thunderbolt (———◁ o ▷———), the symbol of the Egyptian Min, the original form of Amon, god of heaven and thunder (Newberry, *Liv. A.A.A.*, iii. 50 sqq.; Cook, *Zeus*, ii. 767, n. 2).

[2] J. M. Powis Smith, comm. on Malachi, iv. 2, in the Internat. Critical Commentary. Sun-gods were also gods of justice (cf. p. 131).

[3] (a) Seal of 'Hanan son of Jedaiah' (*Eph.* ii. 145), and (b) 'Elzakar son of Yehoḥail (יהוחיל)', an archaic seal said to have come from Galilee (Schroeder, *M.D.P.V.*, xxxvii. 174 sq.); the Jerusalem seal of 'Hananiah (son of) Neriyahu', and the very similar seal of (? his brother) 'R (or D)emaliah (?) son of Neriyahu' (ר]ד[מליהו בן נריהו), Pilcher, *Q.S.*, 1923, p. 94; cf. Torrey, l.c. For intermediate forms, cf. seals of Chemosh-yeḥi, and Sasarel, above.

[4] . . . נגשל (Brit. Mus., no. 1023, Levy, no. 10); עבדכחבן (Br. Mus.,

In its original form, the symbol of the winged sun, the god of righteousness, would evoke or give reality to the idea of the protecting wings under whose shadow men could take refuge. To the familiar words of the Psalms old Oriental art—outside Palestine—supplies the pictures.[1] Winged figures, divine or superhuman, abound. The seal of Chemosh-zadak, whose name (cf. Jehozadak) suggests that he was a Moabite, presents a fine example of a four-winged deity with a pair of wings in his hands (Pl. ix. 11).[2] It has the Egyptian double crown, but its wings are more Mesopotamian, and beneath the name is the winged disk, analogous to that on the seal of Chemosh-yeḥi. Other types of four-winged figures (deities, genii, &c.) are familiar

no. 1028, Clermont-Ganneau, no. 20); Nadab-el son of Gad-marom (גדמרם; Vincent, *Rev. Bib.*, 1910, p. 417); Barak-ba'al (Levy, *Phoen.*, no. 14; device of a lion attacking a bull). Pilcher (l.c.), too, points out that the seals with the double line cannot be regarded as necessarily later than those more ornate.

[1] Ps. xvii. 8, xxxvi. 7, lvii. 1, lxi. 4, and especially xci. 4. Thus the falcon Horus is behind and above king Khepren of the Fourth Dynasty (Gressmann, no. 35); or it clutches the Philistine enemy of Ramses III (*C.A.H.*, pl. i, 152b). The soul-bird of the deceased is embraced or over-covered by the arms of the heavenly *ka* (*Anc. Eg.*, 1914, p. 24). Isis stands behind and protects Osiris with her wings (Gr. 258). On the sarcophagus of Haremheb the goddesses of the dead similarly protect the deceased (Haas, *Bilderatlas z. Rel.-gesch.*, *Aeg.*, no. 123). At Karnak goddesses protect the divine symbols with their wings (*Rev. Bib.*, xxxv. 487). On an Egyptianized Syro-Hittite seal the male figure stands between Isis and Nephthys (Contenau, *Glypt.*, p. 129 sq., no. 84) —these two goddesses occur in Palestine, e.g. at Gezer (ii. 333).

[2] In our drawing the figure has been accidentally reversed. On its genuineness and place in art, see Lidzbarski, *Eph.* i. 136, who compares the seal of Baal-nathan (where the deity holds serpents in his hands). On the seal of M-m-h (Pl. ix. 12) the hands are empty (note the *ankh*). That of Abayau (אביו, ib. 15) was found in the tomb of a Carthaginian woman, of the fourth to third centuries B. C., and is Egyptian (*Rev. d'Ass.*, vi. 84). The name (which could otherwise be read as Joab) recalls the Hebrew Abijah ('Yau is a father') and the Abiaho found in an Egyptian magical papyrus (W. M. Müller, *Egypt. Mythol.*, p. 209).

in combats, &c.[1] It is a four-winged serpent that we seem to have (a) on a Beirut seal with the letters l, b, m, and (b) on that of 'Yaḥmeliah son of Maʿaseiah': the latter sounds Jewish enough; and although the first name is new, it has an excellent meaning, 'may Yahweh spare' (Pl. ix. 16).[2] Of another order is the winged demon with curved tail and dagger, on the seal of 'Adonipelet, servant of Amminadab', possibly the Amminadab who paid tribute to Assyria in the time of Ashurbanipal.[3] Quite Assyrian is the head of a storm-demon, perhaps that of the south-wind, which was found at Jericho in a late Israelite stratum.[4]

To identify the cherubim and seraphim we must look amid the many miscellaneous representations of superhuman creatures. By the cherub we may understand the Akkadian creature, a worshipper or devotee (Akkadian kāribu), to be identified with the šēdu and lamasu who guard the entry to the temples. They are alike male and female, and serve partly as intercessors for men, partly as protectors of the threshold. So, the cherubim guard Eden (Gen. iii. 24), and the six-winged seraphim in Isa. vi. 6 sq., instead of repelling the intruder, prepare the prophet for admission to the god.[5]

[1] C.A.H., pl. i. 226 e; Contenau, Glypt., no. 282; C.I.S., ii. 89, 106; cf. also the winged Adad with thunderbolts (Gressmann, no. 380).

[2] See (a) Lidz., Eph. i. 12, and (b) Gressmann, no. 589 (cf. Stade, Z.A.T.W., 1897, p. 502, Noth, Israel. Personennamen, p. 197).

[3] Torrey, Annual of the American Schools, ii. 104 sq.; Clermont-Ganneau, Études, i (1895), pp. 85–90.

[4] Sellin, Jericho, p. 149 sq. (taf. 40, ii. 2); cf. also Gressmann, no. 386, and the four-winged storm demon of the eighth century (Gr. no. 383).

[5] I am indebted to the admirable study by Vincent and Dhorme in Rev. Bib., 1926, pp. 335 sqq., 481 sqq. (ib., p. 343: four Elamite priestesses prostrate themselves before the lamasāti and karibāti, and pray for their intercession on behalf of the king). The laḥmu serpent is essentially a guardian, as distinct from the youthful and kindly kāribu. (For the commonly cited Akkad. kirūbu there seems to be no authority, A. Jeremias, O.T. in light of Anc. East, i. 236.) For illustrations see, besides Vincent and Dhorme, Gressmann, no. 378, serpent-griffins, ib., nos. 367, 370 sq. The suggestion has also been made that the idea of animal guardians of doors and gates is due to the grinding and groaning

The Hebrew *sārāph* is variously explained from the Egyptian winged griffin *seref* or the Akkadian *šarrāpu* 'the burner', a western name of Nergal. Its six wings recall the figure on the seal of Chemosh-zadak, and the much later form of the god Kronos or El of Byblus (Pl. xxxii. 14).[1] In Isaiah's vision the seraphim belong to the temple, and this raises an interesting point, because in later periods such beings are supposed to take part in the service in a *heavenly* temple.[2] This belief in a temple above does not, however, appear to be an early one, and it seems to take the place of the old conception, common to Egypt and Babylonia, that the temple on earth was, in a sense, a cosmic abode—a heaven upon earth.[3] The ziggurat symbolized the world-mountain, and the great basin (*apsū*), symbolizing the Deep, 'had its parallel in the Temple of Jerusalem, in the great laver supported on the bronze oxen, three looking towards each point of the compass'. Indeed, Gray points out that Solomon's temple may have been built in accordance with cosmical speculation, later forms of which are preserved in the interpretations followed by Philo and Josephus.[4] For the serpent Neḥuštan we may perhaps compare the drawing on a vase of Gudea, where the double serpent, winding about a perpendicular staff, suggests a prototype of the later caduceus.[5] And how Yahweh was conceived to ride upon the cherubim (Ps.

---

of heavy temple doors and the shrieking of the bolts, see L. W. King, *P.S.B.A.*, xxxiv. 276. See further Gray's comment on *Isaiah*, p. 105; Oesterley, *Immortality and the Unseen World*, p. 51 sq.

[1] On the etymology, cf. Lagrange, *Études*, p. 430 (but see *K.A.T.*, p. 415), and for El, see below, p. 168.

[2] So the Phoenixes, Cherubim and six-winged creatures are in the sixth heaven; Charles, *Secrets of Enoch*, xix. 6, xxi. 1; *Test. Levi*, iii. 5, &c., and his commentary on Rev. iv. 6.

[3] Ramses III built a temple to the god Amon in Phoenicia like 'the horizon of heaven which is in the sky' (Breasted, *Anc. Records*, iv. 219, cf. ii. 883, iii. 412).

[4] Gray, *Sacrifice in the O.T.*, p. 152 (cf. 151, 156 sq.).

[5] Gressmann, no. 367.

xviii. 10) we may perhaps see later from the coin of Yahu (Pl. xxxii). The association of alternate cherubim and palm-trees in the Temple recalls the winged genii who fertilize the palm-tree (p. 50).[1] On the other hand, the ark and its cherubim suggest Egyptian chests with the goddesses Isis and Nephthys;[2] and other contents of the Tabernacle and Temple find their analogies at present in Cyprus and South Arabia.[3]

Nothing shows more clearly than the dirge over the king of Tyre (Ezra xxviii)—in spite of its obscure reference to the cherubim, &c.—the variety of the old Oriental lore which must once have been familiar and intelligible. Yet it is noteworthy that the cherub with 'two faces', which Ezekiel knows (xli. 18), has to be illustrated from North Syria—Zenjirli or Carchemish.[4] In spite of the general homogeneity of culture in Egypt and South-west Asia there are some instructive differences. Thus, (a) the vigorous sphinxes of the Euphrates valley contrast with the conventional and lifeless Egyptian type, and (b) those of North Syria are sometimes marked by a certain femininity, which finds a parallel in (c) some Hittite human representations, of uncertain sex, to which may be added the sentimentalism and voluptuousness of Syria of the later periods.[5] Palestine has an individuality of its own; it

[1] This ornamentation (Ezek. xli. 18 sqq.) was perhaps not in Solomon's temple (*Ency. Bib.*, col. 4932, § 9).

[2] For a curious and long-known 'cherub' or griffin from Jerusalem, see Gressmann, no. 395, *Rev. Bibl.*, 1926, p. 489; and for a late Jewish graffito of the ark and cherubim, see ib., p. 494, 2nd or 3rd cent. A.D.

[3] There are S. Arabian analogies for some Hebrew ritual terms ; cf. Hilprecht, *Explorations in Bible Lands* (1903), p. 750 ; and Landersdorfer, *Die Bibel u. die Südarab. Altertumsforschung* (Münster i. W., 1920), p. 69 sq.—*mabsal* (place where meal is boiled), *maslam* (altar of incense), *makānat* (ornamented support for lavers).

[4] See *Rev. Bib.*, 1926, p. 357, pl. ix. 3, 4; Gressmann, no. 388. The horse-like figures in Rev. ix. 7 may be derived from the Mesopotamian archer-centaurs (Jastrow, *Civilization of Bab. and Ass.*, pl. lxxiii).

[5] For (a) see Garstang, *Hittite Empire*, p. 132 sq., (b) ib., p. 261, 274; cf. Gressmann, nos. 390 and 92. For (c) see below, p. 133, n. 4.

shows itself equally in the pottery (Thomsen, *Reallexikon Vorgeschichte*, 'Vase' [§ 18]).

Various kinds of winged figures, sphinxes, &c., are depicted upon the small objects found in excavation (cf. Pl. x. 23). In the 'Philistine' tomb no. 2, was a seal with a man in Persian dress fighting two mixed figures (Pl. xv. 4), and in no. 4 a figure stands before a winged sphinx (Pl. vii. 14).[1] But what can be more distinctive than the fragment of a pottery shrine on each side of which was a small laver and—as the guardian—a quaint seated figure with high peaked cap? It may be as old as the first part of the second millennium B. C. (see Pls. xxix sq.).[2]

Egyptian influence can be discerned in the sphinxes on certain Hebrew and Phoenician seals.[3] Especially noteworthy is the very fine seal of Asaph, found at Megiddo, and ascribed to about 700 B. C.: a winged griffin, crowned, and on the right a cartouche with more or less meaningless Egyptian hieroglyphs.[4] We meet with a basilisk and the *ankh* on the seal of Yoram (son of) Zimriyyahu, and a couple of apes and a flower on that of 'Elsegub daughter of Elishama'.[5] The remarkable seal of Mar-

---

[1] See *Gezer*, i. 292 (fig. 153), 293 (fig. 154, no. 14*b*), and the remarks by Pilcher, *Q.S.*, 1912, p. 35. Other conflicts on *C.I.S.*, ii. 78 and 92.

[2] *Gezer*, ii. 437 sq., figs. 517 sqq.; cf. *Rev. Bib.*, l.c., p. 484 sq.

[3] e.g. the seal of Ṣedek-rimmon (*C.I.S.*, ii. 73), and that 'to Zeker (*or* to the memory of) Hoshea' (Pl. ix. 17 sq., Gressmann, no. 593, Cooke, p. 362, *Eph.* i. 41); for the latter cf. the archaic 'Zeker 'Ezer' (Clermont-Ganneau, no. 4), and, for the device, the seal of Yeḥzaḳ (Pl. ix. 20 sq.; יחזק). On Egyptian influence see further Thomsen, *Reallex. Vorg.*, 'Amulett', 'Siegel' (§ 5).

[4] Gressmann, no. 599 (Steuernagel, *Mutesellim*, i. fig. 148, Watzinger, ib. ii. 64). The cartouche recurs on the ivory brooch 'of Malkiram', which is of about the eighth century (Cooke, no. 150 [1]). In general, the hieroglyphs on Egyptian scarabs were often copied, and badly; and the date of any genuine Egyptian scarab is not necessarily a reliable indication of the date of the stratum or tomb in which it is found; see Macalister, *Gezer*, ii, p. 314.

[5] See (*a*) *Eph.* i. 11, and (*b*) Gressmann, no. 591. Cf. the Askalon

samak (Pl. ix. 29 sq.)—the name may have been added later
—includes, among a variety of Egyptian signs, a scarabaeus
and two uraei. The scarabaeus reappears on (a) the seal
of Ḥanan (Pl. ix. 14), while on (b) that of 'Elishama, the
king's son', the scarabaeus has a double winged uraeus
serpent with the crowns of Upper and Lower Egypt.[1] An
interesting scarabaeus is that of 'Hodu the scribe', where
a figure stands before the seated goddess (the queen of
heaven), with an eight-rayed star above, and, between
them, what seems to be the *ankh* (Pl. ix. 4).[2] Here must be
mentioned the common symbol on South Palestinian jar-
handles, with its affinities both to the Egyptian scarab and
the four-winged figures noticed above. The symbol is four-
or two-winged, and it is possible that the latter type has
been influenced by the winged disk.[3] Although opinions
vary, a date about the fifth century B.C. still seems, to the
present writer, the most probable.[4]

Distinctly Egyptian is the lotus, the symbol of the
renewal of life, of resurrection and immortality. It is found
associated with genii of the dead; and it is the emblem of
royalty (found in North Syria), and—later, and persisting
through the Graeco-Roman age—of the 'child Horus',
Har-pe-Khrod or Harpocrates. The lotus, springing up
daily from the primal waters of Nu, bears the plump little
sun-god who, with his finger to the lips—a conventional
sign of childhood—was erroneously interpreted as warning

---

seal, *Q.S.*, 1913, p. 145 (Torrey, *Amer. Schools of Or. Res.*, ii. 108): a
griffin wearing the *pshent*.

[1] For (a) see *Eph.* i. 10, 277; and for (b) Sayce, *Q.S.*, 1909, p. 155;
Torrey, l.c., fig. 9.

[2] See Gressmann's remarks on no. 573, *C.I.S.*, ii. 84. In Assyrian
scenes the throne of this goddess is on her sacred animal (Gress.,
nos. 257, 335). For the *ankh*-like object, see below, p. 64.

[3] See Driver, p. 74 sq., Handcock, p. 294. Pilcher finds the symbol
on a coin of Datames, 378–2 B.C. (*P.S.B.A.*, xxxii. 93 sqq., 143 sqq.);
cf. below, p. 170 and note 1.

[4] See *Q.S.*, 1924, p. 181, 1925, pp. 91, 100; and for other views,
Thomsen, *Reallex. Vorg.*, 'Siegel' (§ 6), Albright, *J.P.O.S.*, 1926, p. 93.

the initiated not to reveal the mysteries. The type appears on the very similar seals of (*a*) 'Asayau (Asaiah) son of Yokim', and (*b*) 'Abayau (or Abio), servant of Uzziyau'; and on the older seal, acquired at Beirut, of (*c*) 'Birel(?), servant of Gaddiel', where the name is repeated encircling the figure of a bull (*C.I.S.*, ii. 76).[1] Another seal ('to Uzzi'), depicting a cow turning her head to look at the suckling calf, is interpreted by the editors of the *C.I.S.* (ii. 90), as the Egyptian myth of Hathor, as the cow, suckling the young Horus.

A lotus, with a horned animal, star and crescent, appears on the seal of 'Tamak-el son of Malkam' (Pl. ix. 22); and flowers are held by the kneeling figure in the Egyptianizing seal of Par'ōsh.[2] The seal of 'Hananiah son of Azariah', found at Jerusalem, bears a decoration of pomegranates or lilies; and there are palmettes on that of 'Hananiah son of Achbor'—both have the double dividing line—and also on that of Shebanyau.[3] A late seal, with the name Abah, presents the characteristically Jewish *ethrog* and *lulab*.[4]

Much more significant is the fondness for depicting animal life. On the vases sent from Syria into Egypt in and about the Eighteenth and Nineteenth dynasties models of animals are especially common, and in the order: gazelle, ox, lion and sphinx, griffin and eagle. Even at this date the art is pseudo-Egyptian, and Syrian or Phoenician work,

---

[1] See for (*a*) Pl. ix. 25–27 (Cooke, no. 150 [8]), ascribed to the fifth or fourth centuries B.C.; and for (*b*) Gressmann, no. 592 (see no. 300); cf. for the type, the coin of Antoninus Pius (*Coins of Alexandria*, xvii. 1130, p. lxvi). Horus recurs in Phoenician names (חר, *C.I.S.*, i. 46, Cooke, p. 62); but the identification of חור, &c., among the names at Elephantine (Cowley, p. 286 sq.) is less clear; see also *Ency. Bib.* on the names Ashḥur, Ḥur. On the forms of the Egyptian lily, see W. D. Spanton, *Anc. Eg.*, 1917, pp. 1 sqq.; Petrie, ib., 1929, pp. 65 sqq.

[2] See (*a*) *C.I.S.*, ii. 94; (*b*) Clermont-Ganneau, *Rec.*, vi. 374.

[3] See (*a*) Gressmann, no. 583; (*b*) ib., no. 587; and (*c*) Pilcher, *Q.S.*, 1913, p. 143 (cf. Torrey, *American Schools of Or. Res.*, 1913, p. 108).

[4] See below, p. 194, n. 5.

already influenced by Egypt, is being taken to Egypt.[1] To supplement what has been said about the bull (p. 27 sq.), we may note the heifer on the archaic seal of 'Shemaiah son of Azariah' (Gressmann, no. 582), while on the seal of Yish'el (Pl. ix. 23), the combination of bull and star may indicate the god Hadad and his consort.[2] The eagle is found at Gezer (Pl. viii. 2), and the double-headed type points to Mesopotamia (or rather to Elam) and to the Hittite area. It is possible that the story of Etana and his ascent to heaven on the eagle's wings in search of the life-giving plant was not wholly unknown in Palestine.[3] Upon a strange uninscribed seal from Tell el-Mutesellim (Megiddo), a hare and vulture occupy the upper register; in the middle two griffins face a stylized tree, and at the foot a lion, beneath a crescent, springs upon a gazelle (Pl. ix. 10). The hare is a well-known *motif* in Hittite and Palestinian art, down to the Galilean synagogues, and as the third scene is also often met with, we may suggest that the middle register, too, would not be foreign to Palestinian ideas.[4]

[1] So W. Max Müller, *Asien und Europa*, p. 307. At Beth-Shan, beneath the floor of the temple of Seti I, Rowe found, *inter alia*, 'a vase having the head of a lion one end and the head of a bull the other ... a beautiful alabaster jar with two handles in the form of the heads and horns of ibexes ... a very well made pottery model of a hippopotamus' (*Q.S.*, 1927, p. 73). The last is specifically Egyptian and was the animal of Set-Setekh (Vincent, *Rev. Bib.*, 1928, p. 535); see p. 110 n. 3.

[2] Cf. p. 28, n. 1. S. Smith (*Ass.*, p. 326) observes that on a seal impression from Kerkuk Marduk with a double animal or bird head stands between Nabu and a semi-human monster, while his son Nabu is wholly human. This theriomorphic form of Marduk finds a parallel in the close association of Enurta with his symbol, the bird of prey.

[3] *Gezer*, pl. cxxxvii, no. 48, and pl. clxvii. 13, ccxiv. 3, with Vincent's discussion, *Syria*, v. 197 sq.; also Garstang, *Hitt. Empire*, pp. 115, 143. For archaic seals of the story of Etana, see *C.A.H.*, pl. i. 40. Mention may be made, in passing, of the eagles on the seal, *Eph.* ii. 147 sq., and the birds, *Mutesellim*, p. 73, fig. 99. See further, pp. 211 sq., 228 n. 2.

[4] Steuernagel, fig. 212: Watzinger, p. 65 sq. For the hare, see Contenau, no. 315, *Samaria*, i. 378, pl. 57, *a*8; Bliss-Macalister, pl. lxi. 18 (?),

A favourite animal is the lion. On the fine seal of 'Asaniel it has its most typical form; and beneath it is the scarabaeus with the pellet, its egg, symbolical of the sun-god rolling the sun through the heavens (Pl. ix. 24).[1] On the seal of Aḥmah (ib. no. 19) the animal is on a platform, and the device behind it may represent a double-peaked mountain—lion-gods tend to be solar and mountain gods, and other examples will be met with later.[2] But by far the best example is the splendid seal of 'Shama the servant of Jeroboam', of about the eighth century. It was found at Megiddo, where there were some excellent models of lions on the spot, whence the suggestion that the animal may have been specially associated with the ancient battlefields of the plain of Jezreel.[3] The type is Mesopotamian (cf. Gressmann, no. 375), and with the splendid basalt lion at Sheikh Saʿd is one of the several indications of the cultural influences of the north.[4] The now well-known lion and dog panels from Beth-Shan (where several figurines of lions were found) show alike northern affinities and unusual native artistic power; and it is to be noticed that the curious star-like mark on the lion's shoulders, interpreted as possibly an astral symbol, is not infrequent

note also the lamp, Sellin, *Taannek*, p. 44. For the *motif* of the lion attacking an animal, cf. *Pennsylv. Museum Journal*, 1927, p. 424 (a bull [?], Beth-Shan), *Gezer*, iii. pl. cc. 33 (gazelle, Hellenistic).

[1] The name שעיאל, presumably meaning 'God made me', is Hebrew rather than Phoenician.

[2] Similarly the seal of Sarʿ, *Eph.* i. 11, the coin, pl. xxxiii. no. 21; and see p. 117. On the name Aḥmah (? 'his mother's brother'), see W. R. Smith, *Kinship and Marriage in Early Arabia*, p. 185 n.

[3] See Steuernagel, p. 99 sq., Watzinger, p. 64 sq. (for models, see ib., p. 88 sq.). Cf. also Driver, p. 91, Gressmann, no. 578; *M.D.P.V.*, 1904, pp. 1 sq., 83 sq., *Q.S.*, 1904, p. 287 sq., *Eph.* ii. 140. The *ankh* which is painted behind the lion and the tree of life (?) in front of it are scarcely visible.

[4] See Gressmann, no. 399 (*M.D.O.G.*, xxiii. 32, *Z.D.P.V.*, xxxvii. 127 and taf. 37; *Syria*, v. 207 sqq., pl. lii); and for N. Syria, Garstang, *Hittite Empire*, Index, s.v.; Weber, *Hethit. Kunst*, nos. 17, 22; note also the huge lion at Petra (*Q.S.*, 1927, p. 155 sq.).

elsewhere.[1] Accordingly, the lion-decoration in the temple of Jerusalem (1 Kings vii. 29), like the lions that guarded the throne (x. 19 sq.), would be in harmony with oriental usage; although whether the animal was associated with some specific deity (e. g. Nergal) archaeology alone does not enable us to determine.[2]

Animals of the deer, gazelle, and goat kind are very frequently depicted, and at Beth-Shan seals so inscribed were often found, as well as gazelle horns: the animal was probably associated with the mother-goddess.[3] One and two goats respectively appear on the rather similar seals of 'Jehoezer son of Obadiah' and 'Nethaniah son of Obadiah'.[4] How naturally the symbolism of Palestine agreed with that of neighbouring lands—while preserving features of its own —is shown by the unique Taanach terra-cotta incense altar or incense burner of about 700–600 B. C. (Pl. xi).[5] Here

[1] See e. g. Q.S., 1929, p. 87, and pl. xiv. For the mark, see the Megiddo model (p. 88, fig. 128), Samaria (i. 333, pl. lxxx), Gezer (see Pl. xvii. 2 b), also the lions on the carved ivory head-seat from the annexe of Tutankhamen's tomb (Illustrated London News, July 6, 1929, p. 15), the Assyrian art of the time of Ashur-nasir-pal II (Opitz, Arch. f. Orientforschung, v. 189, col. 2, note).

[2] The lion recurs on a scarabaeus at Taanach (Egyptianized; Gressmann, no. 580), also at Jericho (Sellin, pl. xlii); and rude models were found at Gezer (ii. 18, pl. cxxv. 12), Taanach (Sellin, Nachlese, p. 9), Megiddo (p. 190).

[3] As a 'survival' of this note the Christianized story that Justinian hunted a gazelle, north of Damascus. It became the Virgin, who commanded him to build in her honour the Church of Saidnaya. This is a place of annual pilgrimage; and in the district are traces of gross nature worship (Hanauer, Q.S., 1909, p. 137).

[4] Gressmann, no. 585 sq. The former is especially archaic (Lidzbarski, Eph. i. 15; but see Clermont-Ganneau, Rec. iii. 189 sq.). Dalman (Pal. Jahrb., 1906, p. 46) suggests that goats were a symbol of divine strength, and compares the sĕ'īrīm, demons (Isa. xiii. 21, &c.; see Gray, Ency. Bib. 'Satyr'). (A couple of ibexes, or the like, facing a tree, in Sellin, Taannek, fig. 98, Nachlese, fig. 41.)

[5] See Sellin, pp. 75 sqq., taf. xii. sq. (fragments of a second, p. 81 sq.); Driver, p. 85 sq.; Vincent, pp. 181 sqq. (and Rev. Bib., 1926, p. 492 sq.); Handcock, pp. 291 sqq.; Gressmann, no. 396 sq.

are three sphinxes, with a head covering (with projecting ears, decorated border and two tassels on the left side); while, in between are two lions each with a paw upon the head of the sphinx beneath it. On other sides are a tree with a goat on either side, and a youthful figure holding a serpent—a unique scene which we may treat as the native version of a deity piercing the serpent. In any event the youthfulness of the hero is noteworthy.[1] The importance of the object is undeniable for, even if it is not a 'sacred' object, but merely represents a brazier, like that in Jer. xxxvi. 22 sq., it illustrates contemporary culture. It may be observed that much has been written upon the archaeological evidence for the early use of incense and 'incense altars' in Palestinian ritual; and it has been assumed that it refutes the view commonly accepted by O.T. scholars that the 'altar of incense' in the Temple did not exist before the fifth or fourth century B.C.[2] On the other hand, the 'altars' or incense-burners so far discovered are movable objects; and even if they are to be called 'altars'—which is somewhat doubtful—they differ in shape and use from the Jewish altar of incense which was 'a piece of furniture *fixed* in the Holy Place'.[3]

Various cult-scenes can be illustrated by archaeology. Thus, the seal of 'Shebanyau son (*bar*) of Uzziyau', with its double dividing lines, depicts on one side a couple of winged disks, and on the other a figure with right arm

[1] For this view, cf. Griffith, *P.S.B.A.*, xvi. 87 sqq. (and Vincent, *Rev. Bib.*, 1928, p. 517, and notes 1–3). Driver, p. 85, n. 1, compares the Cypriote beast-tamer, Ohnefalsch-Richter, *Cyprus*, pl. cxviii. 7a, cc. 4. Gressmann (no. 400), following Wiegand, observes that the Petra scene, where a boy holds two serpents (?), is rather some 'Eros' with two winged lions.

[2] See e.g. H. M. Wiener, *The Altars of the O.T.* (*Beigabe z. O.L.Z.*, 1927), especially pp. 23 sqq., and M. Löhr, *Das Räucheropfer i. A.T.*, 1927; also Albright, *J.P.O.S.*, ix. 53 (the *ḥammān* as an incense altar).

[3] See G. B. Gray, *Sacrifice*, pp. 142 sqq. For 'incense burners', see *Gezer*, ii. 336, Steuernagel, *el-Mutesellim*, Frontispiece, and p. 127, fig. 190. Löhr (p. 173) also cites the Beth-Shan seal (our Pl. xv. 1).

half raised, and in the left a sceptre similar to that carried by Egyptian gods, but inverted (the hook being at the lower end and the crescent at the top).[1] He is nude from the waist upwards, in this resembling the figure on the seal of 'Jazneel son of Elḥanan', which has the double dividing line and is decorated with three birds. The same attitude of worship reappears (a) on the seal, from 'Ammān, 'of El-amas son of Elisha', where a grave bearded figure, clothed in a long cloak, stands with right arm half raised, palm-upwards (Pl. ix. 13), and again (b) on the seal of El-ram son of Tama (Pl. ix. 5).[2] Sometimes we see a wor-shipper standing solemnly in the presence of the god, so notably the fine Taanach seal of 'Atanaḥil son of Ḥabsi, servant of Nergal'.[3] Or he stands, with hands uplifted, before some object.[4] Especially curious is a seal from Megiddo where the figure holds some conical object, and the scorpion (otherwise known as the emblem of the god Ishkara), star, crescent, and other objects may symbolize deities (Pl. ix. 9).[5] Not less noteworthy is the Gezer seal, with the guilloche pattern that points to northern influence (C.A.H., pl. i, 230 c.), where a figure kneeling on one knee, holds out a seven-branched tree (Pl. ix. 7).[6] Such a tree (five or seven branched) frequently occurs, and an exceptionally interesting example is furnished by the seal

[1] Gressmann, no. 588. The name (שבניו, שבניהו) is not rare on seals (Q.S., 1902, p. 265 sq.); and seems to be of Post-exilic origin (for 'Yah brought me back'). For the sceptre, see p. 110, n. 5 end.

[2] (a) Gressmann, no. 579 (for this attitude, cf. Megiddo, fig. 72d), and (b) C.I.S., ii. 74 (Brit. Mus., no. 1030). The two symmetrically grouped figures each with a hand raised (Megiddo, p. 124, and pl. xxxix) may be taking an oath.

[3] Gressmann, no. 577 (note inter alia the same symbol, ☥, as in Megiddo, fig. 72c; cf. below, p. 65 n. 1.

[4] ? A tree, Samaria, i. 377, fig. 57a 2 (ib. a 1, it is thought, may repre-sent Marduk and an axe).

[5] Steuernagel, p. 139, taf. xliv.

[6] Gezer, pl. ccii, b 5 (Contenau, no. 273). The symmetrical arrange-ment of the animals is very common (Vincent, Syria, v. 91 sqq.; Watzinger, Mutesellim, p. 23).

from Tell eṣ-Ṣafi, where there are two stags on what appear to be an altar, and on the extreme left are to be seen the sun and moon-crescent (Pl. xiii. 1).[1] On Assyrian scenes there is a certain tendency for the stylized tree and candelabrum to coalesce. Indeed, the sacred candlestick of the Temple of Jerusalem was not always represented with the ends of the arms forming a horizontal straight line: the tree shape is known even in the Christian age.[2] The modern custom of hanging lamps upon trees will serve to illustrate the easy transference; and, at the entrance to a tomb in the Wady el-Balāt, Dalman saw a schematic representation of a palm the upper part of which exactly resembled a seven-armed candlestick. Not only has the sacred tree survived, but in the Mishnah tractate against Idolatry the Asherah is not a tree-stump but a tree.[3]

The cult object may be (a) an altar with a flame upon it (Pl. ix. 3); while (b) on the seal 'of Shama', an Egyptianized figure with a sceptre stands with his back to an inscribed obelisk (Pl. ix. 28).[4] Of two Akkadian contract-tablets with seals of about 650 B.C., found at Gezer, one has a conventional seven-branched tree, and a winged disk, beneath which two figures, with half-raised arms, stand on either side of what looks like the *ankh*, but may be an altar, or a fusion of the two (Pl. xii. 1, 2).[5] On

---

[1] Q.S., 1900, p. 19 (Bliss-Macalister, p. 153, and pl. lxxxiii); cf. also Pl. x, no. 21 (Gezer). A seal (Legrain, no. 170), said to come from Gezer, depicts two figures with horned mitres and long robes, standing with raised hands on either side of a palm in a conical vase. On a rough seal from esh-Shihāb are three figures and something resembling an artificial tree or perhaps an altar (Q.S., 1901, p. 350); see Pl. xiii. 2.

[2] Gressmann, nos. 50–112 (cf. Galling on the devices upon lamps, Z.D.P.V., xlvi, taf. iv; Gezer, iii, pl. cxvii sqq.); see also Q.S., 1886, p. 8; Loeb, R.E.J., xix. 100 sqq.; coins of Antigonus Mattathias (Madden, p. 102, cf. p. 116, nos. 5 and 6). See further Ency. Bib., 'Candlestick'; Ohnefalsch-Richter, Cyprus, p. 88 sq., Dalman, Pal. Jahrb., 1906, p. 50.

[3] See Ab. Zar., iii. 1, iv. 4, and Elmslie's edition (1911), p. 60 sq.

[4] The former is the seal of עבדרחבן.

[5] Gezer, i, frontispiece, fig. 1, and p. 23 (see Q.S., 1904, pp. 208, 229 sqq., 400); Gressmann, nos. 595 sq. For the 'altar'(?), cf. the seal of Hodu

the other, the seal of Natanyau, a typical cult object (here with a six-rayed star) resembles a crescent with pendants on a post, with a cross-bar, fixed upon a stand (Pl. xii. 3).[1] Very similar is the object depicted upon a seal from Gerar, where a figure with arms raised stands before it.[2] A good parallel is to be found in the elaborate seal from Baghdad, where a figure stands before the object, which is accompanied by other typical Assyrian symbols.[3] There are other types of cult-objects.[4] In particular, on a seal from eṣ-Ṣāfi, a priest stands before two cult objects fixed upon a base (Pl. viii. 6); and on the late seal of H-n-m-i upon a similar construction are fixed the spear of Marduk and, it would seem, the sticks, the emblem of Nabu.[5] More elaborate is the seal obtained some years ago in Beth-Shan, where the priest is standing before a fire-altar, facing a figure

(p. 57). Here may be noticed the strangely-shaped Hittite 'mushroom' altars (Garstang, *Hitt. Emp.*, p. 134, fig. 8, with refs.); cf. the somewhat similar type in S. Arabia, Nielsen, *Handbuch*, p. 170, fig. 64 (Grohmann, *Göttersymbole*, fig. 88).

[1] *Gezer*, i. frontispiece, fig. 3, and p. 27 sq. (see *Q.S.*, 1905, pp. 206 sqq., 272); Gressmann, no. 610. This second contract is dated in the eponymate of Aḥi-ilai, governor of Carchemish, and is a valuable indication of the political and cultural connexions with North Syria. The cross-bars are a noteworthy feature (cf. Pl. x, nos. 11, 20, 21); they may be for the purpose of carrying the object; cf. also above, p. 63, n. 3.

[2] Petrie (*Gerar*, pl. xvii, no. 12) recognizes a pair of horns at the top of the post. (Ib., pl. xix, no. 27, the crescent and pendants appear to be on a baetyl, and there are other symbols.)

[3] *Eph.* ii. 146.

[4] Pl. viii. 3 (Gezer): a figure between two erect objects and a seated figure [? deity] with half-raised arm; *Eph.* iii. 117, an oval with two ribbons upon a post on a base (Egypt, Assyrian period). In Pl. ix, no. 6 (*C.I.S.*, ii. 97), the worshipper stands before the spear of Marduk, above him are sun and lunar crescent; equally Assyrian is *C.I.S.*, ii. 103.

[5] See Bliss-Macalister, pp. 41 (fig. 16, no. 2), 153. Lidzbarski (*Handb.*) suggests that the second seal is Hebrew (Levy, no. 24, Renan, *Miss. Phén.*, p. 144). A figure seems to stand before an altar with tree and spear in *Samaria*, i. pl. 57, d 7. For the typical combination of the emblems of Marduk and Nabu, see the Neo-Babylonian examples collected by Legrain, pl. 34.

K

standing over an animal (dog?), while behind is the spear of Marduk with tassels, surmounted by a star (Pl. xv. 1).[1] But by far the finest is the sacrificial scene upon the seal found at Gezer among debris of *c.* 1200–1000 B.C. (ib. no. 2).[2] The stylized tree is familiar. The figure with horned head-dress and flowing lock has his foot raised in a way that marks mountain and solar gods, and survives in coins of the Roman age. Behind him is an attendant with a fine vase. The scimitar held by the figure on the left is the *khepesh*, the weapon introduced by the Hyksos. Such a scimitar was found in Tomb 30 at Gezer (perhaps four-teenth century), and, as the later *harpé*, is widely distributed.[3] To interpret the scene in detail would be hazardous; but it is certainly one of the most important illustrations of early Palestinian cult, and points to the rich and elaborate ritual that was in use before or at the time when the Israelite tribes from the wilderness began to intermingle with the earlier inhabitants of the land (Judges iii. 5 sq.).

It is perhaps a baetyl in a shrine that is to be recognized in the rough seal recently discovered in Ophel and dated to the Second Bronze period, i.e., 2000–1600 B.C. (Pl. xv. 3).[4] We may compare the Mesopotamian seals which depict the

[1] *Q.S.*, 1907, p. 130. The dog recalls the lion and dog panels at Beth-Shan (p. 60), and the fact that models of the animal were found there at various levels (*Q.S.*, 1929, p. 87 sq.).

[2] *Gezer*, ii, p. 345, fig. 464 (*Q.S.*, 1907, p. 266).

[3] For the weapon, see *Q.S.*, 1904, p. 334 sq., 1907, p. 266, *Gezer*, i. 313 and pl. lxxv. 16; Gressmann, no. 668. Similar is the fine sword of Adad-nirari I with an ibex carved upon it (*Transactions of the S.B.A.*, iv. 347; S. Smith, *Ass.*, p. 137 sq.). One was found also at Byblus (see Pottier, *Syria*, iii. 301, who notes diverse types), and at Shechem or Nāblus, see *Q.S.*, 1909, p. 74. The Egyptian name likens it to an animal's thigh (Hall, *Anatolian Essays to Sir W. M. Ramsay*, p. 176). Kronos and Perseus received the *harpé* from Hermes, but it is too hazardous to recall the Hebrew *ḥermēsh* 'sickle'! On the distribution of the weapon, see Cook, *Zeus*, ii. 550; and for a general discussion, Dussaud, *Syria*, vii. 253 sq. A fine one was found in Tutankhamen's tomb (*Ill. Lond. News*, Oct. 12, p. 629, fig. 8).

[4] *P.E.F. Annual*, iv. 34, 177, fig. 28.

goddess in a tent or shrine,[1] and more especially those Assyrian types where an object of cult is within some baetyl-like construction.[2] Here, as frequently, Palestine, and in particular Jerusalem, manifests a certain individuality, dating even to pre-Israelite days, and it remains to refer to some remarkable decoration found upon a series of carved stones in Ophel, which not only seem to reflect the usual combination of Egyptian and Mesopotamian elements, but have peculiarities of their own (Pl. xiv. 1, 2). We appear to have (1) a head-dress: the cone will remind us of that at Byblus (Pl. xxxiii. 5), while the boat-shaped structure with the sun has parallels (p. 32 sq.). Underneath may have been a (cow?) head with a pair of horns; that it should have been broken away is not surprising. In (2) we trace a similar head-dress, a cone between petal-like designs, above a head (the top of the face is visible) from which spring horns. On other panels it is perhaps possible to see in one case a tree flanked by two serpents, and in another some solar *motif*. Entirely conjectural though his interpretations must be, Prof. Macalister is probably right in ascribing these fragments to the Ptolemaic age (note the compass-drawn circles in no. 1) and in finding traces of a religious symbolism other than that of orthodox Judaism.[3]

It is, to be sure, a delicate task to determine the contribution of archaeological evidence, *taken by itself*, to our knowledge of Palestinian religion. Much could be attempted by a judicious use of other evidence, literary and monumental,

---

[1] Cf. Weber, nos. 370 sq., Contenau, nos. 138, 144, and perhaps *Jericho*, taf. xlii f. For a seated goddess in a shrine, from Hauran, early Christian period, see Moulton, *American Schools of Or. Res.*, i. 83 sq.

[2] Cf. Weber, no. 471 and the seal *C.I.S.*, ii. 107.

[3] *P.E.F. Annual*, iv. 159 sqq. (cf. Macalister, *Q.S.*, 1924, pp. 119, 137 sqq., from whose tentative suggestions we quote). The editors compare the similar objects—although the actual ornamentation is different—in Weill, *Cité de David*, p. 184, pl. 25*b*; we may also note the schematised Ionic volute from the wall of the citadel at Megiddo (Steuernagel, p. 119 sq., fig. 178).

from around Palestine; but this would involve discussion that would be out of place here. Always there is the risk of reading into our evidence the fullest conceivable interpretation, for, often enough, the object under discussion may have had but the vaguest meaning, or there was no intelligent explanation of its purpose. It was, maybe, something merely prophylactic, an amulet or a charm; it preserved the owner from harm, or, more positively, it assisted him to overcome evil and escape danger. Thus, throughout the Oriental world scenes of conflict were extremely popular, and the myths of gods who fought, conquered, or healed, served as letterpress; but it does not follow that objects inscribed with such scenes were necessarily understood or interpreted intelligently.[1]

Traces of conflicts of gods with dragons survive even in the later parts of the O.T., e. g., in Job xxvi. 12 sq., where reference is made to the winds which overcame Tiamat, the representative of the sea and of the forces of disorder, and to the piercing of this dragon by Marduk.[2] Such may be the interpretation of some of the seals from Gezer, where a winged figure attacks a serpent, or with a scimitar in his hand overcomes a horned animal.[3] Similarly a

[1] On the appropriate myths, see S. Smith, *Ass.*, p. 339 sq. Cf. the Egyptian 'Metternich stele' of the fourth century B.C. (*C.A.H.*, pl. ii. 16) with all its prophylactic emblems: the idea being the victory of the young Horus (the personification of good) over evil. May we compare the youthful figure at Taanach (p. 62)?

[2] See G. B. Gray on Job ix. 13, xxvi. 12 sq.; also *Ency. Bib.* 'Creation'; and Wardle, *Israel and Babylon*, ch. v. It is a striking fact that a good Jew could be called after Marduk, viz. Mordechai (see Paton, Commentary on Esther, pp. 85 sqq.); this fine solar god of Babylon, if any, will have left his mark upon the religion of the western states (see Winckler and Zimmern, *K.A.T.*, pp. 370 sqq.). For the possible identification of Marduk, Asshur and the Egyptian Osiris, see S. Smith, *Ass.*, p. 125.

[3] Our Pl. x, nos. 19, 22, and 15; also *Gezer*, i. 359, fig. 186. Even on the late 'votive altars' (ib., fig. 524, our Pl. xvii. 2*b*) the conflict has a mythological significance; for the star on the animal's body, see above, p. 61, n. 1. For seals with conflicts see, in general, Ward, *A.J.S.L.*, xiv. 95–105. On a late and obscure representation at Suweida in Hauran of a solar hero

seal from Tell Zakariya depicts a fight (see Pl. xv. 5). In the Persian period such conflicts are under the aegis of Ahuramazda (*C.I.S.*, ii, 100), and in Samaria a deity, Persian style, grasps a dragon by its throat.[1] When at Samaria a man stabs an erect lion which he holds by the mane, we may compare the seal, said to have come from Gezer, of the usual Mesopotamian type, with Gilgamesh and Eabāni (Enkidu) each fighting a lion.[2] Indeed it is not unlikely that echoes of this conflict can be traced in the story of Samson, and on a coin from Lachish where the grotesque god Bes is seen attacking the animal.[3] The far-famed Gilgamesh may, in fact, have been the prototype of Bes, models and figurines of whom are frequently unearthed.[4] As Herakles-Melkart of Tyre he is the colossal figure at Amathus rending the lion: the old myth was apparently adopted by the Phoenicians and carried over to Cyprus.[5] But there were other ways of hunting. Gods and hunters trap their foe in nets—compare Job's complaint against the Almighty (xix. 6): such nets are illustrated in the great stele of the Sumerian Eannatum ('the Stele of the Vultures'), and the monolith of Sargon I at Susa and elsewhere.[6]

The victory, whether of gods or kings, over their enemies

fighting a monster (serpent with paws of a lion), see Jeremias, *O.T. in Light of Ancient East*, ii, fig. 160; Dussaud, *Syria*, iv. 170, n. 2.

[1] Bliss-Macalister, pl. 83, no. 2 (*Q.S.*, 1899, p. 187, pl. vii, no. 12); *Samaria*, i. 378, pl. 57*h*; cf. also *Gezer*, i, fig. 153 (*Q.S.*, 1912, p. 34 sq.), our Pl. xv. 4. Serpent or dragon contests also occur in Egyptian mythology (Yahuda, *Sprache d. Pentateuch*, p. 194 sq.).

[2] *Samaria*, i. 378, pl. 56*a*; Legrain, no. 134. At Carchemish are representations of Gilgamesh and his beasts, and of a god (Teshub) killing the lion (Weber, *Hethit. Kunst*, nos. 23, 21).

[3] Pilcher, *Q.S.*, 1921, pp. 134 sqq. See below, p. 135.

[4] W. M. Müller, *As. u. Eur.*, p. 310; Lagrange, *Études*, p. 452. Amulets of Bes at Megiddo, Taanach, &c.; see Gressmann, nos. 555*l*, 558.

[5] Gressmann, no. 605; Burney, *Judges*, p. 497 sq. and pl. vi (see ib., pp. 401, 495 sqq., and pl. ii. sqq., for Gilgamesh and Samson, and seals of Gilgamesh and Enkidu). Bes appears on coins of Ebusus (in the Balearic islands) of *c*. 200 B.C., grasping a serpent (Pilcher, l.c., p. 137).

[6] *C.A.H.*, pl. i. 42; see especially L. W. King, *Sumer and Akkad*, pp.

could be an inspiration to those who knew the old myths or who gazed upon the scenes. The belief in gods who 'save' or deliver is familiar enough in ancient personal names. A Babylonian version of the Fall, it was once thought, was to be recognized upon a British Museum seal: a tree stands between two figures, behind one of which is a serpent. But it is now interpreted as a god with his worshipper partaking of the fruit of the 'tree of life'.[1] The 'rewarding god' is named in Nabataean and Palmyrene inscriptions. Here the god of heaven or sky is called 'the good and rewarding god'. Shē-al-ḳaum, whose name designates him 'the protector of the people', has the same epithet, and is also 'he who does not drink wine', presumably a protest against the dominant Dionysian cult of Dushara.[2] It is fitting, therefore, to conclude this rapid survey with the unpublished British Museum seal of Saʿadath ('fortunate') with its representation of Nikē, goddess of victory, holding the palm-branch and crown for the victor (Pl. ix. 31). Despite her foreign origin she is not out of place in Palestine, and figures of her, with or without a wreath, are to be found, e.g. on coins of Palestine (Herod Agrippa I and II) and in Galilean synagogues.[3]

Looking back, we can see how archaeology enables us to illustrate and supplement our conceptions of the early religion of Palestine. The prophets' denunciation of various forms of idolatry, the necessity for such an injunction as that prohibiting 'figured stones' (Num. xxxiii. 52), the laws against depicting natural objects—such evidence

129 sqq., 220, 229. In the Book of the Dead the man's *ka* escapes from the Net of the Underworld.

[1] Brit. Mus., no. 89326 (Weber, no. 429). See Fr. Delitzsch, *Babel and Bible* (1903), pp. 56, 114 sqq.; A. Jeremias, *O.T. in Light of Anc. East*, i. 220 sq.; and Wardle, *Israel and Babylon*, p. 186 sq.

[2] Cooke, pp. 295, 304.

[3] For the name, cf. Cooke, no. 89, l. 1. See Kohl and Watzinger, *Antike Synag.*, p. 200 and n. 1: and for Nikē and the crown of immortality, Cumont, *Études*, pp. 65 sqq.

proves how prevalent were the beliefs and practices against which the more progressive minds rebelled. Job might declare that he had not kissed his hand in homage to the sun and moon—but Job was not as other men.[1] How some of the devices on Palestinian seals or other objects were explained—or explained away—is left for us to conjecture. Natural curiosity must be satisfied, and we have a few examples of the endeavours to answer questions (e. g. Exod. xii. 26; Joshua iv. 6). In the meantime, the chief need is to form a general idea of the religion of Palestine as a whole, and its place amid other religions; and for this archaeology does not answer all the problems it brings. So far we have been looking at the evidence classified and viewed comparatively. Questions of date have been of secondary importance, because of the close connexion between earlier and later periods. Profound changes have indeed to be noticed, and in the next two lectures we shall see how the Old Oriental and the Graeco-Roman periods illumine and supplement each other.

[1] Job xxxi. 27. The sun and lunar crescent are figured together, e. g. in *Samaria* (i, pl. 57*d*, 6). For the raised hand, cf. p. 40, n. 5.

CHAPTER II

THE OLD ORIENTAL PERIOD

FROM a survey of some of the religious ideas and *motifs* which archaeology illustrates we now pass to a more historical treatment of the subject—at least so far as the nature of the evidence permits. It is, in fact, impossible to present a consecutive sketch of the historical development of Palestinian religion on the basis of archaeology alone, partly by reason of the difficulty, not only of interpreting but also of dating our material, and partly on account of the unequal distribution of the material, and the many gaps in the history. It will, however, have been seen that a certain persistence or continuity can be traced throughout; and this can be demonstrated more decisively as we proceed from the more ancient periods of Palestine through the Israelite period to the Graeco-Roman age. In the present chapter we shall be confined mainly to the pre-Greek periods; and, after some pages on the evidence of the excavations, we shall consider the more important deities, in so far as the external evidence throws light upon them.

Of all the excavations that have been undertaken in Palestine, that of Gezer in 1902–9 still remains in several respects the most complete and instructive; although the subsequent work at Beth-Shan, Byblus, Megiddo (Tell el-Mutesellim), and other sites has corrected many false impressions and made most important additions to our knowledge.[1] For earliest Palestine we may now refer to the Galilee district rich in Neolithic and Bronze Age remains, where, in a Palaeolithic cave (Mugharet el-Zuttiyeh) in the

---

[1] Prof. R. A. S. Macalister's reports in the *Q.S.* of the Palestine Exploration Fund, utilized by Prof. Driver in his Schweich Lectures, are superseded by two volumes of letterpress (with 535 illustrations), and one of 226 plates.

Wady el-'Amud, bordering the plain of Gennesaret, Mr. Turville-Petre discovered in 1925 a portion of a human skull.[1] It was of a woman of Neanderthal type, and, according to Sir Arthur Keith, 'in its mass and in its markings her brain reached at least to the level attained by individuals in living races—such as that represented to-day by the aborigines of Australia'. The skull was associated with traces of an abundant fauna, including hippopotamus (fossilized) and the two-horned rhinoceros.[2]

It is to be noticed that, uniquely interesting as Palestine and Syria are from religious and historical points of view, both the geology and the fauna are no less interesting, and the latter 'reflects the wonderful variety of climate, vegetation, and altitude in this comparatively small area'.[3] Moreover, there seems to be no ground for the view that the fauna of south Palestine can be sharply separated from that of the north at about the plain of Jezreel: the transition from southern to northern types is gradual. Accordingly it is proper to notice that even in the remotest times there is a general tendency for the north and south of Palestine to gravitate respectively to the north and south—to Syria and to Egypt—a tendency which becomes most marked in later history. Next, the skull points to the antiquity of man in Palestine—to a date round about twenty thousand years ago, indeed a date so early that there has been time enough for development and intercommunication long before the dawn of continuous history. There has been time enough for the early recurrence of the movements that are

---

[1] *Researches in Prehistoric Galilee*, 1925–6, by F. Turville-Petre, with a report on the skull by Sir Arthur Keith, three chapters on the animal remains by Dorothea M. Bate, and a chapter on the geology of the cave by Charlotte Baynes (*B.S.A.J.*, 1927).

[2] The fact that this last (R. hemitoechus) was not the 'woolly' rhinoceros and was two-horned removes the last support from the view that it represents the $r^e\bar{e}m$ (A.V. unicorn) or wild ox, which is described as a wild animal unlikely to submit to the plough (see *Ency. Bib.*, 'Unicorn', and G. B. Gray on Job xxxix. 9).

[3] Miss Bate, p. 48.

typical in south-western Asia, e.g. the influx of nomads from the desert, the rival lines of influence from the north and south. It is futile, therefore, as a general principle, to spend much time upon theories of origin and of specific sources of influence. Nor can one speculate upon the vast chronological gaps in our evidence. There are similar gaps or blank periods elsewhere—notably in the early history of Egypt—and it seems that the general culture of these 'dark ages' was not such as to leave obvious traces. Finally, since the Galilee skull was associated with Mousterian culture, pre-historic Palestine is brought into contact with Europe; yet at the same time the Upper Mousterian flints of the Palaeolithic cave of Shuḳbah (17½ miles north-west of Jerusalem) were found to differ markedly from the similar cultural type in western Europe. Consequently, the fact that prehistoric Palestine proves to be not isolated culturally from the world of her time must not obscure the equally important fact that even at this remote period the land has a certain individuality of her own.[1]

Gezer itself was inhabited from Neolithic times by cave-dwellers, of small stature (the males and females average respectively 5 ft. 6 in. and 5 ft. 3 in.), who practised cremation, and were distinct from the 'Semitic' race which must have closely resembled the modern fellahin. From a careful examination of many of the Gezer caves it appears that some were used for occupation and for burial, others for burial only; some served later as store-houses. One of the most interesting lay beneath thirty-six feet of debris representing eight different cultural strata. It is dated round about 3500–3200 B.C. At its south end was the mouth, surrounded by small hollows, and cup-marks. A long narrow passage led into the cave itself, which was oval with irregular

[1] Miss Dorothy Garrod, *Q.S.*, 1928, p. 183. The case of Shuḳbah is not isolated. For a sketch of the prehistoric archaeological development see especially Vincent, *Canaan*, ch. vi; Karge, *Refaim*; Kohn, *Mitt. Anthrop. Gesell.* xxxiv (1914), pp. 81–135; and FitzGerald, *Q.S.*, 1930, April, pp. 85 sqq.

apses round the sides. Its greatest length was 16 ft. 7 in.[1] It was 5 ft. 5 in. high, and around the walls ran a 'frieze' of rock that had been made smooth, and covered with scribings, sixty-seven of which are noted by Professor Macalister. They fall into three classes: (a) variously arranged lines which sometimes cross as on a draught-board; (b) circular dots arranged as a row of dots within a circle of dots, a spiral arrangement, &c.; and (c) rude drawings of animals.

Since the lower part of the walls is rough rock, the presence of even the first class (a) on a prepared surface does not seem motiveless. From the lowest layer of the Galilean cave of Zuttiyeh came fragments of antlers and bones with markings (cross-cuts, longitudinal striae), which the Abbé Breuil definitely regarded as the work of Palaeolithic man.[2] Such marks may well be prototypes of the regular pottery linear patterns of the First and subsequent Semitic Periods at Gezer (Macalister, Pl. cxlv. 1), the draught-board patterns of the Third Period (Pl. clviii, clxiii. 3), the rather cruder example of the same period (Pl. clxvii. 16), and the crossed lines on the late 'box' (i. 358, fig. 185).[3]

The second class (b) recalls the arrangement of the cup-marks: a principal cup surrounded by others, or a spiral grouping of cups, &c. A bowl with knobs arranged spiral fashion was found in the 'crematorium' (*Gezer*, fig. 50; see p. 75), and the spiral pattern is found on pottery, early (some fine examples in Bliss-Macalister, Pl. xl) and late (*Gezer*, Pl. clxxiii. 3). The significance of cup-marks is not certain (see p. 11); but these may be definitely associated with the early cave-dwellers, and it is a tempting suggestion that there is some connexion between them and the pattern on the 'frieze'.

The animals in the third group are distinguished by the rudeness of the linear drawings, analogous to the animals on

[1] *Gezer*, i. 144–52 (Cave 30 iv), Plates xlvi–xlviii; Handcock, *Archaeology of the Holy Land*, pp. 45 sqq.

[2] *Prehistoric Galilee*, p. 47, Pl. xvii.

[3] Cf. the unintelligible marks, *Gezer*, ii. fig. 426, and Pl. ccxxv. 9.

seals (our Pl. xvi, nos. 1, 3, 4).[1] The millipede which Professor
Macalister recognizes (Pl. xlvi, no. 21) tempts comparison
—merely as regards style—with the seal, ib., fig. 438 c
(Fourth Semitic), cf. also the potsherd, Pl. clix. 13 (Third
Semitic). The excellent cow (our Pl. xvi, no. 3) would appear
to have tipped horns to prevent it from doing injury: the
custom, which was in use in Talmudic times, illustrates old
laws.[2] The human foot (no. 24, our fig. no. 2) is more
carefully engraved than the rest. Like the common representation of the hand (see p. 46), it cannot be meaningless,
but may be a part for the whole, a symbol of the owner.
At Gezer were also found rudely cut models of feet in clay,
and a clay tablet with the impression of a child's left foot
(ii. 447). While the former may be interpreted as votive
offerings, the latter seems to represent a bruised foot, and
Macalister suggests that the purpose was a magical one,
to inflict a similar bruise upon the child itself. On the other
hand, the foot on the 'frieze' may possibly be in the hope
that the owner might be protected (cf. Ps. xl. 2).

Besides nos. 48–50, scenes of hunting or driving animals,
and no. 3 (variously explained as bird or fish, or preferably
a boat), the elaborate no. 44 seems to represent an animal
being killed with bow and arrow. Crude linear drawings
persist to the Greek age, but become more ambitious and
reflect a far more advanced environment.[3] The human
figure (no. 48) is not stylized; contrast the triangular convention on a painted sherd of the eighth to seventh centuries

---

[1] *Gezer*, Plates xlvi sqq., nos. 34, 38, 52; also ii. fig. 439; cf. also
Samaria, p. 97, fig. 21 (time of Omri and later).

[2] See Talmud. Bab. *Berakh.*, f. 33a, cf. Code of Hammurabi, §§ 250
sqq. (horns to be cut), Exod. xxi. 28 sqq.

[3] Cf. *Gezer*, figs. 6, 7, 213, 425. Compare nos. 42, 43 in the cave
(the hindquarters of one animal under the snout of another) with the
'votive altar' of the Hellenistic stratum (*Gezer*, figs. 525, our Pls. xvii sq.);
also *Samaria*, i. 333 (and Pl. lxxx). Contrast the linear but stylized
life on the Third Semitic pottery, Pl. clxiii. 1, 3, clxvii. 12. If the vertical
lines in nos. 42 sq. really represent vegetation we may compare the
pattern on the Fourth Semitic sherd, Pl. clxxiii. 10.

from Megiddo.[1] This love of depicting life is common to seals and pottery patterns; and with the 'frieze' we may legitimately compare the friezes with animals and birds on the painted pottery, especially of the Third and Fourth Periods.[2] Nor can we ignore Ezekiel's remarkable vision of the secret cults practised in a dark chamber upon which were carved all sorts of 'abominations, and all the idols of the house of Israel'.[3] It is impossible to resist the conclusion that there was a recrudescence of earlier ideas in Ezekiel's time, although it is not easy to say decisively what meaning was attached to the cults.

On the whole, the scribings in the Gezer cave may be ascribed neither to mere ebullition or *joie de vivre*, nor to definite aesthetic motives. If no. 44 represents the slaying of the animal, the fact that the human figure is left undrawn will remind us of the precautions taken by hunters to avoid offending the animals they slay or propose to kill, and so to free themselves of responsibility for the animal's death.[4] On this view, the drawings are partly magical, or magico-religious: they served in some cases to foreshadow and secure success in hunting—like the representation of the slaying of the bison in the cave at Niaux—in others to preserve the

---

[1] *Mutesellim*, Taf. xxiv, Gressmann, no. 24. See, in general, Deonna, 'Les Origines de la Représentation Humaine', *Bull. Corresp. Hell.*, 1926, pp. 319 sqq.

[2] *Gezer*, ii. 173 sqq., fig. 336 sq. (good examples). In the earlier period the figures are drawn in broad strokes and the spaces filled in, whereas in the later they are drawn in narrow strokes and the spaces empty. The difference may perhaps be associated with cultural changes at the entry of the Philistines (l. c., see Macalister, *Schweich Lectures*, p. 121 sq.).

[3] See commentaries on Ez. viii. 10. The Septuagint omits the reference to the 'creeping things and beasts'; possibly the words are a gloss based upon Deut. iv. 17 sq. (Cornill, Davidson-Streane), or the Greek translators omitted words which might offend Egyptian susceptibilities (Bertholet). See also *Rel. Sem.*, pp. 357, 625, 629.

[4] Cf. Frazer, *Golden Bough*, iii. 204 sq., 219, 223; cf. viii. 188, also iii. 400 (the Algerian lion-hunter points to the beast but says 'he is not there' to disarm its suspicions).

'spirit' of the animal in question.[1] Even the prohibition of making images in Islam is explained by the belief that in some way this encroached upon the function of Allah, who alone endows creatures with life-giving 'breath' (*Rel. Sem.*, p. 573, n. 1). It is, in any event, noteworthy that while some of the scribings appear to be defaced, the animals are left intact; and that this unique 'frieze', dated as it is before 3000 B.C., is roughly contemporary with the remarkable frieze at Ur with all its domestic and pastoral interest.[2]

Another cave in Gezer was in use for many centuries as a dwelling place, a cistern, and as a burial place (in the Hyksos period). It is remarkable, also, for its concentric ovals of cup-marks, and for the curious deposit of miscellaneous human bones in jars (i. 123).[3] Above the shaft of one of its ten chambers was a pile of potsherds which had been deliberately broken on the spot (cf. above, p. 23 sq.). While the original sacral significance of the complex is unquestioned, culturally it is also of great importance on account of its general resemblance to royal burial caves found at Byblus and elsewhere.[4]

What is called 'the rock-cut place of sacrifice' consists of a rock-surface 86 × 76 feet with no less than 83 cup-marks. Beneath it is a row of three caves. One is unusually lofty (almost 11½ feet), another is fed by a channel apparently

[1] For the former, note Ezekiel's symbolical action (ch. iv; *Rel. Sem.*, p. 640), and, for the latter, a possible explanation of the 'foot' (no. 24), and primitive ideas of the 'spirit' (*Rel. Sem.*, pp. 585, 635).

[2] On the interpretation of prehistoric drawings (symbolism, magic, &c.), see R. A. S. Macalister, *Text-book of European Archaeology*, i (1921), pp. 505 sqq.; M. C. Burkitt, *Prehistory*, ch. xxii; Deonna, *Rev. Hist. Rel.*, lxxxix (1924), pp. 1 sqq. At Ophel the figure of a fish (4 ft. long) and remains of two smaller ones were found painted on the side of a cistern in a house (extending into the Byzantine period), *P.E.F. Annual*, iv. 114.

[3] Cave 28 ii. *Gezer*, i. 112–41, figs. 38 sqq. The cup-marks are plausibly explained as equivalent to a gigantic table of offerings (ib., p. 139). For a convenient summary of the Gezer caves, see Thomsen, *Reallex. Vorgesch.*, 'Gezer', §§ 7 sqq.

[4] Vincent, *Rev. Bib.*, 1923, pp. 552 sqq.; 1924, pp. 161 sqq.

connected with some of the cup-marks; and Macalister justly compares the *ghabghab* of the heathen Arabs.[1] At this, the northern end of the cave was an 'apsidal projection', with its floor two feet higher than the floor of the cave, and here were found, *inter alia*, a number of pig bones. They appeared to belong to the earliest history of the cave, whereas cow, sheep, and bird bones were scattered in the debris of the 'Semitic' period. The fact that the pig was a tabooed animal among the Semites may be due to its sacrosanct character among the original inhabitants: at all events little figurines of the pig, pig's teeth as amulets, &c., are found in Gezer and elsewhere, and also in Jericho to the Jewish period.[2]

On the eastern side of Gezer lay what is known as the 'Troglodyte crematorium'.[3] Outside were cup-marks, and steps led to a cave, $31 \times 24\frac{1}{2}$ feet, and 2–5 feet in height. The floor was covered with burnt human ashes. But later, this was succeeded by ordinary burial, bodies buried in the contracted ('embryonic') positions, and round the wall were grave-enclosures and a jar with the bones of a newly-born infant, the special treatment suggesting an inaugural sacrifice (cf. p. 84 below). It is natural to associate the changes with similar changes elsewhere (cf. Vincent, p. 267), and the transition from cremation to inhumation may be taken to point to some change of population. Moreover, outside was found a small standing-stone set up after the rock-surface had become covered with debris. The burning of the dead and the burial in the 'embryonic' position betoken different cultural practices and conceptions of death, and it is an instructive fact, in any event, that a cave once

---

[1] Caves 16 iii, 17 iii, 17 iv; *Gezer*, i. 100 sqq., ii. 378; Handcock, pp. 327 sqq. See *Rel. Sem.*, pp. 198, 339 sq.; similar channels were found at Megiddo and Taanach.

[2] Thomsen, *Reallex. Vorgesch.*, 'Schwein'. See *Rel. Sem.*, Index, *s.v.* 'Swine'; also Burney, *Judges*, p. xvii sq.; I. M. Price, *J.B.L.*, 1925, pp. 154 sqq.; Meissner, *Bab. und Ass.*, i. 220 sq.

[3] Cave 2 i, *Gezer*, i. 74 sq., 285 sqq.; ii. 380; Handcock, p. 303 sq.

associated with one type of burial should still be employed —and elaborated—by Semites who held other beliefs.[1]

Of outstanding interest is a double cave, the use of which goes back to *c.* 2500–2000 B.C. It lies to the east of the line of pillars, the so-called 'Gezer High-place', which must first be briefly described (plan on Pl. xviii).[2] Between the two hills of Gezer is an open space about 150 feet north–south and 120 feet east–west. Here stood eight (originally ten) stones in a slightly curved line, ranging between 5 feet 5 inches and 10 feet 6 inches in height. They were probably not all erected at the same time. As we face the east, no. 1, on the extreme right (south), is the largest (10′ 2″ ×4′ 7″ ×2′ 6″); there were traces of blackening by fire on the western side and near its base. On its top is a curious groove, such as has also been found on a monolith at Taanach; it is scarcely pronounced enough to support the view that it could be a rough equivalent of the horns or bosses upon altars.[3] No. 2 is the smallest, and the smooth patches on its surface are such as are found nowadays on stones venerated by the kisses and offerings of pilgrims. Nos. 3, 5, and 8 have cup-like hollows on the western sides (which are smoother than the eastern). No. 7 is not of local rock like the rest, but of stone that is found elsewhere (e.g. at Jerusalem). The supposition that it had been carried away is supported by the shallow curved line carved on the western face (? for tying a rope round it). Mesha 'dragged'

---

[1] Cremation is found to enter with the age of iron, i.e. at a relatively late date, at Carchemish and elsewhere (*C.A.H.*, ii. 293 sq., &c., see Index). At en-Nasbeh, in the early Eneolithic caves (*c.* 3000–2500 B.C.), 70 or more individuals are inhumed; but whether they are to be called pre-Semitic or non-Semitic has yet to be determined (*Q.S.*, 1927, p. 12). On inhumation in the 'embryonic position', see Vincent, *Canaan*, p. 269 sq.; apart from considerations of economy of space (Handcock, p. 306), this mode of burial associates itself with beliefs of 'mother earth', see above, p. 36, n. 3.

[2] *Gezer*, ii. 381–406 (see plan, fig 486); Driver, pp. 62 sqq.; Vincent, pp. 109 sqq.; Handcock, pp. 345 sqq.; Gressmann, nos. 411 sqq.

[3] See Vincent's discussion, p. 124 sq.

before Chemosh the 'altar hearth' (*ar'ēl*) of Davdoh, and the same verb is used when Hushai proposes to 'drag' away the stones of a city with ropes.[1] No. 8 is phallic; phalli were found in large numbers at Gezer (see further, *Rel. Sem.*, p. 687 sq.).

To the west of and between nos. 5 and 6 was a large block (6′ × 5′ × 2′ 6″) containing a hollow (2′ 10″ × 1′ 11″ × 1′ 4″), the purpose of which has been keenly discussed (Pl. xix). Hardly a trough for ritual oblations (such as were found at Serabiṭ), more probably it was for the purpose of holding a cult-object.[2] As a matter of fact, before excavation a carefully squared stone had been found on the surface measuring 6′ × 2′ 6″ × 1′ 5″, and tapering to 2′ 5″ × 1′ 3¾″.[3] It would be remarkable if this once belonged to the block, and it has been suggested that the block was intended to hold a stela, but one that has long since disappeared.[4] Behind the alinement (i.e. to the east) were two caves connected by a narrow crooked passage.[5] One (A) had the entrance blocked up so that it remained secret, and it would be possible (as Macalister suggests) for a man to enter the other and more southerly chamber (B), and secreting himself in (A), act the 'oracle' to those who entered and were ignorant of

[1] 2 Sam. xvii. 13. The nature of the cult-objects of Yahweh which Mesha also 'dragged' before Chemosh can only be guessed, as there is a fracture in the stone: altar-hearths, or vessels, or (Clermont-Ganneau) calves. For the removal of sacred objects of cult, cf. 1 Sam. iv. 8 sqq. (the ark), 2 Sam. v. 21 (the images of the Philistines, on 1 Chron. xiv. 12 see the Commentaries). At the old sacred site discovered at Bāb ed-Draʿ there were six fallen monoliths, and the fragment of a seventh; all were of a limestone not found in the locality, and must have been dragged for miles (p. 91).

[2] See for (a) Petrie, *Sinai*, pp. 88, 105 sqq., 190; and for (b) Lagrange, *Études*, p. 202; Vincent, p. 131 sq.

[3] *Gezer*, i. 50, ii. 396.

[4] Thiersch, *Z.D.P.V.*, xxxvii. 88 (cf. 65 sqq.), with important illustrations Pl. xxx sq. (in one case a stele was found in its socket). Cf. Przeworski, *O.L.Z.*, 1928, col. 233 sqq. (on North Syrian and Hittite stelae). See also below, on the Tyrian stelae, pp. 161 sqq.

[5] Caves 18 i, 19 iii. *Gezer*, i. 105 sqq., ii. 381 sqq.

its existence. In other words, (A) was an inner chamber, an *adyton* or *megaron*, and confirms Robertson Smith's suggestion that the ancient *adytum* was originally a cave.[1]

To the east of the cave a deep cistern, round whose mouth was an elaborate system of cup-marks (*Gezer*, fig. 490), contained the bones of animals (cow, sheep, deer, and goat) and of a number of human beings.[2] In front (i.e. to the west) were two similar pits, in one of which was found a small bronze serpent: it is one of many indications of serpent cults in Palestine.[3] Near by, a passage led direct from the alinement to a bank of earth 7 feet by 1–2 feet, baked hard, and containing eleven human skulls, a quantity of cows' teeth, and a number of splintered bones and potsherds.[4]

Over the whole area were found infant jar-burials.[5] The infants were new-born, none over a week old. They had been buried head first in large two-handled jars with pointed base; two or three smaller vessels for containing food were in or by the side of them, and at least two showed marks of fire. Besides this, jar-burials of infants or very young children were found under the corners of rooms. The practice was not confined to any one period, though it seems to have become rare in the Hellenistic stratum.

[1] See *Rel. Sem.*, pp. 200, 568; cf. the passage at Hal-Tarxien and other old Maltese sanctuaries (*C.A.H.*, ii. 576), and Bliss-Macalister, p. 262 sq. (cave of Khirbet el-'Ain). The *dĕbīr* in the Temple of Jerusalem was probably dark (1 Kings viii. 12 sq.); the E. V. 'oracle' is an early misunderstanding of the root; the proper meaning is the inner or back room (cf. Ar. *dubr*, hindmost or back part).

[2] Similarly the ruins of a supposed temple on the western hill of Gezer had on the eastern side a couple of circular structures filled with the bones of sheep and goats (ii. 407, fig. 491).

[3] ii. 398 sq., Handcock, p. 368. Serpents' heads at Taanach (p. 112); a bronze serpent from Arabia (Nielsen, *Handbuch*, p. 175). See Thomsen, *Reallex. Vorgesch.*, 'Schlange', and p. 98 sq., below.

[4] *Gezer*, ii. 368. It was by no means the only problematical 'find' of human remains in Gezer (see ib., and cf. i. 342 sq.).

[5] *Gezer*, ii. 402, 406; Driver, pp. 68 sqq.; Handcock, pp. 321, 357 sqq. At Taanach these burials were in the vicinity of a rock-altar with cup-marks.

At Taanach it was a child of about ten (Sellin, p. 51; Vincent, p. 200). More striking is the case at Gezer where a jar-burial and a number of vessels were *under* the wall which had been built over it; while at Megiddo, besides a jar-burial at the foot of a wall, a jar was found between the first and second layers of stones at the foundation of another wall; and the skeleton of a girl lay over the foundation-stone of a third.[1]

In a prepared hollow in the corner of a Gezer building was the skeleton of a woman of advanced age, and in a diseased condition: 'possibly she was selected as a victim because she was useless to the community'.[2] Eduard Meyer entirely dissents, treating it as an ordinary burial.[3] The archaeological evidence by itself certainly does not permit dogmatism, but the transition from a precious sacrifice to one that is relatively valueless is characteristic of the history of religions; and can be illustrated, both by the prophet's condemnation of the indifferent worshippers (Mal. i. 7 sq.), and by the Carthaginian conviction that their disasters at the hands of Agathocles were due to the negligence of the rich who were sacrificing purchased children in place of their own.[4]

Here may be mentioned cases of mutilation. At Gezer the upper half of a girl of about sixteen was found buried along with fourteen males whose skeletons were intact; and, in another case, the skeleton of the upper half of a youth of about eighteen lay over two skeletons (one certainly male), with jugs and bowls. Mutilation ($\mu\alpha\sigma\chi\alpha\lambda\iota\sigma\mu\acute{o}s$) is found in Greece and Italy, though its motive is uncertain.[5] Dis-

---

[1] *Gezer*, ii. 432 sqq., see fig. 514; Megiddo, pp. 45, 54, figs. 41, 59 (cf. Driver, pp. 69 sq., 72 sq.).

[2] Macalister, *Gezer*, i. 67, ii. 427; *C.A.H.*, iii. 449 sq.

[3] *Arch. Anz.*, 1913, p. 76, n. 2. Peter Thomsen, *Reallex. Vorgesch.* 'Gezer', § 12, is sceptical throughout as regards the Gezer evidence.

[4] See also n. 5 end.

[5] Thiersch, *Jahrb. K. D. Arch. Inst.*, xxiv (1909), 360, n. 18, refers to Furtwängler, *Antike Gemmen*, pp. 229 sqq., taf. xxi. 48 (the upper part

memberment in general has been explained (*a*) as a magical rite to fertilize the soil, or to distribute the virtues of the dead (Frazer, *Adonis*, ii. 97, the story of the scattering of the remains of Osiris); or (*b*) as a means of preventing the dead from doing mischief (ib., p. 188); or again (*c*), the parties to a covenant pass between the two halves of the victim.[1]

Foundation-sacrifices are well known everywhere, and there is a general tendency to soften the practice.[2] Of this there is an interesting example in the jar found at Gezer in the corner of a building containing a thin bronze sheet, the rude figure of a man ($2\frac{1}{4}$ in.), and about nine similar but smaller figures in silver, more or less incomplete, together with small silver saucers.[3] Dead infants often receive special

---

of the body of a young sacrificial victim over the altar). Macalister (*Q.S.*, 1909, pp. 102 sq., citing *The Times*, Jan. 21, 1909) records similar dismemberment from Moro Land in the Philippines: a boy placed against a tree is cut in two, one half is cut up and carried off by those present, the other is buried. The Bilanes sacrifice their own people, but the Bagobos use old and decrepit or useless slaves captured from other tribes.

[1] Frazer, *Folk-lore in the O. T.*, i. 408, 418 sq., 422 sqq. (cf. *Rel. Sem.*, p. 691 sq.). The dismemberment of the Levite's concubine (Judg. xix. 29), and of the oxen by Saul (1 Sam. xi. 7), united irrevocably in a supreme common cause all those who received the pieces. It is difficult to explain the burial in Jerusalem of *c.* 7th to 6th cent., where the skulls had been severed from the bodies of a row of skeletons (*Q.S.*, 1922, p. 18). As regards (*a*), Osiris was known as 'the one in the tree' (Frazer, *Adonis*, ii. 111); cf. Petrie, *Anc. Eg.*, 1928, p. 40. In some way the tradition arose that Isaiah took refuge in a tree which was sawn in two (see Charles, *Ascension of Isaiah*, pp. xlv sqq.; Galling, *O.L.Z.*, 1930, col. 99 sqq.). 1 Chron. xx. 3, though corrupt (see 2 Sam. xii. 31), can be taken to show that the barbarous practice was not unknown.

[2] See Driver, pp. 69 sqq.; *Rel. Sem.*, pp. 376, 632 sq. The case of Hiel the Bethelite (1 Kings xvi. 34) is mentioned as something notorious and in need of an explanation.

[3] ii. 434. At Byblus two jars contained about sixty small bronzes (5–10 cm.): armed men, some with pointed caps, others nude, and with spikes in their feet for fixing them in position (*Syria*, viii. 95). On the other hand, at the base of two columns in the southern temple of Ramses II at Beth-Shan, Rowe found deposited merely a pot full of

treatment, and in the East peasants bury still-born infants and premature births in the corner of rooms.[1] Hence, although the first-born in particular were often sacrificed, so often as to arouse the indignation of the reforming prophets of Israel, it does not follow, of course, that every jar-burial represents a sacrifice. Yet, whether the infants died a natural death or not, and whether they were buried in the home or at a sacred place, ideas prevailed that the spirit or soul of the dead was there, on the spot, so to say, waiting to be reborn. If men died and were 'gathered to their fathers', infant burial would seem to ensure the presence of young life about a house waiting to be born, while the burial of the infants at a shrine would give concreteness to the practice of childless women of resorting to sacred places.[2] Hence between this treatment of infants who were born dead or died young and the deliberate sacrificial rites for this or other purposes there is no great gulf, and infant-sacrifice as a means for procuring prosperity was only too common in both Palestine and Phoenicia (cf. below on Kronos, p. 168).[3]

jewellery. In Babylonia figurines were buried under the floors, and generally by the doorway, to protect the households (Woolley, *J.R.A.S.*, 1926, pp. 689–713).

[1] See generally, A. B. Cook, *Zeus*, ii. 1059; Canaan, *J.P.O.S.*, iv. 8 n. (children buried in large broken jars), vi. 118, n. 3 (some Palestinian shrines reserved specially for children); Vincent, pp. 282 sqq.; cf. also Mishnah, *Ohol.*, xviii. 7, *Nidd.* vii. 4 (the houses of heathen are 'unclean' on this account). A case of burial of a premature birth was found at Megiddo, p. 60.

[2] Driver, p. 69 n., cf. Frazer, i. 78, 96, 108 sq., 214 sqq.; *Rel. Sem.*, p. 689. Burney explains the place-name Eltolad to mean the place where children could be obtained, cf. also the name Iptaḥ-el (*J.T.S.*, xiii. 84, cf. S. A. Cook, ib., xxviii. 379 sq.).

[3] At Carthage were found thousands of urns containing the bones and relics of children, newly born and up to twelve years of age; see Bryon Khun de Prorok, *Digging for Lost African Gods* (1926), pp. 89 sqq.; Contenau, *Civ. Phén.*, pp. 138, 230, and esp. Dussaud, *Rev. Hist. Rel.*, lxxxvii. 55 sq., 66 (other similar sanctuaries, e.g. Motya in Sicily). With them were the bones of small animals, and it has been conjectured

A deliberate effort to banish the barbarous rite has been seen in the 'lamp and bowl' deposits at Gezer, which begin in the middle of the Third Period, are common in the Fourth, but are infrequent in the Hellenistic. They are found in corners or under thresholds, and consist typically of a lamp with a bowl below and another inverted above. There were some signs that the lamps had been lit.[1] A somewhat similar custom has been discovered in Babylonia, as late as the early Christian period. Under rooms were placed bowls inverted or mouth to mouth; and they were, an inscription states, 'covers to restrain the sacred angels (i.e. the accursed spirits) and all evil spirits'.[2] The procedure is called a *kibshā*, to repress or suppress demons, and, though in itself of ancient origin, it is not on all fours with the Palestinian deposits. Yet the two practices are not entirely unrelated. The repression of evil spirits gives more scope for the benevolent ones; and men aim either at driving away evil, and thereby securing protection and happiness, or at securing protection, and thereby escaping harm. Now in Palestine the lamps are the essential feature, and at Gezer they are frequently found in tombs (from the Second Period), and often with traces of smoke-blackening.[3] Even at the present day lamps are hung up to cure

that these were substitutes. The urns were under the altars; and an inscribed Punic stele has been found upon which a priest seems to be holding a child before sacrifice (de Prorok, p. 98, see Dussaud, pp. 47, 62). The inscription has been translated: 'offering of a son which thy servant has vowed' (cf. also Chabot, *C. R. Acad. Inscr.*, 1922, p. 112); similar inscriptions (*C.I.S.*, i. 166, 194) are too uncertain (*Rel. Sem.*, p. 630, n. 4). It should, however, be mentioned that in some cases in Egypt where children are represented as being held by priests, they are child gods (Spiegelberg, *Arch. f. Rel.*, xxi. 228). In any event, the barbaric dances witnessed and described by de Prorok vividly illustrate the orgiastic rites of the Carthaginians, and of their Phoenician and other kinsmen.

[1] Macalister, ii. 435 sq.; Driver, 72 sq.; Vincent, pp. 198 sq., 290 sqq.; Gressmann, no. 233.

[2] J. A. Montgomery, *Aramaic Incantation Texts from Nippur*, p. 41 sq.

[3] Cf. Ain Shemesh (*P.E.F. Annual*, ii. 58). At Carthage there were

the sick. In tombs of the Christian period lamps are inscribed 'the Lord (or the Christ) is my light' (φωτισμός), 'the light of Christ shone for all', or the like, and the mottoes tend to degenerate into unintelligible lettering and finally become mere ornamentation.[1] It is obvious that such lamps were intended positively to enlist the help of Christ: it is the divine help and not the expulsion of evil that is besought. But the Christian *practice* is not an isolated one, nor is the *idea* without earlier analogies.[2] Yahweh was the light of Israel and of the Israelite (Is. x. 17, Ps. xxvii. 1); and the name Neriah (which occurs also on Israelite seals) designates Yahweh as the bearer's lamp (*nēr*), cf. 2 Sam. xxii. 29. David has a 'lamp', as long as his dynasty lasts (1 Kings xi. 36, 2 Kings viii. 19); and to destroy the last of the family is to 'extinguish the coal' (2 Sam. xiv. 7). David's death, in turn, would extinguish the lamp of Israel (2 Sam. xxi. 17). Accordingly lamp and light are symbols of prosperity and of life itself, and the god is the source and preserver of life.[3] Hence, although the lamp and

'hundreds of lamps' along with babies' bottles and toys, and 'thousands of urns' containing the remains of children (de Prorok, op. cit., p. 98). For the varieties of Palestinian lamps—important for questions of dating—see K. Galling, *Z.D.P.V.*, xlvi. 1–50.

[1] See *Gezer*, ii. 228, and Plates civ. 3 (cf. i. 357), cx. 2, cxviii. 16; also *Q.S.*, 1905, p. 164, and *P.E.F. Annual*, iv. 194 sq. Such evidence goes to show that the lamps, as a general practice, were not merely for the purpose of relieving the gloom of the deceased (on which cf. Oesterley, *Immortality and the Unseen World*, p. 187 sq.).

[2] Note the Egyptian lamps of the Graeco-Roman period with the frog (a symbol of the goddess Hekt), and the words 'I am the resurrection' (Budge, *Eg. Magic*, p. 63). As a general principle there is a real difference between objects of positive cult and those that have a vaguer apotropaic significance, although it was and still is easily obscured.

[3] Noth, *Israel. Personennamen*, p. 165 sq.; Pedersen, *Israel*, p. 465 sq.; Galling, *Z.D.P.V.*, xlvi. 36 sq.; and for later Rabbinical ideas, Abrahams, *Studies in Pharisaism*, ii. 16, and in general, Wetter, *Phōs* (Upsala, 1913). Note also the cosmic life-giving power of the sun's rays in Ikhnaton's hymns (*C.A.H.*, ii. 117 sqq.; Baikie, *Amarna Age*, pp. 322 sqq.), and the Jewish Festival of Lights (Gray, *Sacrifice*, pp. 292 sqq.).

bowl deposits are for long contemporary with infant-sacrifice, it is possible that while the lamps in tombs were a symbol of light and life, these deposits were intended to preserve the family 'life', and secure the prosperity of the household.[1]

In course of time the whole area of which the alinement formed part was built over. Are we to suppose that it lost its former sacred character, or may we compare the way in which the Jewish sanctuary at Elephantine in the fifth century B.C. was closely surrounded by private houses?[2] The figurines and emblems, the representations of Bes, and the unique bronze statuette of a 'horned Astarte' which were found there, may have been the property of the later dwellers rather than votive offerings at the original sanctuary (Macalister, ii. 403). We know that when Simon the Maccabee captured Gezer he cleansed it of all idolatry, and placed therein men who feared the Mosaic Law (1 Macc. xiii. 43–8). Hence all the religious objects unearthed at Gezer and earlier than the second century B.C., either escaped the iconoclastic reform, or were tolerated, or re-interpreted and regarded as harmless, or, perhaps, lay hidden beneath the debris already accumulated. Yet even before the work of excavation began, the tops of two of the standing stones already projected above the surface of the ground; and beside it to the west lay a third (1 Macalister, i. 50 sq.). Why had these been allowed to remain ?

It is conceivable that it had become possible to give the whole alinement a harmless meaning; and, as a matter of fact, what is commonly known as 'the Gezer High Place' is regarded by some scholars as a line of pillars, mere memorials, devoid of sacred significance. Certainly it

---

[1] The burial of the lamps under the threshold is in keeping with ideas of its sanctity, cf. Clay Trumbull, *Threshold Covenant* (1896); Cheyne, *E.Bi.* 'Threshold'. Such ideas were maintained by the Philistine neighbours of the Jews; see 1 Sam. v. 5, and Targum on Zeph. i. 9 (cf. M. A. Meyer, *Gaza*, p. 123).

[2] See van Hoonacker, *Schweich Lectures*, the plan facing p. 14.

is not necessary to suppose that the stones represented so many gods or—on the analogy of Josh. iv.—tribes. And even if they were, as Eduard Meyer has suggested,[1] memorials to ensure the existence of the dead (cf. Absalom's monument, 2 Sam. xviii. 18), not only was the area as a whole undoubtedly a sacred place, but such stones received more than mere respect or honour.[2] What to the modern mind seems to be of merely 'political' or 'secular' interest was often the centre of religious beliefs and practices among early or primitive peoples, and although it is hazardous to speak of the alinement as a 'high place', it is safe to regard it and the area as possessing a sacred value.

Indeed, somewhat to the west of this area were the remains of a large building with the traces of a line of pillars, running north–south for 44' 4", and of monoliths too unequal in height to serve merely as supports for a roof. East thereof were a couple of circular structures with fragments of sheep and goat bones (no signs of burning).[3] Here we have, as Macalister recognized, a temple—and roughly of the age of the monarchy; but we are left with the curious fact that whereas only its foundations remain, so much of the line of pillars was allowed to survive.[4] Not without reason was Gezer a priestly 'Levitical' city; but from what can be seen of its early religion it was of the general type that is to be expected when one considers the specific denunciations of the great reforming prophets, and the character of the reforms in the temple of Jerusalem itself attributed to King

[1] *Arch. Anz.*, 1913, p. 83 sq.; Thiersch, loc. cit., p. 376 sq.

[2] Cf. the sacrifices offered to Assyrian dedication tablets, and see *Rel. Sem.*, pp. 569 sqq., 582 sq.

[3] *Gezer*, ii. 406 sq.; Vincent, p. 150 sq.; Handcock, pp. 359 sqq. Note that the pillars at Megiddo (pp. 110 sqq.) and Tell eṣ-Ṣafi (Bliss-Macalister, pp. 32 sqq.) are of more equal height; of the five 'baetyl-like' pillars at Ain Shemesh not enough is known (Mackenzie, ii. 16).

[4] Perhaps, as Thomsen suggests, this temple, lying as it did near an Egyptian building (? temple, *Gezer*, ii. 307 sq.) and the royal graves (28 ii, *Gezer*, i. 111 sqq.) was the real sanctuary (*Reallex. Vorgesch.*, 'Gezer', §15).

Josiah (621 B.C.). The archaeological history of Gezer is one of continuity in spite of change; and this, on the whole, is true of the religion of Palestine itself. Unfortunately there is no written evidence to throw light upon the deities venerated, whether in Gezer [1] or (with rare exceptions) elsewhere, although, as we shall presently see, there is much miscellaneous evidence for the deities of Palestine, and of its immediate neighbours.

The religious development of Palestine was in full swing by the closing centuries of the third millenium B.C. (the Middle Empire), and the invasion of Egypt by the Hyksos (c. 1750–1600 B.C.) makes a definite landmark. The invaders appear to have come from Syria with a medley of peoples, some of whom were from beyond the Taurus, and they are distinguished culturally by their use of horse and chariot, their free control of bronze, and their weapon the *khepesh*.[2] To these successful warriors we may attribute the deep impression made upon the Egyptians by the war-deities of South-West Asia, though this invasion was not by any means the first occasion that Semites or other Asiatics had influenced Egypt.[3] After successfully expelling the Hyksos (c. 1600 B.C.), Egypt extended her victories, and for the next few centuries Palestine and Syria were in the thick of the conflicts in the Near East. Only with the decline of the great powers after the Amarna Age did the petty peoples of the coast-land gain their independence, and the rise of the Israelite monarchy or monarchies was one of the

[1] For Thiersch's view that there was a cult of Iao—Inasios, see Macalister, *Gezer*, ii. 441 sq.; and for Iao-Yahu-Yahweh, see below, p. 145 sq.

[2] P. 66, n. 3. See Hall, *C.A.H.*, i. 311 sqq., and, of more recent writers, Sidney Smith, *Assyria*, pp. 216 sqq., who points out the connexion between the Hyksos and the semi-Iranian and other adventurers who settled down in Syria.

[3] On very early cultural relations between Syria and Egypt see Frankfort, *Studies in Early Pottery*, i. 104, 117 *et passim*; Hall, *C.A.H.*, i. 577 sqq.

results. The date of the entry of the tribes of Israel is still a vexed question; but in any case the pre-Israelite period, that is, the period before there could have been any distinctive Israelite culture, is of the utmost importance. The invading Israelites, as we gather from Judges i, iii, settled down among a people by whose religious beliefs and practices they were deeply influenced, and the question of the relations between Yahwism and (*a*) the earlier religions and (*b*) the religions outside Israel is one of absorbing interest.

Upon the early pre-Israelite period increasing light continues to be shed, and we may probably recognize a distinctive 'Amorite' period about 2300–1800 B.C.[1] Outside Palestine itself, the turquoise mines at Serabiṭ el-Khādim in the Sinaitic peninsula were known to the Egyptians, who worked them especially in the XIIth and XVIIIth Dynasties. By whom they were otherwise exploited it is hard to say; for there are the remains of un-Egyptian temples and their appurtenances, and of the cult of a Baalath who was identified with the Egyptian Hathor.[2]

Roughly contemporary with the Middle Empire are the remains recently found to the east and south-east of the Dead Sea. At Bāb ed-Drā', near Kerak, are traces of a great fortified camp (1,050 × 325 feet), and, hard by, seven pillars and a number of tombs. The obvious importance of the site and the absence of cities in the neighbourhood have suggested that it was a place of pilgrimage, a large necropolis—as was Petra in the Roman age—the religious centre of a district which on all accounts was once exceedingly fertile and wealthy. The place seems to have been abandoned after the Early Bronze Age, and the explorers have naturally been tempted to comment upon the approximate coincidence of this date with the traditional destruction of

[1] Cf. the First Babylonian or 'Amorite' Dynasty of Babylon; see Albright, *Bulletin of American Schools*, vi. 66 sqq.; *J.P.O.S.*, viii. 251.

[2] See Sir Flinders Petrie, *Researches in Sinai* (1906); Lina Eckenstein, *History of Sinai* (1921); also Gressmann, nos. 498 sq., 677; and *Ency. Brit.* 14th ed., 'Sinai'.

the cities of the Ghor.[1] North-east of Kerak were found remains of 'the first Moabite temple as yet known'. It was perhaps of rather later date, and here as elsewhere in Transjordania the cultural connexions were with the north.

The technical skill of the pre-Israelite age is admirably exemplified in (a) the walls of Jericho, (b) the Gezer 'water-passage', and (c) the not dissimilar earthworks and citadels which range over a wide area, including the eastern Mediterranean, and demonstrate the place of Palestine within the architectural or rather the cultural development of the Near East.[2] As regards Jericho, in spite of its antiquity and situation the religious remains prove to be relatively poor. It is not mentioned—at least under this name—in the Amarna Letters, and until it has been more extensively excavated it would be unsafe to speculate upon the religious conditions of a city whose climate alone, encouraging indolence and luxury, would tell against the *argumentum e silentio* that a 'purer' type of religion was preserved there.[3]

Each site brings its own contribution. Especially imposing have been the prolonged French excavations at the ancient city of Byblus (Gebal, modern Jebeil); the full

[1] M. G. Kyle, *Explorations at Sodom*; cf. Mallon, *Biblica*, v. 413–55; Albright, *Bulletin of American Schools of Or. Research*, April 1924, and their joint article in *Bibl. Sacra*, 1924, pp. 262–91.

[2] See (a) Gressmann, nos. 639–47; (b) *Gezer*, i. 256 sqq. For (c) see Mackenzie, *Q.S.*, 1913, pp. 65 sqq., and Albright, *J.S.O.R.*, x. 252 sq.: the similarities extend from Tell el-Yehudiyeh and Heliopolis in Egypt to Askalon and Tell Fara in Palestine, and Tell el-Mishrifeh, Sefinet Nuḥ (near Kadesh on the Orontes), &c., in Syria. More detailed inquiry is necessary: for example, the Palestinian citadels may be of North Syrian rather than of Anatolian derivation (Gustavs, cited *Q.S.*, 1927, p. 232), see Thomsen, *Reallex. Vorgesch.*, 'Hilani'.

[3] On purely archaeological grounds it was inferred that Jericho, whose 'Golden Age' was contemporary with the Middle Empire, was destroyed, *c.* 1700–1400; see Garstang, *Q.S.*, 1927, p. 100. [Recent excavation points to the lower date, i.e. *c.* 1400 B.C., Garstang, *Q. S.*, April, 1930.] Also it has been urged that many of the great sites of Syria and North Mesopotamia were abandoned between the Early and Late Bronze Ages. Fuller evidence is to be desired.

significance of the rich discoveries there can hardly as yet be estimated.[1] Intercourse with Egypt goes back before the Middle Empire. There was discovered a vase of Khase-khemui (IIIrd Dynasty), who also worked the mines at Sinai (*Syria*, ix. 181), and a seal of the Thinite period demonstrates the great antiquity of the mutual influence of the Egyptian and Phoenician religions. It had already been inferred that there was an Egyptian colony—if not also a Nubian contingent—in Gezer in the Middle Empire;[2] and this is now confirmed by Vincent's comparative study of the hypogaeum at Gezer with one at Byblus, both illustrating the close relations between Egypt and Palestine, and the attention paid by the Pharaohs to their vassal kinglets.[3]

The 'lady (Baalath) of Byblus', assimilated to Hathor, was then known in Egypt, and women called themselves after her. Remains were found of a grand temple—one is mentioned in the Amarna Letters (no. 137, l. 61 sq.)—with three great colossi (deities) guarding the entrance; and besides a 'lord' of Byblus (the ram-headed Amon-Re), a 'Re of the mountains' and a lion deity were members of the pantheon. Numerous objects pointing to intercourse with Egypt, the Levant, and Babylonia combine to illustrate the importance of the city, and they enable us to understand that the fusion of Semitic, Egyptian, and Levantine culture which characterizes Phoenicia, and indeed the whole littoral

---

[1] The results published by Montet and Dunand in the journal *Syria*, and elsewhere, have been noticed periodically by Vincent in the *Revue Biblique* (esp. April 1925), and by Gressmann (and others) in the *Z.A.T.W.* (esp. 1925, pp. 225 sqq.), where full bibliography will be found, pending the publication of a complete memoir. See also Contenau, *La Civilisation Phénicienne* (1926), esp. pp. 150 sqq., Thomsen, *Reallex. Vorgesch.*, 'Byblus.'

[2] viz. traces of a building with hieroglyphs (*Gezer*, ii. 307 sq.; cf. 311 sq.). On interrelations between Jerusalem and Egypt at and before the Middle Empire, see Mallon, *J.P.O.S.*, viii. 5 sq., and above, p. 5.

[3] See Vincent, *Rev. Bib.*, 1924, pp. 161 sqq.; also Thomsen, *Reallex. Vorgesch.*, 'Gezer', § 10 (Cave 28 ii, the tomb of the Gezer princes). At Gezer and Byblus the royal tomb is near the citadel and sanctuary.

in the Graeco-Roman period, had its roots in the distant past.[1]

No less brilliant have been the results of the excavations undertaken by the University of Pennsylvania at Beisan, the ancient Beth-Shan (1925–29). There is no doubt that when they are finally co-ordinated and the work at Byblus more complete our knowledge of the religion of ancient Palestine (with Phoenicia, &c.) will be immensely increased.[2] At Beth-Shan the fortunate excavator found the remains of several superimposed temples which—to judge from the scarabs, &c.—ranged from the age of Thutmose III to Ramses II (i.e. 15th–13th cent. B.C.). Of the presence of Egyptian officials there are many traces, not to speak of two royal stelae, of Seti I and Ramses II.[3] From this it follows that in spite of the intrigues and invasions which the Amarna Letters so vividly depict, and in spite of the weakness of which the reforming king Amenhotep IV (Ikhnaton) has been accused, the hand of Egypt still lay over Palestine. With this it agrees that the treaty between Ramses II and the Anatolian Hatti (Hittites) was a greater achievement for Egypt than has been thought;[4] and from a rude statue of Ramses III found at Beth-Shan and other data, e.g. the Harris papyrus, it appears that the Egyptian domina-

---

[1] Even the sarcophagus of Aḥiram with its mourners (p. 35) recalls the classical 'weeping women' at Sidon. It is of the age of Ramses II, and is of unique value for its Phoenician inscription which, on any reckoning, is the oldest of its kind; although the archaeological evidence may suggest that it was inscribed at a date rather later than that of this Pharaoh. See v. Bissing, *Arch. f. Orientforsch.*, iv. 57 sq., and Galling, *Z.D.P.V.*, 1928, p. 131 sq.; Ed. Meyer, *S.B.*, Berlin, 1929, p. 204, proposes the Xth cent.; contrast, however, *Syria*, x. 368.

[2] See, meanwhile, Mr. Alan Rowe's reports in the *Museum Journal of the University of Pennsylvania*, and *Q.S.*, April 1928 and April 1929.

[3] Ramses refers to his Delta city Raamses; but not, as was once believed, to the building of it or to Israelite prisoners (Rowe, *Museum Journal*, 1929, p. 95).

[4] See Ed. Meyer, *Gesch. d. Altertums*, ii. 1, p. 466; Pieper, *O.L.Z.*, 1929, col. 7 (see also Götze, ib., col. 832 sqq.).

tion over Palestine must have extended into the twelfth century.[1]

At Beth-Shan, as at Gezer, we pass imperceptibly from the pre-Israelite temples of the Egyptian period to the Greek age. There is nothing distinctively Israelite or Jewish; the Israelites appear to have been content to utilize the older buildings. In view of the part played by Beth-Shan when Saul's kingdom was overthrown by the Philistines (1 Sam. xxxi), it would be reasonable to look for a 'Philistine' phase between the earlier periods—call them Canaanite or Amorite—and the later. But here as elsewhere the contribution of archaeology to the relations between the Philistines and Israel is scanty. In a sense it is true that the Philistine invasion was the climax of the interrelations between the mainland and the Aegean, and that it marks the severance of Occident and Orient.[2] A 'Philistine' ware has been confidently recognized, and variant types distinguished (at Dor); but the so-called 'Philistine' graves at Gezer would seem to be some centuries later, and although cultural connexions with the Levant are indubitable, doubts have even been cast upon the legitimacy of recognizing specifically *Philistine* ware.[3] Certainly a clear line of demarcation has been traced by

---

[1] On the statue, see Hall, *Q.S.*, 1925, p. 118; and for the papyrus, Breasted, *Eg. Records*, iv. §§ 219, 225 (l. 15), 226 (l. 11), 229 (l. 8), 368 (l. 7?), 376 (l. 12), 384. For the independent position of Phoenicia, as illustrated by the story of Wen-Amon (*c.* 1100 B.C.) see Macalister, *Schweich Lectures*, pp. 29 sqq.: the record is of special interest for its light upon the Phoenician attitude to Egyptian religion.

[2] See Hempel's illuminating essay on western cultural influences upon early Palestine, *Pal. Jahrb.*, 1927, pp. 52–92, esp. p. 89.

[3] For Dor (Tantura) see *Bulletin of the British School, Jerusalem*, iii. 34, iv. 42; the graves at Gezer, p. 38, n. 3, above; the doubts, Saussey, *Syria*, v. 169 sqq.; a 'Philistine' helmet among the mercenaries at Carchemish (Smith, *Ass.*, Pl. xix); supposed traces of Philistines near Jerusalem in the ware found in tumuli at Malḥah (*Bulletin of American Schools*, 1923, p. 2; Vincent, *Rev. Bib.*, 1924, p. 420 sq.). On the diffusion of the 'Philistine' ware, see Hempel, op. cit., pp. 61 sqq.

excavators at Askalon and at Ain Shemesh—where the burnt stratum has been ascribed to Israelite invaders; and the signs of conflagration at Beth-Shan have been attributed to David's expulsion of the Philistines from that city.[1] Whatever be the correct interpretation of the archaeo- logical developments at the close of the second millennium B.C., the vicissitudes of the various sites, as judged from the archaeological point of view, are very instructive.

Thus the Danish excavations at Shiloh, incomplete though they are at present, appear to show that its history begins with the Later Bronze Age (c. 2000–1600 B.C.).[2] Older is Tell en-Nasbeh (Mizpah), whose history is interpreted as extending from the Eneolithic period (c. 3000 B.C.) to the sixth century B.C., and whose remarkable walls (16 feet thick, and once considerably over 25 feet high) raise the question of the earliest history of the Holy City and its environs.[3] Of Jerusalem itself it can only be said that it has suffered so much from pillage, iconoclasm, and reconstruc- tion, and the practical difficulties of excavation are so serious, that every particle of evidence bearing upon the history of its religion is invaluable.[4] One of its rivals, Shechem, has already contributed much of interest from c. 2000 B.C. onwards. Two cuneiform tablets supplement those found some years ago in Taanach, and tell us of the nomenclature of about the Amarna Period; and a temple (several times repaired) stood on a terrace, with altars, pillars (maṣṣēbōth), &c.; and on purely archaeological grounds it is suggested that these pillars (and an altar) continued to

[1] See (a) Phythian-Adams (Q.S., 1923, pp. 66 sqq. and p. 77); (b) Mackenzie, Annual, ii. 28 (with Vincent's cautious comments, Q.S., 1911, p. 149 sq.).

[2] Mallon, Biblica, 1929, pp. 369–75 (cf. Kjaer, Q.S., 1927, pp. 202 sqq.).

[3] Badé, Q.S., 1927, p. 11 sq., cf. Elihu Grant, ib., p. 159. On the history and identification of Mizpah, see Hertzberg, Z.A.T.W., 1929, pp. 161 sqq., and Badé's reply, Q.S., 1930, p. 8 sq.

[4] Its archaeological history is summarized by Thomsen in Ebert's Reallex. Vorgesch., vol. vi.

be venerated even when the temple itself lay in ruins (cf. similarly Jerusalem, Jer. xli. 5).[1]

So, also, life at Samaria did not cease when the northern tribes were carried off into exile; the city was reoccupied and old material used again.[2] On the other hand, the statement has been ventured that archaeological survey indicates that many towns in South Judah and Simeon were not reoccupied after the exile, and that the Babylonian invasion must have been disastrous in the extreme.[3] Samaria is especially important as a *terminus a quo*, as its archaeological history does not begin before the ninth century when it was founded by Omri (1 Kings xvi. 24). But unfortunately, considering the historical importance of the site, the objects of religious significance were not so numerous as might be expected, and the best remains were of the Graeco-Roman period. It is the same period that is illustrated in a most interesting way by the little Greek site, Tell Sandaḥannah, fuller excavation of which is much to be desired. On the other hand, numerous ostraka at Samaria, probably of the time of Ahab (about 860 B.C.), are of the first importance for the political organization and the nomenclature of the period.[4] It is, to be sure, by no

[1] See Sellin's reports in *Z.D.P.V.*, xlix sqq. Gustavs (*Z.D.P.V.*, li. 169–218; cf. *Q.S.*, 1927, p. 231 sq.) has discussed the character of the population on the basis of the names. A jar-handle with the impression of a scarabaeus and a seal of about the Middle Empire (*Z.D.P.V.*, l. 267, Taf. xxx) illustrates the common blend of Egyptian and Mesopotamian elements already noticed (p. 46). Other examples (not from Shechem) are (a) the seal of 'Aḥ-li-ib-sar servant of Teshub' with an *ankh*, &c. (Winckler, *M.V.A.G.*, 1896, iv. 18 sq.) ; (b) the British Museum seal of c. 14th–12th cent. with *ankh*, ape, sun-disk, moon, tree, &c. (*Brit. Mus. Quarterly*, 1927, p. 95, no. 64); (c) the seal of Yakin-ilu in Akkadian, with Egyptian hieroglyphs (*J.E.A.*, vii. 196, Albright, *Sellin Festschrift*, p. 9).

[2] Reisner, Fisher, and Lyon, *Harvard Excavations at Samaria*, 1908–10 (Cambridge, *U.S.A.*, 1924); see also Gressmann, nos. 648–52.

[3] *Bulletin of the American Schools*, 1924, p. 5.

[4] On the latter see Gressmann, *Z.A.T.W.*, 1925, p. 148 sq., and C. W. Jack, *Samaria in Ahab's Time* (1929). Jack (op. cit., p. 157)

means improbable that its fine Herodian temple, with its
giant statue of Augustus, was built upon an earlier sacred
site; and its triple arrangement has led to the conjecture
that three gods were once venerated: e.g. Baal, Astarte, and
(cf. I Kings xx. 23) some mountain god.[1]   There is no
doubt that a careful application of the principles of continuity and similarity in temple architecture, and in religious
archaeology in general, has much to suggest. So, to return
to Beth-Shan, a temple of the Greek period was constructed
on a plan similar to that of the smaller temple at Baalbek;
but it is another question whether, if the latter was dedicated to Bacchus—or, as has also been argued, to the
Mother Goddess (Atargatis)—the one at Beth-Shan was in
honour of a similar deity; or, again, whether the earlier
pairs of temples at Beth-Shan were, always, the larger of the
two for a god, and the smaller for his female counterpart.[2]

Of Beth-Shan it must suffice to say that the cultural
history of the city points to Egypt, to Crete (linear signs)
and Cyprus, to the Anatolian Hatti, and to Babylonia. It
supplements the discoveries at Byblus, and gives us a vivid
picture of the religious and other conditions in this part, at
least, of Palestine, and of the nature of its indebtedness to surrounding lands. The name itself is of special interest, since
there is reason to believe that serpent cults were once widely
prominent, and the name *Shān* (or *Shĕ'ān*) may be directly
connected with Shaḥan or Sakhan, the Semitic name of an
old Sumerian serpent deity. Upon a bowl is depicted an
undulating serpent; and a pottery model of a serpent has
female breasts, and a cup below for collecting the milk.
Besides curious models of shrines with human figures and
serpents, there were two-storied structures with birds
(? doves)—in one a nude female figure holds birds in
both hands—while serpents are coiled around the base.

remarks that of fifty-two names six are compounded with Baal and
that two begin with and nine end in Yo (Yau).

[1] Galling, *Z.D.P.V.*, l. 302.

[2] Cf. also Vincent, *Rev. Bib.*, 1928, p. 135 sq.

That the Mesopotamian cults of old serpent mother-goddesses extended into Palestine is also suggested by a fragmentary stele at Tell Beit Mirsim where a serpent is coiled round the legs of a walking figure.[1]

Beth-Shan more than any other Palestinian site has told us of its temples and deities. In particular, what may be called the Temple of Mekal, the god of Beth-Shan, may be briefly summarized on the basis of Mr. Rowe's discoveries.[2] The site (see Pl. xx) commands a good view facing the south-east, where the modern village and remains of the Roman theatre are visible. The walls, which have been

[1] Vincent, *R.B.*, 1929, p. 105 sq. (the figure is walking to the left). The identification of this site with Kirjath-jearim has been recently urged (Albright). The stele will recall the Syrian cult of the Janiculum, where a bronze deity (? Atargatis) is entwined seven times by a serpent and seven eggs are ranged between the folds (Gauckler, *Le Sanctuaire Syrien du Janicule* [1912], see Gressmann, *Die hellenist. Gestirnreligion* [1925], Taf. iii). Isis was serpent-bodied (Haas, *Urchristentum*, no. 14, cf. 109 sq.; other Eg. parallels, Mallon, *Biblica*, ix. 250). Sumerian seals depict a serpentine body with human head and bust (Langdon, *Tammuz and Ishtar*, p. 120 sq., see ib. pp. 114 sqq.). Ward describes a unique seal with 'Hittite' signs: a cult-object surmounted by a crescent, and a priest standing before a pole on which is coiled a serpent; he recalls the Neḥushtan cult (no. 796). Alan Rowe finds a combination of a goose (? symbol of Amon-Re) and a serpent on a unique vessel from Tell eṣ-Ṣafi (Bliss-Macalister, p. 98 sq., Pl. xlvii). For the 'shrines,' which resemble those some fifteen centuries earlier at Ashhur (*M.D.O.G.*, liv. 33, fig. 7), see the discussions in *Z.A.T.W.*, 1926, pp. 73 sqq.; *Z.A.* xxx. 79; Galling, *Altar*, p. 22; Contenau, *Kerkouk*, p. 31 sq.; Smith, *Ass.*, p. 67 sq. and Pl. ix. On the female at the window as a *motif* see Evans, *Palace of Minos*, ii. (1928), p. 410, and Herbig, 'Aphrodite Parakytusa', *O.L.Z.*, 1927, col. 917 sqq., cf. Zimmern, ib., 1928, coll. 1 sqq.; and the illustration, Binns, *From Moses to Elisha* (*Clarendon Bible*), p. 233. Grant reports at Beth-Shemesh jugs with serpent-ornamentation (becoming conventionalized), and a figurine of the nude mother-goddess (cf. pp. 123 sqq. below) with a somewhat ram-like face, a lotus in one hand and papyrus in the other, while over the shoulder falls a serpent with its head on her thigh (*Annual of Amer. Schools*, ix. 2, and figs. 3, 6–8).

[2] *Museum Journal*, March 1929; and *Q.S.*, April 1929. The explanations are, of course, often conjectural.

carefully treated for their better preservation, point to an
extensive complex of buildings. A long corridor (A A),
maximum measurements 127 feet by 25 feet, severs the
buildings from the outer fortification walls. To the left (B)
is a room with the *Maṣṣebah* (Pl. xxi), near which was found
the stele of Mekal. The baetyl is a conical basalt stone on a
base of unhewn stones, the whole 2½ feet high. Behind are
stone bases upon which cult objects were perhaps set; and
about 45 inches in front (to the SW.) a libation bowl was
sunk in the floor. Away to the left (outside the photograph) is a room with an oven for roasting the sacrifices,
and, beyond, is a well 43 feet deep. Behind it is a corner
of the inner sanctuary (C), in another part of which were a
stone altar and a brick-stepped altar. Next to the *Maṣṣebah*-
room was the great stepped altar of sacrifice (D), it is between the letters D and E, and behind the pole. A hole (E)
in which the (modern) pole is fixed, may conceivably have
been for some post on which the skin of the sacrificed animal
was hung. It is in the great courtyard (F), 82 feet east–west,
114 feet north–south, where many finds were made. The
three bases (G) were possibly used as tables. The room (H),
near which stands the man, is 14½ ft. by 16½ ft., and has a
low seat (*mastabah*) running round the northern and eastern
sides. In it was found a conical basalt baetyl, 10 in. high.
Against its south wall is built (I) a larger stepped altar,
16 ft. 10 in. wide, 3 ft. in height; and by its side steps (J)
lead from the corridor of the Mekal temple to the southern
corridor. Away to the west (in the foreground) are remains of the fortress and other buildings (K), with a large
silo (on the right) 12½ feet in diameter and about 11½ feet
in depth.

In turning to a survey of the ancient deities of the land
it will be convenient to start with the curious clay tablet
from Gezer, found in about the 'Amarna' stratum, though
it may be of much older origin. It bears two bands, the
impressions of a cylinder seal; and is commonly inter-

preted as a 'zodiac tablet' (Pls. xxii and xxiii).[1] We seem to
have (a) a ladder surmounted by (b) an inverted vase, to the
right is (c) an ibex, above which is (d) an animal with its
young, (e) a bird with a cone (? egg), while above is (f) a
T-shaped object. Then (g) another horned animal, below
which is (h) a sign like Libra, and above is (i) a bird. Next
(j) the sun and lunar crescent have (k) a star and serpent
on the left, and below (l) are a fish and scorpion; finally
(m) a palm tree and (n) an inverted amphora. With these
we may compare another clay impression from Gezer,
where (o) a seated figure holding a bird has beneath him
(p) a horned animal (? a sphinx), behind which are (q) a
similar animal, (r) a bull, with (s) an amphora below, and
above (t) something like the palm (m above). In the upper
left corner is (u) a human figure, while (v) the vertical bar
may be simply a divider.

If we agree that we have no mere collection of meaningless devices it is possible to recognize some astral signs.
Thus, apart from the more obvious sun, moon, and serpent,
we may have in (a) not the ladder (cf. the ladder to the
realm of Osiris), but Libra; in (c) Aries; (d) Leo or Taurus;
(g) Capricorn; (h) Saggitarius; (l) Cancer; (m) Spica;
(n) Aquarius; and, to the left of the serpent's tail, the Babylonian sign for Gemini. It is along such lines that zodiacal
interpretations have been hazarded, though it seems
impossible to carry them—or indeed any other interpretation—through to the end. The signs are clearly too
heterogeneous to suggest some symbolical scene; nor can
we venture to think of some picture-writing, e.g. the
Phaestus disk.[2] Certain of the signs (e.g. c, d) occur singly
elsewhere; but the combination may more probably be
explained on the analogy of the symbols of deities found
upon *kudurrus* ranging from the Kassite to the neo-Babylonian period. These were conical blocks of stone which

---

[1] *Gezer*, ii. pp. 347 sqq. (cf. *Q.S.*, 1908, pp. 26 sqq., 78 sq., 162 sq.);
Gressmann, no. 597. For the second tablet, see our Plate x, no. 26.

[2] On this, cf. Macalister, *Schweich Lectures*, pp. 83 sqq.

defined the boundaries of estates, or recorded grants and business transactions.[1] Their object was to place the owner's rights under the protection of the gods; and while in the case of written treaties various deities may be named as parties to and protectors of the treaty, the *kudurru* bears the symbols of those deities whose aid is directly invoked or taken for granted. So, too, a king will specify the names of the deities under whose protection he stands, and a priest of Nebo (*c.* 750 B.C.) utters a curse upon those who destroy, mutilate, or cancel his monument: 'may the gods as many as are found on this stone destroy him'.[2] In one case the names of the deities Adad and Shala are actually written within their emblems (Ward, no. 475). Although the symbols engraved on these stones are not necessarily those of the deities specified, they are evidently believed to be efficacious in themselves. Indeed, the symbols of deities are usually thought to be effective agents, and consequently it is possible that the Gezer tablet, or tablets, bear divine symbols, and that they would be considered powerful talismans.

The symbols are, in any case, hardly zodiacal; the *systematic* association of certain symbols with stars and constellations, and of the latter with certain deities, belongs to a later period. That some of the Babylonian symbols were familiar in the west has already been seen. Thus on monuments from North Syria we find, besides the winged sun (Shamash), the lunar crescent (Sin), a star in a ring (Ishtar), a horned head-dress (Anu–En-lil), an obscure bridle-like sign remotely resembling (*h*) above.[3] The scorpion, (*l*) above, found at Megiddo and Carchemish,

[1] L. W. King, *Babylonian Boundary Stones* (1912); Jastrow, *Bildermappe*, cols. 30 sqq.; Contenau, *Rev. Bibl.*, 1916, pp. 537 sqq.; Steinmetzer, *Die babylonischen kudurru* (1922); Gressmann, nos. 142–4; Unger, *Reallex. Vorgesch.*, 'Götter-symbol'.

[2] *M.D.O.G.*, 1899, no. 3, pp. 14 sqq.

[3] See Lidzbarski, *Ephemeris*, iii. 196, 221 sq. (p. 236 on the god of the yoke of horses); Sayce, *P.S.B.A.*, 1912, p. 27. For the 'bridle', cf. the reversed yoke, King, no. xxviii, pl. 14.

was the symbol of Ishkara, a goddess of the Ishtar type; and the serpent (*k*) was that of Siru.¹ Hence, since on any theory the Gezer tablets are unique, it might be conjectured that some of the signs represent purely native symbols of otherwise well-known gods; or, again, it may be preferable to suppose that here, as on the seal from Megiddo (p. 59), a number of symbols have been collected together, some with a meaning—one may surely include *a* and *b*—and that a typical *horror vacui* has prompted the insertion of other signs, including the horned animals so dear to the old-time artists.²

If the Gezer tablet or tablets are only another illustration of the individuality of Palestinian religious archaeology, we may set against them a third tablet. It is of hard-baked red clay and is covered with cross lines. This is not merely, as Macalister suggested, 'possibly used for magical purposes', but, as Vincent remarks, it appears to be an illustration of ancient hepatoscopy, a mode of divination by means of the liver that can be found among Babylonians and Etruscans and seems to have been not unknown in Israel (see Pl. xxiii, fig. 2).³

¹ See *K.A.T.*, p. 432, and ib. p. 504 sq. For the sake of completeness we may add to the list of Babylonian symbols the horned head-dress on altar (Anu–En-lil; see on this *M.D.O.G.*, lxiv. 40 sqq.); the ram-headed crook and goat-fish (Ea); the lion-headed mace (Nergal); the eagle-headed mace (Zamama); the seated goddess (Gula); the seven stars (Sibitti). The lamp was the symbol of Nusku (p. 120, n. 4); the column with spear-head of Marduk (p. 65); the wedge or double rod and stylus of Nabu (p. 65); and the lightning fork, or bull and thunderbolt, or thunderbolt on throne, the sign of Adad (p. 131). A fine cylinder seal with Ea and the bird-scorpion was found by Petrie at Gerar.

² Cf. the accumulation of symbols on Syro-Hittite seals, Hogarth, *J.E.A.*, viii. 214, no. 15 (no. 8 on p. 213 contains Libra).

³ *Gezer*, ii. 453 sq.; Vincent, *Rev. Bib.*, 1909, pp. 614 sqq. See further *Rel. Sem.*, p. 634. It may be mentioned, in passing, that a tablet with a quadruple maze carved upon it, found at Beit Mirsim, is explained by Albright (*Arch. f. Orientforsch.* v. 120) as perhaps connected with the 'face of Humbaba', on which see Smith, *Assyria*, p. 34, Pl. vii (*a*).

For the names and representations of the members of the old Syro-Palestinian pantheon our best and earliest evidence comes from Egypt. Without going back to prehistoric times and questions of the earliest relations between Egypt and south-west Asia, we may start with the prominent warring deities of the Semites who impressed themselves upon the Egyptians.[1] These were generally known as 'lord (or lady) of heaven', an old title typical of a culture more 'advanced' than the local and more telluric Baals of the peasantry. To begin with the goddesses, the most famous name is undoubtedly that of Anath, who appears in Hyksos royal names,[2] and persists in the Elephantine papyri of the fifth century B.C.; and in a bilingual inscription from Larnax Lapēthos is equated with Athene. She leaves her name in Anāthōth ('Anaths') hard by Jerusalem and the Judaean and Naphtalite Beth Anath (or Anoth); and in both tribal districts there is a Beth Shemesh, or 'house of the Sun'. In Babylonia she appears to be a pale reflection of the male Anu, the supreme god of heaven, whose name is not found in the west, unless it appears in the form Anammelech.[3] In Egypt she was 'lady of heaven and mistress of the gods'. Thutmose III built her a shrine at Thebes, and established a priesthood; and in the following dynasty she is often mentioned. Thus Ramses II is 'companion of Anath and Bull of Set'; and she and Astarte are the shield of Ramses III against his enemies.[4]

There are two types. On the 'Kadesh' stele (Pl. xxiv, no. 2)

---

[1] Similarly, war-deities—especially goddesses—were very prominent among the warlike Assyrians; cf. Ishtar of Asshur and Arbela, *C.A.H.*, Pl. i, 230 c.

[2] Especially, Anath–El, 'Anath is god'. Against the alternative transcription, 'A.–her', 'A. is contented', see W. Wolf, *Z.D.M.G.*, 1929, p. 69 (pp. 67–79 a good résumé of the Hyksos question).

[3] For 'Anu is king', 2 Kings xvii. 31; see *K.A.T.*, p. 353 sq., cf. also Albright, *A.J.S.L.*, xli. 73 sqq.

[4] On the spelling of the name ('n-ty, 'n-ty-t, &c.), see W. M. Müller, *Asien u. Europa*, p. 195. For Anath with her hand on the shoulder of Ramses II, see Montet, *Rev. Bib.*, 1930, pp. 21, 27 (from Tanis).

Anath is seated with shield and spear in her right hand, and in her left a club or stick is held horizontally, in a way that recalls the god Resheph who, however, stands erect. Or she stands clad in a panther skin holding her papyrus sceptre in one hand and in the other the *ankh*. Her crown sometimes has a pair of horns at the base.[1] The latter is the type found on a little basalt fragment in the northern temple of the age of Ramses II at Beth-Shan: long dress, the *was* sceptre and *ankh*, but her crown has no horns (Pl. xxiv, no. 1).[2] Here Ḥesi-Nekht, who dedicated the object, stands before the goddess, while between is an altar over which is a flower.[3] On the Phoenician bilingual which identifies her with Athene Sōteira Nikē she is called 'the strength of life', as though she were a personification of vital force.[4] It is true that we shall find Anath and Astarte associated, apparently as goddesses of fertility; on the other hand, Eduard Meyer observes that her temple in Idalium is noteworthy for the absence of the votive images common elsewhere in Cyprian temples; and Vincent, too, contrasts the more noble character of Anath with Kadesh, Astarte, and other mother-goddesses.[5] Since Hebrew usage suggests that a god is not only the 'strength' of a man, but his 'place of refuge', it may be the protective care of Anath rather than her vital power that is here meant.[6]

[1] Budge, *Gods of Egypt*, ii. 277.

[2] *Museum Journal*, 1926, pp. 294 sqq. She is called 'Antit lady of heaven, mistress of all the gods', and the inscription runs: 'May the king give an offering. Antit, may she give all life, strength and health to the *ka* of Ḥesi-Nekht'.

[3] There is a third type, however, if we may cite the coin, with a deity with sceptre in the left hand and holding an offering over a thymiaterion. On the reverse is Anath (so de Vogüé reads the letters) seated on a lion, both facing the left; there are also an *ankh*, a star, and other signs (de Vogüé, *Mélanges*, p. 47).   [4] Cooke, no. 28; *C.I.S.*, i. 95.

[5] See (a) *Ency. Bib.*, col. 3748; and (b) *Rev. Bib.*, 1928, p. 541.

[6] The point lies in the existence of two distinct Hebrew roots *'āzaz*, 'be strong', and *'ūz*, 'take refuge', see Brown, Driver, and Briggs, *Hebrew Lexicon*, p. 732, col. i (*mā'ōz*). The identification with Athene may not be substantial, but suggested by the similarity of name; see

Kadesh is called 'mistress of all the gods, the eye of Re (the sun-god), without a second'. She is depicted nude— a Mesopotamian trait—though later she wears a long garment.[1] Her name, which means 'sacred, holy', has been connected with the important city of Kadesh on the Orontes, the chief centre of opposition to Egypt after the expulsion of the Hyksos, on the view that she was the goddess of that city. But the name may be merely an epithet—like the Greek *hagios*, later (p. 196 and n. 3)— although it would not necessarily have by any means an ethical connotation. In the best-known scene (of the XIXth Dynasty), in the British Museum, she has her characteristic attitude (fig. Pl. xxiv, no. 2).[2] She stands upon a lion or panther (Asiatic type) which faces our right—an Aegean and Anatolian trait. Full-faced and nude, her coiffure is, as is usual with the Syrian goddesses, treated after the model of Hathor. In her right hand is a lotus flower (? and a mirror); in her left are two large serpents. On her left stands Resheph, whom we shall consider later, and on her right is Min, god of Coptos, whom the Greeks identified with Pan.[3] This triad recurs with minor variations—e.g.

Baudissin, *Adonis*, pp. 18, n. 2, 457. Baudissin cites an inscription from Carvoran where of the great goddess Caelestis it is said: *lance vitam et iura pensitans*.

[1] Nude goddesses appear to be rare in Egypt. For exceptions see some from Karnak, Pillet, *Rev. Arch.*, 1928, pp. 36 sqq., and the Hyksos scarab, *J.E.A.* viii. 203 (figs. 14, 15). For 'eye of Re', cf. p. 42.

[2] Budge, ii. 276, 280; see W. M. Müller, *Egyptian Researches*, i. Pl. xli; Gressmann, no. 270. (Her name here is Ḳent, for Ḳedeshet.)

[3] Min, guardian of the desert road to the Red Sea, protector of roads and herds, and god of gardens, was also embodied in a stake or in a heap of stones (like Hermes). Min with the lettuce was a symbol of generation (*Aeg. Z.*, lix. 140 sqq.; cf. Ar. *manā*, Albright, *A.J.S.L.*, xxxiv. 231; see also F. Hommel, *Grundriss*, pp. 51, n. 2, 59, n. 1, 72, n. 1, 831 sq.). It may be noticed that the Anatolian Men was associated with fertility (his symbol being the pine cone) and the bull (A. B. Cook, *Zeus*, i. 642), and that it has been suggested that the thunderbolt was the symbol of the Egyptian Min (Newberry; see *Zeus*, ii. 767). The bull was the animal of Hadad whose emblem was the thunderbolt.

she wears a crescent and a disk (Pl. xxiv, no. 3).[1] In the Cairo Museum a stele of about the ninth century shows her holding a serpent (?) in her right hand and lotus flowers in her left, and she stands between Setekh and a female worshipper.[2] On another she is alone on a pedestal with an altar or table of offerings, her head crowned with flowers; and again a female worshipper stands before her.[3] As 'Kadesh the beloved of Ptah' (the god of Memphis), she is represented alone, with a serpent in each hand; there are some half-dozen circles marked upon the stele, which may be stars.[4]

Astarte is often mentioned together with Anath in Egyptian texts. They are 'the great goddesses who conceive but do not bear'; and while one Egyptian story ascribes their origin to Set, another tells how Astarte became one of the deities at Memphis, as daughter of Ptah.[5] A prophet of A-s-r-ta-tu is named on a Louvre amulet, and a prince bears the name 'favourite of Astarte'.[6] She had a temple near Lake Serbonis, and another in Memphis, where

On the other hand the Egyptian Min may represent Tammuz-Adonis (Müller, op. cit., i. 32, *Eg. Myth.*, p. 156), or Pan (E. Hommel, *J.S.O.R.*, 1926, pp. 46, 57).

[1] See de Rougé, *Acad. des Inscr.*, xx. 2, pp. 174–82 ; W. M. Müller, *Asien und Europa*, p. 314; Vincent, *Rev. Bib.*, 1928, p. 530, n. 4.

[2] Gressmann, no. 272 (the god was formerly identified as Resheph).

[3] Gressmann, no. 271. Müller (*Eg. Res.*, i. 32 sq., *Eg. Myth.*, p. 411) adopts an astral interpretation: Virgo on Leo with Hydra and Spica in her hands.

[4] Gressmann, no. 276 (Roeder, *Alte Orient*, xx. 63). May one compare the red-coloured and degenerated Astarte plaque at Gezer on which are pricked a number of small holes (*Gezer*, ii. fig. 501, our Pl. xxviii)? See below, p. 127 and n. 1. We can hardly identify as Kadesh the long clothed and winged figure standing on a lion, both facing the right (Gressmann, no. 275). Vincent suggests Resheph (*Rev. Bib.*, 1928, p. 531, n. 3, Pl. xxv, no. 9a); see p. 111, n. 3.

[5] See (a) the Harris magical papyrus, ed. Chabas, p. 55; and (b) *P.S.B.A.*, xxiv. 42; Gressmann, *Texte*, p. 7 sq. (here her realm is the sea, she is 'lady of the oceans', and appears to collect 'the tribute of the sea'—a tax on imports, cf. Neit of Saïs).

[6] Müller, *Eg. u. As.*, p. 313, n. 5.

there were Jewish and Tyrian quarters. This was the 'Aphrodite temple' (Herodotus, ii. 112); it was in the vicinity of the Serapeum, and had two-and-forty ever-burning lamps, and an *adyton* in which stood the *naos* of the goddess.[1] Astarte was among the deities of Pi-Ramses or Pelusium (*J.E.A.*, v. 255); and in the famous treaty between Ramses II and the Kheta (Hittites) of Anatolia, the first goddess to be named, after Re and Setekh, is Antheret of Kheta, a name presumably to be corrected, not into Anath, but Astarte.[2]

The Semitic mother-goddesses were, from the first, identified with Hathor, and to the title 'Hathor lady of Byblus' corresponds the Egyptian representation of the Baalath of that city on the Phoenician stele of Yeḥaw-melek (c. 400 B.C.). Here she stands as Hathor with the solar-disk between her horned head-dress, wearing the uraeus, but is marked out by her nudity and the chain round her neck.[3] Otherwise Astarte can be seen on a late Ptolemaic stele from Edfu, where, lion-headed, like the Egyptian Sekhmet— with whom she becomes identified—and surmounted by a disk, 'Astarte, lady of the chariot horses' stands in a four-horsed chariot which she drives over the body of the foe. As a warrior, too, on a Memphite stele of the XIXth Dynasty, she carries a shield.[4]

[1] Wilcken, *Urkunden der Ptol. Zeit*, i (1927), p. 37 sq. On an ex-voto from Memphis a bearded Semite burns incense before an Astarte seated in an Egyptian shrine, see Aimé-Giron, *Bull. de Inst. Franç. d'Arch. Orient.*, xxv (1925), 191 sqq. (with valuable analysis and comparative study of the various elements in the scene); see also id., xxiii. 11 sqq., on the deification of Astarte-Berenike and the vitality of the Astarte cult.

[2] So Breasted, *Ancient Records of Egypt*, iii. 386, and many others; the form is retained, though not explained, by Petrie (*Hist. of Eg.*, iii. 66, Anetharta) and Roeder (op. cit., p. 44).

[3] *C.I.S.*, i. 1. Gressmann, no. 516. Note the fragment of the Saïte age with the Baalath as Isis-Hathor (Renan, *Mission*, pp. 179 sqq., see *Syria*, iv. 312, n. 4). The identification goes back to the third millennium B.C. at Byblus, while at Serabiṭ the Baalath, whose name can be deciphered on the inscribed stones, and Hathor, the 'lady of turquoise', were evidently identified.

[4] Wilcken, l.c. For the throne of the goddess flanked by lions

Of uncertain identity are the Egyptian representations of the riding Asiatic goddess. From the south of Edfu comes a bas-relief of about the XIXth Dynasty: a female on horseback with a shield in her left hand and in her right a weapon; from her head-dress (the crown between two feathers) falls a ribbon (Pl. xxiv, no. 4). She appears to be some warrior-goddess of the desert; and, in fact, a gazelle-goddess, a wild huntress from Lebanon, was known at an early date in Egypt.[1] We have her name: 'Asi(ti) of Kharu (Palestine), the lady of heaven, the mistress of the two lands, the mistress of all the gods'. The word is enigmatical: scholars have thought of el-Aṣi, the Orontes river, of Asia (cf. the goddess Europa), or of some feminine form of the Semitic Esau ('*ēsāw*).[2] Esau is a wild desert-haunting figure, and with his name has been connected the hunter-god Ousōos of the Phoenician mythology given by Philo of Byblus. The variation in gender is no objection—we may compare Anu and Anath (Akkadian Antum), and the male South Arabian Athtar and Astarte. Nor is the distribution of the deity unusual. And if this view be right, we find support in the name Edom which also seems to have been used as a divine name (p. 112).

Of the Semitic or Asiatic gods in Egypt, the first place must be given to Sutekh or Setekh, later the everyday name for any hostile Asiatic god, and identified with the old Egyptian Set.[3] God of storm and war, he was venerated

---

in the Beirut Museum, see *Syria*, v. Pl. xxxii; Contenau, *Civ. Phén.*, p. 178 sq. and fig. 34.

[1] Sethe, *Untersuch.*, v (1912), 112 sqq.; Müller, *As. u. Eur.*, p. 316 ; Gressmann, no. 273. Note Gressmann, no. 274, where a female on horseback, nude, with ear-rings and necklace, brandishes a weapon (?) in the right; also Davis, *J.E.A.*, iv. 238 sq., where she seems to ride side-saddle. The gazelle was especially the animal of the Astarte-goddesses —notably at Beth-Shan, to judge from the recent excavations.

[2] For the last see Müller, l.c.; Ed. Meyer, *Gesch. d. Alt.*, ii. 2, p. 492. The name of the goddess can be vocalized 'Oseye, 'Asiye, or the like (Dr. Hall: private communication).

[3] On the forms see Roeder, *Aeg. Z.*, l. 84 sqq.: the older *štš* or *šth* was

by the Hyksos king Apophis, who took Setekh for his lord, built him a temple, and served no other god in all the land.[1] His temple was at Avaris in the neighbourhood of Pelusium;[2] and as the god of the Eastern Delta he embodied Egypt's hostile neighbours and gained his evil reputation.[3] In the Egyptian-Hittite treaty of 1272 B.C., of which both the Egyptian and the Hittite versions are extant, Re (or Shamash) lord of heaven, and Re (or Shamash) of the city of Arinna are followed by Setekh, lord of heaven, and the Setekh of various northern cities.[4] Setekh corresponds to the Mesopotamian Teshub, Addu, Hadad, &c.; and Egyptian texts couple Setekh and Baal as gods of battle, or use either more or less indifferently. His wife is Anath.

The best-known representation of Setekh is that on the Tanis stele 'of the year 400' (time of Ramses II). He stands erect with the typical crown of Upper Egypt, from which hangs a ribbon with a bifurcated end. In front of his helmet is, not the Egyptian uraeus, but, as it would seem, horns, also with bifurcated ends; and with the *was* sceptre in his left hand and the *ankh* in his right he makes a characteristic figure.[5] The forked ends are unusual—they recall

shortened into *st* (Sēt). Wolf (*Z.D.M.G.*, 1929, pp. 67 sqq.) doubts whether Set is older than the Hyksos.

[1] See Gunn and Gardiner, *J.E.A.*, v. 40 sqq.

[2] Gardiner, *J.E.A.*, v. 254; cf. Hall, *C.A.H.*, i. 323 sq.

[3] Traces of the cult of Setekh-Set in Palestine have been found in the models of animals specially associated with him (e.g. the hippopotamus), and in the fact that they are *red*, notably the model of an ass coloured red at Gezer (ii. 9). See Vincent, *Rev. Bib.*, 1928, p. 537, who points also to the Syrian seal with the Egyptian inscription of 'Ara beloved of Set' (*Gezer*, i. 312, fig. 163; ii. 330, no. 8). To one of Set's opponents will belong the fragment of a hieratic inscription at Beth-Shan referring to 'the fiend in the house of the ruddy beings' (Rowe, *Museum Journal*, 1929, p. 59).

[4] For this treaty, of the first importance for the light it throws upon the recognized deities of the age, see Langdon and Gardiner, *J.E.A.*, vi. 179 sqq.; cf. also Roeder, *Ägypter u. Hethiter* (*Der Alte Orient*, 1919), pp. 36 sqq.

[5] Gressmann, no. 344; Roeder, op. cit., p. 63; see in general the

the forked tail of Set's animal (the okapi ?). Ordinarily the god's horns are slightly curved, like those of Resheph. This is the case on a Kadesh stele (p. 107, n. 2), and on a representation found by Petrie at Serabiṭ el-Khādim.[1] Similarly in a scene from Thebes (*c.* 1300–1000 B.C.) a worshipper stands before the god Amon, who is offering him the *ankh*; behind is his spouse Mut, and behind her a diminutive Amon, the meaning of which is obscure (? his *ka*). Below, the god Khnum of Elephantine has Ptah in front of him, and behind is Setekh (called Set), whose long band ends in a tassel (Pl. xxv, no. 1).[2] Once he stands horned, bearded, and winged as usual, upon a lion, both facing right.[3] In Palestine we may no doubt recognize him between Amon and Montu, the god of war, upon the fragmentary stele of Seti I at Tell Mend—now identified with Kadesh on the Orontes. This is suggested especially by the god's title 'the great in might, very strong'.[4] Again, on the fine seal of Ramses II from Beth-Shan he holds out the *khepesh* in his left, while the *ankh* is in his right; his typical conical head-dress (made of plaited rushes) has a double streamer, and in the place of horns there is the head of a gazelle (Pl. xxv. 3).

illustrations collected by Vincent, *Rev. Bib.*, 1928, pp. 514 sqq., Pl. xxiv. Very similar is the figure found not far from Tanis at Nebesheh (Griffith, *P.S.B.A.*, 1894, p. 87). The *was* sceptre survives as a bedouin camel-stick (Seligman, *J.E.A.*, iii. 127).

[1] Petrie, *Sinai*, p. 127, fig. 134.

[2] In the Berlin Museum; Gressmann, no. 305. The tassel will recall those at the bottom of the tunics of the Semites in a tablet of Seti I (Gressmann, no. 1); cf. perhaps the 'fringes' (*gĕdīlīm*) of Deut. xxii. 12; see *Ency. Bib.* 'Fringes'.

[3] Petrie, *Hyksos and Israelite Cities*, Pl. xi, no. 209, and p. 15. This indubitably Semitic god bears a very close resemblance to the deity referred to on p. 107, n. 4.

[4] Gressmann, no. 91. See *Syria*, iii. 108, and especially ix. 128 (Mallon). Amon and Setekh offer Seti I, the one the Egyptian *khepesh*, the other some token of victory—the lower part of the left arms is missing. Montu holds a club, and behind can be traced the head-dress of some deity—Kadesh (Moret, Mallon) or Khonsu (Pezard, Gressmann).

The god seems to be Setekh, although the bellicose attitude will recall the fighting god Resheph.[1]

The history of Resheph is lengthy and highly interesting. He is hailed in Egyptian texts as 'great god, lord of the Enneads, lord of heaven, hearer of prayer'. Officers of Ramses III are said to be mighty—'like the Reshephs': the plural is noteworthy.[2] With a number of other deities he was worshipped at Memphis; and the name of his spouse, Atum ('-t-m), resembles, on the one hand, the Palestinian compound place-name Shamash-Atum mentioned in the lists of Thutmose III and Amenhotep II, and, on the other, the name Obed-Edom ('Servant of Edom'). The two names suggest that Atum, Edom, or the like, was the name of an old deity of either sex (like Shamash, p. 134, n. 3), and equally the name of a land or people (cf. Gad, &c.).[3] In the eighth century Resheph is among the leading gods of Syria; and Panammu in his inscription to Hadad (see p. 38, n. 4) names him between (a) Hadad and El, and (b) Rekub-el and Shamash. He adds that these four gods gave into his hand the sceptre of... (the word is obscure) and 'Resheph stood with me'.[4]

---

[1] See Mallon, *Biblica*, 1928, p. 254 sq.; Vincent, 1928, p. 529 (both hold that the god is not Resheph); on the scene, see above, p. 44. Setekh may conceivably be recognized at Shechem, *Z.D.P.V.*, l. Taf. xxviii A *a*, p. 266 sq.; Taf. xxviii A *c*., p. 270 (Sellin, however, describes the former as typical Hyksos work with a Horus-like god, perhaps an Adonis).

[2] Budge, *Gods of Egypt*, ii. 282; Müller, *As. u. Eur.*, p. 312, n. 4. On an altar-list of gods is 'Resheph in Hat-Reshpu' (*T.S.B.A.*, iii. 429, no. 67); also 'Anath who loves her mother' (p. 427, no. 11). That Resheph should be placed over the Enneads or cycles of nine deities is in accordance with the old Oriental practice whereby an important local city would place its own local god at the head of the pantheon.

[3] See Breasted, *Anc. Rec.*, ii. 783 (*sh-m-sh–y-tu-my*), and W. C. Wood, *J.B.L.*, xxxv. 264 sq.; on Edom see *Rel. Sem.*, pp. 42, 509 (where on l. 1 sq. *warrior*-god goes beyond the evidence).

[4] Cooke, no. 61. Resheph is also called Ark-resheph (l. 11), as obscure a name as Arṣ-reshaphim on the later Sidonian inscriptions (Cooke, p. 402; cf. Pilcher, *P.S.B.A.*, xxv. 128; Clermont-Ganneau, *Rec.*, v., §41; *Répertoire d'Épig. Sém.*, i. 234 sqq.; Eiselen, *Sidon*, p. 144 sq.).

In the Old Testament Resheph—which occurs as an Ephraimite clan-name (1 Chron. vii. 25)—is the name of the flame or lightning flash, the fiery darts which Yahweh sends forth (cf. Ps. lxxviii. 48, Hab. iii. 5). But Post-biblical Hebrew preserves a recollection of the word's ancestry when it uses it of demons of the smithy, of the hot season, and of roofs.[1] Outside the Old Testament Resheph continued to flourish. He had a temple at Carthage (*C.I.S.*, i. 251); and in Cyprus of the fourth century B.C., where bilingual inscriptions identify him with Apollo, there are several forms or phases of Resheph, as well as proper names meaning 'Resheph gives' and 'servant of Resheph'.[2] The identification with Apollo is confirmed, at least indirectly, by the place Apollonia near Jaffa, whose modern name Arsūf doubtless points to an older Resheph. Here was unearthed a colossal hawk, the bird of Horus-Apollon, and, near by, the sacred place of 'our lord Ali' is still the resort of pilgrims.[3] In fact, there was an 'upper temple of

---

[1] See S. R. Driver on Deut. xxxii. 24. Apollo, the Greek counterpart of Resheph, was, in one aspect at least, god of pestilence; and Resheph resembles the fire-god Nergal, one epithet of whom was *rashbu, rashubbu* (*K.A.T.*, p. 478). The emblem of Nergal was the Vulture's head, and Albright (*Haupt Commemoration Volume*, p. 149 sq.) suggests that this explains the versions on Deut. l.c. (e.g. Vulg. *devorabunt eos aves*). Driver, however, points to Job v. 7 (see his note there), where 'the sons of *resheph*' that *fly* upward were taken by the versions to be birds. Thackeray, *Schweich Lectures*, p. 52 sq., refers to the belief in the great birds that were supposed to attend the sun.

[2] The Cypriote god *Resheph–ḥ-ṣ* may be 'R. of the street' (cf. Apollo Agyieus, guardian of streets), or 'R. of the arrow' (cf. e.g. Ps. lxxvi. 3). *Resheph—al-h-y-th-s* (Greek ἀλασιῶται) may preserve the old name of Cyprus, Alashiya (see Cooke, p. 57, for these and other combinations). For the Cypriote *Resheph–m-k-l* see below, p. 129. The god Resheph doubtless also appears on the Phoenician seal of 'Baal-yathon, a man of the gods (אש אלם) who belongs to Melḳart-Reṣeph' (רצף; Cooke, no. 150, 5).

[3] Clermont-Ganneau, *Recueil d'Archéol. Orient.*, i. 176 sqq.; G. A. F. Knight, *Nile and Jordan*, p. 423. There is also a 'cave of Apollo', a burial place to the south-east of Sidon (*Syria*, i. 21 sqq.; *J.A.O.S.*,

Apollo' in Memphis in the second century B.C., and the Egyptian name 'she of Resheph' was still in use.[1] And not only may other traces of the name of the Semitic god be suspected, but echoes of him may lurk in the stories both of Perseus and of St. George.[2]

There are two main Egyptian types. In one, where he appears with Kadesh and Min, he is a Semite, his long hair is bound with a fillet in front of which is a gazelle head (Pl. xxiv. 2).[3] In the other he is in a fighting attitude, with spear and shield in his left hand, and a spear or club raised and held horizontally, level with the middle of his typical conical helmet; sometimes another club hangs from his shoulders. A specimen of the XIXth Dynasty depicts the club separately; the inscription runs: 'a royal offering which Reshpu gave, the great god who hears those who pray'.[4] Once, where he is named with Horus and Ptah, he seems to have a quiver, which will recall one of the interpretations of the Cypriote Resheph–ḥēṣ, 'R. of the arrow' (?).[5]

xxix. 192 sq.); for Resheph at Sidon, see p. 112, n. 4. Resheph is no doubt the 'Apollo' of the treaty of Hannibal, Polybius vii. 9 (Contenau, *Civ. Phén.*, p. 110).

[1] See (a) E. Bevan, *History of Egypt under the Ptolemaic Dynasty*, p. 108; (b) Müller, *O.L.Z.*, 1908, col. 401.

[2] Clermont-Ganneau notes in Cicero, *de Nat. Deorum*, iii. 22, 57, that an Arsippos (? Resheph) takes the place of Apollo as the father of Asklepios-Eshmun (*Rec.* vii. 173). Also αβεδραψας on a tomb of 324 A.D. at Frīkyā in N. Syria may be Abd-resheph—his wife αμαθβαβεα is 'handmaid of Bab(a)ia', a Damascene goddess (*Rec.* viii. 47). See also his study of Horus and St. George (Paris, 1877), and for the identification of Resheph with first Perseus and then St. George, *Rev. Archéol.* xxxii. (1876), 372 sqq.

[3] Gressmann, no. 270; similarly the Louvre Kadesh stele (our Pl. xxiv. 3); see Vincent, *Rev. Bib.*, 1928, p. 531 and Pl. xxv (fifteen examples of the types). Müller, *Eg. Res.*, i. 33 (and Pl. xli), notes that the gazelle head generally points forward (except Lanzone, *Dizionario*, Pl. cxci).

[4] Besides Vincent, see further Gressmann, nos. 346–51. The inscribed razor from Carthage (Delattre, *C.R. de l'Acad. d. Inscr.*, 1900, p. 501; cf. *Zeus*, ii. 630, fig. 536) recalls Resheph in so far as the spear and shield are concerned.

[5] Spiegelberg, *O.L.Z.*, 1908, col. 529, no. 2; above, p. 113, n. 2.

We show an Egyptianized representation with the legend 'Reshpu great god hearing prayer' (Pl. xxv, no. 2).[1] A very interesting scene of the XXth or following Dynasty depicts the god facing a table of offerings behind which stands the worshipper. The god is called *Resheph–Sh-r*(or *l*)-*m-n*.[2] This is interpreted to mean 'R. who is Ramman' (a god of the Addu-Hadad type); or, if we treat the whole as a compound divine name, the second part may be identified with Shulmān, a god of war. This name itself may be properly an epithet, 'he who requites, recompenses', it would be one particularly appropriate to a god 'hearing prayer'.[3] An old Phoenician representation of the god is supplied by two seals with Akkadian inscriptions, one the seal of 'Addumu of Sidon beloved (*na*[?]-*ra-ma*) of the gods', the other of An-ni-y his son, prince of Sidon. As usually interpreted, Set has long asses' ears and the *was* sceptre, and Resheph holds spear and shield in the usual way. The second cylinder has, in addition, the Egyptian sun-god with solar disk and the hawk's head of Horus.[4]

It is rarely possible to determine the local name of any given deity, for there were many gods and goddesses who because of their similar functions or attributes were easily associated or identified. There is, in particular, one very familiar and widespread type of statuette, commonly identified with Resheph: a martial deity with conical hat, his right hand is bent and raised, his left is held out; sometimes

---

[1] From Berlin (no. 14462).

[2] The 'Aberdeen' stele, Griffith, *P.S.B.A.*, 1900, p. 271 (cf. Spiegelberg, *Z.A.*, 1898, p. 120; Winckler and Zimmern, *K.A.T.*, pp. 224, 474; Albright, *Paul Haupt Commemoration Volume*, pp. 143 sqq.).

[3] Cf. Heb. *shalmōn*, 'reward', Is. i. 23. Yahweh Shālōm (Judges vi. 24) may no doubt be used in a pacifist sense to mean Yahweh who is peaceful, &c.; but a god who 'hears prayer' also works actively, cf. the meaning of the 'righteous' acts of Yahweh in Judges v. 11, 1 Sam. xii. 7.

[4] De Clercq collection, *Catal.* 386, i. 217; Pietschmann, *Phoen.*, p. 151; Winckler, *Altorient. Forsch.*, iii. 177 sq.; Contenau, no. 87; Sayce, *Q.S.*, 1893, p. 241.

there are tenons on the feet for fixing it in position. These figures are generally mutilated, and it is not possible to determine what, if anything, they held—no doubt there were various sub-types. The 'Reshephs' spread over the Mediterranean. Schliemann, who found a specimen at Tiryns, observed its resemblance to one from Tortosa in Spain (now in the Louvre); while W. M. Müller speaks of one at Munich said to have come from Pompei.[1] We give an unusual type, from the Berlin Museum, it is Egyptianized, and of about the XIXth Dynasty; it is noteworthy for the sun on the top of the reed crown, while on the breast is a solar ornament (Pl. xxvi. 1).[2]

It is Set with some attributes of Horus, or perhaps it is Resheph, who is represented in the unique Egyptian scene of a bearded winged deity with conical reed head-dress slaying the serpent with his spear.[3] And it is presumably not merely a Moabite warrior, but a warrior-god—Chemosh

[1] Schliemann, *Tiryns*, fig. 97; Müller, *As. u. Eur.*, p. 311 sq. (the Munich specimen at all events comes from Italy); Vincent, *Rev. Bib.*, l.c., p. 531 n. (end); Gressmann, no. 347. We may also compare the attitude of the Assyrian 'dagger-bearers' (*C.A.H.*, Pl. i, 234 c.).

[2] Berlin, no. 12621 (the white is a bit of oxydized lead); Gressmann, no. 350. Resheph has the attributes of Onouris, and the ornament may be descended from one often worn by early Egyptian kings (Dr. Hall, private communication). Of the same period is Gressmann, no. 347 (Roeder, p. 62, fig. 25). A specimen was found at Gezer in the vicinity of the alinement; it was of native workmanship, with traces of gilding (ii. 344, see our Pl. x, no. 33); a similar bronze one, in the Beirut museum, was plated with silver (*Syria*, v, Pl. xxxi, no. 1); see Vincent, loc. cit., p. 523, n. 3. A fine specimen from Minet el-Beida in N. Syria had a gold mask over the face, and the body was silver-plated (*Illustr. London News*, 2 Nov. 1929, p. 764; *Rev. Bib.*, 1930, pp. 20, 152; *Syria*, x. 228 sq.).

[3] Griffith, *P.S.B.A.*, 1894, p. 89; Vincent, l. c., p. 517. Griffith suggests that the attitude explains the mutilated figurines which originally held a spear in the right and a serpent in the left. At Tell Fara Petrie found a scarab representing a 'Syrian horned god', with a long streamer hanging from his peaked crown, striking with a spear the tail of a gigantic uraeus which he holds (*Ancient Egypt*, 1929, p. 12).

himself—who is depicted upon a relief which was found be-tween Dibān and Shiḥān in the land of Moab.[1] A beardless figure with long trailing coil, and in his hands a spear, he is of quite uncertain date (? 800 B.C.). Another piece of work, more Syrian than Egyptian, is the elaborate bas-relief from Amrit (Marathus). Here a figure with a band hang-ing from the head-dress holds a throwing-stick in one hand and a young lion in the other; he stands beneath the winged sun and the crescent moon upon a lion which is walking upon the mountains.[2]

The god is presumably one of the mountain-gods, and the lion, haunting mountains rather than plains, is his appropriate animal (1 Kings xx. 23, cf. 2 Kings xvii. 25 sq.). The antiquity of this conception has been remark-ably illustrated by an Egyptian seal at Byblus of about 3000 B.C. which describes a man as 'beloved of the god-dess ... the son of the lion, son of Re of the mountain, (beloved) of the god with the two lions'.[3] From Jebel Salaḥiyeh near Barada, in the region of Damascus, comes a broken slab, now in the British Museum, depicting a figure in a tunic with a chain round his neck, in the left hand is a stick or the like, and in the right something re-sembling a quatrefoil. It looks early (c. 1000), and is

[1] Dussaud, *Monuments Pal. et Jud.*, i. 3; *Syria*, vii. 345; Gressmann, no. 617; Vincent, p. 521 (who associates Shiḥān with the serpent deity of Beth-Shan, see p. 98 above). A somewhat similar sculpture was found at Rukkad in Golan (Kittel, *Z̧.D.P.V.*, xxxviii. 149 sqq., Taf. xix).

[2] Gressmann, no. 307 (cf. the Assyrian god, ib., no. 331). The Phoenician inscription is very obscure; it may be a dedication to Sad-repha (? a 'satrap' god, Adonis), so Clermont-Ganneau, *Rec.*, iv. 334 sq.; or to some god Sadid . . ., cf. the son of Kronos in Philo of Byblus; so Lidzbarski, *Eph.*, i. 282 sq. Contenau (*Civ. Phén.*, p. 181 sq. and fig. 37) dates the stele before 1000 B.C. The *motif* of the king with a weapon uplifted in one hand and holding a lion with the other is well illustrated from the tomb of Tutankhamen (*Ill. London News*, 12 Oct. 1929, p. 631).

[3] See further Montet, *Syria*, iv. 181 sqq. Gressmann (*Z̧.A.T.W.*, 1925, p. 230 sq.) compares the late Greek inscription (A.D. 147) where a man, after dreaming of two lions, makes an offering to Ζεὺς ὄρειος (Renan, *Mission*, p. 397).

supposed to represent some Syrian king or, more probably, a god.[1]

Equally obscure, though not nameless, is the deity on the 'Job stone' at the Mohammedan shrine at Sheikh Sa'd. The district was an important one. At Tell esh-Shihāb ('the mound of the warrior') Sir George Adam Smith found (in 1901) a basalt monument of pure Egyptian work, representing Seti I, adoring Egyptian gods.[2] Presumably there was an Egyptian station there. Its strategic value is attested by the Amarna Letters (C.A.H., ii. 311 sq.); and to a somewhat later age belong the fine lion of Sheikh Sa'd (p. 60), and other remains of Syro-Hittite cultural influence.[3] As a border-city it was one where a Pharaoh might well erect his stele (cf. C.A.H., ii. 343 foot)—such a one as Shalmaneser III set up at Lake Van, and which is now in the British Museum (Gressmann, no. 534). The 'Job stone' itself, a little to the north of esh-Shihāb, shows Ramses II holding a bowl with the image of Ma'at, goddess of Truth and Right, before a deity with high hat (horned?); above is a winged disk. The name of the god can be read as 'kni-spn, which seems to be a compound of some such forms as Yachin and the deity Ṣaphon: 'Ṣaphon establishes', cf. the analogous names of Jechoniah, and Eknibal king of Tyre (6th cent. B.C.).[4] Clermont-Ganneau conjectured that the 'Job stone' might represent some lunar goddess, the prototype of the 'lady (κυρία) Artemis' to whom is dedicated a Greek inscription at Tell el-'Ashari, some seven miles to the north.[5]

---

[1] Sir Charles Wilson, Q.S., 1869–70, p. 43, cf. p. 210; Conder, 1889, p. 87 sq.; see now Contenau, Syria, v (1924), 210 sq., Pl. liii.

[2] Q.S., 1901, p. 348; W. M. Müller, ib. 1904, p. 78.

[3] On the district, see also Maisler, Untersuch. Syr. u. Pal., i. 43 sqq.

[4] Gressmann, no. 103. See, in the first instance, Schumacher, Across the Jordan, p. 189; Z.D.P.V., xiv (1891), 142, xv. 205, xxxvii. Taf. xxxviii; Aeg. Z., xxxi (1893), 100 sq.; Q.S., 1902, p. 23. For the suggested Yachin, see Cheyne, Ency. Bib., col. 2304, and cf. the names יבונעתה, יבנשלם (Lidzb., Handb.). Albright reads Adon-Ṣaphon (Annual of the American Schools, vi. 45, n. 104).

[5] See Q.S., 1901, p. 354 sq., 1902, pp. 23 sq., 27 sq. Artemis was

A deity Ṣaphon (or the like) is to be found in the place Baal-Zephon on the Eastern Delta (Exod. xiv. 2); while at Memphis a corresponding Baalath was worshipped.[1] Her cult is connected with that of the solar god Sapdu, who was known as 'lord of the east and of the Asiatics', and whose city and temple probably survive in the modern Saft, a few miles south-east of Bubastis. It is the (Pi-)Saptu, the 'gate of the east' of Ashurbanipal's day. At Serabiṭ the sanctuary and outbuildings of Sapd or Sopd run along the southern side of the longer buildings of Hathor; and Petrie suggests that his symbol was identified with the goddess, since at Elephantine and Abydos she herself is called Sapd.[2] A Baal-Ṣapun is named with Baal-Shamim (the sky-god) and Baal-ma-la-gi-e (? the salt sea) in Esarhaddon's treaty with Tyre; and the name is given to a land rich in copper-mines, north of Phoenicia—cf. the regional god Baal Lebanon. It is perhaps his temple at Carthage which is referred to in the famous temple-tariff found at Marseilles;[3] and Phoenician personal names testify to the persistence of a god Ṣapun. His name would suggest that he was a god of the northern region; cf., besides the Baal of Lebanon (*C.I.S.*, i. 5), the Baal of Hermon (Judges iii. 3), and the North Syrian district of Sam'āl, the name of which ('left') means

worshipped also at Jerash, and no doubt represents some earlier Semitic goddess distinct from Aphrodite. On the locality see G. A. Smith, *Ency. Bib.*, 'Ashtaroth', and note the place-name Ash-tar-ti in the Amarna Letters (with Weber's note on no. 197, l. 10).

[1] See W. M. Müller, *E. Bi.*, col. 409 (the reading *ba'aly* is incorrect). A Set (Setekh) of Zaphon (?) seems to occur on a stele from Minet el-Beida, north of Laodicea, where very important discoveries are now being made (see Montet, *Rev. Bib.*, 1930, p. 20; *Syria*, x. 294).

[2] *Sinai*, p. 192; cf. Lina Eckenstein, *Sinai*, pp. 25 sqq., 55. On points of contact between Yahu and Sapdu, see Furlani, *Giornale d. Soc. Asiat. Ital.*, 1925, pp. 1 sqq. If Pi-Sapdu is the later φακουσα (Müller), note the late Edomite or Idumean god Kos, and the presence of Idumaeans with names compound with Kos in Memphis (see p. 203).

[3] *C.I.S.*, i. 165; Cooke, no. 42; Lagrange, p. 471. The opening words are fragmentary.

North. But a more cosmic interpretation is possible. Ṣapun
was the god of the sacred northern mountain of the gods,
a conception common to Mesopotamia and Palestine; for in
the recesses of the north was the Mountain of Assembly,
above which sat the Most High (Isa. xiv. 13 sq., Ezek. xxviii.
16). Scanty though the biblical references are, they belong
to a world of ideas for which Palestinian archaeology has
already prepared us.[1]

These close relations between the Delta, Phoenicia, and
Syria find a further illustration, later on, in the appearance
of the mountain god, Zeus Kasius, at Pelusium and near
Antioch (p. 157). Pelusium, or Avaris, was a centre of the
old Hyksos with their cult of Setekh, and a fuller knowledge
of the history of civilization in the Delta would undoubtedly
give us a more proportionate view of the religious interrelations between Egypt, the Levant, and south-west Asia.
Among the Semitic deities that entered Egypt some are
distinctly Akkadian. Memphis was especially catholic.[2]
Besides Baalath Zephon we meet with Nu-ka-ra or Nikal,
i.e. Nin-gal, the 'great lady', wife of the 'high god'.[3] This
is of twofold interest, first because of the distribution of the
cult of the moon-god Sin at the three points, Ur, Harran,
and to the south of Palestine; second, because at Nerab,
near Aleppo, Nikal appears with the moon-god Sahr, their
son the fire-god Nusku, and the sun-god Shamash (c.
600 B.C.).[4] Now while the Akkadian goddess Nikal occurs

[1] See, beside the commentaries, K.A.T., p. 355 sq.; the god Bel was
šadū rabū, 'the great mountain', and his temple E-kur, 'the house mountain'. The 'mountain of the north' was also an Iranian conception
(Meinhold, Baudissin Festschrift, p. 352).

[2] For the Ptolemaic period, see E. Bevan, Ptolemaic Egypt, p. 108.

[3] See Gardiner, Aeg. Z., xliii. 97; W. M. Müller, M.V.A.G., xvii. 38
(274). The 'high god' (or 'god on high') seems to be a sun rather than
a moon-god (so Gardiner).

[4] Cooke, no. 64 sq. Sahr is named with Shamash, Baal-Shamin, and
others in the Zakir inscription from North Syria. Nusku's symbol was
the lamp. In the 'Doctrine of Addai', a Syriac work of c. 300 A.D., the
pantheon of Harran includes Bath Nikal, Tar'atha (Atargatis), Sun,

in various personal names in the Harran district, in the seventh century (e.g. N. knows, N. is my mother), Nusku is found in personal names from Nerab, and also among the Jewish, Aramaean, and other colonists of Elephantine a couple of centuries later.

Nergal, the Akkadian god of war, pestilence, and death, the parching sun, was known in the west. Although he is mentioned among the gods introduced into Samaria by men of Cuthah (2 Kings xvii. 30), seven or more centuries earlier, Atanaḫil, whose seal was found at Taanach, calls himself 'servant of Nergal'. The name Nergal-Tallim (?) has been read on a cuneiform tablet found at Samaria, and a Phoenician-Greek bilingual from the Piraeus names the 'chief priest of the god Nergal', and his son Yathan-Bel.[1] While one line of argument tends to connect him, through his 'western' name *sharrab(p)*, with the seraph (p. 54 above), and through his destructive character with the god Molek (or Milk)—Kronos—Saturn (Lagrange), another line would associate Nergal with Resheph and with the lion, and finds traces of his cult in the lion-*motifs*, &c., at Beth-Shan.[2] Be that as it may, among the Akkadian tablets discovered at Amarna were copies of two well-known myths which, to judge from the marks upon them, were used for teaching Egyptians the use of cuneiform. One of these was the myth of Ereshkigal and Nergal, the queen of the Underworld, and her spouse with whom she shares the sovereignty. The name of Ereshkigal itself persisted in

Moon (Sahra), and the eagle Nashra. For the last some would read Nuskā (see Cooke, p. 188) or the Nabataean Dushara (Burkitt, *J.T.S.*, xxv. 403). But an eagle is not necessarily out of place, see *Rel. Sem.*, p. 579. Bath Nikal is Ishtar (Winckworth, *J.T.S.*, xxv. 402 sq.).

[1] *C.I.S.*, i. 119, Cooke, no. 35. In the Amarna Letters, the 'hand of Nergal', i.e. pestilence, falls upon Alashiya (Cyprus, or perhaps rather Cilicia, Knudtzon, no. 35). The Akkadian ideogram could, however, stand for some native god similar to Nergal. On Nergal in the west, see *K.A.T.*, pp. 412 sqq.; Lagrange, pp. 107 sqq., 430.

[2] Rowe, *Q.S.*, 1929, p. 89; *Museum Journal*, 1929, p. 50 sq.; Albright, *Paul Haupt Commemoration Volume*, pp. 150 sqq.

Greek magic, and under her other name Allatu she was known to the Carthaginians.[1] The other myth was that of Adapa, who forfeited immortality by refusing to take of the food and water of life.[2]

Naturally we cannot say how far Egyptians were influenced by Babylonian lore: whether it reached them directly or, as the finds at Byblus suggest, through Syro-Phoenician channels. It is possible that the name of Ishtar—as distinct from the more western Astarte ('-s-ty-r-t)—reached Egypt and may be seen in Istaram, the name of a slave of the Hyksos fortress of Avaris.[3] Moreover, besides Babylonian and Assyrian seals that have been carried into Egypt, there are those that bear *motifs* of Mesopotamian origin, or are Egyptian representations of Assyrian scenes.[4] One, perhaps of the seventh century B.C., is the seal of a man who calls himself 'servant of Addu'; it depicts two royal (Egyptian) figures on either side of a tree, performing some ritual with the tree such as is well known in Assyria. A Babylonian seal of about 2,000 B.C. bears the words 'Addu son of Anu'. Here the god Amurru with a club in his right hand faces a divine figure whose head-dress has four pairs of horns; in between are sun and moon, and above is the lightning trident of Addu; and there are other objects. On another seal are Addu's lightning-fork, and the gods Shamash and Amurru.

The mountain god Amurru (Amor), or Martu, though probably of western origin, cannot be recognized in the art-objects of the west, at least in his Babylonian form. Nor can we definitely pick out his consort the goddess Ashirat

---

[1] See Knudtzon, i. 25, ii. 1357, 1584; and for the myths, Jastrow, *Rel. Belief*, pp. 369 sqq.; Wardle, *Israel and Babylon*, pp. 62, 97.

[2] Jastrow, pp. 366 sqq.; Lagrange, pp. 391 sqq.; Wardle, pp. 188 sqq. Contenau sees in the myth a prototype of the lament over Adonis (*Civ. Phén.*, p. 142 sq.).

[3] *J.E.A.*, v. 53; but it is interpreted as Ishtar-ummi (I. is my mother) by Burchardt.

[4] Sayce, *P.S.B.A.*, xxxiii. 259 sq.; Sidney Smith, *J.E.A.*, viii. 207 sqq.

(Ashratu), who however is named upon one of the cuneiform tablets at Taanach, where she gives oracles by moving her finger.[1] She was the 'wife of the king of heaven' (in a Babylonian inscription of c. 2000 B.C.), or of the 'lord of the mountain' (Amor), and was also associated with Ramman. In old Arabia her husband was the moon-god. At Tēma in north Arabia she seems to be mentioned—appropriately enough—after the moon-god Sin-galla, 'great Sin'.[2] Clearly Ashirat was one of the prominent goddesses of the west.

It is Ashirat or Astarte, or some local Baalath, who is to be recognized in the innumerable plaques and figurines of a female turned up in course of the excavations.[3] Usually nude, with pronounced marks of maternity, and all the associations of a goddess of fertility, it is of course an open question whether popular opinion always definitely identi-fied the objects with this or the other goddess, whether they were often merely talismans, or again, whether in some cases they symbolized a companion to accompany the dead. The fact that the figurines are generally found broken can be easily explained by the collapse of the walls upon which they sometimes seem to have been fixed. But sometimes the mutilation is thought to be deliberate, perhaps some ritual act, corresponding, on the one hand, to the sacrifice of wives and concubines on the occasion of the death of their lord (as at Ur), and on the other, to the broken models

---

[1] Sellin, *Taannek*, p. 114 (Gressmann, *Texte*, 1st ed., p. 129, 2nd ed., p. 371). This form of divination is found in Babylonia; see Behrens, *Ass. Bab. Briefe* (1906), p. 68 sq. Egyptian deities replied to questions by nodding (Breasted, *Anc. Eg. Records*, iv, §§ 615, 617, &c.).

[2] *C.I.S.*, ii. 113; Cooke, p. 198; Lagrange, p. 503; Lidzbarski, *Handbuch*, ii, Taf. xxvii.

[3] Macalister, ii. 411 sqq.; Vincent, pp. 158 sqq.; Driver, pp. 56–9; Gressmann, nos. 279–96; Benzinger, nos. 19 sqq., 230 sqq.; Reifenberg, *Pal. Kleinkunst*, pp. 92 sqq.; Pilz, 'Die Weiblichen Gottheiten Kanaans', *Z.D.P.V.*, xlvii. 129–68; Watzinger, *Mutesellim*, ii. 61 sq.; cf. also, on the Cretan types, H. Prinz, *Mitt. d. K. D. Arch. Inst. Athens*, xxxv (1910), 155 sqq.

of offerings placed in tombs.[1] But such a conjecture will not apply throughout; and if it be supposed that the mutilation was often due to iconoclasm, it is surely surprising that it has not been more thorough.

The figurines, usually 4 to 8 inches in height, were turned out wholesale, and moulds have been found. They abound in the Amarna age—the type begins earlier in Babylonia—are numerous c. 1000–500, and last on into the Greek age.[2] A survey of the numerous types, their distribution and persistence, illustrates in a striking manner the character of the prevailing religious ideas which it was the endeavour of the reforming prophets of Israel throughout the eighth to sixth centuries to purify.

The types point to influences from almost every quarter. As a rule the figure is represented holding her breasts or with some object or objects in her hands, e.g. a dove, serpent, tambourine, lotus flowers (held in the hands or placed on either side). The type with hands crossed *under* the breasts is rare (Gressmann, no. 292).[3] The dove (one at Beit Mirsim has outstretched wings) has distinct Cypriote parallels. With the tambourine (?)—found e.g. at Gezer (fig. 499), Megiddo (fig. 156), and Samaria (i. 384, Pl. lxxv *a*)—we may compare the mirror held by female figures in the Graeco-Roman period.[4] On plaques from eṣ-Ṣafi

---

[1] Broken foundation-offerings have been found in Susa (Vincent, p. 163, n. 1), and a broken plaque of a goddess at Nerab (*Syria*, ix. 311 sq.). The human sacrifices at Ur of *c*. 3000 B.C. are unique, though the practice is well known elsewhere and later, and leaves its traces in milder forms, in offerings to the dead (see p. 38).

[2] Macalister and Duncan comment on the absence of figurines (except the pillar type) at Ophel (*Annual*, iv. 184). On the relevant Akkadian seals, see Contenau, *Glyptique*, p. 106.

[3] From a house in Taanach comes a figurine, clothed, with conical head-dress, and tenons on the feet in order to fix her in position. She is presumably some household deity (Gressmann, no. 288, Vincent, p. 163).

[4] Ronzevalle, *Q.S.*, 1921, pp. 173 sq.; see id. *Mélanges Beirut*, xii. 151–76 (esp. p. 166).

and el-Ḥesy the figure holding the lotuses stands in a shrine; and the former is noteworthy for its Mesopotamian astral symbols and is reminiscent of the Egyptian goddess Sekhet.[1] The lotus-*motif* naturally recalls the representation of Kadesh (p. 106 above). A characteristic 'turreted' head-dress recurs at Taanach and Megiddo, and persists from about 1500 to 800 B.C. It resembles the Hittite head-dress at Iasily Kaya (see p. 138) and the crown of Cybele, and is the prototype of the mural crowns of the later city goddesses.[2]

Of Egyptian styles we may note first the fine golden pendant of the goddess, nude, with Egyptian head-dress, *was* sceptre, and right hand held out in greeting; it comes from the courtyard of the Temple of Mekal at Beth-Shan (Pl. xxvii, no. 1).[3] More familiar is the Hathor type with typical head-dress and hanging locks. The Hathor cow-horns are well seen on a Gezer plaque where the goddess wears the two feathers of Ma'at (the goddess of Truth and Right) and a uraeus.[4] An Egyptian figure of the nude goddess was found at Jericho (Gressmann, no. 294), and at Kuyunjik there was an ivory figurine of Ishtar as an Egyptian goddess (*J.E.A.*, i. 108). At Beth-Shan an Egyptian stele represents the goddess with open dress, plumed helmet, two horns, sceptre, and

---

[1] Bliss-Macalister, Pl. lxvii. 15 (Vincent, p. 160), and lxviii. 2.

[2] *Gezer*, fig. 497; Gressmann, no. 286, cf. no. 282; Vincent, p. 161, and Driver, facing p. 57; also no. 293: the more slender specimen from Gezer which, Pilz suggests (p. 144 sq.), is the prototype of the Venus of Medici. For the crown, see S. Smith, *Ass.*, p. 233, and Langdon, *J.R.A.S.*, 1930, p. 26 sq. For Mesopotamian coins see S. Smith, *Bab. Hist. Texts*, p. 66 sq.; also Zimmern, *Islamica*, ii. 579 n. Garstang observes that the style still survives (*Hitt. Emp.*, p. 104 n.).

[3] Alan Rowe, *Museum Journal*, 1929, p. 40.

[4] Driver, p. 57; *Gezer*, fig. 498; Gressmann, no. 281. In Jer. xlvi. 20, Egypt is appropriately personified as a heifer. At Tell el-Ḥesy the goddess seems to have the head of the cat Bast (Gressmann, no. 289). Of Egyptian origin, too, may be the curious symbol on the forehead of two Taanach figurines (Vincent, fig. 105, Gressmann, nos. 283 sq.; uraeus, bee, flower ?).

ankh, while before her stands a woman, also uncovered, presenting a lotus (Pl. xxvii. 2). An 'unveiled' goddess with ear-rings, necklace, and crescent amulet, is to be seen on Gezer plaques of the Third Semitic period; the nudity is sometimes emphasized, but a long veil with embroidered border is thrown over the head and falls down the back.[1] The best example of this style is a remarkably fine marble statue of the inscrutable goddess, found at Tell Khalaf, Rās el-'Ain.[2]

The veil is the symbol of Ishtar, and two leading ideas are involved: (1) no deity may be seen unveiled—e.g. to unveil the statue of Isis at Saïs meant death; but (2) the deity is revealed to the worshipper, and such unveiling of the goddess is to be seen on old Akkadian seals.[3] Another 'horned' goddess, with hollow eyes (perhaps once jewelled), is represented in the small bronze from Gezer with ram-like horns, found in one of the chambers built to the west of the alinement (*c.* 1000 B.C.). Such a type was not unusual if we may suppose that the place-name Ashteroth Karnaim (Gen. xiv. 5) refers to a goddess known as 'Astarte of the two horns' (Pl. xxviii. i. 12).[4]

Extremely conventionalized forms begin early. One of the most remarkable dates from before the Amarna age, and its curious holes are not without analogies as far afield

[1] *Gezer*, ii. p. 414, fig. 499, see our Pl. xxvii. 3 (it is the figure with a tambourine noted above).

[2] von Oppenheim, *Alte Orient*, 1908, i. 24 sqq., 36; Benzinger, no. 80 (cf. ib., no. 81 from Cyprus). There are veiled goddesses at Petra (Brünnow, i. 220, no. 60 [2]), at Caesarea Arca (Macrob. *Sat.* i. 21, 5; Hill, *Coins of Phoen.*, p. lxxii), and elsewhere.

[3] Contenau, *Glyptique*, p. 41, nos. 139 sq. (see p. 176 and n. 2). According to old Assyrian law veils were worn by daughters of freed men (who in due course would be unveiled to their husbands), but the wearing of the veil was forbidden to hierodules.

[4] *Gezer*, fig. 504; Vincent, fig. 107; Gressmann, no. 285. Cf. Speiser, *Bulletin Amer. Schools of Oriental Research*, April 1927, p. 9 (a rude stone representation of a horned goddess); and *Bulletin of the Palest. Museum, Jerusalem*, No. 2, 1926, p. 7, Pl. iii *b* (head of goddess of Eg. type with some suggestions of horns: found at Tell el-Jerisheh). On Ashteroth Karnaim, see Driver, p. 58, *Rel. Sem.*, p. 602 sq.

as Susa (Pl. xxviii. 2).[1] Rather later, yet more realistic, is the Gezer 'Astartoid vase' (Pl. xxix. 1).[2] The rudeness of figurines, idols, &c., is not *in itself* a criterion of age, even as rudimentary religious beliefs and practices which might seem to bespeak an early date will persist by the side of those more highly developed. The archaic bird-like type with huge ear-rings found at Taanach of about 800 B.C. has Cypriote and northern affinities.[3] A male figurine, also beak-nosed, found in a tomb at Ain Shemesh, has analogies elsewhere in the Shephelah, and notably in the curious Gezer 'pottery shrine' which is dated to the Second Semitic Period (Pls. xxix. sq.).[4] Of Cypriote affinity also is the 'pillar type' of mother-goddess (Pl. xxvi).[5] The type persists, and a crude figurine from Kirjath-jearim near Abu Ghosh comes from an untouched cave as late as the sixth or fifth century B.C. Well might the discoverer remark: 'il faut bien avouer sur certains indices . . . que les usages cananéens persistaient encore vivaces sous la domination juive.'[6]

Here may be mentioned the red pottery model of a prognathous head found in one of the oldest of the caves of Gezer (i, fig. 24). None the less, even if it illustrates one of the early troglodytes, prognathism is not confined to the prehistoric periods, and in art can be mere caricature or convention.[7] So, too, the shapeless limestone anthropoid

[1] *Gezer*, fig. 501; Vincent, p. 157, n. 2, Pl. iii. no. 2. With the holes, cf. the dotted incisions on the figurine from the temple of Thutmose III at Beth-Shan (*Museum Journal*, 1927, p. 418 sq.); see also p. 107.

[2] *Gezer*, fig. 505.

[3] Gressmann, no. 280; see Driver, no. 3, facing p. 57, Vincent, fig. 108.

[4] Mackenzie, p. 76, Pl. xlii; Bliss-Macalister, fig. 51; Macalister, ii. 437, figs. 517–19; cf. above, p. 56. With the figurine at Ain Shemesh (found in tomb 5) was the upper half of a corresponding female, and it is suggested that they represented a divine pair.

[5] *Gezer*, no. 502, cf. Ain Shemesh, p. 54 sq., Pl. xxiii (found with the thrones, see p. 22).

[6] Father Abel, *Rev. Bib.*, xxx (1921), 97 sqq.

[7] Cf. the human and animal heads from Sidon (*Syria*, i. 306 sq.), and the head (from Abu Ghosh), Vincent, *Canaan*, p. 156, fig. 100.

figures found at Gezer are of no particular date, but ranged from before 2000 B.C. to the Fourth Semitic Period.[1] To speculate on the identity of such objects would be futile—note, for example, the late male figurines at eṣ-Ṣafi, with the right hand clasping the beard,[2] or the grotesque male with protruding tongue, braided cap (from which hang six streamers), and a hole in the chest, evidently for fastening it to a wall (Pl. xxx. 3).[3]

Beth-Shan, which has contributed more to our knowledge of early temples than any other site, has revealed both its god and his name. A stele (about 12″×8″) of 'the god of Beth-Shan', found in the southern of the two temples of Thutmose III, depicts a venerable bearded Semitic god, by name M-k-l or M-k-r, with conical horned head-dress (with two bands behind). In his right hand he holds out the ankh, while in his left is the usual sceptre, above and behind which are emblems no longer intelligible. The stele, which is broken, is inscribed above, 'made for the builder Amen-en-Apt, true of word, by his son Pa-Ra-en-Heb'; and below it speaks of the offering made by the king on behalf of the man's ka to Mekal the great god, that he may give life, health, &c., and that the father may reach his place in peace. We are shown the father and son, each with a lotus in the left hand, and with the right arm raised. The whole work, thoroughly Egyptian in sentiment, testifies to the veneration of Palestinian gods by Egyptians—such as has already been illustrated—and to the readiness with which they could associate with them the familiar Egyptian ideas. See Frontispiece.[4]

[1] *Gezer*, ii. 421 sq.; Vincent, p. 153 sq.

[2] Bliss-Macalister, fig. 53. Cf. also the wooden figure with pointed head-dress at Elephantine of c. fifth cent. B.C. (*Aeg. Z.*, xlvi, p. 32, fig. 10).

[3] *Gezer*, ii. 77, fig. 271 (see further, *Q.S.*, 1908, p. 23 sq.). It was found along with objects bearing the name of Ramses II.

[4] See also p. 100. See Rowe, *Museum Journal*, 1928, pp. 149 sqq.; *Q.S.*, 1928, pp. 79 sqq.; Mallon, *Biblica*, 1928, pp. 253 sqq.; *Syria*, ix. pp. 124 sqq.; and especially Vincent's very valuable monograph, 'le Baal Cananéen de Beisan et sa Parèdre', *Rev. Bib.*, 1928, pp. 512–43.

The name of the god has been variously explained: 'devourer' (from *ākal*, to eat), or 'king', or Molek (metathesis for *m-l-k*). Naturally it at once recalls that of Michal, the daughter of Saul, which, as Nöldeke has suggested, may possibly mean 'power'.[1] Vincent, too, suggests the meaning 'powerful one', comparing Omnipotens and Νίκη (p. 527). Equally uncertain is the real meaning of the name of the Cypriote god *M-k-l*, who seems to have had a temple at Kition in the fourth century B.C. (*C.I.S.*, i. 86, 89), and in the form Resheph–M-k-l was an Apolline god identified in a bilingual inscription with Apollo Amyklos.[2] But here again it is not clear whether this identification (with Apollo of Amyclae in Lacedaemon?) is substantial; the Greek might be merely an ingenious adaptation of an authentic Cypriote or Semitic god M-k-l.[3] If the god of Beth-Shan were Dagon (1 Chron. x. 10), whose name stamps him as a food-god, some such meaning as 'he who gives to eat' would be more tempting.[4] On the other hand, the 'temple of Dagon' in this passage has usually been treated as an error for 'Beth-Shan' in the older parallel passage, 1 Sam. xxxi. 10. The Chronicler lived in an age when Dagon was still a prominent god—whence perhaps Dagon for Nebo

[1] *Ency. Bib.*, col. 3301. It is at least a coincidence that Saul's fate should be so closely linked with Beth-Shan (1 Sam. xxxi), and that his other daughter Merab has a name of similar form that may mean 'increase' (Nöldeke, l.c.). For attempts to connect lunar-*motifs* with Saul, as a moon-god, the curious reader may refer to Jeremias, *O.T. in Light of Ancient East*, ii. 177 sq., Winckler in *K.A.T.*, p. 225.

[2] *C.I.S.*, i. 89, cf. 86 A 13, B 5; see Cooke, p. 76 and no. 20.

[3] Cf. Anath and Athene (p. 105, n. 6), and see the article by E. Power in *Biblica*, x (1929), 131 sqq. Clermont-Ganneau's suggestion may be noted (*Rec.* iv. [1901] 324), that Apollo Mag(e)irios of Cyprus has a Semitic epithet which can be explained by the Akkadian name Sin-magir, 'Sin is benevolent'; at all events 'the benevolent one' would be an admirable name for the venerable god of Beth-Shan, but the term is not found in West Semitic.

[4] The loss of the first radical would find an analogy in the spelling of the Aramaic word for 'food' in one of the Elephantine papyri (Cowley, no. 24, l. 35).

s

in some Greek MSS. of Isa. xlvi. 1—and it is not improbable that he was thinking of the Philistine country (*v.* 9 in both chapters) rather than of the plain of Jezreel.

Whatever be the best explanation of the name of 'the god of Beth-Shan', as he is styled, this somewhat aged and paternal deity is scarcely to be compared to the warrior god Resheph, as we have found him. He more naturally resembles the great god Setekh, though this does not exclude the possibility that the god, the Baal of Beth-Shan as we may call him, combined the attributes of Resheph and Setekh: for in this period the great gods were not clearly divided from one another.

In any case the little stele is unique, and the fact that it should ever have survived to illustrate the god of the important city of Beth-Shan is not without significance. For not only is there no gap between the pre-Israelite and Israelite religious history of Beth-Shan, but the god himself—to judge from the fair condition of the stele— has not come under the eye of later iconoclasts.

To the Egyptians, especially of the XIXth Dynasty, 'Baal' was perhaps the best-known Semitic deity, a war-god whose roaring spread terror. The name itself occurs as early as the Hyksos period, and in the Amarna Letters Baal appears to be identical with Addu or Adad. Properly speaking, Baal is a title and not a proper name, e.g. the Baal of Harran was the moon-god Sin; but it could become the name of a specific deity, just as El ('god') was a distinct god in North Syria in the eighth century (named between Hadad and Resheph) and later.[1] From the Amarna Letters it appears that the two dominant deities were (*a*) the sun-deity, and (*b*) the god of mountain and rain whose animal was the bull. Their names varied among different peoples,

---

[1] As a divine title the name Baal falls out of use in Palestine, and it is not found in the personal names at Elephantine (note Cowley, p. 215, l. 95). But there was a Baal temple later, in Memphis, near the Astarteion and with a hereditary priesthood (W. M. Müller, *As. u. Eur.*, p. 309, n. 2; Erman, *Aegypten*, p. 616, n. 3).

e.g. (a) Re and Shamash, (b) Addu or Adad, Hadad, Ramman, Teshub. The tendency was to fuse them. Thus
although the sun-god was essentially the god of justice, in
Kassite times Hadad (to use the Aramaic name) has this
attribute; [1] and the Assyrian name Shamshi-Adad, borne
by several kings of 1800–1000 B.C., combines them, even as in
Egypt the Pharaohs are spoken of in terms that refer to both
gods. Even though they are not explicitly thought of as
one god, the doctrine of the king's unique relationship to the
god or gods was part of a tendency to what has been
called monarchical monotheism, or rather henotheism.[2]
Moreover, the readiness to recognize first one and then
another deity as above the rest has already been observed
in the Egyptian titles of Asiatic gods and goddesses; and in
Palestine the writer of one of the cuneiform tablets found
in Taanach starts off with the wish: 'may the lord of the
gods guard thy soul'.

The storm and rain god (Hadad, &c.) is distinguished
by his weapon the thunderbolt, and his animal the bull.[3]
On an Akkadian seal 'to the god Hadad and the goddess
Shala', he stands on the bull holding the thunderbolt, before
him is a worshipper. It is the type found (a) on seals, and on
the bas-reliefs at (b) Maltia (near Nineveh) and (c) Malatia
(near the Upper Euphrates), and (d) among the symbols
on Esarhaddon's stele at Zenjirli.[4] Of quite another type

---

[1] Cf. p. 27, n. 3. So too in the Graeco-Roman age the bull is often
associated with the sun in Syria (Lidzbarski, *Ephemeris*, iii. 153, 162).
See A. B. Cook, *Zeus*, i. 577 sqq., also p. 635 (the sun being the heavenly
cause of things and the bull the telluric, the two were readily combined).
Dölger, *Die Sonne der Gerechtigkeit* (1918), p. 100 sq., remarks that
Philo speaks of the Logos as the sun.

[2] See *C.A.H.*, ii. 351.

[3] For symbols of the god, see Contenau, *Rev. Bib.*, 1916, pp. 537 sqq.,
554, 557, and, for the thunderbolt in particular, *Zeus*, ii. 764 sqq., with
illustrations (also pp. 722 sqq.).

[4] See (a) Ward, nos. 456, 461 (*Zeus*, ii. figs. 715 sq.), (b) Gressmann,
no. 335 (seven deities on their respective animals, Hadad's bull is
winged), (c) Garstang, *Hittite Empire*, p. 205, and (d) Gressmann, no.

are the two grim figures at Zenjirli, the one where he stands on a pedestal supported by lions, while the other bears Panammu's inscription to Hadad.[1] Again, he is no doubt the god at Zenjirli with hammer or axe in the right hand, and the lightning-fork in the left; he has Hittite upturned shoes, conical head-dress (some trace of horns), long curled band or pig-tail, and he wears a sword in his belt.[2] It is especially noteworthy that a votive offering dedicated by Esarhaddon to *Marduk* is inscribed 'the seal of *Hadad*'. So also the horned and winged god fighting the winged lion with a couple of thunderbolts is Hadad, though it recalls Marduk's fight with the female demon Tiamat (10th cent.).[3] In later centuries the storm and mountain god Hadad has solar elements, while as far back as about 3000 B.C. an Egyptian seal at Byblus mentions 'Re (sun-god) of the mountains'.[4] How extremely complex this god could become can be seen in the Louvre bronze of a beardless figure, whose head-dress blends the conical hat, bull-horns, solar disk, &c.; see below, p. 221, and Pl. xxxi. 1.

143 (*Zeus*, ii. fig. 730). For a bull on a conventionalized mountain (Hittite), see von der Osten, Chicago Orient. Instit., *Communication* vi. 92, 94.

[1] Hogarth, *Schweich Lectures*, figs. 12 (Gressmann, no. 345), 14 (Cooke, no. 61, see p. 38, n. 4); cf. the burly Hadad of Carchemish in Hogarth, fig. 40, and Binns, *From Moses to Elisha*, p. 207.

[2] Gressmann, nos. 339 sq., *Zeus*, ii. figs. 724 sq., Garstang, op. cit., p. 253, Pl. xlv. On a bas-relief of Tiglath-pileser III, where Assyrian soldiers are carrying a number of gods—presumably captured, cf. Isa. xlvi. 1 sq.—there is a fine Hadad with axe, thunderbolt, and two pairs of horns (Gressmann, no. 336). In Assyria Hadad is also shown with a typical feathered head-dress, standing on the mountains (ib. no. 326; cf. *Zeus*, fig. 731); on his chest is depicted a *ziggurat*, and there are astral symbols on his dress (so also no. 330).

[3] Gressmann, no. 380, cf. *Zeus*, ii. 769, n. 1 and fig. 728.

[4] Gressmann, *Z.A.T.W.*, 1925, p. 231, compares Ζεὺς ὄρειος. In the Xoïte nome of the Delta the mountain and bull belong to the cult of the apparently foreign mountain-god Aḫu; and a 'priest of the double axe' seems to be connected with it (Newberry, *Oxford Congress of Religions*, 1908, i. 212 sq.).

The Hittite war god is sometimes armed in more anthropomorphic fashion with a bow.[1] Although Hadad was so well known in Palestine he is not to be found there in any of these types. None the less, Yahweh is spoken of in terms appropriate to storm- and sun-gods, and, as a god of war, he has his arrows (Ps. vii. 13, Lament. ii. 4). Indeed, he also wielded a battle-axe, if we may rely upon a favourite interpretation of *segōr* in Ps. xxxv. 3 (R.V. mg.).[2] The Aegean god with the double axe is also Hittite, and this type survives on coins of Ake (Accho) and in Zeus of Doliche (p. 222). The weapon was certainly not unknown in Palestine;[3] and conversely, one, found in a fifteenth-century temple at Beth-Shan, of unusual shape, resembles that held by a Hittite figure representing the king or rather a war god.[4]

The Akkadian sun-god has for his emblem a disk containing a four-rayed star and bundles of flames.[5] One of the

[1] On seals (Hogarth, *Hitt. Seals*, p. 90, fig. 114, cf. nos. 313 sq.; *J.E.A.*, viii. 216, no. 17), and monuments (Garstang, *Hitt. Emp.*, pp. 177, 203, cf. *Zeus*, i. fig. 500).

[2] See commentaries *ad loc.*; esp. Cheyne, *Psalms* (1888), who traces this interpretation back to the medieval Jewish exegete Kimchi. The *sagaris* itself, however, was not a *double* axe (*Zeus*, ii. 560).

[3] Karge, *Refaim*, p. 213 (Jerusalem museum), cf. *Gezer*, ii. 242 sq. (Pl. cxcii. 7). The axe as an amulet at Ain Shemesh (ii. 61 sq.); set up on a base, on Assyrian seals (*Zeus*, ii. 545 sq.).

[4] Cowley, *Schweich Lectures*, p. 24, fig. 10; *C.A.H.*, Pl. i. 238a; Gressmann, no. 341. Garstang (*Hitt. Emp.*, p. 85, Pl. xix) comments upon the femininity of the figure, and takes it for an Amazon—note that the sun-deity was female (p. 134, n. 3 below). Others are not of this opinion. The prominent breasts upon which Sayce relies (*J.R.A.S.*, 1929, p. 896) recur upon the Cappadocian bronze god, see Hogarth, *Schw. Lect.*, p. 17 n.; *C.A.H.*, Pl. i. 238b. The delicacy and femininity of face on some of the Hittite sculptures are no criterion: 'on the same argument several of the Pharaohs of the XVIIIth and XIXth Dynasties would appear to have been female' (Garstang, p. 97 n.). Note also the graceful and rather girlish Mithras stabbing the bull (see Legge, *P.S.B.A.*, xxxiv. 140, Pl. xiv, in the British Museum), and the ambiguous Hittite deity, *Syria*, i. 265, fig. 5. Cf. further, pp. 55, 205 n. 4.

[5] Gressmann, no. 316.

best-known scenes depicts the sun-god of Sippar (British Museum, ninth century). Here Shamash sits within a shrine supported by palm-columns, before him on a table is his solar disk, above are the symbols of Sin, Shamash, and Ishtar. It is one of the familiar introduction scenes, and takes place, not on the top of a mountain, as in Exod. xxiv. 9–11, but on the waters of the heavenly ocean.[1] On the stele bearing Hammurabi's code of laws—where the sun-god and the king are characteristically alike—rays spring out of the god's shoulders. This is common on the old seals; especially typical also is the god, with horned head-dress and rays, standing between the mountains, and entering the sky through the eastern gate.[2] Although it is the solar emblem rather than an anthropomorphic Shamash of this type that can be recognized in Palestine, the sun-god has left his name in such places as Beth- and En-Shemesh, the 'house' and 'well' of the god. There is reason to believe that there were solar cults at Jerusalem.[3] Moreover, in Zechariah's vision of the four chariots coming from between the mountains, there may be a reference to the double-peaked mountain where the gods were wont to appear before Shamash. It was the 'place of decisions'. But

[1] Above, p. 40 sq. See L. W. King, *Hist. of Babylon*, facing p. 260; *C.A.H.*, Pl. i. 74; *Zeus*, i. fig. 190; Gressmann, no. 322, and on details, S. Smith, *Hist. Bab. Texts*, p. 70 n.

[2] Cf. Gressmann, nos. 319 sq.; King, *Bab. Rel. and Mythology*, pp. 32, 182; Ward, ch. xiii.; Kraeling, *A.J.S.L.*, xli. 175.

[3] See p. 32; and Thackeray, *Schweich Lectures*, pp. 64, 78. The eastern gate of the temple was especially sacred. The view that the Parbar of 1 Chron. xxvi. 18 is the Akkadian [*E*]-*barbar* ('the shining house'), the name given to the sun-temple of Sippar, &c., is questioned by Kahle and Sommer, *Kleinasiat. Forsch.*, i. 35. The name of Abdi-Khiba of Jerusalem, in the Amarna Letters, contains the name of a Hittite solar goddess (Burrows, *J.R.A.S.*, 1925, p. 280), and Shamash is construed as feminine in Letter no. 323 (l. 22 sq.), where the king of Askalon speaks of the Pharaoh as the Shamash of heaven, the son of Shamash, whom Shamash loves (*ti-ra-am*). Garstang suggests that the old Hittite sun-goddess was the ancestress of Ma–Bellona of Comana (*Hitt. Emp.*, p. 195, cf. Winckler, *M.D.O.G.*, xxxv. 53).

whereas the Babylonian Shamash is in the east, here the scene is transferred to the west, and, at the best, there is now only an echo of the myth.[1]

Samson, as his very name and exploits indicate, may have been a native sun-god who became a solar hero, or a Danite hero who was blended with a sun-god.[2] But Samson also reminds us of Gilgamesh. Reminiscences of the epic of Gilgamesh are to be found on a slab at Carchemish; and the colossal Herakles-Melḳart, from Amathus in Cyprus, which suggests both Gilgamesh and Enkidu, can be supplemented by the scenes of Herakles and the lion upon a Phoenician—or, to be more precise, Cypriote—bowl from Larnaka.[3] As for Melḳart, the Baal of Tyre, he is simply 'the king of the city', as his name indicates. He is mentioned

---

[1] Van Hoonacker, *J.T.S.*, xvi. 251 sq. In the Aramaic version of the story of Aḥikar which circulated at Elephantine (fifth cent. B.C.), certain things are said to be pleasing to Shamash (Cowley, p. 215, l. 92 sq.); and even the later versions preserve several traces of old Oriental 'heathenism'.

[2] On the strength of the name Timnath-Ḥeres, Ed. Meyer suggests that Joshua was originally a solar hero (*Die Israeliten*, p. 476, n. 3; for Samson, see ib., p. 529). S. Klein (*Jüd.-Pal. Corpus Inscript.*, p. 30, n. 2) cites an old Haggadah (preserved by Rashi on Joshua xxiv. 30, Judges ii. 9) to the effect that a solar emblem was placed on the grave of Joshua, the name of whose burial place was interpreted to mean 'likeness (*tĕmūnath*) of the sun'. Solar ideas lie at the back of Ps. xix. 1–6; and with the 'going forth in the morning' Burney compares Samson at Hebron (*Judges*, p. 407)—for an expansion of this theme see Kraeling, *A.J.S.L.*, 1925, p. 174 sq. On the solar elements in the Samson-story, see further Burney, *Judges*, pp. 392 sqq.; *Schweich Lectures*, p. 56 sq.; Hans Schmidt, *Jona* (1907—with Gressmann's review, *Z.D.M.G.*, lxi. 945 sq.). G. A. Cooke (*Judges*, p. 137) observes that it cannot be without significance that Beth-Shemesh lay so near Zorah (2 miles across the valley), in the very neighbourhood of Samson's home.

[3] Burney, *Judges*, p. 497, Pl. v; Hogarth, *Schweich Lectures*, p. 35, fig. 38; Contenau, *Civ. Phén.*, p. 207 sq. and fig. 67 (the bowl, after Longperrier, *Musée Napoléon*, iii, Pl. xv). See the discussion by Baudissin, *Adonis und Esmun*, p. 296 sq. (Taf. vii sq.), who suggests that by the side of the senior and bearded god Herakles-Melḳart was the younger and beardless Eshmun-Melḳart=ʼΑσκληπιὸς Λεοντοῦχος of Askalon.

with other gods in Esarhaddon's treaty with Tyre, and his cult spread to Egypt, Malta, and Carthage. In view of the close and persistent relations between Tyre and Jerusalem, especially at the building of Solomon's temple, and after the marriage of Ahab and Jezebel, we should expect this Baal to be well known in Judah (see 2 Kings xi. 18), though not necessarily as an exclusively Heraklean god.

Herakles of Tyre continued to be prominent, and is found on Phoenician coins of the fifth and subsequent centuries B.C. (cf. Cooke, p. 347 sq.), and notably on coins of Tarsus, of the fourth century (viz. shortly before 333 B.C.). In the latter, the Baal ('Baal Tarz') closely resembles Zeus, while on the obverse is Herakles-Melḳart. Hence these coins would enable East and West to unite in recognizing an oriental Baal and Melḳart and a Greek Zeus and Herakles.[1] Such syncretism was so natural in the Near East that it is unnecessary to ascribe the type to the genius of Alexander the Great.

It is not going too far afield to observe that this Baal of Tarsus, like other popular deities, had attributes of fertility. His prototype is to be seen in the imposing and very well-known rock-sculpture at Ivriz a few miles north-west of Tarsus.[2] A simple, thick-set, and muscular Armenoid figure, Hittite in dress, with quadruple horned cap, he holds bunches of grapes and ears of corn.[3] A lusty god of the soil, he is 'the peasant god', subsequently to be a Herakles who left his name hard by in Eregli, the last echo of the

[1] C. T. Seltman, cited by A. B. Cook, Zeus, ii. 761 sq.

[2] C.A.H., Pl. i. 246 b; Zeus, i, fig. 453, Cowley, fig. 20, Hogarth, fig. 48. Garstang, Hitt. Emp., p. 165 sq., gives a new and improved photograph, Pl. xxxiv. Discussions by Sir J. G. Frazer, Adonis, &c., i. 119 sqq., and Sir W. M. Ramsay, Luke the Physician, and other Studies (1908, ch. v on 'the peasant god').

[3] Ears of corn are represented on a Syro-Hittite seal (Hogarth, Hitt. Seals, p. 69, no. 179), and on coins of Datames (below, p. 169); cf. the story of the pre-Islamic idol at Damascus with grapes in one hand and wheat and barley in the other (Q.S., 1910, p. 85 sq.).

Greek Herakleia.[1] Facing him, and far more elaborately dressed, is the appropriately smaller figure of the priest or king, or most probably the priest-king, in an attitude of adoration.[2] This is no 'introduction': the more direct relationship between the god and the priest-king, who is, in a sense, the intermediary between god and people, and 'represents' each to the other, is characteristic of the old religions. It is very clearly indicated in the Amarna Letters, where the loyal chiefs of Palestine and Syria freely use—however conventionally at times—the conception of the divine sonship of their Egyptian suzerain, and even of his divine nature; and this relationship is elaborated, with the utmost realism, on the temple-walls in Egypt.[3] Such beliefs involved the recognition of the more supreme gods, on the one hand, and, on the other, their human representatives, the less supreme sacred beings. Traces of this are to be looked for in Palestine, especially in the cult of Molek (or Milk), the king-god.[4]

The theory that there was a dominant Semitic triad comprising the father-god, the son-god, and the mother-goddess has recently been maintained.[5] At all events, a 'son-god' may no doubt be recognized on the frequently described procession at Iasily Kaya a little to the east of Boghaz-Keui.[6] The scene, which may. be dated about

[1] Hogarth (p. 65 sq.) identifies him with the bearded god of Carchemish, with horned mitre and battle-axe, but questions the identification with the Cilician Sandon (Frazer, *Adonis*, i. 125, after Sayce, Jensen, &c.), or Tarkhu (Contenau, *Kerkouk*, p. 23).

[2] The swastika appears on the highly decorated dress (Garstang, p. 161). On the Palestinian swastika, see p. 183, n. 5.

[3] Frazer, *The Magic Art and the Evolution of Kings*, ii. 131 sqq. For the Amarna Letters, see *C.A.H.*, ii. 341.

[4] Cf. Lagrange, *Études*, pp. 99 sqq., and Frazer, *Adonis*, ii. 219 (with Kennett's view that Molek, to whom first-born children were sacrificed outside Jerusalem, 'may have been originally the human king regarded as an incarnate deity').

[5] Ditlef Nielsen, *Die dreieinige Gott* (Copenhagen 1922); also *Handbuch d. altarab. Altertumskunde* (ib., 1927), i. 206 sqq.

[6] Garstang, *Hitt. Emp.*, pp. 95–119, Pl. xxi–xxiv; *Zeus*, i. 604

T

1200 B.C., is placed on the tops of the mountains, and probably represents a divine marriage to ensure the fertility of nature. Here, the bearded god with conical hat has, by his side, an animal, interpreted as a bull (or even as a goat), with a similar head-dress, and stands on the neck of two bowed figures, at the head of a line of male gods and attendants. Facing him, the goddess with turreted crown stands upon a panther or lioness. Behind her, a young beardless figure stands upon a lioness (?) holding a staff and a double axe. Behind him are two goddesses above a double eagle, and other figures (female), and the line is brought up by one who is probably the priestly king standing upon two mountains. The whole symbolism of this remarkable scene is extraordinarily interesting.[1] It is perhaps the same youthful god who in the inner sanctuary embraces the priest-king; cf. also the Egyptian description of the Hittite-Egyptian seal (p. 43 above).

There can hardly be any doubt that the leading goddess is the great mother-goddess, by whatever name she was everywhere known: Ishtar—Cybele—Ma—Ammas—Atargatis (Derketo)—Rhea. The similar male deities, the one bearded, the other beardless, appear farther to the west at Giaour Kalesi.[2] With Eduard Meyer we might interpret the pair as the supreme god of heaven (Attis-Papas) and Teshub (=Setekh) respectively. On the other hand, the younger seems to be more naturally the forerunner of Attis; but this very name appears to mean 'father', and Attis was a father-god, at once the son and lover of the goddess.[3]

sqq.; Gressmann, no. 338; *C.A.H.*, Pl. i. 236 *a*. Cf. also Frazer, *Adonis*, i. 128 sqq.; Meyer, *Gesch. d. Alt.*, i, §§ 477 sqq.; Garstang, p. 116. (Note the origin of 'circus processions', Martin Nilsson, *Archiv f. Rel.*, xix. 82.)

[1] As regards some details: for the persistence of the conical head-dress, see Cumont, *Fouilles de Doura-Europos*, p. 59 sq.; Conder has observed that it still survives (*Q.S.*, 1889, p. 89); Hempel (*Pal. Jahrb.*, xxiii. 69 n.), after Karo, contrasts the *god* holding the double axe with the similar Minoan *goddess*.

[2] Garstang, p. 147 and fig. 9.

[3] See Frazer, *Adonis*, i. 137 sq., and esp. p. 281 sq.

Again, if the older male is the prototype of Zeus of Doliche, Jupiter Dolichenus, the latter, as A. B. Cook remarks, bears some resemblance to the younger, the son-god, who is the forerunner of Herakles-Sandas, the Baal of Tarsus.[1] The close resemblance between them points not, as was once suggested (by Perrot), to the twofold representation of one god with different attributes, but to their father-son relationship. The problem of the youthful son-gods of the Near East lies outide the scope of these pages; but the intricacy of the archaeological data is hardly surprising when we consider, on the one hand, the Amarna Letters, where the Pharaoh is at once the god and the son of the god, and, on the other, the Akkadian conception of Bel the older and his son Bel-Marduk.[2]

Concerning the Tammuz-Adonis cult, it may be noticed that its antiquity in Byblus is confirmed by the letter of Rib-Addi of that city, who, in one of the Amarna Letters, speaks of 'my Tammuz'.[3] Moreover, an ivory found at Byblus, representing a swallow in flight, recalls Plutarch's story of Isis as the swallow lamenting over the tree containing her dead brother Osiris.[4] Indeed, the old myth has been traced back to the time of Pepi I of the VIth Dynasty.[5] The suggestion has been made that the circular rings of pottery with vases found at Beth-Shan and Megiddo were used in the cult of Adonis; but although the 'Adonis gardens' are evidently referred to in the 'plantings of Naaman', in Isa. xvii. 10, the proposed identification needs

[1] See (a) Zeus, i. 604, 631, and (b) ib., i. 599; ii. 560.

[2] On Adonis and Eshmun as youthful gods, see the great work of that title by Baudissin (Index, s.v. 'Jugendliche Götter'); cf. A. f. R. xvi. 413 n.

[3] No. 84, l. 33: Da-mu-ia (see Schroeder, O.L.Z., 1915, col. 291).

[4] Gressmann, Z.A.T.W., 1925, p. 233. For Plutarch's story, see Frazer, Adonis, ii. 9 sq.

[5] Ib., p. 230 (after Montet, Syria, iv. 185), with Contenau, Civil. Phén., p. 117 (see ib., p. 142 sq., on a possible connexion between the laments for Adonis and the Adapa myth, p. 122 and n. 2 above).

confirmation.[1] Representations of Adonis are, as a matter of fact, very rare even in Phoenicia.[2]

The Israelite period of the history of Palestine follows so closely upon the Amarna Age that the religion of Israel could not but be influenced by the conditions that preceded its rise. No obvious images of Yahweh have been found in Palestine.[3] But the same might be said of Shamash, Hadad, and Baal. The cult of Asshur was imageless, his was the winged sun-disk, and he too was without a consort. Further, the cult of the Khaldian or Urarṭian national god of ancient Armenia required no image.[4] On the other hand, it is

[1] For Beth-Shan and Megiddo, see *Q.S.*, 1927, pp. 74, 149, *Z.A.T.W.*, 1926, p. 75, and Steuernagel, p. 137, fig. 204 (identified by Gressmann, no. 676). At Bethlehem, where the cult of Adonis persisted into the Roman period (Frazer, *Adonis*, i. 257), 'Adonis gardens' are still prepared by some of the women, and set on the table for good luck every Easter (*Bulletin, American Schools of Or. Research*, 1921, Sept., p. 4). On the gardens of Adonis, see also *Syria*, v. 333 sq.

[2] Sculptures of Adonis have been recognized near Byblus at el-Ghineh and Mashnaka, see Baudissin, *Adonis und Esmun*, p. 78 sq., and Taf. i–iii, also *Syria*, ix. 176. For el-Ghineh (where Adonis is attacked by a *bear*) cf. also Gressman, no. 209. A weeping goddess is depicted (a Niobe-like 'mother of weeping', *Baki-umme*, is cited by C. H. W. Johns, *P.S.B.A.*, 1899, p. 1). For a cult scene at Umm el-'Awāmid (two women watering a plant), see Heuzey, *Comptes Rendus*, 1902, p. 203 sq., pl. facing p. 204. The god Adonis may also be recognized on coins of Tripolis in Syria (Dussaud, *Syria*, iv. 305); and he is identified with the young Horus and Harpocrates on coins of Byblus (Baudissin, op. cit., pp. 153, 167 sq.), and with the Triptolemus on a bas-relief near Byblus (below, p. 147, and our Pl. xxxi. 3).

[3] Jerusalem has kept its secrets: apart from the god in the boat (p. 34, n. 2 above), mention should be made of a seal found on the Mount of Olives: a deity standing on or behind three lions, in his left hand a sceptre, in his right a three-thonged whip (see Grimme, *O.L.Z.*, 1913, p. 156). It may be the forerunner of the coin-type of Herod Agrippa I (a figure in a quadriga holding a sceptre; Madden, p. 135). The whip reminds us of Jupiter Heliopolitanus (cf. p. 151).

[4] Rowe suggests that in the stele of Mekal and in the stone column or *maṣṣēbah* in the temple of Thutmose III at Beth-Shan we may see the difference between the anthropomorphism of the local Egyptians ('who could hardly visualize a god other than in human, animal, or other

possible that a Setekh or a Resheph could be interpreted as Yahweh; and we have found symbols in Palestine which could belong, not to some Shamash or Marduk, but to the god of Israel who, it must be remembered, was readily known as Baal.[1] Ward (*A.J.S.L.*, xxv. 175–87) has illustrated from Akkadian seals how Yahweh might have been thought of as a mountain god; and it is far from unlikely that the familiar title El Shaddai betokens a 'mountain-god', or rather 'god-mountain', of the type that can be traced in the ancient 'Re of the mountain', in Zeus Oreios, and in the emperor Elagabalus, the very 'god-mountain' himself.[2]

Again, the view has often been held that Yahweh was a moon-deity, or that Yahwism contains elements of a moon-cult.[3] One may even ask whether the venerable Mekal represents a moon-god. In any event, it is noteworthy that in the O.T. we can contrast the conception of an aged deity, 'the ancient of days' (Dan. vii. 9), with the active warrior-god, with blood-sated sword (Isa. xxxiv. 5 sq.), or clothed in brilliant blood-red garments fresh from the annihilation of Israel's foes (Isa. lxiii). Indeed, it is possible that the animal of the Hadad type of gods was a relatively young animal, presupposing a relatively young god.[4]

shape') and 'Canaanite custom', which was satisfied with the stone (*Q.S.*, 1928, p. 78 sq.).

[1] We cannot say how the Palestinian would interpret the representations of Osiris (*Q.S.*, 1903, p. 39), Ptah (Vincent, fig. 118), Sekhmet, Khnum (*Gezer*, iii, Pl. ccx. 16), Anubis (*M.D.P.V.*, 1906, p. 56), Isis (with child, *Gezer*, iii, Pl. ccx. 18), Nephthys, Bes, &c.; see further Macalister, *Gezer*, ii. 331 sqq.; Thomsen, *Reallex. Vorgesch.*, 'Amulett', § 5.

[2] Cf. G. R. Driver, *The Psalmists* (ed. Simpson), p. 123. The god Amor was a mountain god (*bel shadē*), and his consort was Ashirat, 'lady of the plain' (*Rev. Bib.*, 1928, p. 178); cf. above, p. 123.

[3] Cf. e.g. Burney, *Judges*, pp. 249 sqq., *Schweich Lectures*, p. 55, n. 4.

[4] A figure of Jupiter Heliopolitanus published by Dussaud (*Syria*, i. 10) is flanked by bulls with barely developed horns, and he observes that the 'golden bull' of Exod. xxxii. was a heifer ('*ēgel*). The remains of a *three-year-old* animal were found at Beth-Shan, cf. the age in 1 Sam. i. 24 sq. (*Q.S.*, 1928, p. 77). On aged gods see Nielsen, *Der dreieinige Gott*, pp. 199, 208 sq., 214.

Special interest is attached to a monument from Tahpanhes (Daphnae) near Pelusium where Jeremiah and
his not too orthodox companions took refuge. It is a stele
of the Persian age, now in the Cairo Museum, and is shaped
like the front of an Egyptian shrine. Within it is the god,
bearded, and with long hair, standing upon a lion not unlike the usual type on the seals (cf. p. 111). Facing him is
the smaller figure of a priest on a pedestal (which Meyer
derives from the Hittite mountain), offering incense upon a
fire-altar. The god wears a mitre and holds in his left hand
the Egyptian *was* sceptre, and in his right the typical Asiatic
curved throwing-stick (the Greek *lagobolon*). In the field
are two crescents, the crescent disk, and two large ears
(Pl. xxxi. 2).[1] While the curved stick reminds us of Marduk
and other Asiatic gods (e.g. the god of Amrit, p. 117), the
ears recall Marduk with the big ear and eye, symbolical
of his wisdom (p. 42), and the attributes of Resheph
('hearing prayer') and other deities.[2]

The Tahpanhes stele illustrates a syncretism which finds
a ready parallel in the monuments from Tēma in North
Arabia on one of the routes between Egypt and Babylonia.
Here, Aramaic monuments of about the same age (fifth
cent. B.C.?) depict a priest with an Egyptian name, with
Assyrian representations of the god Ṣalm and his attendant,
and the pantheon includes a 'Great Sin' and Ashirat.[3] At

[1] Gressmann, no. 354 ; W. M. Müller, *Egypt. Researches*, i. 30 sq., Pl.
xl, and ii. 186; cf. G. A. F. Knight, *Nile and Jordan*, p. 340, E. Meyer,
Gesch. d. Alt., i. 2, p. 631; and see also Müller, *E. Bi.*, 'Tahpanhes.'

[2] The epithet *tashmītum* (i.e. readiness to hear) is applied to the wife
of Nebo; cf. Burney, *J.T.S.*, xiii. 83 sq., on the place-name Eshte-
moa. The Zoroastrian Sraosha is essentially a fine personification of
hearing. For the 'gods that give ear' (θεοὶ ἐπήκοοι), see Weinreich,
Mitt. Deut. Arch. Inst. Athen., xxxvii. 1–68 (p. 25: they are especially
of Oriental origin). Both ear and eye symbols have been found on
a Minoan gold signet-ring (Evans, *Minos*, ii. 842, fig. 556).

[3] See p. 123 and n. 2. A fragment of a local sacrificial scene (the cult
of Dushara-Dionysus?) is given in Euting, *Nabat. Inschr.*, p. 12: cf. *Rev.
Bib.*, 1913, p. 153 and n. 5.

Tahpanhes we are in a district long known for its Semitic connexions; and the name of the place Sīn, mentioned by Ezekiel (xxx. 15), which was near Pelusium, doubtless points to the old moon-god. Hence the god at Tahpanhes need not be due to fugitive Israelites of the time of Jeremiah;[1] nor need we accept Müller's tentative suggestion that the monument represents their god. None the less it testifies to the complex tendencies to which the Israelites were exposed, both here and elsewhere. The 'Queen of Heaven' (Jer. xliv), whose old cult was maintained by the women of Israel,[2] could very easily be identified with the similar goddesses of their neighbours, and Jephthah's readiness to treat Yahweh of Israel and Chemosh of Moab as corresponding deities (Judges xi. 24) is entirely typical of a process a striking example of which has now to be mentioned.

At Elephantine (Yeb) in Upper Egypt there flourished during the sixth and fifth centuries B.C. a curiously mixed colony, some of whose business and other papyri (written in Aramaic) have been brought to light.[3] Here Jews or Aramaeans mingled with Babylonians, Persians, and Egyptians; and although most of the Jewish personal names are of a familar Hebrew or 'biblical' type, several are new. They worshipped 'the god of heaven', by name Yahu (i.e. Yahweh); they were in touch with Jerusalem and Samaria; but they had their own temple, a not inconsiderable building, provided with five stone gates, bronze hinges, cedar-

---

[1] Traces of Israelites, or rather Hebrews, are to be found both earlier and later: cf. Petrie, *Expository Times*, xxxvi. 155 sq. (before Psammetichus I): from the south of Goshen comes the name Yahu-nama, perhaps 'Y. is good' (the word for 'good' being Phoenician rather than Hebrew); it is of the time of Ramses II.

[2] With the 'cakes' used in the cult of the Queen of Heaven (on which see G. F. Moore, *E. Bi.*, col. 3992; Kennedy, ib., col. 460), Rowe compares the cigar-shaped mud-models of bread-cakes, about $3\frac{1}{2}$ in. in length, found at Beth-Shan (*Q.S.*, 1928, p. 81).

[3] See A. van Hoonacker, *Schweich Lectures* (1915), and for the documents, A. E. Cowley, *Aramaic Papyri of the Fifth Century B.C.* (1923), with bibliography.

wood roof.[1] Oaths are taken by the *masgedā* and by Anath-yau (Cowley, no. 44). By the former is meant a stele or altar (see above, p. 17 sq.): compare the oath by the altar in Matt. xxiii. 18 sqq. The latter associates the great and ancient goddess with the god, much in the same way that Mesha king of Moab recognizes both Chemosh and Ishtar-Chemosh.[2] The oath is also taken by the god Ḥerem-bethel (no. 7), a name which could be translated 'sanctuary of Bethel', Bethel being a divine name.[3] In a papyrus of 419 B.C. (no. 22) money is shared between Yahu (12½ parts), Anath-bethel (12) and Ashima(?)-bethel (7). This triad has been keenly discussed. Its significance is obvious when we observe the intimate relations between the Jews and Egyptians in Elephantine, and the fact that the city was the seat of the cult of the ram-headed Khnub or Khnum, who is the member of a triad with Sati and Anuki. This triad can be traced from the time of Sesostris I to Ptolemy V and Tiberius; and a local Greek inscription names two triads, of which the first is Knub who is Ammon, Sati who is Hera, and Anuki who is Hestia.[4]

---

[1] We use a conventional transliteration of the name יהו which appears once as יהה (Cowley, no. 13). Clermont-Ganneau is said to have found fragments inscribed יהה צבאת, i.e. Y. of Hosts (Lagrange, *Rev. Bib.*, 1908, p. 261, n. 2). On jar-handles of Jericho and Ophel the form is more often יה. The different forms are exhaustively discussed by G. R. Driver, *Z.A.T.W.*, 1928, pp. 7–25. The temple is called *egūrā* (אגורא), a testimony to the familiarity with the common Babylonian name E-Kur (cf. Hoonacker, op. cit., p. 53).

[2] The goddess precedes in Atar-gatis (Athtar [Ishtar]+Ate), but follows in the Phoenician Milk-'Ashtart, Eshmun-'Ashtart and Ṣid-Tanith.

[3] See G. R. Driver, *J.T.S.*, xxv (1924), 293 sq. (Lidzbarski, *Eph.*, iii. 248 sq.), and cf. the 'divine seat' (*mautebā*) in Nabataean inscriptions (Cooke, nos. 80, 94). Perhaps Ḥerem-bethel was a god of oaths and contracts, like Mithra, Themis, Dikē, Zeus ὅρκιος and the 'Covenant-god' of Shechem.

[4] *C. I. Gr.*, iii. 4896; see E. Bevan, *Ptolemaic Egypt*, p. 295: Weigall, *Antiquities of Lower Nubia*, p. 44, *Antiquities of Upper Egypt*, p. 475, &c.; Breasted, *Records of Anc. Eg.*, iv. 991, cf. Klio, iv. 155 (where Khnum is

Sati, 'mistress of Elephantine', was the chief goddess, a sun or sky deity, goddess of fertility; she is sometimes represented armed with bow and arrows. In one of the papyri a Jewish woman who had become an Egyptian swears by Sati (no. 14, l. 5). Khnub and Sati form a natural pair, like Yahu and Anath, or Ammon and Hera (or Juno). Moreover, later, on Gnostic gems, Iao (i. e. Yahu) and Chnubis are found associated.[1] But Anuki is more difficult to place: rare elsewhere, she is represented with a feather head-dress;[2] and still more problematical is '-s-m—bethel, the pronunciation and meaning of which are purely conjectural. Bethel itself enters into various Mesopotamian and western personal names as that of a deity; and when the prophet declares that Moab shall be ashamed of Chemosh as the house of Israel of Bethel (Jer. xlviii. 13), it follows that Bethel and Chemosh are comparable deities, and the former, 'the place of the god' (cf. p. 18 above) is a god (or goddess).[3]

Now since Anath-bethel introduces a goddess fairly corresponding to the Egyptian Sati and the classical Hera and Juno, there is a presumption that the third name corresponds to Anuki and Hestia. In this cosmopolitan community the Jews were wont to use the formula 'may the gods seek thy welfare'; they intermarried with Egyptians and others; a Pa-Khnum is the father of a Hanan and the

---

joined with Re). Cf. also the Latin inscr. Dessau 4424 sqq. (*Zeus*, i. 353 n.): *Hammoni Chnubidi Iunoni Reginae*. In the Elephantine papyri the god is called Khnub, but in personal names the form is Khnum.

[1] Gressmann, *Z.A.T.W.*, 1915, p. 13 sq.

[2] See Budge, *Gods of Egypt*, ii. 57, and plate facing p. 56 (Weigall compares the Philistine head-dress). The identification with the Phoenician *onka* (*onga*) of Thebes—an Athene type of goddess—is denied by E. Meyer, *Z.D.M.G.*, 1877, p. 722 sq., and Wiedemann on Herod. ii. 50.

[3] For analogies see *Rel. Sem.*, p. 562, and for the name, R. S. Cripps, *Book of Amos*, p. 293 sq. Compounds of Bethel occur at Elephantine, in papyri (Cowley, p. 279) and on an ostrakon (*C.I.S.*, ii. 154). The god Baitil is named on the treaty between Esarhaddon and Tyre (Winckler, *Altor. Forschungen*, ii. 10; *K.A.T.*, p. 437 sq.). We may include the name Bethel-shar-eṣer in Zech. vii. 2.

son of Zaccur (no. 23); and a priest of the Egyptian deities Khn[um and Sa]ti lives in closest proximity to the temple of Yahu (no. 13, l. 15).[1] Hence, while the Egyptians recognized the great god Khnub, the god who created man on the potter's wheel,[2] and his two associates, the Hebrew had, on this view, his supreme god and two accompanying goddesses. After all, the second or 'fellow-wife' was well known in Semitic custom (Deut. xxi. 15; Lev. xviii. 18), and a prophet will even speak of Yahweh as having two consorts, Oholah and Oholibamah (Ezek. xxiii. 4).[3] And since the second wife was not infrequently of lower status—cf. the relation between Sarah (a name meaning 'princess') and Hagar—we may assume that the second deity was not only a female, but of another status, like Hestia. Indeed, even in a very late text an Ethiopian king is said to be 'son of Khnum, born of Sati and nursed (or suckled) by Anuki'. Finally, since Anath and Bethel are well known in Palestine, it is probable that the name '-s-m is the goddess Ashima, who is of the city of Hamath (in 2 Kings xvii. 30), and who may plausibly be read in Amos viii. 14 (for 'ashmath): they who 'swear by Ashima of Samaria'.[4]

Not only can we thus connect the god Yahu with Yahweh and with Iao, there would always be a tendency to identify Yahweh the national god of Israel with one or other of the great gods of other peoples: with Amon, Re, or Khnum, with Bel, Marduk, or Asshur, and, not least, with

---

[1] In the place of figurines of the 'mother-goddess' were found un-Egyptian representations of a nude woman with a small child by her side; also a wooden figure with sharp-pointed head-dress (Aeg. Z., xlvi. 30 sqq., figs. 9 and 10).

[2] See the illustration of this in the British Museum Guide to the Egyptian Collection, p. 135; cf. Yahuda, Sprache des Pentateuch, i. 146 sq.

[3] See S. R. Driver's note on the ṣārāh in 1 Sam. i. 6 (R.V. 'rival'); and for the custom, C. H. W. Johns, Bab. and Ass. Laws, p. 134 sq.; Campbell Thompson, C.A.H., i. 523; S. A. Cook, Moses and Hammurabi, pp. 115 sqq.

[4] See Cripps, Amos, p. 316 sq., also p. 293 sq., and below, Additional Note, pp. 149 sqq.

the grand ethical god of Zoroastrianism, Ahura-mazda. Finally, as we enter upon the Graeco-Roman age, the identification would be with Zeus-Jupiter. Now, one of the numismatic treasures of the British Museum is a south Palestinian coin (? of Gaza) bearing in Aramaic lettering of somewhere about 400 B.C. the name Yahu (Pl. xxxii).[1] On the obverse is an unidentified head with Corinthian helmet; it has been identified with Hadran, a god of Hieropolis, or with Minos the eponymous founder of Gaza. On the reverse within a square frame sits a male bearded figure, his right hand is wrapped in his himation, his left is extended and holds an eagle or hawk. He sits upon a winged car, and in front of him is a curious and obscure face. This last has been identified with Bes; or, on the assumption that it is a satyr-mask, it supports the view that the god is Iao-Dionysus.[2] The identification of Iao and Dionysus appears to be relatively late, and the god is rather a solar Zeus.[3] At the same time, the winged and wheeled car suggests Triptolemus, an excellent representation of whom was found at Gharfin near Byblus (Pl. xxxi. 3). He stands in a car drawn by snakes, scattering seed; above is the moon-disk, and the *naïskos* in which he is placed bears the familiar solar disk of Egypt.[4] At Alexandria the myth of Triptolemus was Egyptianized, and he becomes a son or follower of Osiris; in

---

[1] See now, A. B. Cook, *Zeus*, i. 232 sqq., to whom we are indebted for our plate (also the coin, Pl. xxxiv. 30 sq.). The lettering resembles that on the papyri of Elephantine and is rather more archaic than the jar-handles of Jericho; it is Aramaic rather than Phoenician (note the form of the *h*).

[2] Gressmann, no. 362 sq.

[3] *Zeus*, i. 234 n. 4. Iao was also equated with Zeus and Helios. Dr. A. B. Cook cites an incantation on a papyrus from Thebes: 'come foremost angel of Great Zeus Iao', and a magical papyrus summoning 'the ruler of the gods' Ζεῦ Ζεῦ τύραννε Ἀδωναῖ (for αδαιναι) κύριε Ἰαωούηε (cf. Legge, *Forerunners and Rivals of Christianity*, i. 106). On Iao and Yahu, see now Baudissin, *Kyrios*, ii. 193 sqq.

[4] Cook, *Zeus*, i. 227 sq. (we reproduce his fig. 166); Gressmann, no. 365; Dussaud, *Mythol. Syr.*, p. 153 sq.

Seleucia he was associated with Zeus Kasius. But here at Byblus he is a vegetation god, a Greek representative of a Baal or Adonis,[1] and he may be associated with the Zeus Arotrios of Philo of Byblus, i.e. with Dagon, the corn or food god.[2]

The coin is a telling illustration of religious syncretism; and, with its identification of Yahu with a Greek god, would have a meaning for both Greek and Semite. Its solar Zeus, with suggestions of Triptolemus, could be readily interpreted by either; and, as we shall see, the connexion between Triptolemus and Io in Greek mythology would even encourage the association of Io and Yao (see p. 182). Nor would the winged car be altogether un-Semitic; and while Yahweh has the chariot of the cherubim (1 Chron. xxviii. 18), the flying wheels of Ezekiel's vision (chs. i, x) prepare us for such a scene as is here depicted.[3]

The coin is a vivid object-lesson of the way in which the great and well-known gods could be brought together—and their individuality obscured. It was by such means that the sway of Yahweh would seem to be extended. Yet although the equation Yahweh = Zeus would seem a great step towards universality, it would be at a price which Judaism could not pay, that is if the uniqueness of Yahweh was to be preserved. See further, pp. 186 sq., 188 sq.

The coin bridges the gulf between the period we are leaving behind and that upon which we shall now enter. In the Graeco-Roman world we shall meet with other intricate combinations of types which, after all, will be only later forms of what we have already encountered. The divine kingship of the Ptolemies and the solar monotheism

---

[1] Gressmann ; so also Baudissin, *Adonis*, p. 162.

[2] On Triptolemus as corn god, see Frazer, *Spirits of the Corn and of the Wild*, i. 70 sqq.; *Zeus*, i. 211 sqq. (p. 214: the close relationship between the god and Dionysus).

[3] At Arslan Tepe (Anatolia) a god has a chariot the body of which has the form of an eagle, Von der Osten, *Chicago Orient. Instit. Communication*, no. 6, pp. 89, 92.

or henotheism of the Roman age have their parallels centuries earlier in the Amarna age; and the emperor Elagabalus, who so astounded the Romans, has a far-off ancestor in the no less 'amazing emperor', Amenhotep IV. Ikhnaton. Throughout, the points of resemblance are not to be exaggerated or pressed unduly; but it will be helpful to remember that what we have already found and what we shall find are but different forms of the same process.

The differences are profound. We are gradually leaving an old Oriental world which had a lengthy history. As we pass through the Persian period and enter upon the Graeco-Roman age a new mentality is growing up, a new epoch is being born. Men are looking out upon the world with newly-opened eyes; and the Palestine of the Jews is an integral part of a world of life and thought alien to it. Palestine, or rather Judaism, will still be standing apart from and reacting against the religious conditions of the day; and the history of Judaism and Christianity in and about the first century A.D. gains a new interest when we look at the religion of their environment in the light of archaeology.

ADDITIONAL NOTE ON THE TRIAD OF ELEPHANTINE
(p. 144).

THERE are several varieties of triads. The Babylonians divided the cosmos among Anu god of heaven, his son Bel-Enlil, the earth god, and Ea the god of the waters beneath the earth. Also in Egypt Nut the mother of Re was sky-goddess, Geb her brother-husband was the earth-god, and corresponding to Ea was Nu. There was a Babylonian astral triad: Sin (moon), Shamash (sun), and Ishtar, the source of fertility; or, otherwise, Shamash, Adad, and Ishtar. Much later, Apuleius gives a new triad: fixed stars, seven planets, earth.[1] Family triads are represented in Adad, the divine son of Adad, and his mother Shala;[2] in Osiris, his wife Isis, and their son Horus; and there were other groupings, e.g. Amon, Mut, and

[1] Cumont, A.f.R., ix. 330 sq.
[2] See Dussaud, Myth. Syr., p. 114.

Montu (or Khonsu). At Byblus we may recognize the triad Baal-ath, El-Kronos, and Adonis-Eshmun; at Carthage, Tanith, Baal-Hamman, and Iolaos (Eshmun); at Ammān (Philadelphia), Asteria, Herakles (Melḳart), and Asklepios (i.e. Eshmun); at Palmyra, Bel, Shamash, and Nanai; and there are others.

In view of such triads the identity of the third deity at Elephantine, '-s-m–bethel, cannot be determined *a priori*, although it may be supposed that the triad was a natural one, and that there was some essential relationship between it and the similar Anath-Bethel. This is confirmed by the Egyptian triad at Elephantine itself and by the corresponding Greek interpretation: Anuki = Hestia.[1] The element '-s-m has been explained (a) as an abbreviated form of Eshmun, whose own name, however, is itself of uncertain origin. Thus Lidzbarski explained Eshmun as 'name' (Heb. *shēm*) with *aleph* prefixed and the common ending -n; both in old Babylonian and in late Jewish times '(the) Name' is a divine title and takes the place of the god's proper name.[2] The *Name* whether of gods or men connotes the *nature* of the bearer. Next (b), '-s-m has in turn been explained to mean 'name', and the deity's name is therefore interpreted 'Name of the Bethel (or temple)'. Astarte is called 'name of Baal' (*C.I.S.*, i. 3, l. 18), and the idea of a deity as the 'name' of a superior is not strange, whereas 'name of (the) Bethel' would stand in need of explanation. A third view (c) enlists the Babylonian fire-god Ishum, a name which actually occurs at Elephantine in Ishmu-kudurri, a form analogous to the name Nebo-kudurri.[3] The fire-god Nusku appears in names in North Syria and in Elephantine (p. 121); but there is a gap between this and the tempting conjecture that the third deity corresponded precisely to Hestia (Vesta) and had the care of the family hearth.[4] Finally, the enigmatic element has been con-

---

[1] On the statement of Herodotus (ii. 50) that Hera and Hestia were unknown, see Wiedemann's commentary *ad loc.*

[2] *Eph.*, iii. 262 sqq.; cf. Baudissin, *Adonis u. Esmun*, pp. 203 sqq., and *Kyrios*, iv. 197 (Eissfeldt): for Eshmun and *sumāna* 'quail', see *Rel. Sem.*, p. 690 sq.

[3] Cowley, nos. 53 and 5. See, however, Noth's discussion, *Israel. Personennamen*, p. 124.

[4] The custom, however, is Persian, and it reached Egypt (Otto, *Swoboda Festschrift*, pp. 194 sqq., cf. Leuze, *O.L.Z.*, 1928, col. 83 sq.). Moreover, the notion of the burning coal as a symbol of family life occurs in 2 Sam. xiv. 7 (see p. 87); and although the passage stands alone, it implies ideas of life and fire which must have been intelligible.

nected with (d) Simē or Sima, the goddess at Hieropolis, daughter of Zeus-Hadad and of Hera-Atargatis;[1] and the whole name with (e) *Sumbetulos* who is cited after Seimios (a masculine form of Simē) and the Lion-god in a Greek inscription of A.D. 223 from Kefr Nebo.[2] Now since a *sumbetulos* points to a god who is associated with another, as Herakles is *sunnaos* when associated with Zeus (cf. Dionysos and Apollo at Delphi), it is possible to think of Mercury—Hermes (Nebo) who is joined with the Zeus of Heliopolis the Lion-god and Aphrodite.[3]

The name of Simē of Hieropolis suggests some connexion with the *xoanon* called $\Sigma\eta\mu\dot{\eta}\iota\text{o}\nu$ which stood between the god and the goddess.[4] It should no doubt be restored in a Greek inscription, probably from Palmyra originally, which runs: $[B\dot{\eta}]\lambda\omega\ '\text{I}\alpha\rho\epsilon\beta\dot{\omega}\lambda\omega$ $'\text{A}\gamma\lambda\iota\beta\dot{\omega}\lambda\omega\ \kappa\alpha\dot{\iota}\ \Sigma\epsilon[\mu\ \ldots].$[5] Here Athene stands between two deities, but it is not clear whether Yarḥibol is united with Aglibol, or, preferably, with Bēlos. The name occurs again in a bilingual (of the 3rd cent.) from Deir el-Ḳalʿa behind Beirut in the sanctuary of 'Bal-markod'. The dedication is to him and to the goddess Hera, and $\Theta\epsilon[\hat{\alpha}]\ \Sigma\dot{\iota}\mu\alpha\ \kappa\alpha\dot{\iota}\ \nu\epsilon\omega\tau\dot{\epsilon}\rho\alpha\ "H\rho\alpha = e(t)\ I(unoni\ R(eginae)\ e(t)$ $I(unoni\ S(imae)\ e(t)\ C(aelesti)\ S(ohaemiae).$[6] Here the mother of the emperor Elagabal, who appears on coins as Juno Regina, Virgo Caelestis, is identified with the great Mother-goddess. The god, the Baal of Dancing, is otherwise called $\kappa\dot{\upsilon}\rho\iota\text{o}\varsigma\ \Gamma\epsilon\nu\nu\alpha\hat{\iota}\text{o}\varsigma$; and in the church which stands on part of the old temple at Deir el-Ḳalʿa was found an altar showing Jupiter of Heliopolis flourishing his whip and standing between two bulls.[7] At Dura on the Euphrates it is only by conjecture that a Greek inscription names Zeus Megistos and (Hes)tia; but if this conjecture is right, Hestia, as Cumont remarks, is probably a fire-goddess. Atargatis was also worshipped at Dura, and a Greek inscription unites Zeus and Athene, the latter elsewhere corresponding to the Semitic Allath.[8]

---

[1] See *Zeus*, i. 583; Dussaud, *P. W.* 'Simea'.

[2] See *Zeus*, i. 571 n., *Eph.*, ii. 323 (after *Bull. Corr. Hell.*, xxvi. 161 sqq.).

[3] See Lagrange, *Études*, p. 196. The name Kefr Nebo is significant; see Dussaud, *Myth. Syr.*, p. 114.

[4] Lucian, §§ 33, 49; see Clemen in the *Baudissin Festschrift*, p. 101. Meliton calls Simē the daughter of Hadad (Cureton, *Spic.*, xxv. 10).

[5] *Eph.*, ii. 83 sq., 310 (Ronzevalle, *Rev. Arch.*, i. 385 sqq.).

[6] *Eph.*, ii. 325 (see Ronzevalle, *Rev. Arch.*, ii. 29 sqq., Dussaud, *Myth. Syr.*, pp. 107 sqq.).

[7] L. M. Angus, *Q.S.*, 1920, p. 160. See Cumont, *P.W.*, 'Balmarcodes'.

[8] *Fouilles de Doura*, p. 387 sq., no. 25*b* (no. 25*a*: $\Delta\iota\text{o}\varsigma\ '\text{A}\theta\eta\nu\hat{\alpha}\varsigma\ '\text{A}\theta\eta[..?].$).

Simē, in any case, occupies a subordinate position; and there are changes of sex (Seimios above) which, however, are not without analogy. The name seems to have been fairly well known.[1] But the meaning of the crucial names (Eshmun, Ashima, Simē) can only be conjectured. Obviously it is far from certain that they are to be identified with one other or even that they are essentially related. As for Simē, it has been conjectured that she is deified Fate, corresponding to the Greek Tyche and the Arabic Manāt.[2] And this interesting suggestion, too, is not without support if Simē found her counterpart in the female Tyche, the guardian of the well-being of cities. The evidence as a whole is incomplete; but whether the third of the triad of Elephantine be the Name, or the Hearth-deity, or the Fortune, we gain the result that with the great pair of male and female deities Oriental cults would associate a third—male or female—as a working representative of one or other of the more august couple.

[1] Syr. ab-samya (= αβεδσεμίος), barsamya, βαρσάμεος of Hieropolis, see Eph., iii. 264, 302; also αμασσημια ('handmaid of S.'), Q.S., 1915, p. 144 n. Clemen (op. cit., p. 102) cites the name of Simmas the foster-father of Semiramis, and this name in turn may, according to Ronzevalle, contain the name Simē. According to Clermont-Ganneau (Rec., iv. 238), Simē was a name often borne by courtesans.

[2] Zimmern, Islamica, ii. 574 sqq. (The Shi-mi-i-gi of the Amarna Letters, no. 24 [Weber, in Knudtzon, p. 1056 sq.] is too remote.) In the triad Malakbel, Gad-Taimi, and Atargatis (Cooke, no. 112), the second is the Luck or patron deity of the clan Taimi; the cult of Gad-Tyche was very popular; see Ency. Bib., 'Fortune'.

III

THE GRAECO-ROMAN AGE

THE Graeco-Roman age upon which we now enter seems short indeed compared with the lengthy history of Oriental culture which occupied the preceding chapter. The age is one of culmination and decay, and the rise of Christianity is its swan-song. To be sure, the cultural history of the maritime coast had never been entirely severed from that of the Levant as a whole; and the new and intensive Greek influence which had already begun to make itself felt on the Syro-Palestinian coast-lands before the conquests of Alexander the Great may be said to have had its forerunner, many centuries previously, when these lands came within the Aegean orbit. Palestine, never an isolated land, is now part of a world living in close contact with the ripest fruits of Greek thought; and while many of the consequences can be marked, it is unfortunately far less easy to determine exactly the influence of the west upon the east in that earlier period when Palestine, Cyprus, and the rest of the Aegean were parts of one and the same world.

Taking a long view of the past, we may legitimately recognize a swing of cultural influences, now westwards and now eastwards.[1] Nor need we confine it to the few thousands of years of recorded history. Hence, although it seems natural to assume that 'civilization' first arose in the Near East, it is not to be forgotten that our evidence for Syro-Palestinian man goes back to an exceedingly remote day (see p. 73 sq.), and that influences from the western Mediterranean littoral eastwards in absolutely prehistoric times are not to be ruled out on *a priori* grounds.

[1] See Hempel, *Palästinajahrbuch*, xxxii. 88 sq. 'Dark' periods intervene; so even as regards Egypt and Phoenicia, the intercourse between them after about the 11th cent. B.C. seems to have relatively little effect, until we enter upon a new and more energetic age under the Saïtes.

As we consider the Near East century by century from a purely archaeological point of view it is astonishing to observe how insensibly we pass from, say, the earlier Persian age to the Byzantine. Throughout there is a certain continuity in the religious background; and in the light of the facts the vicissitudes of Judaism and Christianity gain a new interest. In the Graeco-Roman age we reach one of sophistication and antiquarianism, of mysticism and theosophy; the crudest cults mingle with sweeping universalizing ideas, and the proselytizing zeal of a Judaism, conscious that it had something to give the world, found a rival in the young Jewish sect that became Christianity. The age, as a whole, is one of a powerful, though by no means permanent, influence of the West upon the East, and of a powerful reaction, which had permanent results. No one can fail to be impressed by the extent to which the East was Hellenized; yet not less impressive is the spread westwards of cults, beliefs, and ideas of Oriental origin.

We shall find ourselves in the midst of archaic beliefs and customs, which had persisted, or had re-emerged in some not unfamiliar form. Yet, at first sight, we seem to be in a Greek world, with Zeus, Apollo, Dionysus, Athene, and Aphrodite among the leading deities. A Ptolemais replaces an Accho; and instead of Beth-Shan we meet with Nysa–Scythopolis. The numerous Greek and Latin words in the Rabbinical Hebrew and in the Aramaic of the day would seem to have altered the language as surely as Greek thought gave a new turn to the Judaism of the Jews of Alexandria. But Alexandria may be said to have contributed more effectively to the history of Christianity than to the growth of Judaism; the Greek and Latin words dropped out of use; and the factors that preserved the old place-names Akka and Beisan will account for the preservation of much that is characteristic of the older ways of life and thought.[1]

[1] See, in general, E. Schürer, *Geschichte des jüdischen Volkes im Zeitalter J.C.*, ii (1898); *Schweich Lectures* for 1926 (1929), ch. ii by J. W. Hunkin,

In fact, the archaeological data point not so much to
any deep-reaching influence of Hellenism as to a syncretism
becoming increasingly unnatural and too artificial to endure.[1] There are syncretistic and pantheistic speculations,
sometimes attractive, often extremely bizarre. The literary
evidence and the evidence of archaeology converge when,
on the one hand, we read of the many names under which
Isis is worshipped—mere names, we are told, for she *is*
Isis—and, on the other, when the artist has fused together
the attributes of a variety of deities.[2] Again, the coinage
of Phoenicia reflects an almost complete Hellenization of
the native deities along with (in the Roman age) the re-
assertion of old religious elements which, it is clear, had
never been suppressed.[3] And these are not necessarily
mere antiquarian relics or of purely literary interest.[4] The
movements of Arab tribes in the Syrian desert were encouraging the recrudescence of old Semitic religion, and

ch. iii by F. C. Burkitt; *C.A.H.*, vol. vii. ch. 5, vol. viii. ch. xvi; and the
useful survey by E. S. Bouchier, *Syria as a Roman Province* (1916).

[1] Note, e.g., the promiscuous combination of Phoenician and Greek
ideas and myths in Philo of Byblus (1st cent. A.D.), the very nature of
which indicates the vitality of the beliefs preserved by his source
'Sanchuniathon' (Baudissin, *Adonis und Esmun*, p. 236). No doubt
we have Philo's syncretism and euhemerism; but while there are
different estimates of his trustworthiness, where he can be checked he
proves his value (cf. id., *A.f.R.*, xvi. 411). It is to be observed that outside Phoenicia (Carthage in particular), where Oriental religion was
less Hellenized, more of the old usage remains, e.g. human sacrifice
(id., after Nöldeke, *A.f.R.*, xvi. 391).

[2] For Isis, see the well-known passage in Apuleius, *Metamorph.*
xi. 5; cf. Hehn, *Die biblische Gottesidee*, p. 149 (see p. 394 sq. for the
Mixobarbaron of Ausonius); *Ancient Egypt*, 1927, pp. 19 sqq.; Weiss-
häupl, *Jahreshefte d. Oesterr. Archäol. Inst.*, xiii. 176–99. Cf. the goddess
with the attributes of Isis, Tyche, Nemesis, Sun and Moon in the
Lewis collection, Corpus Christi College, Cambridge. Note also the
many-named Arabian goddess in the Sabaean inscriptions, see Ditlef
Nielsen, *Der dreieinige Gott*, p. 321 (Umm-'Athtar).

[3] See G. F. Hill, *Church Quarterly Review*, lxvi. 124.

[4] e.g. the survival of Dido on a Sidonian coin (Hill, *Coins of
Phoenicia*, pl. xxiv, no. 13).

we see something of the background upon which Islam was one day to develop. The Biblical student can find many interesting traces of old Oriental religion in the Apocalypse of St. John,[1] and Oriental activity accounts both for the vigour of pagan religion and philosophy in the world of Rome and for its ultimate defeat. To cite Cumont: 'la même race sémitique qui a provoqué la chute du paganisme est aussi celle qui fit l'effort le plus puissant pour le sauver'.[2]

As the contents of this chapter will be classified according to the nature of the material—a strictly chronological arrangement being impossible—we may observe at the outset the retention of archaic features on coins. The omphaloi and baetyls are especially striking, for although stone-cults are inveterate, it must not be supposed that the stone objects always meant the same throughout the ages.[3] It is, in fact, of great significance that the 'Bethel' names, already noticed above (p. 145), are of about the sixth and later centuries B.C., and that to Neo-Babylonian seals we owe the illustrations of stones or baetyls set up on altars (pp. 24 sqq.). Now while, on the one hand, the shaped and anthropomorphic image imposed its interpretation upon the worshippers, the cone or the shapeless stone, on the other hand, gave greater freedom to the worshipper, who could focus his profoundest and most private convictions of deity upon the object, the vehicle or embodiment of his god. And how impressive they could be when the *vis praesens* was a Zeus![4]

[1] See R. H. Charles's Commentary (1920), ii. 490, Index, *s.v.* Origins.

[2] *Acad. des Inscr. et Belles-Lettres, Mém. p. diverses Savants*, 1908, p. 479.

[3] In the Mishnah period (*Abodah Zarah*, iv. 1 sq.; ed. W. A. L. Elmslie, 1911, pp. 62 sq., 74) the venerated Mercurius or Herm was a familiar object against which it was necessary to warn the Jews. In front were three stones side by side or arranged as a dolmen, and coins, grapes, wine, oil, sheaves of corn, &c., were offered upon an altar.

[4] *Rel. Sem.*, p. 209; Lagrange, *Études*, p. 215. Cf. Lucian's account of the honourable Rutilianus and his worship of stones (in the account of

An old mountain-god of the Hadad type is to be seen in the Greek Zeus Kasius, whose sacred stone is represented upon coins from Seleuceia Pieria of the first century B.C. and after (Pl. xxxiii, no. 1).[1] It has a fillet attached to it, and stands within a shrine with four pillars and a pyramidal roof; above is the eagle, the bird of Zeus.[2] The scene of the cult is the sacred Mons Kasius (Jebel el-Aḳra'), above Antioch, a few miles from Pieria, described in Baedeker as 'the most conspicuous landmark of North Syria'. Not far off there was a Heraclea on the coast, near el-Lādiḳīyeh;[3] and the sun-cult on the mountain which was so well known in antiquity is still maintained by the Nosairis.[4] The name itself, which is one of the four great mountain-gods of Phoenician myth, recalls that of the sacred mountain Jebel Ḳasyūn outside Damascus, also with a fine view. But Zeus Kasius is elsewhere found firmly established in Egypt at Mount Kasion to the east of Pelusium, where there was a famous sanctuary of the god. From his temple at Pelusium comes a statue of a youthful Apolline figure holding a pomegranate. It is a Harpocrates type of god, and although it is not necessarily Zeus Kasius, the cult of *young* gods is often to be found in this period.

Alexander of Abōnoteichos); and Arnobius's confession of his veneration of any 'well-lubricated stone begrimed with olive-oil, which he would venerate as though there were in it a *vis praesens*' (F. C. Conybeare, *Oxford Congress of the History of Religions*, ii. 178 sq.). Also, A. B. Cook (*Zeus*, ii. 814) on Zeus Keraunios: the thunderbolt as the symbol of superhuman power and not a reversion to an earlier pre-anthropomorphic type of religious thought.

[1] The coins referred to by their numbers are collected on Plates xxxiii. sq. The descriptions given by the respective editors have been freely used. No. 1 is from the Fitzwilliam Museum, Cambridge (McLean, 9437), cf. Wroth, *British Museum, Coins of Galatia*, p. lxxii. A good plate of typical coins is given in Bouchier's *Syria as a Roman Province*.

[2] On local coins we also have the thunderbolt with a fillet—a symbol of Zeus Keraunios who may have been identified with Zeus Kasius (Wroth); but see otherwise A. B. Cook, *Zeus*, ii. 981 sqq.

[3] *Revue Biblique*, 1920, p. 178.   [4] Cumont, *Études*, p. 352 sq.

Pelusium itself is in a district which for many centuries was the meeting-place of diverse elements, Egyptian, Semitic (or Asiatic), and Aegean (p. 120); and it is at least a coincidence that the late Testament of Naphtali (Aramaic version) speaks of a ship belonging to the son of Berakel, and thus recalls the merchant-fleet of Berket-el in the old story of Wen-Amon's visit to Phoenicia (c. Ramses XII).[1] Zeus Kasius, who is also found in Spain,[2] would seem to have been a seaman's god, one of the deities of the estuary or promontory who cheered and guided the anxious mariner.[3] This may account for the late and extraordinary allusion to Kasius, the ship-owner of Pelusium.[4] The name, however, has not been satisfactorily explained. It might be primarily that of a mountain; cf. Tacitus (ii. 78) on Carmel: *ita vocant montem deumque*. In Nabataean inscriptions (1st century A.D.) it is the name of a cult-founder: A'ra, the 'god of Kaṣyu', is introduced at Bostra, and a descendant introduces Allath at Ṣalkḥad.[5] This interest-

---

[1] Charles, *Pseudepigrapha*, p. 362 (Naphtali, iv. 8); Breasted, *Ancient Records*, iv. § 574. This coincidence, or this persistence of trading-intercourse by a long-established firm (cf. the cuneiform business documents of Murashu Sons from Nippur), is pointed out by R. Eisler, *Z.D.M.G.*, lxxviii. 61.

[2] *Syria*, viii. 330.

[3] See Ellen C. Semple, 'The Temple Promontories of the Mediterranean,' *American Geographical Review*, July, 1927, pp. 353–83. The deities include the Tyrian Melkart and Poseidon. In the Aegean their place is taken by St. Nicholas, and in the western Roman Catholic Mediterranean the Virgin Mother inherits the prestige of Artemis or Aphrodite (ib., p. 369). Sir Arthur Evans (*Minos*, ii. 843), with reference to the maritime aspects of the great Minoan goddess, observes that she becomes fused with Isis and Pelagia, and that the Christian churches of St. Pelagia overlook what were once Minoan harbours.

[4] Cited in *Zeus*, ii. 987.

[5] Cooke, *North Semitic Inscriptions*, p. 253; M. Hartmann, *Z.A.*, xxvii. 43 sqq. The god of one Kaṣyu seems to be worshipped as an ox on a Nabataean inscription found near Bostra; illustrated by Sachau, *S.B.*, Berlin, Oct. 22, 1896; but his reading '*image* of Kaṣyu' is not confirmed, see Lidzbarski, *Handbuch*, p. 148 n., *Ephemeris*, i. 74, Clermont-

ing evidence for family gods—cf. the 'God of Abraham'—finds further illustration from this period.[1]

More famous than the baetyl of Zeus Kasius was the black conical stone of Emesa (modern Ḥoms), which was supposed to have fallen from the sky. On coins it is to be seen conveyed on a quadriga; or it is in a temple on a base, or surmounted by an eagle; sometimes a star is marked upon it. The temple also possessed a fine monumental fire-altar, standing on a base: it has a cornice, and on the side are niches containing statues (no. 2).[2] Our coin (dated A.D. 215) is of the Syrian princess Julia Domna, whose sister's grandson, Varius Bassianus (A.D. 205–222), was the high priest of the sacred stone of the god Elagabal. Afterwards he assumed the name of the deity whom he incarnated; and with the stone and the cult settled at Rome, where his ecstatic rites as emperor (218–222) make him one of the most remarkable figures of the old Oriental paganism.[3] Elagabalus, or Heliogabalus—a subtle change to indicate his solar affinity—was a member of a dynasty of Arab origin, as various personal names prove (Soaemias, Sampsigeramos); and the name itself is formed on the same analogy as other contemporary names, Ila-Samsos, 'the god sun', Ela-bēlos, 'the god Bel'. While the name of the god Ela-gabal, in fact, is naturally explained as 'the god mountain', the god is also a solar deity;[4] and to the many

Ganneau, *Recueil*, iii. 75 sqq., Cooke, p. 245. Apropos of the two-peaked temple on the coins, note that Newberry (*Liverpool A.A.A.*, i. 27 sqq.) connects the old Egyptian deity Khas(ti), the double-peaked mountain. For sundry speculations on the name, see E. Hommel, *J.S.O.R.*, 1926, p. 36 sq.

[1] See Lagrange, *Études*, p. 462, and especially A. Alt, *Der Gott der Väter* (Stuttgart, 1929), pp. 34–48, 75 sqq.

[2] British Museum: see Wroth, *Galatia*, p. 238, no. 9, and p. lxiv. sq.; cf. also Leipoldt in Haas, *Bilderatlas: Urchristentum*, nos. 91–93.

[3] See J. S. Hay, *The Amazing Emperor Heliogabalus* (1911).

[4] On the name Elah-gabal (אלהגבל), see *Rel. Sem.*, p. 570. The god is named in the Cordova inscription (see Cumont, *Syria*, v. 343); cf. also *C.I.L.*, iii. 4300, from Pannonia, *Deo soli Alagaba[lo]*. The sacred

points of interest in this strange cult of the third century
A. D. it is to be added that the name corresponds to what is
probably the best explanation of the old title El-Shaddai
(see p. 141). The very persistence of this archaic type of
god is in itself noteworthy; and it should be observed that
on independent grounds there is reason to believe that the
biblical compounds of Zur (ṣūr), 'rock', and of Shaddai
(Zuri-shaddai) are relatively late, viz. of about the sixth
and fifth centuries B.C.[1]

Among other sacred stones may be mentioned those of
(a) Artemis at Perga, (b) Aphrodite of Paphos, (c) the
moon god at Harran—and at Edessa. At Petra (d) the
omphalos-shaped stone in a niche, evidently an object
of cult, will be the symbol of Dushara, like the stone
(or stones) on the coins of Adraa and Bostra (nos. 3
and 4).[2]

There is much to be said concerning the baetyls on the
coins of Byblus and Tyre. The well-known coin-type of
Macrinus (c. A.D. 218) illustrates a temple at Byblus
(no. 5). An obelisk stands upon an altar which appears
to have 'horns' at the corners (see p. 31), though they
are so pronounced as to suggest small pillars or maṣṣēbōth.
The altar is within an enclosure of lattice-work, with which
it is tempting to compare the sōreg of the Temple of Jerusalem. At one end—the northern—is a colonnade with steps;
and adjoining—on the east—is the side-view of a temple

stone at Emesa may probably be recognized in the North Syrian
bronze where an eagle (the bird of Zeus and the sun) stands upon a
discoid base inscribed Helios (Zeus, i. 604, fig. 475).

[1] See G. Buchanan Gray, Hebrew Proper Names, pp. 196 sqq.

[2] See for (a) Frazer, Adonis, i. 35 n.; (b) Zeus, ii. 424; (c) G. F. Hill,
Coins of Arabia, p. xcii, and p. xcvi (pl. xiii, 7, 8); (d) Gressmann,
no. 429 (cf. no. 426): at Petra the omphalos shape is rare, the
square or rectangular block being much more common. For
nos. 3 and 4 (from the British Museum) cf. also above, p. 25.
There is still much that is obscure in the cult at Petra, see W. R. Smith,
Kinship and Marriage, pp. 298 sqq.; Rel. Sem. (Index, s.v. Dusares),
Lagrange, p. 189; Burkitt, Schweich Lectures for 1926, p. 104 sq.

approached by steps. In the entrance is a small incense-altar upon a tripod—or, it may be, a turreted or radiate crown (so Grose).[1] There seems to have been a triad at Byblus: El-Kronos (p. 167 sq.), the Baalath of Byblus (p. 93), and the more youthful Adonis-Eshmun-Aesculapius. The temple on the coin, however, is not necessarily that of the Baalath, the mistress of the city; it is unlike that of Astarte, which is depicted upon other coins.[2] The type is an important contribution to our knowledge of ancient temples, and has been fruitfully studied along with the excavations at Byblus (p. 93), and the Phoenician inscription from Byblus where King Yeḥaw-milk describes his work on behalf of the temple to the Baalath (*C.I.S.*, i. 1).[3]

Upon Tyrian coins of the third and fourth centuries A.D. there are representations of (1) large baetyls or omphaloi on bases with an olive tree between (no. 6), or (2) veritable stelae between a crescent and a flaming incense-altar—on the reverse are a star and olive tree (no. 7).[4] They find their explanation in the traditions preserved by that portentous writer Nonnus of Panopolis (*c.* A.D. 400), who testifies at length to Tyre's pride in her ancestry and sacred lore. It was said that the 'ambrosial rocks' floated in the sea along with the sacred olive, and that after a sacrifice had been offered they came to rest, and the city of Tyre was founded upon them (xl. 428 sqq.). The stones are 'ambrosial' (αμβροσιε παιτρε), i.e. anointed with fat, oil, or honey—one of those oily (λιπαροί) objects for worshipping

---

[1] British Museum: *Coins of Phoenicia*, p. 103, no. 38; Gressmann, no. 521, Haas, no. 89; Grose, *Fitzwilliam Museum: Greek Coins*, iii. 370; Frazer, *Adonis*, i. 14. On the style of the perspective, see P. Thomsen, *Z.D.P.V.*, lii. 164.

[2] See e.g. Gressmann, no. 522; and Hill, *Phoen.*, p. lxx (coins of Elagabalus).

[3] See Dussaud's interesting article, *Syria*, viii. 113 sqq., and Dunand, ib. x. 212 (the oldest temple at Byblus has Isis-Hathor-Baalath in *human* form).

[4] British Museum. See Hill, *Phoenicia*, p. 281, nos. 429 and 430; cf. Hill, p. cxl sq., Cook, *Zeus*, i. 530, Lagrange, *Études*, p. 417.

which Clement of Alexandria ridicules the pagans.[1] Now, according to the Phoenician myth, which Philo of Byblus tells after Sanchuniathon, the old culture-hero Usōos (cf. the name Esau) went to sea and found an island upon which he dedicated two pillars, the one to fire, the other to wind, and watered them with the blood of the beasts he had taken in hunting. Thus originated the island-city of Tyre and the cult of the pillared stones. It seems pretty clear that (after Dr. Hill) the stelae on the coins may be connected with those of Usōos; and we may recognize (after Father Lagrange) a confused recollection both of the Deluge and of that sacrifice which, in the Babylonian and the biblical versions, followed thereupon. According to the biblical tradition, the Deluge was followed by an entirely new world order and a new covenant; and man was allowed to eat animal flesh provided he ceremonially poured out the blood (Gen. ix. 1–7).

There are several points of contact between the relatively early Hebrew narratives and the relatively late Phoenician traditions, and it is not always possible to determine whether the latter are based upon the former, or whether they go back to some independent source.[2] The Rabbis

[1] Cited by Conybeare (p. 156, n. 4 above). For the anointing, cf. Jacob at Bethel (Gen. xxviii. 18), the small stone at Gezer (p. 80 above), and the twin bedaubed stones of the Arabs (ghariy; Rel. Sem., pp. 157, 210 n.).

[2] For Esau-Usōos, see p. 109 and Ed. Meyer, Israeliten, p. 278. On Hebrew and Phoenician versions of the drought in Elijah's day see C.A.H., iii. 369. The 'Cainite' antediluvian names in Genesis may have come from the Phoenicians, see Skinner, Genesis, p. 138 n., and cf. below, p. 199. Late tradition seems to have localized the discovery of the vine (i.e. Gen. ix. 20, after the Flood) at Tyre (Baudissin, Adonis, p. 235 n., citing Achilles Tatius). The tradition in Herodotus (ii. 44) that the temple of Herakles-Melkart was founded 2,300 years previously, points to the 28th cent. B.C., which falls between the date of the Flood according to the Hebrew text (2501 B.C.) and that of the other versions (Samaritan, 2936; Septuagint, 3066); see, for the figures, S. R. Driver, Genesis, p. xxviii. The other tradition, which would date the beginning of Phoenician history some 30,000 years previously,

themselves spoke of the 'Noachic commandments' which were binding upon all men; and in the Jewish literature from about 100 B.C. there are traditions of tablets written after the Flood and containing various enactments and lists of festivals.[1] Tablets of this nature could very easily have been illustrated by such stones as the Carthaginian tariffs and lists of sacrifices and religious offerings (*C.I.S.*, i. 165–7): the 'Marseilles' stone, in particular, must have been an especially fine one. Sanchuniathon himself was supposed to have utilized the secret wisdom contained in the *ammouneis* or *ḥammān*-pillars of the Phoenician temples;[2] and, without discussing the genuineness of this sage—who at least bears a good Phoenician name—we may observe that stelae were set up in temples or in sacred areas, and, even if they were not actually inscribed, were often suitably prepared for that purpose.[3]

This being so, it is tempting to recall the Tables of Stone which were placed in the Ark in the Temple of Jerusalem (Exod. xxv. 16, 21; 1 Kings viii. 9). But while the Ark tended to become Yahweh's throne in the city of his choice, elsewhere, as we shall presently see, 'arks' or shrines were wont to be carried about, even as the ark of Israel was once borne by the Levites (especially 2 Chron. xxxv. 3). Moreover, it is a matter of argument whether the 'Tables' in the

approximates the old Akkadian scheme preserved by Berossus (*C.A.H.*, i. 150 sqq., 365). In a word, Phoenician tradition cannot be severed from the biblical narratives, which contain only a part of the lore and history of the Hebrews (cf. p. 199).

[1] Cf. Charles, *Book of Jubilees*, vi. 17 (cf. iii. 10–14), also the two Sethite pillars, Josephus, *Ant.*, I. ii. 3. For antediluvian tablets see *Vita Adae et Evae*, § 50 (lives of Adam and Eve, written to be preserved after the Flood), and the Sippar tablets buried for safety's sake at the Flood (Bousset-Gressmann, *Rel. d. Judentums*, p. 492 sq., with references).

[2] Ed. Meyer, *Ency. Bib.*, col. 3741; Cooke, p. 104, n. 2; Lagrange, p. 399, n. 2; *contra*, G. F. Moore, *Ency. Bib.*, col. 2976 and notes 8, 9. Cf. the inscribed stones mentioned by Pausanias, VIII. xv. 1, xxxvii. 2.

[3] Note the shape of the stelae of Yeḥaw-milk of Byblus, Mesha of Moab, and Seti I at Tell esh-Shihāb; see Thiersch, *Z.D.P.V.*, xxxvii. 65–7, and above, p. 81, n. 4.

Temple were merely sacred stones (e.g. like the Tyrian omphaloi) or were engraved with laws; and, in the latter case, the view has been maintained that they probably contained, not the relatively brief Decalogue, but a series of laws as extensive as those in the 'Book of the Covenant' (Exod. xxi–xxiii).[1] At all events, relations between Tyre and Jerusalem go back to an early period, and Tyre had proud traditions of her own importance. Tyre was a world-city, and there is reason to believe that at Tyre, as at Hieropolis, Jerusalem, and elsewhere, there was believed to be a chasm leading into the bowels of the earth.[2] Hence the *late* Tyrian version of the Flood, older versions of which are lost. And while Tyre was supposed to be founded upon two sacred stones—omphaloi or stelae—the theocracy of Jerusalem could claim to be founded, more metaphorically, upon the two Tables of Stone. In fine, Tyre, like Jerusalem, claimed to be a centre of the earth—hence the omphaloi; and the conjecture that there were stelae or *hammān*-pillars, which were supposed to be inscribed with ritual or other laws, would account for the alternative coin-types, and is confirmed by usage elsewhere.

Another Tyrian type represents a portable shrine with an omphalos-like stone.[3] It is similar to that on coins from Ake-Ptolemais, where the projecting-poles stand out clearly (no. 8), like those of the Ark in the Temple at Jerusalem —a notice that is preserved also in the post-exilic Book of Chronicles (2 Chron. v. 9 = 1 Kings viii. 8). The type, which is of the third century A.D., represents a shrine, with a deity on a base, holding a double axe and the *harpe*.[4] It is the god who otherwise is seen flanked by the fore part of

---

[1] So Eerdmans, *O.T. Essays*, ed. D. C. Simpson (1927), p. 83; while Morgenstern ('The Book of the Covenant', *Hebrew Union College Annual*, v. 68 sq., 119) thinks it was in *scroll* form, and (p. 116 n.) draws attention to the *two* copies of the Koran in the Mohammedan *mahmal* (with which the Ark has points of contact; see further, p. 32 sq.).

[2] The chasm at Hieropolis has perhaps been located (*Syria*, x. 178).

[3] See Cook, *Zeus*, i. 356, fig. 273.

[4] British Museum: *Phoen.*, p. 138, n. 50 (coin of Gallienus).

two bulls (no. 9).[1] This Zeus of the double axe has an ancient ancestry, going back as he does to the Hittite god with the double axe.[2] In his present form, he reminds us of Zeus of Doliche, Jupiter Dolichenus; and the influence of North Syrian and Anatolian religion upon the south illustrates the rival tendency to that exerted by Egypt upon her northern neighbours.

Shrines were carried around on cars. So, e.g., on the coin from Sidon of the time of Elagabalus the baetyl of the solar and mountain god appears to rest upon a draped stand flanked by four small figures (?); it is within a four-columned frame, above which rise two or, in this case, four branches (no. 10).[3] The practice of ceremonially conveying deities or their symbols has already been noticed (p. 32), Philo Byblius speaks of the Phoenician ναὸς ζυγοφρούμενος, a venerated xoanon drawn by oxen; and he explains it as the god Agrouēros or Agrotēs, whom the men of Byblus call the greatest of gods. As this was an agricultural god, it is only natural that his presence and the virtues it distributed should be extended far and wide; and the car on the Sidonian coin seems, by its branches, to refer to some agricultural ritual.[4] Another well-known car was that of Herakles at Philadelphia (Rabbath-Ammon); he had a sacred chariot, with a canopy stretched over four pillars, drawn by four (or two) horses. The Semitic name of the god is not known; but besides the Herakleion there was a cult of a veiled Thea Asteria, some Astarte.[5]

[1] British Museum: p. 135, n. 41; see further, Hill, *Phoen.*, p. lxxxv; Cook, *Zeus*, ii. 553.

[2] See p. 133; and Garstang, *The Hittite Empire*, p. 253, pl. xlv (2).

[3] British Museum: *Phoen.*, p. 186, no. 250. Hill (*Phoen.*, pp. cxiii, cxl sq.) interprets the device as a baetyl placed between the 'horns of consecration' (see also *J.H.S.*, xxxi. 61 sqq.).

[4] Compare also Triptolemus in his car (p. 147). Lagrange (p. 419) identifies Agrouēros with Adonis. For the procession of deities, see Nock, *J.E.A.*, xi. 130 sq. Objects containing deities or their symbols were thought to be self-moving; see Morgenstern (p. 164, n. 1 above), pp. 20 n., 26, 88 sq. [5] See Clermont-Ganneau, *Recueil*, vii. 147 sqq.

The Sidonian goddess herself appears on a contemporary coin in a car (with two branches) between a crescent and a star (no. 11).[1] The surrounding zodiacal signs are not merely an indication of the celestial character of this Astarte. They appear also in Alexandria; and on a coin of Antoninus Pius (A.D. 138–161) the bust of Sarapis is placed within the gods presiding over the days of the week, while outside are the signs of the zodiac (no. 12).[2] In his day the old Sothic cycle of 1460 years was completed, and the turning-point at the commencement of a new cycle would certainly play a large part in the current convictions of the dawn of a new age. At the same time, however, zodiacal ideas, or ideas of a general astral nature, pre-vailed even among the Jews of Palestine (p. 207).[3]

From coins, too, we obtain illustrations of twin pillars such as we may suppose Jachin and Boaz to have been. Sidonian coins of the first century A.D. depict a temple with four columns which support a pediment with scroll ornamentation; in front is an altar between two palm-branches, and on either side of the building is a column (no. 13).[4] The early parallels include pillars at the entrance

[1] British Museum: *Phoen.*, p. 187, no. 260, and Introd., p. cxiii.

[2] British Museum: Poole, *Coins of Alexandria*, p. 126, no. 1079; ib., p. lvii.

[3] Poole, no. 1078, represents two zodiacs outside the busts of Sarapis and Isis. The coincidence indicates that of the civil and Sothic years. In N. Syria astral ideas were spread by 'Chaldaean' priests, devotees of Mithraism, and the cult of Zeus Oromasdes (Hormuzd = Ahura-mazda) in Commagene. Certain Syrian cities were associated with certain signs, under whose auspices they were presumably believed to be founded: Nisibis and Ares, Edessa and Aquarius (also Leo), Singara (also Rhesaina) and Sagittarius, Palmyra and Libra—though Palmy-rene tessarae also have sun, moon, bull, lion, or scorpion (Lidzbarski, *Ephem.*, iii. 154). Note the horoscope of Antiochus I (69–38 B.C.) in Commagene (*Zeus*, i. 750 sqq.). For a bull's head covered with stars, see *Liverpool A.A.A.*, vi. 52, pl. xi, no. 71 (Old Syrian, of the XVIIIth Dynasty?). For the style of the coins (outer rings and central panel), cf. the old Hittite seals, Hogarth, *J.E.A.*, viii. 214, no. 15; 215, no. 16.

[4] British Museum: *Phoen.*, p. 169, no. 165; a coin of 9/8 B.C.—the type ranges from 10/9 B.C. to A.D. 116/17.

to the ancient temple of Byblus (*c.* 1500 B. C.); two stones at the entrance to that at Shechem (Sellin, *Z.D.P.V.*, li. 120); and pairs of stones before the houses at Taanach (Sellin, *Taannek*, p. 104). There were twin-pillars at Hieropolis (Lucian, § 28 sq.); and at the temples of Aphrodite of Paphos.[1] At Sī' in Transjordania there were found before the temple two square structures called 'guards' (*maṭṭe-rāthā*). Hence, although the gilded glass found in a Jewish burial place (3rd–4th cent. A. D.), with its representation of the Temple of Jerusalem and the twin pillars, is too late to be evidence for the days of Solomon's temple, it does at least reflect the vitality of a tradition which late parallels elsewhere served to maintain.[2] Such pillars have been variously explained as cressets or candelabra, as phalli, as cosmic pillars, or as symbols of the mountains between which the sun-god stepped forth (cf. p. 134). Whether they were usually named cannot be said; the custom of naming gates and walls was familiar in Babylonia, but the meaning of the names Jachin and Boaz is still uncertain: perhaps 'establishes' and 'in him (*or* it) is strength'.[3]

Coins of Byblus of the second century B. C. represent a god, nude, with head-dress of feathers (or rather a four-branched ornament); like the seraphim in Isaiah's vision (p. 54) he has three pairs of wings (no. 14).[4] The god is Kronos; he had four eyes, for he watched while sleeping, and slept while watching; and the feathers on his head-dress are explained as symbols of intelligence and feeling. His Semitic

[1] Coins from Cyprus, Sardes, &c., see *Zeus*, ii. 424. Cf. also the clay model of a temple from Idalion, Gressmann, no. 523; Benzinger, *Hebr. Archäol.*, p. 318, fig. 403. For discussions of the Tyrian pillars, see A. B. Cook, *Zeus*, ii. 423 sqq., and Lagrange, *Études*, p. 213. It should be noticed that at Petra the two giant obelisks have no connexion with the 'High Place'. For Edessa, see below, p. 177, n. 6.

[2] Reproduced in *Ency. Bib.*, art. 'Temple', col. 4934; Cook, *Zeus*, ii. 427; Gressmann, no. 504.

[3] See further, *Ency. Bib.*, cols. 2304 sq., 4933.

[4] British Museum: *Phoen.*, p. 98, no. 16; see p. lxiii sq.; also Cooke, p. 350; A. B. Cook, *Zeus*, ii. 552 sqq.; Lagrange, p. 72 (and pp. 104 sqq.).

name is El; and, as the god to whom children were sacrificed, it is little wonder that eventually he was regarded as
the malignant star associated with Nemesis and Saturn.[1]
El-Kronos, whom Greek authors call 'king', appears to
correspond to the old Melek or Milk, the 'king-god'—the
Mōlek, as the Jewish scribes perverted the name, in order
to suggest the idea of a 'shameful thing' (bōsheth). The
Phoenician tradition that Kronos, the founder of Byblus,
killed his only son (ἰεούδ) or his beloved son (ἰεδούδ)
serves to explain and justify a grisly rite; whereas the
Biblical story of Abraham and Isaac permits the obedient
though tortured father to use an animal surrogate. Phoenician and Hebrew religion had much in common—as the
'Marseilles' tariff tablet and other evidence prove[2]—but
it is necessary to observe step by step where usages converge or diverge, and, in this case, to mark the contrast
between the late persistence of human sacrifice among the
Carthaginians and the much earlier narrative in Gen. xxii
which virtually abolishes it.

The Phoenician ceremonial burning of human victims—
cf. the holocausts of *animals* at Hieropolis (Lucian, § 49)—
and the tradition that the Tyrian Herakles-Melkart offered
himself up to be burnt on a pyre, justify a brief reference to
the so-called Pyre of Herakles-Sandon on coins of Tarsus
from the middle of the second century B.C. (no. 15).[3] Upon
a garlanded altar is a triangular structure surmounted by

[1] See F. Ll. Griffith, *P.S.B.A.*, xxii. 162. When Kronos is explained
as the sun, it is possible that his Semitic name El was connected with
Helios (Cumont, *A.f.R.*, xix. 344; Jüthner, *P.W.*, v. 2218). He was
the inventor of the *harpe*, the symbol of royalty, such as was actually
found at Byblus (see above, p. 66); his very name, Kronos, may have
conveyed to the Greeks the idea of a 'chopper' (*Zeus*, ii. 549).

[2] For a general comparison, see esp. R. Dussaud, *Les Origines
Cananéennes du Sacrifice Israélite* (1921).

[3] Fitzwilliam Museum, no. 9344, coin of Antiochus Grypus (range
of type 116–113 B.C.), cf. British Museum, *Lycaonia*, &c., p. lxxxvi.
See Frazer, *Adonis*, i. 111 sqq., 117 sq., and for the type, ib., p. 126,
and Leipoldt, *Urchristentum*, no. 124.

an eagle with outstretched wings; the eagle, though commonly taken to represent the apotheosis of the victim, may be a solar symbol. Within, the god, holding a double axe, stands upon a lion; on either side is a small cone. The usual interpretation of the scene is contested on cogent grounds by Dr. A. B. Cook, who compares the pyramidal plates of Zeus Dolichenus (p. 220 sq.). What we have, then, is the natural symbol of a mountain-god; or, rather, 'like the Babylonian *zikkurat* or "high place", it was the conventionalized form of a mountain' (*Zeus*, i. 603). The conception of the mountain as the abode or, indeed, as the embodiment of the god comes from Babylonia, where the *E-kur*, or divine house, subsequently became the *ekurru* or 'god', and the temple-tower, as a sort of cosmic mount, unites the earth with the realm of the sky.[1] This persistence of the mountain(-god), especially as the link between heaven and earth, has already found one of its latest and most remarkable illustrations in Elagabalus, the man-god of Emesa (p. 159).

The god of Tarsus who is represented on coin no. 15 is of interest, not only as a descendant of an old Hittite Baal, but also for the symbols of fertility (grapes, ears of corn, &c.) with which he is elsewhere accompanied. For though mystical cults, philosophy, and astral speculation are prominent in this age, practical and popular religion demands gods who shall attend to the daily elemental needs of their worshippers; cf. the old Baal of Tarsus at Ivriz (p. 136). Ancient elements survive in the tall head-dress, and in the type (no. 16) where the god, with outstretched hand, an axe in his left, and a bow-case on the shoulder, stands upon a horned and winged lion.[2] Another type from Tarsus (4th cent. B. C.) is of interest on account of the conventional winged disk—if it be that—which somewhat

---

[1] See Lagrange, p. 192 sq., who finds an illustration in the *conical* stele of Naram-Sin ascending the sacred mountain (cf. *C.A.H.*, plates. vol. i. 52*b*). See also above, p. 25 sq.

[2] Fitzwilliam Museum, no. 9111; cf. *Zeus*, i. 599.

z

resembles the enigmatical symbol on Jewish pottery stamps (no. 17).[1]

Of Semitic origin is the Zeus Hagios ('holy') of Tripolis in Phoenicia, whose coins (of the 3rd cent. A. D.) give an excellent idea of the lofty doorways and lattice-work of the Temple (no. 18).[2] The squared-top structure by the side may be a Persian fire-altar. Another type depicts a temple with four pillars or bases (no. 19).[3] The radiate bust of the god in the pediment suggests that he was solar. The figures on either side represent, on the left, the sun, radiate, and on the right, the moon, with crescent on the head, holding a torch across the body. Hence it is not improbable that Zeus Hagios, whose epithet ('holy') points to a Semitic or Oriental god, was above sun and moon, and that he was a Sky-Baal or Baal Shamim (p. 217), just as, on the Jerusalem seal of Menaḥemeth, Ahura-mazda is over the symbols of sun and moon (p. 49). The two recumbent figures, joining hands, on the pediment of no. 18 may represent the Dioscuri, who are to be found elsewhere on coins from Askalon and Aelia Capitolina. Their presence is not altogether unexpected, see p. 222.

New questions arise when we look at the well-known coin of about the fourth century B.C. which bears on the obverse a half-fish figure, and on the reverse the lion on the mountains (nos. 20 and 21).[4] Votive lions have often

---

[1] Fitzwilliam Museum, no. 9097; cf. Cooke, p. 345, *Zeus*, i. 596 (and for the date, ii. 761, n. 4). See above, p. 57, and Pilcher, *P.S.B.A.*, xxxii. 150 sq. The coin represents the satrap Datames (378–372 B.C.), preparing his weapons for the Egyptian campaign. (On the reverse is a representation, by means of projections, of the temple in which he is seated or of the battlements of the city; there is a similar artistic device in Assyria, Gressmann, no. 538.)

[2] British Museum: *Phoen.*, p. 216, no. 79; cf. p. cxxi sq.; *Zeus*, i. 192.

[3] Fitzwilliam Museum, no. 9515, dated A.D. 219/20.

[4] From an electro cast in the British Museum; see Hill, *Phoen.*, p. xxi, pl. xlv, and *J.H.S.*, 1911, p. 63. See, in the first instance, Babelon, *Les Perses Achéménides* (1893), p. 47, who dates the coin to

been found in Phoenicia; and at Halalieh Renan found two with dedications to the mountain Zeus. The combination of the sea-coast (indicated by the fish-figure) and the mountain-land is instructive, and has parallels elsewhere.[1] Thus, behind Aradus (Arvad) at Ḥuṣn Suleiman is the 'holy heavenly' Zeus of Baetocaece, a famous sanctuary with reliefs of a lion, and a lion standing before a cypress— the symbol of the goddess. At Aradus itself not only is there a maritime god, but coins of the third century A. D. place a cypress between a bull and a lion. Near Ḥuṣn Suleiman at Meshta was found a relief on which a lion and bull ready for sacrifice stood before an altar.[2] Again, while Beirut has a Poseidon, behind in the *hinterland* is the sanctuary of Baal Markod (p. 151).

The half-fish figure holds trident and diadem, and the tail ends in a tuft seized by a scorpion. As a whole, it recalls the early coins of Aradus (4th cent. B.C.) where the man holds a wreath and a dolphin (or else a trident), or swings a dolphin in each hand. It is an open question whether he is to be identified as the Baal of Aradus, or more precisely as Dagon. But Dagon is the name of a very ancient deity, by no means confined to the Philistine (or Phoenician) coast; and, on the strength of the Hebrew words *dāg* 'fish', *dāgān* 'corn', we may regard him as primarily a *food*-deity.[3] On the other hand, the fish-*goddess* Atargatis (Derceto) was well known at Hieropolis and at Askalon. At Askalon, it was said, 'Semiramis' had the face of a woman and the body of a fish; and her fish-pond, near the city, corresponds to that of the 'Syrian Goddess', to whom fish and

about 350 B.C., assigning it to Askalon or Ashdod. (The meaning of the letters אן on the reverse is quite uncertain.)

[1] Hill, *Church Quart. Rev.*, lxvi. 133 sqq., *J.H.S.*, xxxi. 57 sqq.

[2] The combination of animals can be illustrated from a coin of Hieropolis (3rd cent. A.D.), where Hadad (Zeus Adados) and the goddess Atargatis are flanked by a bull and lion respectively. See Gressmann, no. 364; *Zeus*, i. 586, fig. 449; Garstang, *Hittite Empire*, fig. 42; cf. Wroth, *Coins of . . . Syria*, p. liii. sq.

[3] *Rel. Sem.*, p. 578.

doves were alike sacred. And while the latter had her ceremonial 'descent' to the sea (Lucian, § 47 sq.), outside Askalon, at the village of Jōra, the vernal procession of the
goddess Atargatis from her temple to the sea, where her
statue received a bath, still survives in a slightly modified
form, and young men and women go down in procession
and bathe together unclad.[1] Unfortunately the excavations of the Palestine Exploration Fund at Askalon, greatly
impeded by the size of the area and the quantity of debris,
brought to light little that bore upon the old cults: Apollo, a
small statuette of a kneeling goddess, an Isis-like Tyche, &c.[2]
On the other hand, at Tell Zakariya was found a bronze of a
female head, with body and tail of a fish, the left arm holding
an animal (? or child), see Plate xxxv. 1.[3] This may well
be Atargatis. Besides a bath of Aphrodite at Accho, known
to the Mishnah (Abodah Zarah, iii. 4), there was possibly a
sacred pool at Memphis at the temple of Aphrodite and the
fish-god Proteus (Herodotus ii. 112).[4] The antiquity of the
conception of a fish-goddess is vouched for by the old
North Syrian seal, representing a nude goddess with fish
attributes (Hogarth, Hittite Seals, no. 170); while undoubtedly the finest illustration of the influence of the cult
is afforded by the discovery, in the excavations at Carthage,

[1] Bulletin of American Schools of Oriental Research, 1921, Sept.: p. 4;
1922, May, p. 16.

[2] Phythian-Adams, Q.S., 1921, pp. 76–90; 1923, pp. 11–36; Garstang,
1924, pp. 24–35 (also Thiersch, M.D.P.V., xxxvii. 67–73). The fine
basilica and the later arcade were perhaps connected with the sacred
lake (Hogarth, Q.S., 1922, p. 106), but of the latter nothing was discovered more topical than a potsherd depicting a fisherman landing a
couple of fish (Q.S., 1921, p. 15)! By the tank outside the middle of
the southern façade of a large temple built in the Roman style was
found a 'Victory' poised upon a globe upheld by Atlas, and on the
other side of the tank was a statue holding a palm-branch, possibly
'Peace'; cf. the Puteus Pacis mentioned by Antoninus Martyr, A. D. 560–
570.

[3] Bliss and Macalister, Excavations in Palestine, p. 148; Vincent,
Canaan, p. 173 sq., Handcock, Archaeology of the Holy Land, p. 200.

[4] Lagrange, p. 131.

at Bord el-Jeded (in 1897), of the anthropoid sarcophagi of a priest and priestess: the latter holds a dove in her left hand, and her body is enfolded by the closed wings of the sacred vulture so as to give the extremity of the body the appearance of a fish's tail.[1]

A goddess of Askalon appears in coins of the second century A.D., draped, dove in her right hand, sceptre in left, crescent on head; she is standing on a triton (no. 22).[2] The dove is commonly found with representations of the city-goddess or Tyche; and among the images forbidden by the Mishnah tractate against Idolatry are those which hold in their hand a bird, a staff, or an orb.[3] There were, in fact, two Askalonite goddesses, for a native dedicates an altar at Delos to Zeus, Astarte of Palestine, and Aphrodite Urania.[4] The latter of these goddesses possessed the most ancient of temples (Herodotus i. 105), and, as sky goddess, associates herself with a goddess of the Anath-type (cf. p. 104 sq.),[5] rather than with Astarte or with the Atargatis who replaced her. At Ashteroth Karnaim there was also an Atargateion (2 Macc. xii. 26), and it was possibly round about 400 B.C. that this Syrian goddess made her way into Transjordania and South Palestine.[6]

Maritime rites and maritime deities are not un-Semitic. At Tyre there was a ritual 'descent' to the sea. At the small seaport of Dor-Tantureh there has been found a

---

[1] See Mabel Moore, *Carthage of the Phoenicians* (1905), p. 147; frontispiece and plate facing p. 146.

[2] Fitzwilliam Museum, no. 9545; coin of A.D. 156/7; cf. British Museum, *Palestine*, pp. lviii sq. and 130.

[3] *Abodah Zarah*, iii.

[4] R. A. S. Macalister, *Schweich Lectures*, p. 94 (with references).

[5] The temple may be seen on the type which (after de Saulcy) was wrongly supposed to represent Derceto's fishpond. (Thiersch, *Z.D.P.V.*, xxxvii. 73, Hill, *Pal.*, p. lxi and pl. xiv. 9.)

[6] A very crude bas-relief from Askalon of three nude females, the middle one wearing the Egyptian Hathor headdress, is of the early Christian period, and may—Gressmann suggests—represent different phases of the native Astarte (Gressmann, no. 618).

deep deposit of fish-scales and sea-shells by the side of what seems to have been a temple to a deity probably of the Poseidon type.[1] At Tripolis there was a maritime city-goddess, and Beirut was the scene of the legend of Poseidon and the nymph Beroë (Beirut).[2] Upon a coin of Beirut of A.D. 240 the local goddess is represented by a richly-draped bust of an Astarte, whose head-dress appears to be turreted (no. 23).[3] With her is associated a lion, and on a Sidonian coin Astarte is seen riding upon the animal; it is perhaps the symbol of the god of Heliopolis who was venerated at Beirut. River-gods appear on the coins of Eleutheropolis, Ptolemais-Ake, Tyre, Aradus, Orthosia, and Caesarea Arca ad Libanum. On the coins of Nysa-Scythopolis the river-god is presumably a reference to the Jordan.[4] Whether the river-god appears on coins of Aelia Capitolina is very uncertain.[5] At all events, in the triumphal procession on the Arch of Titus, three Romans may be seen carrying an aged figure leaning on an over-turned urn.[6] But S. Reinach explains it as a symbol of

[1] *Bulletin* of the British School of Archaeology in Jerusalem, vi (1924), 67.

[2] *Abodah Zarah*, iii. 3, condemns utensils with representations of Sun and Moon and Dragon or Serpent (*darkōn*). By the last some well-known sea-monster may have been meant, and Elmslie thinks of the one at Joppa (the legend of Perseus). For the legend of Beroë see Lagrange, pp. 422, 427 (on the name, p. 177); Hill, *Church Quart. Rev.*, lxvi. 137 sq.; *Zeus*, ii. 886.

[3] Fitzwilliam Museum, no. 9471; cf. British Museum, *Phoen.*, p. lviii sq. (see ib., pl. xxv, no. 8, for the Sidonian coin).

[4] Hill, *Palestine*, p. xxxvi, pl. xl, no. 4; for the river-god Belos at Ptolemais and the maritime deities at Tyre, see *Phoen.*, pp. lxxxiii, cxlii.

[5] See no. 37. See Madden, *History of Jewish Coinage* (1864), p. 217; *Coins of the Jews*, p. 255, no. 14. De Saulcy (*Numism. de la Terre Sainte* [1881], p. 89, no. 14) describes the object on the coins as 'un fleuve vu a mi-corps'; Madden in the former work suggests with a query that it is a helmet. May it be an inverted urn? See p. 191.

[6] Hunkin, *Schweich Lectures*, p. 84, pl. xii, fig. 34; see Montfaucon, *Antiquity Explained* (Eng. by Humphreys), iv. 102, pl. xxxiii; and for the description, S. Reinach, *R.E.J.*, xx (1890), p. lxxx.

Palestine, just as the Rhine and Rhone typified the conquered Gaul at the first triumph of Caesar, while at his
second triumph the conquest of Egypt was typified by the
Nile. It is far from certain, therefore, that we have archaeological evidence for any *cult* of the river Jordan. On the
other hand, a mosaic of about the third century A.D. at
el-Mas'udīyeh on the Euphrates personifies the river as a
bearded man seated between two females (Syria and Mesopotamia), the one with sceptre and turreted crown, the
other with a cornucopia. A Greek and a (vertically
written) Syriac text designates him 'king Euphrates'.[1]
The river is otherwise personified as a young child on a
wall-painting of Dura (p. 217 n.).[2] It is true that Jerusalem
seems to have claimed a mystic stream (p. 34 above); but
it is disputed whether any definite cult of the Jordan can
be deduced from the prominence of the river in the late
cosmogony of the Mandaeans, to whom every stream of
running water was a Jordan, and who, by reason of their
habitation in South Babylonia, would hardly have made so
much of the distant Jordan unless—so it can be urged—
the sect arose in the neighbourhood of that river.[3]

One of the most instructive examples of early antiquarianism is afforded by the reverse of the Sidonian coin
already referred to (no. 13). It depicts Europa as the bull,
with raised veil (no. 24). The type, which begins *c.* 174 B.C.,
shows that Astarte has been fused with Europa, and partly
influenced by Selene. The Pseudo-Lucian relates that
Zeus as a bull carried Europa to Crete; but Zeus Asterios
the white bull-god of Cortyna was the male counterpart of
Astarte, and consequently the design could be interpreted
as the astral or rather the solar god carrying off the moon.[4]

---

[1] See, on the cult of the Euphrates, Cumont, *Études*, pp. 247 sqq.

[2] Cumont, *Fouilles de Doura-Europos*, 1922–3 (1926), pp. 66 sq., 120,
and pl. liv.

[3] For a recent argument in favour of a Jordan cult, see Kraeling,
J.A.O.S., xlix. 206, 212.

[4] Lucian, § 4; see *Zeus*, i. 538 sq.; cf. the late story of the rape of

The Semitic equivalent of Europa can only be guessed: it was perhaps the feminine of El, viz. Elat, or Allath.[1] The type itself has obvious Oriental associations: the inflated veil reminds us of the uncovering-*motif* on old Syro-Hittite seals, where the goddess is especially associated with the bull, i.e. Teshub, or some other god of Hadad type. Of such seals one comes from Hauran.[2] Accordingly, the Phoenician story is concerned to tell, *not* how Europa ever came to Phoenicia, but how this evidently Phoenician goddess found herself in Crete.[3] Indeed, we may go further and observe that the fusion which we postulate would be facilitated, by the superficial resemblance between (1) Europa as a goddess of willows (A. B. Cook, *Zeus*, i. 531, and n. 3) and the Hebrew *ʿarābīm* 'willows' (rather, 'poplars'); and (2) the coins where Europa sits pensively in her willow tree (*Zeus*, i. 528) and the conception of the virgin daughter of Zion under the willows by the waters of Babylon (Ps. cxxxvii. 2). As will be seen when we come to Marnas of Gaza, there were repeated traditions associating Crete and the Phoenician coastlands. But while the cultural interrelations are, in point of fact, of great antiquity, the extant traditions are in a very late form, and it is the work of criticism to disentangle the old elements from the later accretions.[4] It was as easy then as it is now

Britomartis (or Diktynna) by Minos (see A. B. Cook's criticisms, *Zeus*, i. 524, 541 sq.).

[1] Lagrange, p. 73, after Bérard, *Cultes Arcadiens*, p. 123; Cooke, p. 158 n.; *Zeus*, i. 525.

[2] Ward, *Seals*, pp. 296 sqq., esp. no. 914; see also *Zeus*, i. 526, n. 2; Contenau, *Glyptique Syro-Hittite*, p. 41.

[3] So also, if Aphrodite comes to Crete from over the sea, viz. Askalon, 'this Philistine city owed much of its culture to Crete and may have brought its goddess thence' (Farnell, *Aegean Arch.*, *Essays to Sir Arthur Evans*, p. 17).

[4] Baudissin (*Z.D.M.G.*, lxvi [1912], 171–188: on Tammuz at Harran) comments on the zealous but extremely uncritical antiquarianism of very late writers, and the blend of old material with much that is of quite late invention. The vicissitudes of the stories of Tammuz can be

to indulge in rash comparisons; and sometimes there is very little to choose between the etymologies of ancient writers and those of to-day.[1]

The Semitic god behind Herakles of Ammān is unknown (p. 165). As for Moab, a native deity no doubt reappears in a Greek form in the warrior-god on coins of Rabbah (A.D. 193–211). He stands upon a base, with helmet, cuirass, and boots, a sword is in the right hand, and in the left a spear and a round shield; on either side is an altar with a flame, not an ordinary incense-altar (no. 25).[2] Semitic gods were often represented in Greek dress;[3] and if we may assume that this is a descendant of Chemosh and akin to the great Transjordanian Dushara, the Jews at all events were able to confuse these two deities.[4] Now Rabbah of Moab was called in Greek Areopolis; and although this may be due to a misunderstanding of the old 'city of Ar' (Is. xv. 1), the city may also have been the seat of the cult of Ares, who was god of war, but also a vegetable god, and not narrowly confined in his functions.[5] At Edessa Ares and Hermes formed a pair, and they were identified with the Semitic Azizos and Monimos, the 'strong' and the 'benevolent'.[6] As Aziz is *Deus bonus puer phosphorus* in Latin inscrip-

followed step by step, and they illustrate the processes that could and did happen at those much earlier stages where we have little evidence wherewith to check them.

[1] e.g. Mt. Tabor and Zeus Atabyrios, Hermon and Hermes, Cassiopeia as 'throne of beauty', cf. also the ancient etymology of Atargatis cited by Macalister, *Schweich Lect.*, p. 97.

[2] British Museum: *Arabia*, p. 44, no. 2 (p. 44, no. 1, pl. vii. 1, is a 'horned altar', as on the coin from Petra, p. 36, pl. v. 14).

[3] e.g. Aesculapius (Baudissin, *Adonis*, p. 299, Taf. ix (from Hauran, Gaulanitis and Gadara). There are notable examples at Dura, see below, p. 224.

[4] G. F. Moore, *Ency. Bib.*, col. 738, n. 1.

[5] cf. Schwenn, *A.f.R.*, xxii. 224 sq.

[6] Lagrange, pp. 135, 210; *Zeus*, i. 706 n., ii. 428; Dussaud, *Mythol. Syr.*, pp. 9 sqq.; Nielsen, *Der dreieinige Gott*, pp. 122, 233, and *Handbuch*, p. 229 sq. The two great pillars at Edessa can hardly be connected with any pair of gods, still less with the cult of the Twins; it is not even

tions it is argued that he was the morning star, and consequently his associate could be the evening star. In a Palmyrene inscription Azziz and Arṣu (? = 'gracious') are associated as 'good and rewarding gods'; and in Arabia we find the corresponding feminine forms Uzza and Ruḍa.[1] While, on the one hand, the name Arṣu may conceivably be identified with the god *A'ra* whom we find joined to Dushara, the name *A'ra* certainly recalls that of Ares who, however, is already identified with Az(z)iz.[2] Hence it is possible that there has been—besides the change of sex—some duplication of a single deity.[3]

We have another youthful and warlike deity in Phanebal of Askalon, on coins of A.D. 132–159 (nos. 26–28).[4] He stands erect, with Phrygian cap, pointed chin and beard, his right hand is raised and seems to hold a *harpe*, in his left are a shield and palm-branch.[5] The attitude reminds us of Resheph. But it is noteworthy that the types differ somewhat, and the body is found clothed in a long chiton, and the figure might be that of a female. Such variation of sex is, however, not surprising; e.g. although Tyche or Fortune is commonly feminine, it once appears as a male

quite certain (as Prof. Burkitt points out, in a private communication) that they are a pair, they may be merely two survivors (see id., *P.S.B.A.*, 1906, pp. 149–55).

[1] They also appear, one on a dromedary, the other on horseback, see further, Cumont, *Syria*, x. 31 sqq. (with refs.).

[2] Dushara-A'ra are united in a Nabataean inscription of A.D. 147 (*Ephem.* ii. 262); and Suidas evidently identified Theusares (i.e. Dusares) with Ares. The meaning of A'ra, however, is very uncertain, see Cooke, pp. 238 sq., 295, n. 1; *Rel. Sem.*, p. 603 sq.

[3] See *Zeus*, ii. 430. Burrows, *J.R.A.S.*, 1927, p. 319, suggests that Pax Virtus on the Carvoran inscription represents the morning star Azizos and the evening star Monimos as aspects of Virgo, i.e. the Syrian Goddess (Atargatis).

[4] British Museum: *Palestine*, p. 129, no. 188, p. 133, no. 216, p. 134, no. 225. See Hill, p. lix sq.

[5] On a coin of A.D. 219 there is a thunderbolt in the field (*Palest.*, pl. xiv. 13); and on a coin of Hadrian the sign of Tanith (p. 47 above) seems to occur (ib., pl. xiii. 18).

with the mural crown usually worn by goddesses.[1] Indeed, the title 'face of Baal' is the common epithet of the Phoenician goddess Tanith, and the 'face' or manifestation of a deity (see Exod. xxxiii. 14) need not, as such, be regarded from the point of view of sex.[2] In any event Phanebal is a youthful deity, and the points of contact with Resheph, later identified with Apollo, are strengthened by the traces of the Apollo cult, not only at Askalon itself,[3] but also at Apollonia-Arsuf (p. 113), Pelusium (p. 157), Gaza (p. 181), and among a Sidonian colony at Marissa-Eleutheropolis (p. 203). Now Apollo is found hailed as 'foremost angel of great Zeus Iao' (cf. p. 147), and the identification of Zeus and Yahu (Yahweh) goes back at least to the fourth century B.C. Moreover, since Baal would be an obvious name for a great Semitic god, whether a Yahweh or a Zeus, the 'face of Baal' (Phanebal) is an appropriate name for his

---

[1] Dussaud, *Syria*, v. 50 sqq., pl. xx, fig. 2 (Ghariyeh-Shubeih, south of Jebel ed-Druz): probably Dushara. Gad ('luck'), too, is male.

[2] Cf. Kadesh the 'eye' of Re (p. 106) and Astarte the 'name of Baal'. The latter (שמבעל, see Cooke, p. 37) is interpreted by Ed. Meyer (*Ency. Bib.*, col. 3745), Baudissin (*Kyrios*, iii. 4 n.), and others, as 'heaven of B.'; the ordinary view, however, involves no 'mystic doctrine of theology' (Meyer) and is in accord with ideas of the 'name'. As for the title 'face of Baal', W. R. Smith (*Rel. Sem.*, p. 478) held that Tanith had Baal's face, i.e. was bearded; certainly in *C.I.S.*, i. 401 sq. we read of 'lord (אדן) Tanith'. Others compare the place-names Phanouēl, Penuel and Theouprosopon (Baudissin, *Adonis*, p. 23 n.). But Penuel, like the Phoen. male name פנסמלת (as though 'face of the image'), finds a parallel in Babylonian compounds of Panu- in the Persian period (L. W. King, cited by G. F. Hill, *Proc. of the British Academy*, v. 421 n.), and the name Ea-ṣalam-ili(ilani) styles Ea the 'image of the god(s)' (Hehn, p. 114). Tammuz is called Ea's image. Salambo (צלמבעל), 'image of Baal', is identified with Aphrodite by Hesychius (see Cooke, p. 106), but may rather have been male: Adonis (*Rel. Sem.*, p. 412 n.) or Melḳart (Hoffmann, *Z.A.*, xi. 244). Salambo was venerated at Seville at least up to A.D. 287 (Cumont, *Syria*, vii. 330 sqq.).

[3] Herod was said to be descended from a hierodule of Apollo in the temple of Askalon (Julius Africanus, Schürer, i [1901], 292 n.). For Apollo on coins of Raphia see Hill, *Pal.*, p. lxxxiii.

representative or messenger.[1] Beyond this we can scarcely
go. Nothing is known of the temple of Ṣeriphā mentioned
in Abōdāh Zārah: it was possibly that of Sarapis. Later
coins depict a figure riding upon a lion: this may be
'Asklepios *leontouchos*' (the lion-borne), that is, the young
Eshmun of Askalon.[2]

Gaza, the famous city of pagan culture, so long the
stronghold against Christianity, has some especially interesting coins. Most noteworthy of all are those of the god
Marna(s). The type, ranging from A.D. 130 to 240, is inscribed *Gaza Marnas* and shows an Apolline figure, nude,
with a bow in the left hand, facing Artemis (no. 29).[3]
The Marneion, the destruction of which in A.D. 401, with
seven other temples, was a turning-point in the history of
Christianity, was round, like the temple at Harran, and with
a sort of dome and a double cloister it may have resembled
the Dome of the Rock.[4] Some resemblance to a Cretan
labyrinth has also been suggested.[5] The most sacred part
of the Marneion might not be entered by women, and it
retained its sanctity even when the Christians replaced

---

[1] Yahweh is represented by his 'presence' (*pānīm*) in Exod. xxxiii. 14,
or by his 'messenger' or 'angel' (*mal'āk*) in the similar passage, Exod.
xxiii. 20 (cf. Malakbel, p. 219 and n. 5 below).

[2] See Baudissin, *Adonis*, p. 221. Phythian-Adams, *Q.S.*, 1921, p. 82,
suggests that Phanebal was a fusion of Baal, Sarapis, and Eshmun; see
also Dussaud, *Myth. Syr.*, p. 77.

[3] British Museum: *Palestine*, p. 146, no. 17 (reverse of a coin of
Hadrian, A. D. 133/4). In the latest coin (p. 168, no. 147) Marnas, nude,
holding a thunderbolt, is crowned by Nikē. See Hill, pp. lxxi sq., lxxv
sq., and *Proc. of British Academy*, v. 424 sqq., also *Mark the Deacon's Life of
Porphyry* (1913); R. A. S. Macalister, *Schweich Lectures*, pp. 106 sqq.;
M. A. Meyer, *Gaza* (New York, 1907), pp. 63 sqq., 158; and on Gaza
in general, Bouchier, *Syria as a Roman Province*, pp. 240 sqq.

[4] See Hill, *Proc. of British Academy*, v. 425 n.; also Conder, *Q.S.*, 1880,
p. 8; Macalister, p. 111; and cf. K. A. C. Cresswell, *Origin of the Plan of
the Dome of the Rock*, p. 19 n. Madden, *Coins of the Jews*, p. 137 (2),
recognizes the Marneion upon a coin of Herod Agrippa I. The round
churches of medieval Europe are derived from this type.

[5] A. B. Cook, *Zeus*, i. 478.

it by a cruciform church. Besides the Marneion there were temples of (1) Sun, (2) 'Aphrodite Venus'—on the 'day of Roses' Aphrodite and Adonis were celebrated; the cult was Christianized by the bishop Marcianus. There was also (3) a temple of Apollo large enough to hold 500 people (Josephus, *Ant.* XIII. xiii. 3). (4) The temple of the Maiden (Korē, Proserpina) was perhaps that of the consort of Marnas (Hill, p. xxxi). In (5) the temple of Hecate, we may perhaps recognize the cult of Allath. (6) The so-called Hiereion or Sacerdotum was presumably a 'Heraion' dedicated to Hera. Finally (7) the 'Fortuna civitatis' would be a Tycheion.

Gaza was celebrated for its fair (Maiuma) and games.[1] Outside Gaza was the mound Aldioma, from which stones were taken to pave the Christian church.[2] If this is the Zeus Aldēmios or Aldos of Gaza, referred to by Methodius, some would identify with him the fine statue found south of Gaza, at Tell Ajūl.[3] It has not attracted the attention it merits, and it is better interpreted as a Zeus-Sarapis, or rather Sarapis.[4] Marnas was god of growth and fertility, a 'dominus imbrium'; and when in Porphyry's day (A. D. 395)

[1] There was also a Maiuma at Askalon, Accho, Antioch, and one beyond the Jordan near the old Baal-Peor (p. 208 sq.). See Elmslie, p. 33 (the fair at Gaza forbidden to Jews); Roscher, 'Maiumas'; Bouchier, pp. 70, 83; Cumont, *Syria*, v. 355 sq. (with citation from Chrysostom on Matt. vii. 6 [Migne, lvii. 79], on the rites of bathing, &c.); M. Meyer, pp. 120, 124.

[2] See *Zeus*, ii. 675, 1187. The usual view—apart from the conjecture Maioumas—is that of the *Etymologicum Magnum*, 'lord of duration', a title corresponding to the Palmyrene 'lord of eternity' (see p. 216), but with the Hebrew *ḥeled (ḥald)*, on which see S. R. Driver on Job xi. 17.

[3] See C. R. Conder, *Q.S.*, 1880, p. 7 sq., 1882, p. 147 sq.; M. Meyer, *Gaza*, p. 152 sq. Of neighbouring sacred sites Sheikh Hasan is in the north-west, and to the south-east is the shrine of Ali Muntar (*Q.S.*, 1918, pp. 75, 82 sq., M. Meyer, p. 110 [who naturally rejects the suggested connexion with the Minotaur]).

[4] See Vincent, *Rev. Bib.*, 1920, p. 173 sq. (good illustration), who suggests that there was a Sarapaeum founded between 260 and 255 B.C.

there was a drought the Christian prayers alone brought rain, and 'Christ conquered'.[1] Human sacrifices were also offered to him.[2] As regards his identity, the old god Dagon who was venerated at Ashdod (1 Macc. x. 83 sq.) and other Philistine cities naturally suggests itself. On the other hand, Marnas was identified with Cretan Zeus.[3] In fact, Gaza more than any other city was traditionally connected with Crete, and the trading and other relations were undoubtedly of great antiquity. Minoa, it was said, was the old name of Gaza, and the fact that 'Minaean' traders from South Arabia used the port would facilitate appropriate traditions and etymologies, as early as the days of the 'Cherethites' (Cretans), if not earlier.[4]

On some coins of Gaza, from A.D. 131, the city Tyche has by her side, either a bull, cow, or heifer, or, otherwise, the moon-goddess and her name Io. Gaza, it was said, was called Iōnē because Io settled there (Stephanus Byz.), and the sea from Gaza to Egypt was called Ionian. Now to the Semites of Gaza the animal would suggest a Baal, and with the *name* Io they could readily associate Iao or Yo.[5] Here indeed was room for speculation and confusion, and Greek writers went further, and connected Gaza with Azōn, son of Herakles, who left his 'treasure' (*gaza*) there! Some of the coins of Gaza actually give the head and club of this god (Meyer, p. 122). In an age when Osiris could be eruditely explained as ὅσιος+ἱερος, it is not surprising that popular opinion was not less unrestrained. To the Semite Marna(s) would undoubtedly suggest the meaning

[1] See M. A. Meyer, p. 63.

[2] Cf. the citations from Mark the Deacon in Macalister, *Schweich Lectures*, p. 109 sq.

[3] Hill, p. lxxi sq., Cook, *Zeus*, i. 149, n. 1 (n. 2, the triad Hestia, Zeus Kretogenēs, and Hera are adjured in an oath, see p. 144 n. 4).

[4] Minos is named on Gaza coins of A.D. 131/2. On the Cretan associations see Bethe, *Rhein. Mus.*, lxv. 204 sq. Greek influence can be seen on South Arabian coins of about the second cent. B.C.

[5] See *Zeus*, i. 236, and note the view that Yahweh (Yao) was a moon-god (p. 141).

'Our Lord'.[1] Yet, on the other hand, Marnas might well have been a Cretan god. Near by, at Raphia, Dionysus was worshipped as Eiraphiōtēs, and a Semitic equivalent can with difficulty be found. In fact, Marnan(s) was said to be a Cretan word for young women. Thus the question arises whether this explanation is to be taken seriously, or whether it is a bit of late etymologizing, like 'baetyl' (βαίτυλος) from the Cretan baitē, 'goat (skin)'.[2] In view of the 'face of Baal' at Askalon the question of the primary meaning of the god is of no slight importance.

The name is not confined to Gaza. There was a Marneion at Ostia, due to men from Gaza, and perhaps also at the Portus Trajanus, where men of Gaza at the command of the 'national god' erected a statue to Gordianus III.[3] But if Marnas be purely Cretan, it is surely remarkable that it should be met with in Transjordania in a Greek dedication: Διὶ Μάρνᾳ τῷ Κυρίῳ (Waddington, iii. 2412 g). Passing over the river Marnas at Ephesus, we may note the Cypriote name 'servant of Marni', and the more remarkable Marna-yau (or the like) on one of the Samarian ostraca (9th cent.).[4] It is probable enough that the Phoenician m on some coins from Gaza (and also on the back of a weight) is rightly explained as standing for Marnas.[5] The sign is

---

[1] The shorter form (mar-nā—contrast, e.g., Maranatha—is in accordance with a tendency found also in Babylonian-Aramaic (C. Levias, *Aramaic of the Bab. Talmud*, §§ 107, 112).

[2] For *Marnan*, see Stephanus Byz., cited in *Zeus*, i. 149 n.; and for the Cretan *baitē*, G. F. Moore, *Ency. Bib.*, col. 2977, n. 16. Epiphanius speaks of Μαρνᾶς δοῦλος Ἀστερίου τοῦ Κρητὸς παρὰ Γαζαίοις (Asterios is Cretan Zeus). Hill, *Proc. of Brit. Acad.*, v. 415, thinks the Aramaic appearance of the name fortuitous, and identifies Artemis with the Cretan Britomartis. (Ib., p. 415, Raphia is connected by Greek etymologists with ῥαφή, 'seam', and the story of Dionysus sewn up in the thigh of Zeus: a good example of ancient erudition not to be taken seriously.) [3] Meyer, p. 148.

[4] See (1) *C.I.S.*, i. 16 (מרני[ד]ר[עב]), and (2) Baudissin, *Kyrios*, ii. 37 sq. (מרניו): 'our lord is Yau'.

[5] Damascius, cited by Hill, p. lxxi. On an alternative view it is a

of some antiquity, to judge from the *m* (repeated) on an object from the Philistine district.[1] Again, it is possible to suppose that the name is Egyptian or Assyrian.[2] But it is most naturally treated as some part of the word *Mār*, 'lord', which, familiar as a title, occurs in proper names on seals and other objects from about the sixth century B. C. onwards.[3] Like κύριος, the title is applied to a king, governor, procurator, &c.; but while a king might be considered divine, the title *mār* is not usually applied to a god: note, for example, Dushara as 'the god of our lord' (i.e. the king).[4]

In any case, a divine name with a suffix, like the Hebrew *Adōnāy* (properly 'my lord'), does not stand alone.[5]

quasi-swastika, see *Zeus*, i. 478, and cf. Dowling, *Q.S.*, 1912, p. 100. The swastika is found at Gezer (ii. 191, accidental?), and Beit Jibrin, see Bliss-Macalister, p. 225 (cf. p. 264).

[1] Torrey, *Annual of American Schools*, ii. 106 (a winged genius holds a horned animal with one arm, in the other is a three-branched flower; Assyrian style).

[2] e.g., Ramses II refers to the 'chiefs' (*m–r*) of the peasantry (Breasted, *Anc. Records*, iii, § 322). On the other hand, in Assyrian *māru* means 'son', and Clay (*Empire of the Amorites*, p. 69) cites compound names, e.g. Mar-sham-si.

[3] מרסמך (above, p. 56 sq.); מרברך (*C.I.S.*, ii. 85); מריחי (*C.I.S.*, i. 60); מראהד (*C.I.S.*, ii. 79, cf. the seal with Assyrian and Egyptian elements, *Z.D.P.V.*, xxxvii. 178 sq., מרחד), and perhaps the name on a Jerusalem tomb (*Eph.*, i. 187, 312, 351); also a Palmyrene tessara, 'to my lord (מרי) Bel' (Euting, *Florilegium De Vogüé*, p. 238), and the dedication to Θεῷ Βεελμαρι on a lamp from Tyre (*Rev. Arch.*, xxix. 267), and Μαρηαβδηνου (מריהב) at Askalon (Meyer, p. 145).

[4] Cf. in Palmyrene, the 'god' Hadrian, the 'god' Alexander Caesar, (Cooke, nos. 121 sq.); and in Nabataean, the 'god' Obedath of Petra (Cooke, no. 95). On the other hand there are important exceptions in note 3 above.

[5] Zimmern (*Haupt Commemoration Volume*, pp. 282 sqq.) cites as proper names Da-mu-mi ('my D.'), Bēlti[n] ('my [our] B.'). Jensen (*S.B.*, Berlin, 1919, p. 1049) cites מרתן as the title of Asshur's spouse Sheru'a in an Aramaic text of the Seleucid period. That the βαλανίου of Heliopolis is derived from a ba'alan, 'our Baal', is very doubtful. Rendel Harris (*Z.N.T.W.*, 1914, p. 105 sq.) explains the name Marinus among the priests of Doliche as 'our lord', and cites the mocking title Marin ('our

Moreover, in a Phoenician inscription from Ur (*c.* 700 B.C.) we read of the handmaid of 'our lord'—the title is used absolutely, while in another, a late one from the temple area of Byblus, there is a dedication 'to our lord and to the image-of-Baal'.[1] If, as seems highly probable, the 'image-of-Baal' here refers to some deity, it is improbable that 'our lord' refers to the reigning emperor (Augustus). Either the emperor is mentioned before the deity, and this seems unlikely, or 'our lord' stands for another deity, in which case the combination finds what is surely a striking parallel in the existence, down in the south of Palestine, of a Marna ('our lord') and a Phanebal (the 'presence of Baal').

The district of Gaza was one of mixed dialects.[2] Greek was in use as well as 'the language of the Syrians', though not everybody could speak it; and among the personal names several are, as is to be anticipated, of distinctly Semitic type.[3] Hence, if Marna(s) were primarily a purely Cretan god, the name of this the most important deity of Gaza would have had no meaning for the people; though they could easily have given it a very natural Jewish-Aramaic interpretation. On the other hand, if it were primarily a Semitic name, this would not exclude a 'Cretan' etymology, for which, by the way, our sole authority is Stephen of Byzantium, i.e. the sixth century A. D. No doubt, in practice, Greeks and Semites often found common ground, even as the Jews were ready to associate Sabazios and Sabaoth. It is on much the same principle

lord') which the Alexandrian mob bestowed upon Carabas (Philo, *In Flaccum*); cf. Baudissin, *Kyrios*, iii, 59 n., iv. 28, 195 sq., and (on Marna in general) ii. 38 sqq.

[1] *Syria*, vi. 269 sqq., *O.L.Z.*, 1927, col. 457 sq. (the term is אדן).

[2] Cf. Ashdod, Neh. xiii. 24, the Aramaic Atargatis at Askalon, Aramaisms in Phoenicia (*Eph.*, iii. 53, n. 1); and, for the persistence of Aramaic, see Nöldeke, *Z.D.M.G.*, xxxix. 333.

[3] Hill, *Life of Porphyry*, §§ 66, 68. Among the personal names are the bishop Natiras (Meyer, p. 70, n. 50), a deacon Barochas, there is also a maid Salephtha (?) or Irene.

that the Septuagint sometimes translates by a Greek word that more or less closely resembles the Hebrew.[1] If, then, we may with some confidence explain Marna(s) as 'our lord', and as a parallel to the Jewish Adōnāy, it is not difficult to imagine how the very name would feed the fanaticism of Gaza, whether it was directed against the Jews—who did not forget how Hadrian sold so many of them to the men of the city in A.D. 119—or against the progress of Christianity and its *Kyrios*. And so the god of Gaza held his ground, and in the days of Hilarion when the Christian in the chariot race beat his pagan rival it was taken as an omen: *Marnas victus a Christo est.*[2]

The coins of Marnas at Gaza thus recall that much earlier coin, commonly supposed to be of Gaza, where a Zeus-Triptolemus is, as the Aramaic lettering indicates, no other than the Hebrew Yahu (nos. 30, 31).[3] Indeed Yaho (Yo) would be easily connected with Io, and between Io and Triptolemus there are other points of contact. How Yahweh and Zeus could be associated, if not identified, is known from other sources. As the writer of the Letter of Aristeas says (§ 15), Greeks and Jews worship the same God, the Lord and Creator of the Universe, as all other men, 'though we call him by different names, such as Zeus or Dis'. The 'Most High God' (Zeus Hypsistos) was invoked by Greeks and Jews, and later by Christians;[4] and the common recognition of one and the same name broke down religious differences, but at the cost of destroying the distinctiveness of each god to whom the title was applied.

There were Jews in Palestine who watched with jealous

---

[1] See Driver on 1 Sam. v. 4. It is interesting to see how Joh. Lydus (*De Mens.*, iv. 53) even explained the Jewish Sabaoth as ὁ ὑπὲρ τοὺς ἑπτὰ πόλους, connecting the word with the Hebrew 'seven' (see Cumont, *A.f.R.*, ix. 334).   [2] Meyer, p. 61.

[3] British Museum: *Palestine*, p. 181, no. 29; see above, p. 147 and Plate xxxii.

[4] See *Zeus*, ii. 885 sqq., and 888 n. 32 ; Baudissin, *Kyrios*, iii. 83.

eye a universalizing process which weakened the preroga-
tives of their Yahweh. Their Samaritan neighbours, closer
to Syria and Phoenicia, were never so exclusive as the
orthodox Jews of Jerusalem. Their coins, too, present
some interesting features, and to those of Samaria and
Jerusalem we now come.

The Baal of Baalbek, Zeus of Heliopolis (p. 219), appears
on coins of Neapolis (from A.D. 158), as also at Nicopolis
(Emmaus) and Eleutheropolis.[1]

The goddesses are noteworthy. One, standing on a
running lion, recalls the Syrian goddess Atargatis, who is
also shown seated between two lions. A veiled mummy-
shaped goddess with plumed head-dress and a structure resembling a temple-façade appears on coins of Neapolis
from A.D. 158/9 (no. 32).[2] Her hands rest on supports
flanked by stags and topped by birds which, if doves—as is
probable—give this, the ordinary Ephesian Artemis, the
attribute of a goddess of the Astarte-Aphrodite type. Her
sheath-like form, with its panels, recalls the Heliopolitan
Zeus, and it is possible that she is his consort, even as Hera
(accompanied by Athene) on other coins will be the consort of Zeus Hypsistos whose cult Hadrian established
on Mount Gerizim.[3] This Zeus was appropriately explained, according to Damascius, as the god of Abraham,
though on another view the cult introduced was that of
Zeus Sarapis.[4]

At Shechem was the cult of the Heavenly Virgin Korē,

---

[1] *Zeus*, i. 572, 590. The type 'may have been prompted by the
erection of the great temple of this god at Heliopolis by Antoninus
Pius' (Hill, *Palestine*, p. xxxi sq.).

[2] British Museum: *Palestine*, p. 54, no. 61; see *Zeus*, ii, fig. 312, and
on the complicated symbolism, ib., p. 408 sq. The sheath bears a
certain resemblance to old forms at Susa (Vincent, *Canaan*, p. 166,
fig. 112) and Jericho (Sellin, p. 120, fig. 107).

[3] Hill, *Proc. of British Academy*, v. 417 sq., *Pal.*, pp. xxx sqq.

[4] Damascius, cited, *Zeus*, ii. 887; for the second view, see A. R. S.
Kennedy, *Q.S.*, 1914, p. 195 sq.; J. A. Montgomery, *The Samaritans*
(1907), p. 92 n. (after Clermont-Ganneau).

and on the summit of Gerizim the Emperor Zeno founded a temple in honour of the Virgin (Theotokos).[1] The Jewish accusation that the Samaritans venerated the dove may find here its basis.[2] The coins depicting Gerizim with its 300 steps represent the temple of Zeus (Jupiter Capitolinus) on one summit, and on the other a small altar (? or cone), lying to the west of the former. As Dr. G. F. Hill has pointed out, this is perhaps the Khurbet Lōzeh, whose name preserves the tradition that here was Luz-Bethel.[3] The summits are sometimes surmounted by an eagle, the bird of Zeus. Earlier, however, it had been another Zeus to whom Antiochus Epiphanes dedicated the temple on Mount Gerizim, though again reports differ: Zeus Xenios (2 Macc. vi. 2), or Zeus Hellenios (Josephus, *Antiq.*, xii. v. 5). The former, the hospitable Zeus, would reflect Oriental ideas illustrated both in the old 'covenant god' of Shechem, and in Allah as the protector of guests and clients.[4]

Antiochus IV was one of many who attempted to unify rule and universalize religion. Previously Ptolemy I had introduced the cult of Sarapis, the spread of which in

---

[1] Burney, *Judges*, p. 332, observes that Epiphanius (*Adv. Haeres.*, iii. 2, 1055) associated the cult with the commemoration of the daughter of Jephthah. The rape of Korē-Persephone appears on coins of Neapolis (Septimus Severus and after, Hill, *Pal.*, p. xl). Korē is mentioned in a much discussed inscription from Nablus, which is translated: 'Courage, fair sister! Sacred attendant now thou art of Korē, Pluto's wife, for thou knewest the mystery of Eleusis' (see Torrey, *J.A.O.S.*, xlvi. 244 sqq.).

[2] Otherwise explained as a reference to the cult of Semiramis (cf. p. 171), or to that of the Samarian Ashima (p. 146); see further, Montgomery, op. cit., pp. 169, 320 sq.

[3] Hill, *Pal.*, p. xxviii. sq., *Proc. of British Academy*, v. 415 sq.; cf. Montgomery, p. 236 (and facing p. 88), *Zeus*, ii. 887. The Tyche holds Mt. Gerizim in her hand (Hill, p. xxxii, pl. vii, no. 7), or is it a (conical?) stone (ib., pl. viii, no. 8).

[4] Wellhausen, *Reste Arabischen Heidentums*, p. 223. The Shechemite god (Baal Berith) cannot be etymologically connected either with the god of Berytus (Poseidon) or with the Cretan Britomartis.

Palestine is attested by the coinage.[1] Antiochus went further. He regarded not the god of his fathers (Apollo), nor the 'desire of women' (Adonis); but identified himself with Zeus, setting himself—like Zeus—above every god.[2] What is said of Nebuchadrezzar in the book of Judith (iii. 8) would at least illustrate his policy. Zeus Olympios, whose cult was imposed upon the temple of Jerusalem, was also the god of the temple of Herakles-Melḳart at Tyre.[3] The 'abomination of desolation' that was set up on the altar (1 Macc. i. 54) has, since Nestle (in 1884), been explained as the Sky-god, Baal of Heaven, whose cult was more readily accepted by the Jews of the Diaspora than by their more rigid brethren of the mother-city.[4] For three years the Jews were forced to submit to the desecration of their sanctuary, and on the 25th of Chislev in the year 164 B.C., the holy place was cleansed and rededicated.[5]

The claim to divine ancestry made by kings or ruling houses is well known.[6] The stages can sometimes be traced: dead kings are deified by their descendants, or are divine already in their lifetime. Their divine nature is manifested by actually portraying them on coins, by adding a horn (p. 29), and finally by visibly assimilating in some way the king and his god.[7] The steps in the self-deification

[1] See G. A. F. Knight, *Nile and Jordan*, pp. 412 sqq.; *C.A.H.*, vii. 145 sq., E. Bevan, *Egypt under the Ptolemaic Dynasty*, pp. 41 sqq.

[2] Dan. xi. 36 sqq. The identity of the 'god of strongholds' is uncertain.   3 Josephus, *c. Ap.*, i. 17; cf. *Eph.*, i. 252.

[4] See commentaries on Dan. xi. 31 sq. The 'abomination that maketh desolate' (*shōmēm*) stands for Baal *shāmayim*. Such perversions were not infrequent, e.g. Beth-Aven (house of iniquity) for Beth-el (house of El), see *Ency. Bib.*, 'Bethel', § 4; cf. the Gemara on *Abodah Zarah*, iii. 6. The Syriac in 2 Macc. vi. 2 has Baal-shamin Olympius and B.-s. Xenius where the name has lost its distinctiveness.

[5] On the chronology, see E. Bevan, *C.A.H.*, viii. 515 n.

[6] Cf. Dionysus as the founder of the Attalids, Herakles the ancestor of Marcus Antonius, Ares and Aphrodite of Julius Caesar. The Ptolemies were descended from Zeus and Dionysus, and the Seleucids from Apollo.

[7] Cf. Seleucus I deified by Antiochus I, and the latter by Antiochus

of Antiochus can be followed on the coins.[1] We show, first, an earlier stage where, on the obverse, the youthful Antiochus has curls and diadem, while on the reverse, Zeus, seated on a throne with high back, holds in his right hand a Nikē bearing a wreath (nos. 33, 34). Later, Zeus remains unchanged, but on the obverse is a bearded figure which is interpreted either as another head of Zeus, or, rather, Antiochus assimilated to Zeus (nos. 35, 36).[2]

In the Roman period, the coins of Aelia Capitolina have three special points of interest for us. (1) They are of architectural importance in that they represent a temple of four columns with bases, central arch and pediment. In the middle is the Tyche, Fortune, or City-goddess, and on either side, Nikē on a globe (no. 37). This domed temple is probably that which was replaced by the Church of the Holy Sepulchre.[3] Next (2), the Tyche wears the mural

II. But Ptolemy IV tends to identify himself with Dionysus (cf. E. Bevan, *Ptol. Eg.*, pp. 230, 233 sq.). Alexander the Great in due course has the head-dress of Herakles and the ram's-horns of Ammon; see I. Abrahams, *Schweich Lectures*, p. 21 sq. and plate (on the 'little horn' of Daniel); and Hunkin, *Schweich Lectures*, p. 61 and pl. 2. The head of Herakles is often assimilated to the portrait of the contemporary Caesar, as at Philadelphia Amman (Hill, *Coins of Arabia*, p. xxxix). Demetrius Poliorcetes appears on coins with the bull's horn, and in the garb of Pallas Athena (*Amer. J. of Phil.*, xlix. 218). Antiochus I of Commagene, who was θεὸς δίκαιος ἐπιφανής, was the human representative of Zeus Hormazd (Ahura-mazda), and his effigy resembles that of Zeus (see A. B. Cook, *Zeus*, i. 742 sqq.).

[1] For the coins see, in the first instance, Babelon, *Les Rois de Syrie*, pp. xcii sqq.; also E. Bevan, *House of Seleucus*, ii, pl. ii. 7 and 8; Cook, *Zeus*, ii. 1189 sq.; Hunkin, op. cit., pl. vi, fig. 16; Driver's *Daniel*, p. 191 sq. (with head of the king radiate).

[2] (a) Fitzwilliam Museum, Leake collection, kings of Syria, p. 26; cf. *Zeus*, ii. 1189, fig. 991, British Museum, *Coins of Seleucid Kings*, p. 35; (b) Fitzwilliam Museum, Leake collection, ib.; cf. British Museum, *Seleucid Kings*, p. 36, no. 22, pl. xi. 9, and Head, *Hist. Num.*, p. 762 sq.

[3] British Museum: *Palestine*, p. 95, no. 76 (coin of Diadumenianus). Hill (p. xli) dissents from Heisenberg's view (*Graberkirche u. Apostelkirche*) that the Church of the Holy Sepulchre more or less resembled

crown—of the sort known to the Mishnah (*Shabb.* vi. 1)
as 'the golden city'—and her right foot rests on some
object (a familiar attitude, p. 66), though of quite uncertain
identification (p. 174, n. 5). In her right hand is a
human bust, presumably that of the reigning emperor.[1]
The famous Tyche, designed by Eutychides, representing
Antioch as a woman with the river-god Orontes at her feet,
is very rare in Phoenicia, where the preference is for the
goddess with mural crown and cornucopia.[2] Such a Tyche
with her symbols of fertility and abundance corresponds to
the Baalath of old.[3] The Tyche of Gerasa was Artemis,
and Atargatis was the Tyche of Hieropolis and also evidently of Neapolis. On a Sidonian coin the crescent on the
mural crown of the city-goddess identifies her with Astarte.
Hence the city-goddess of Jerusalem, if not strictly an
Astarte, is at least a modified form of her.[4] The old conception can be also traced (3) in the coins descriptive of the
fate of the unhappy city and land. The types on the coins
of Vespasian and Titus are well known: *Iudaea Capta* or *Iudaea
Devicta*, with the mourning woman seated beneath a palm
tree, or standing by it with hands bound, or sitting on one
side of the tree with a male figure with hands bound on
the other.[5] In striking contrast is the type, elsewhere, of

the Astarte temple (cf. *J.H.S.*, xxxi. 60). For the traditions, see Sir
Charles W. Wilson, *Golgotha and the Holy Sepulchre*, pp. 63 sqq., 179, 186;
also his notes on the coins, pp. 69–71.

[1] Similarly on coins of Neapolis, Sebaste, &c. Sometimes the bust
is carried by a male (e.g. Caesarea); for a male Tyche see p. 179, n. 1.

[2] Hill, *Journal of Hellenic Studies*, xxxi. 58.

[3] On a coin of Herod Agrippa II she has a modius on her head and
holds ears of corn and cornucopia (Madden, p. 148). On the Tyche
as the 'Luck', see Zimmern, *Islamica*, ii. 579, n. 4.

[4] Haas, *Urchrist.*, nos. 82 sq., calls her the 'Astarte of Aelia Capito-
lina'. See Hill's discussion, *Proc. of British Academy*, v. 413 sq. Years ago
Clermont-Ganneau reported the discovery at Jerusalem, under the
Mehkemeh, of a lead figurine of a semi-nude female, with arms folded
and raised above her head, 'which reminds one of certain statues of
Venus' (*Q.S.*, 1874, p. 104).

[5] See I. Abrahams, *Schweich Lectures*, plate, nos. 8 and 9; Hunkin,

the *Restitutor Provinciae* where the emperor Hadrian offers his right hand to assist the kneeling Provincia to arise. A monument with such a scene may be recognized at Paneas.[1] The Jewish female is, of course, the personification of the city or land, and the conception can be illustrated, on the one hand, by the old Jewish idea of the Virgin Daughter of Zion, while, on the other, it is developed into the representation in late art of the Jewish and Christian Churches by two female figures, as in Strasbourg Cathedral.[2]

Besides the stone of Elagabal in a quadriga (also at Neapolis), and the war-god 'whom we call Ares for want of a better name',[3] there are representations of the temple of Jupiter Capitolinus, erected on the site of the old temple, with Jupiter, Juno, and Minerva, and containing an equestrian statue of Hadrian. The god himself is also probably symbolized on the coins with an eagle on the thunderbolt.[4] Sarapis, too, appears here, and at Neapolis he is seated on a throne and holds a globe in his hand, thus resembling the 'lord of the world' (p. 216), and illustrating a type which was subsequently taken over into Christianity.[5]

Schweich Lectures, p. 83, pl. xii, no. 33. The seated and weeping Judaea is already found on coins commemorating the defeat of Antigonus. On the sorrowful Venus Architis (Caesarea-Arca in the Lebanon), see Hill, *Church Quart. Review*, lxvi. 131 sq., and cf. p. 140, n. 2.

[1] W. Weber, *Deissmann Festgabe*, pp. 38 sqq. On the Arch of Trajan at Benevento the favoured province is Mesopotamia (Domaszewski, *Abhand. Röm. Rel.*, p. 41 sq.).

[2] Similarly, the Christian Church is hypostatized, and the Virgin Mother and the Virgin Church are corresponding figures (Conybeare, *A.f.R.*, ix. 73 sqq.).

[3] Hill, p. xlv (pl. ix, no. 5).

[4] Sir Charles W. Wilson, *Golgotha and the Holy Sepulchre*, pp. 62, 70.

[5] A coin of Caracalla; *Zeus*, i. 45, 49 sqq. An inscription of Sarapis (A.D. 115–117) was found at Jerusalem (*Q.S.*, 1896, pp. 133, 137 sqq.; *Z.D.P.V.*, xliv. 1), and Wilson suggests that his temple was not far from the Zion gate (*Golgotha*, p. 94, n. 2). Sarapis, though of Greek-Egyptian origin, may have been to some extent influenced by the Babylonian Marduk (Winckler and others, see Wilcken, *Urkunden d. Ptolemäerzeit*, i, p. 82).

Turning to the native Jewish coins we cannot fail to observe the numerous strange and even inexplicable elements.[1] For example, there is the peculiar omphalos-like helmet which, with minor variations, appears on the coins of Herod I; it has flaps, on the top is a star, and on either side are palm-branches (no. 38).[2] Apparent 'solar' emblems are also found.[3] The caduceus appears upon coins of Jerusalem, Askalon, and Sepphoris, and is usually winged (no. 39).[4] It would be difficult to say what meaning was attached to it; probably it was interpreted not, as in Egypt, as part of the cult of the Agathos Daemon, the 'good genius' of the city, but rather as the symbol of the guardian god and messenger, Hermes.[5] The temple-vessels were renowed for their beauty (Ben Sira, l. 9; Jos., *Ant.*, xvii. ii. 10), and coins depict lyre, trumpet, chalice, &c. There is a predilection for palms, grapes, and baskets of fruits and cornucopias.[6] On coins of Antigonus Mat-

[1] Hill, *Palestine*, pp. xcv sqq. (see p. lxxxix sq. and F. W. Madden, *Coins of the Jews* [1881]); a typical selection in Cooke, *North Semitic Inscriptions*, pp. 352 sqq. and pl. x; Wilson, *Golgotha*, p. 71 sq., pl. vii.

[2] British Museum: *Pal.*, p. 220, n. 1. See Hill, p. xcvii. It may be an inverted chalice (cf. those on coins of the First Revolt). Hunkin, *Schweich Lectures*, p. 79, pl. viii, no. 23, associates the type with the celebrations at Herod's marriage with Mariamne.

[3] Madden, pp. 90, 109, n. 2; otherwise interpreted as wheels (Hill, p. xcv), partly on the ground that, though a star might be tolerated, Jews would hardly permit the representation of heavenly bodies. But see the synagogue zodiacs, below, p. 207 sq.

[4] British Museum: *Pal.*, p. 2, no. 14, from Sepphoris; for the winged caduceus, see p. 110, no. 39 (Askalon), p. 222, nos. 15, 17 (Jerusalem). The caduceus also occurs on seals, &c.; at Samaria it is held by a naked god (i. 379, pl. 57 *d* 2 and *f* 2).

[5] Dussaud, *Myth. Syr.*, pp. 23 sqq.; Cook, *Zeus*, i. 564 sqq. The Agathos Daemon was regarded as a snake, and in fact the caduceus may be derived from a double serpent; see Ward, *Seals*, p. 408; *A.J.S.L.*, xxxvi. 274; Fotheringham, *Amer. J. of Arch.*, xx. 176.

[6] Palm-tree between two baskets of fruit (Hunkin, op. cit., pl. vii, fig. 18)—perhaps a reference to the offerings of first-fruits. Palms on some coins of the procurators, see ib., p. 81, pl. xi, fig. 30. For palms on festal occasions, see 1 Macc. xiii. 51; 2 Macc. x. 7 sq.; cf. John xii. 13.

tathias the double cornucopias are on the obverse (no. 40), while on the reverse is an ivy wreath tied at the top (no. 41).[1] The latter is particularly remarkable, seeing that ivy wreaths were worn on the festival of the Dionysia. The story that Ptolemy tried to force the Jews to worship Dionysus may be a fiction based upon the persecutions by Antiochus Epiphanes half a century later.[2] But it is at least noteworthy that the most important of the Dionysian festivals corresponded nearly to the time of the Passover. Dionysus with thyrsus appears on coins of Aelia Capitolina; and Scythopolis, the old Beth-Shan, adopted the name Nysa, evidently because of the cult of Dionysus.[3] The god appears on coins of Scythopolis (from c. A.D. 163) and Raphia (A.D. 180), and on Phoenician coins he may represent, to some extent at least, the native god Eshmun.[4]

That rites, more or less Dionysiac, were familiar in Palestine is borne out by the Dionysiac character of the Feast of Booths or Tabernacles. Characteristic of this festival are the lūlāb and ethrōg which are to be seen on coins, synagogue ornamentation, and a seal.[5] The lūlāb is here shown in the middle, with palm-branch, myrtle and willow, on a coin 'y[ear] two of the freedom of Israel' (no. 42, A.D. 133).[6] The ceremony itself goes back to old agricultural rites for the fertility of nature: rain and abundance

---

[1] British Museum: Pal., p. 212, no. 2. On other coins of his is one of the earliest representations of the seven-branched candlestick, and on the obverse an enigmatic device: a horizontal line on which are four verticals thicker in the middle than at their ends (Madden, p. 102; Hill, p. 219, no. 56).

[2] E. Bevan, Ptolemaic Egypt, p. 230.

[3] Abel, Rev. Bib., 1912, p. 413 sq.

[4] Baudissin, Adonis, pp. 231 sqq.; Hill, Proc. of British Academy, v. 414 sq.

[5] The seal is that of 'Judah, the —— (Levite? wise? officer?) son of Abah', see Lidzbarski, Eph., i. 141; Torrey, Annual of American Schools, ii. 107; Schroeder, M.D.P.V., xxxvii. 176 sq. (? the Amora, R. Abbahu of A.D. 279–310).

[6] No. 42, British Museum: Pal., p. 284, n. 2, cf. Cooke, pl. x. 9.

of food. Myrtles had apotropaic and fertilizing virtues; the *lūlāb* itself seems to have been a symbol of justification.[1] Such rites were certainly of long standing, although it is possible that some features (e.g. the *ethrōg*) came in during the Persian age, and that, under the influence of the Hellenizing Jews, a Dionysiac festival was 'Judaized'.[2] Hence it was possible for Plutarch to describe Jewish ceremonies as Dionysiac, while Tacitus saw that in spite of the resemblances the identity was to be repudiated.[3]

Finally, the coins of the Second Revolt (A.D. 132–135) display a temple with four fluted columns, and a row of dots to represent the architrave. Above is seen a wavy line, or, in this case (no. 43), two letters of the name Jerusalem, or, on others, a star, explained as a reference to Bar Cocheba who claimed to be the Messiah.[4] The scene is interpreted as 'the four pillars for the veil before the Holy of Holies in the Tabernacle, with a conventionalized representation within of the ark and mercy seat'.[5] Otherwise it is held that we have the temple which the followers of

[1] See A. Marmorstein, *Doctrine of Merits in Old Rabbinical Literature* (1920), p. 18 n., and *Q.S.*, 1921, p. 187 sq. On the *ethrōg*, &c., see Kohl and Watzinger, *Antike Synagogen*, p. 186; Grünbaum, *Z.D.M.G.*, xlii. 251 n. (the citron as the 'Apple of Paradise'); Strack and Billerbeck, ii. 780 sqq. On the Feast of Tabernacles and water-drawing ceremonies to ensure rain (Zech. xiv. 16 sqq.), see Lévy, *R.E.J.*, xliii. 193; *Ency. Bib.*, cols. 269, 4880; and on the unrestrained character of the celebration, see the Second Targum on Est. iii. 8 and Burkitt, *J.T.S.*, xvii. 141 sq.

[2] Wellhausen, *Nachrichten* of the Göttingen University, 1905, p. 131; cf. Ed. Meyer, *Ursprung Christentums*, ii. 209, n. 5.

[3] Plut., *Sympos.*, iv. 6; Tac., v. 5. See Büchler, *R.E.J.*, xxxvii. 181–202.

[4] British Museum: p. 284, n. 1 (see pp. 287 sqq., pl. xxxii sq.); see Hill, p. cvi sq. On the star, see an ingenious article by Clermont-Ganneau, *Rev. Bib.*, 1920, pp. 542 sqq.

[5] Hill (after Edgar Rogers, *Numism. Chron.*, 1911, pp. 205 sqq.). Hunkin (*Num. Chron.*, 1916, p. 253) recalls the representation of the ark in the Catacombs, where, by a curious association of ideas, room is found for Noah.

Bar Cocheba hoped to restore, and that the central structure is the podium.[1]

After written sources (e.g. Lucian's 'Syrian Goddess'), the most important aids to the interpretation of coins and other archaeological objects are the Semitic and Greek inscriptions. These often have a more objective value than the descriptive works of early authors. Two Greek inscriptions may be mentioned for special reasons. One, on an inscribed altar, was discovered by Sir Charles Wilson in 1865 at the site of the ancient Kadesh Naphtali. The stone itself appears never to have been rediscovered, the squeeze was lost, and the outline sketch here given (Pl. xxxv. 2) remained unnoticed until it became the subject of one of Clermont-Ganneau's many brilliant studies.[2] We have (1) a Greek inscription between two palm-trees, (2) the carved outline of a cippus on the side of the stone, and (3) a bearded man covered with a sort of veil, and on his head a six-rayed disk. He is presumably the deity to whom the altar is dedicated, in fact the Greek inscription speaks of the 'holy god . . .'. The epithet points to some Semitic deity.[3] The word above the figure should—with Clermont-Ganneau—probably be corrected to *bōmos* ('altar'), and we may compare the two dedications—within a day's journey of one another—the one (A.D. 160) to Zeus Bōmos, from a temple in the district west of Aleppo, the other (A.D. 70–120) to the Aramaic equivalent, Zeus Madbakhos, and to Selamanes, 'gods of the country', from a locality (north of Jebel Sheikh Berekāt) where the tomb of a Mohammedan saint now takes the place of the earlier god.[4]

[1] A. R. S. Kennedy, *Q.S.*, 1914, p. 198 sq. Some temple front appears to be shown on the Byzantine lamp, *Gezer*, pl. ci *a* (foot).

[2] Clermont-Ganneau, *Q.S.*, 1903, pp. 131 sqq. (*Rec.*, v. 341 sqq.).

[3] Cf. Clermont-Ganneau, *Rec.*, iii. 330, v. 322; examples in Cumont, *Oriental Religions* (Eng.), p. 249; *Syria*, vi. 355, n. 4 (a 'holy heavenly god', at Baetocaece and also at Kadesh); Baudissin, *Kyrios*, iii. 209 n.

[4] For these see *Zeus*, i. 519 sq., and for the 'god-altar' (cf. the 'god-mountain', p. 169), *Rel. Sem.*, p. 562. Lévy, *R.E.J.*, xliii. 102, compares

Unfortunately there is nothing more to be said, save that the stone may be of the latter part of the third century A.D., and that there are traces at Kadesh of an old pagan temple oriented to the east.[1]

Kadesh occupied an important position and was an asylum city. Its name 'holy' befitted a place which lay along the line severing 'Galilee of the Nations' from Jewish territory.[2] Boundaries were sacred: an Aramaic boundary inscription from Cilicia invokes the curses of the Sky-god (Baal-shamin), Moon (Sahr), and Sun upon the transgressor and his seed.[3] Besides the boundaries of Gilead (Gen. xxxi. 44 sqq.), Egypt (Isa. xix. 19), and presumably Kadesh-Barnea (Judah and Edom), there were city-boundaries at Gezer, where Macalister (i. 37–40) found traces of half-a-dozen, at Ikhnaton's sacred city of Akhetaton (fourteen stelae), and no doubt elsewhere.[4] Sacred places had their boundaries: Mount Sinai (Exod. xix. 12), a garden of Adonis at Latakiyeh (*Syria*, v. 334), and in the Temple of Herod the Great pillars with Greek and Latin inscriptions warned non-Jews against trespassing within the sacred precincts on pain of death.[5]

Another example of such a boundary inscription seems, at first sight, to be furnished by the 'Hermon inscription'

the temple of N-d-b-kh-h at Accho, mentioned in the Talmud, *Abodah Zarah*, 11*b*. (According to Rashi a *bōmōs* was worshipped as well as the image on it, Elmslie on *Ab. Z.*, iii. 7.)

[1] *M.D.O.G.*, 1904, no. 23, p. 22 sq.

[2] See Hölscher, *Q.S.*, 1909, p. 150, on the temple to the 'goddess Athene the lady (*kyria*)' at Khurbet Harrawi, a place on the border line between the Jews and the district where pagan temples begin to appear.

[3] *Eph.* iii. 64; Montgomery, *J.A.O.S.*, xxviii. 164 sqq.; see further, *C.A.H.*, ii. 343 sq.; *Rel. Sem.*, pp. 561, 570.

[4] James Baikie, *The Amarna Age*, pp. 266 sqq.; Breasted, *Anc. Records*, ii. 949–72, one of the stelae is about twenty-six feet high.

[5] Jos. *B.J.* v. v. 2. One of the Greek inscriptions has been found; see Deissmann, *Light from the East*, fig. 8. A new squeeze is given in *Syria*, i. 192, pl. 18.

(Pl. xxxvi). This is a large stone $3\frac{1}{2}$ ft. by 19–20 in., originally weighing 18 cwt., which was found by Sir Charles Warren in 1870. Brought to London it eluded decipherment until a clue was found, once more by Clermont-Ganneau, who published the inscription in 1903. He renders it: 'by the order of the god most great and holy, those who take the oath, hence!'[1] The stone, which is perhaps of the third century A.D., comes from the summit of Hermon, the sacred mountain, where traces of several temples have been found, built to face the rising sun. On the summit is a sort of natural altar and a cave; and an inscription to Zeus Megistos, found on the eastern declivity of the mountain, is in all likelihood to the Baal of Hermon, the god whose sacred *enceinte* is here referred to.[2] If Clermont-Ganneau is right, the 'Hermon inscription' is no interdiction, 'away from here', warning off the layman, but a liturgical notice marking some point in the ritual circumambulation, for which the summit was adapted, and regulating the movements of the worshippers. He goes on further to remark that the allusion to the oath suggests some Ζεὺς ὅρκιος; even the word Hermon suggests ideas of consecration, devotion, and anathema; cf. the oath by Ḥerem-bethel at Elephantine (p. 144).

The 'Hermon inscription' has attracted very little attention, and its explanation remains somewhat obscure. But still following Clermont-Ganneau we are led to what is virtually another discovery, of hardly less interest. Traditions in the Book of Enoch and elsewhere knew that Mount Hermon received its name because of the rebellious angels

---

[1] *Q.S.*, 1903, pp. 135 sqq., 231 sqq. (*Rec.*, v. 346 sqq.). It is now in the British Museum. The Greek reads: κατὰ κέλευσιν θεοῦ μεγίστου κ(αὶ) ἁγίου υ(=οἱ) ὀμνύοντες ἐντεῦθεν.

[2] See Warren, *Q.S.*, 1869, pp. 210 sqq. (with plan of the summit), *Our Work in Palestine* (1873), pp. 245 sqq., Conder, *Q.S.*, 1881, p. 82, Baedeker, p. 294; *Ency. Bib.*, col. 2022. The Greek inscription in question (*Q.S.*, 1903, p. 140 n.; *Zeus*, i. 420) has an obscure reference to a pot (? some survival of human sacrifice, Clermont-Ganneau, *Rec.*, iv. 250).

who bound themselves by oaths—the same verb as in the Hermon inscription (ὄμνυμι) is several times used. Of these traditions—the earliest of which appears quite isolated in the fragmentary passage, Gen. vi. 1–4—those now preserved speak of the descent of angels, the introduction of the evils of civilization, the cries of suffering humanity, and the deluge. Now the writer of Enoch seems to have been familiar with *north* Palestine,[1] and according to another tradition, while godly Sethites live in purity on the summit of Hermon, and have an oath 'by the blood of Abel', below live the wicked Cainites, the inventors of civilization. Indeed, near by are the tombs of Seth and Noah, so that there seems to have been a general localizing of traditions of civilization and the flood in the Hermon district.[2] The district is scarcely outside the ideal limits of Israel (Deut. iii. 8); indeed the cities of Abel and Dan claimed to be true homes of the genius of Israel, as we know from the original text of 2 Sam. xx. 18 sq. Accordingly, we are able to lay our finger upon what seems to have been a corpus of antediluvian traditions flourishing in the *hinterland* of Tyre and Sidon. Like the Tyrian story of the 'ambrosial rocks' and the flood (p. 162 sq.), the traditions are partly within, partly without, the horizon of Israelites or Hebrews. Late though they all are, they testify to the vitality and continuity of old lore outside strictly Israelite canonical tradition. And when we consider the coins and other archaeological material on the one side, and these fragments of myth and legend on the other, it is certain that there must have been a considerable amount of material lying outside the stories that were accepted and preserved in the Jewish canonical literature.

[1] Burkitt, *Schweich Lectures*, 1913, p. 28, cf. p. 53 sq.; note the mention of Dan, Lebanon, and Seniser (or -el) = Senir (i.e. Hermon, Deut. iii. 9). So also Clermont-Ganneau (l.c., pp. 238 sqq.), who conjectures *inter alia* that the name Abel-beth-Maacah suggested the 'mourning' to which the tradition alludes, and that the mourning may have been some laments (*Adonia*) for Tammuz or Adonis.

[2] So Clermont-Ganneau. Note also Sanchuniathon's cosmogony of the mountain-giants inventors of the arts.

Greek inscriptions of quite another character were discovered in the excavation of Tell Sandaḥannah in the Shephelah or Lowlands, the district of Mareshah, Eleutheropolis, Beit-Jibrin.[1] The site, a fine specimen of a Jewish-Greek town, is named after Saint Anna (Ḥannah), whose church, of Byzantine origin, faces a cave which goes back to Jewish times. Apart from the fragmentary claw of a colossal statue of an eagle—perhaps (to judge from the reading . . . ωνι) a dedication to Apollo (p. 70)—and apart from the usual coarse figurines of the mother-goddess (pp. 138, 146), one of the most interesting finds was that of a statuette nearly one foot in height, representing an Astarte on a stand, with a head-dress with seven bosses (Pl. xxxvi).[2] It is tempting to suppose that we have here the 'pagan' forerunner of Saint Anne. Further, there were found little leaden figures two to three inches in height. Their hands were bound in front or behind, or the legs were bound, or both legs and hands were bound together. They illustrate the *peridesmos*, the binding and knot-tying of 'sympathetic magic', whereby men believed they could fetter and torment their foes.[3] Another example was found at Samaria: a small naked leaden figure with its right arm and leg twisted off.[4]

As letter-press to these objects Tell Sandaḥannah furnished a number of limestone tablets containing Greek exorcisms and imprecations. One of them actually mentions the dreaded *peridesmos*. The writers curse the hand and heart of their enemy; one curses his enemy's marriage.[5]

[1] For the P.E.F. excavations in 1900, see Bliss and Macalister, *Excavations in Palestine*, pp. 52 sqq. For the famous caves of the district see ib., pp. 204 sqq. (Some have apses, not necessarily in the east, p. 255; for a Christian chapel, see pp. 209, 253 sq.; other possible sanctuaries, pp. 262 sq. and 264.)

[2] Op. cit., p. 139 sq., fig. 52.

[3] Op. cit., pp. 154 sqq. (pl. lxxxv), Wünsch, ib., pp. 158 sqq.; Thiersch, *Arch. Anz.*, iii (1908), 400 sq.

[4] *Samaria*, p. 384, no. 10.

[5] The Jerusalem Targum on Deut. xxiv. 6 explains that verse as a

In one very elaborate text (no. 35) a man worsted in a law-suit writes an appeal to a god for help: he languishes in prison, an innocent victim, 'it is high time if ever I am to be saved (σώζω) and delivered that thou shouldst save me to-day; I am constantly beaten, my life endangered thereby, and I can no longer endure my fetters. . . .' It is noteworthy that the god is not named. The tablets as a whole appear to come from the slave-class, but magic of this sort was in-veterate, and not confined to slaves.[1] Corresponding to the *leaden* figures is the use of lead in the *tabellae devotionis*, one of which from Carthage appeals to the 'ladies Ḥawwath, Allath, and Milkath', evidently a triad of chthonic deities.[2] To judge from the abundant Jewish superstitions practices of 'binding and loosing' were familiar; indeed, it has been urged that many of the Psalms, wherein the afflicted cry for help against their enemies, refer to the magic of which they were the victims.[3] 'Magic' of another sort at Tell Sanda-ḥannah was afforded by the many fragments of masks, re-sembling the *oscilla* which were hung up in the wind, and were supposed to make the vines fruitful.[4]

reference to the 'fettering' of a newly-married couple (see Levy's Dict., *s.v.* אסר).

[1] The tablets are dated by Wünsch to the 2nd cent. A.D. (p. 187); Thiersch, however, from a comparison of Hellenistic papyri and the Marissa inscriptions (p. 202 below), would place them earlier, 2nd to 1st cent. B.C.

[2] See Cooke, no. 50; Lidzbarski, *Eph.*, i. 29 ; cf. Macler, *Rev. Hist. Rel.*, lxxxviii. 264 sqq. It was probably owing to the use to which lead was put that Christians disliked the deadly metal.

[3] See H. Wheeler Robinson, *Ency. Brit.*, 14th ed., 'Psalms', xviii. 663*b*. For Jewish superstition in general, see Grünbaum, *Z.D.M.G.*, 1877, pp. 252 sqq.; D. Joël, *Der Aberglaube* (1881–3); L. Blau, *Das alt-jüdische Zauberwesen* (1898), especially pp. 157, 164 sq.; Le Blant in *Journ. d. Savants*, 1890, pp. 309–20 (on Abodah Zarah); Gaster, *The Wisdom of the Chaldaeans*; Nicolsky, *Spuren magischer Formeln i. d. Psalmen* (1927); and especially Strack and Billerbeck, *Komm. z. N. T.*, iv. 501–35.

[4] p. 140; cf. Hanauer, *Q.S.*, 1894, p. 209; 1903, p. 190: specimens from the districts of Jaffa and Gaza.

Opposite Tell Sandaḥannah, to the north-west, lies Marissa, famous for the painted tombs discovered in 1902 Sadly mutilated by fanatical natives, and gradually losing their colour, the tombs are an important contribution, partly by reason of the paintings, and partly because of Greek inscriptions which testify to the presence of a Sidonian colony of the late third and second century B.C.[1] As a whole they afford an admirable illustration of the care taken to provide for what was known to Egyptians and Semites as the 'eternal home'.[2] In particular, a large *klinē*, over six feet wide, is unique of its kind. Paintings of various ceremonial vessels (with and without flames) include a fine candelabrum, part of a scene of introduction (p. 41 above). Two minstrels (one a girl) are depicted going down to the dead to honour and cheer them. A lively hunting scene recalls the fine tomb at Sidon with the skulls of the hunting hounds buried together with the royal occupant. There are large paintings of eagles, cocks and a Cerberus, and a number of African animals, as well as some fabulous or imaginary beasts, among them a man-headed lion.[3] The fondness for animals is typical of the age.[4]

[1] See J. P. Peters and H. Thiersch, *Painted Tombs in the Necropolis of Marissa (Mareshah)* (1905), to be supplemented by W. J. Moulton, *Amer. J. of Arch.*, March 1915, pp. 63–70, and Abel, *Rev. Bib.*, 1925, pp. 267 sqq. See especially Vincent, *Rev. Bib.*, 1906, pp. 317 sqq., and Thiersch, *Arch. Anz.*, 1908, pp. 407 sqq.; and for brief accounts, G. A. F. Knight, *Nile and Jordan*, p. 425, Hunkin, *Schweich Lectures*, p. 67 and pl. v. An Aramaic inscription is reported by Albright (*Bulletin of Amer. Schools of Or. Res.*, Oct. 1924, p. 4).

[2] Jewish, Eccles. xii. 5 (Tobit iii. 6); Phoenician, *C.I.S.*, i. 124; Palmyrene, see Cooke, p. 307; for the Greek, cf. the poorly-painted tomb in the district, described by Bliss-Macalister, p. 201 and pl. xci. It had 'remarkably spirited' figures of birds, and two figures of flying genii, nude, and supporting a wreath in the centre of which was the inscription *OYTOC OIKOC AΩNIOC*.

[3] Each has its name, and this engaging creature is called *H . . C* (two or three letters are illegible).

[4] Antiochene kings collected animals, and there was a 'zoo' at Alexandria. In the ' Zeno papyri' we read of men in Transjordania

·The rather dull and slovenly art of the Marissa tombs shows Greek influence, though, indeed, not of any very deep-reaching character.[1] Persian influence, more noticeable in Sidon and the north, may be seen in the painting of the fire altar. The Phoenician element in the south was intermittently strong;[2] and the names of the dead, written in the tombs, testify to their Phoenician origin.[3] Names compounded with Apollo, frequently found over Syria and the coastland, and in the Zeno papyri, are here especially prominent, and the fact is in harmony with the evidence for Apollo in South Palestine (see p. 179). The Semitic equivalent would presumably be Resheph (cf. p. 113), and the Apollodorus of the tombs bears a name both characteristic of the period, and corresponding to such a Semitic name as Resheph-yathon.[4] But it is noteworthy that in the personal names of the colony compounds of Kos are also prominent. Kos was an Idumaean god, and similar compounds are found in Egypt, notably in Memphis of about 200–150 B.C., where Idumaeans were in the habit of meeting in 'the upper temple of Apollo'.[5] Kos may be

who collected animals to send to Egypt. Centuries later, Timotheus of Gaza (c. A.D. 500) wrote on the strange animals to be seen conveyed through his city. (On the Palestinian interest of the Zeno papyri, see Vincent, *Rev. Bib.*, 1920, pp. 161–202; Abel, 1924, pp. 566–74; Harper, *Amer. Journ. Phil.*, 1928, pp. 1–35.)

[1] Moreover, the Greek of the inscriptions tends to be barbaric (p. 13), even as the style of the paintings deteriorates.

[2] *Marissa*, p. 10 n. (Thiersch); cf. the Greek inscription to the Phoenikarch of Gaza (M. A. Meyer, *Gaza*, p. 147).

[3] e.g., Sesmaios, Meerbalos. The son of the former, Apollophanes, is called χρηστότατος καὶ φιλοικειότατος, of which the first is not found in funereal inscriptions, while the latter recalls Nabataean usage (see Cooke, p. 215).

[4] Cf. Lidzbarski, *Eph.*, i. 150.

[5] E. Bevan, *Ptolemaic Egypt*, p. 108 (citing Dittenberger, ii. 737). The Marissa compounds include Kosbanos and Kosnatanos (also in Nabataean inscr.), and the latter is found at Memphis along with Kosmalakos, Kosadaros (also in Sinaitic inscr.), and Kosgeros. See Miller, *Rev. Archaeol.*, lxx. 109 sqq., and for compounds from Ashmunen

found as early as the name Barḳos ('Son of Ḳos'), a family
of the Nethinim, who include other non-Jewish names
(Ezra ii. 53). The name also may not unnaturally be connected with the older Edomite god who appears in two
names of the time of Tiglath-Pileser III, viz. Kaush-gabri
and Kaush-malaka, if not in the biblical Ḳushaiah, a
Levite, and in the form Ḳos in Nippur contracts of the
Persian period.[1]

Some additional light is thrown upon the god when we
recall the allegation that king Herod was descended from
a hierodule of Apollo in the temple of Askalon, and that
the ancestors of his sister's husband (Kosgabaros) had been
priests of Koze (or Kozai). Either the latter or Kos will be
the Idumaean Apollo to whom Josephus refers (c. Apion.,
ii. 10), and although the two names are not connected
philologically, there is a functional relationship. Koze is
the Arab Ḳozaḥ, the divine archer whose bolts were lightning and his bow the rainbow. He was a mountain-god of
rain and thunder, and the early Arabs maintained his cult
near Mecca.[2] Kos, then, associates himself with the warlike, young, and Apolline deities who are the late representatives of such bygone deities as the ubiquitous Resheph
and other war-gods.

The Greek inscriptions of Marissa include familiar warn-
ings, e.g. 'let no one disturb (the) daughter' (no. 17). Of
special interest, by reason of the verb employed, is the
warning against interfering with Apollodoros son of Zab-
baios: 'let nobody touch this, else, may he not be saved

(Hermopolis Magna), Eph., ii. 339 sq. Other names are Kosbarakos,
and especially Kostobaros (the husband of Herod's sister Salome),
which should no doubt be corrected to Kosgabaros.

[1] K.A.T., 473. If—to argue from the name Ḳushaiah (on which see
Ency. Bib.)—the god Ḳush (Kaush) was once known in Israel, he has
been eliminated as successfully as Hadad (found in Edom and Syria).

[2] Wellhausen, Arab. Heid., pp. 81 sq., 146; W. R. Smith, Kinship and
Marriage, pp. 236, 302, 304 sq. (a god of the same type as the archer-
gods Hobal and Dushara). For the archer god, cf. the Cypriote
'Resheph of the arrow' mentioned on p. 113, n. 2.

(i.e. have no peace).'[1] Another seems to be erotic.[2] This can be more definitely said of the tantalizing four-lined inscription in well-written Greek on the wall of one of the passages.[3] It is 'a striking confirmation of a passage in Athenaeus (xv. 679 B), where he tells us that all Phoenicia was full of the so-called "Locrian" songs, which are, he says, songs with adultery for their theme'.[4]

There are other painted tombs in the vicinity of Marissa. In a Byzantine tomb are paintings of birds and flowers, peacocks—symbols of immortality in the belief that their flesh was incorruptible—and cocks—either for a similar reason or as harbingers of the dawn of the coming of Christ.[5] Moreover, among the many mosaics discovered in Palestine,[6] one in the neighbourhood, belonging to what was a fine Roman villa of about A.D. 100–300, depicts animals in five pairs, separated by panels which represent Spring, Earth, Summer, in the shape of appropriate female figures, and with their Greek names.[7] Mosaics of

---

[1] Μηθένα κινεῖν, εἰ δὲ μή, μή αὐτῶι σώζεσθαι (no. 29, p. 54).

[2] No. 34, p. 60 (see the Addenda to the volume), is too obscure. At Tell Sandaḥannah a Roman soldier has scribbled his love for little 'snub nose': σιμὴ καλὴ δοκεῖ ἐμόι (Bliss-Macalister, p. 245, see Clermont-Ganneau, Q.S., 1901, p. 116 sq., Rec. iv. 238). Cf. the Sidonian Simotera on a Jewish tomb at Alexandria (Rec., viii. 60).

[3] No. 33, pp. 56 sqq.; see Wünsch, Rhein. Mus., 1909, pp. 433 sqq.; Macalister, Q.S., 1906, pp. 54, 158 (cf. Conder, ib., pp. 147, 238).

[4] E. A. Barker, in The Hellenic Age, p. 62. Mr. A. D. Nock kindly points out to me that in metre the poem corresponds closely to the Locrian song cited by Athenaeus. He himself questions the explanations given by the editors, and thinks it possible that the last line is an addition to make the poem relevant to a particular situation. As he remarks, it is another illustration of a sentimentalism that seems to be characteristic of 'Syro-Greek' culture, and—as he rightly adds—goes with a certain cruelty.

[5] Q.S., 1915, p. 93 sq.; Moulton, Art and Archaeology (U.S.A.), i. 62–71; Abel, Rev. Bib., Oct. 1924, pp. 583 sqq.

[6] The chief literature is given by P. Thomsen, Z.D.P.V., lii. 163 n.

[7] See further, Vincent, Rev. Bib., xxxi (1922), 259–81. Spring (Ἔαρ) is a veiled nymph with flowers in her hair; while the rather emaciated

the seasons are common enough in the Oriental world, especially during the Antonine period.[1] Although they are allegorical rather than religious, they are frequently of interest for the 'survivals' they preserve, or for the way in which earlier *motifs* have been reinterpreted. On a mosaic in a Christian church at Medeba in Moab of about A. D. 500, the seasons are represented by delicate busts of almost identical females draped, and with the turreted or mural head-dresses found on Tyches and goddesses. Similarly, on a contemporary mosaic at Hiram's Tomb the seasons appear as female busts, draped and winged, but in this case each has some slight variation.[2] This personification of the seasons cannot be severed from the earlier beliefs that there were 'angels' over winds, clouds, snow, waters, and the four seasons.[3] Such ideas were not very far removed from genuine polytheism and demonism, and they have been still further refined in the graceful figures on the Christian mosaics.

An extremely interesting example from a Jewish synagogue was discovered at the end of the Great War at Ain Dūk, north-west of Jericho. First laid bare by a Turkish shell in the middle of September 1918, opened up by an Australian regiment, and then covered again for safety's sake, the site was scientifically examined by the Dominican École Biblique of Jerusalem, to whose labours Palestinian archaeology is so vastly indebted.[4] Once a fine synagogue by the side of the Wady Nu'aimeh, and described in one of

---

bust, with head covered, a poor-looking tree by the side, and an overturned amphora, is presumably winter.

[1] Vincent, l.c., p. 275, nn. 3, 4.

[2] Vincent, l.c., pp. 275 n. 4, 276, 278 n.

[3] See Book of Jubilees, ii. 2; cf. 1 Enoch lxvi. 2; note also the presiding or patron 'angels' of the Seven Churches (Rev. i. 20, &c.), see R. H. Charles, *Comment. on the Apocalypse*, i. 34, 203, ii. 44, with references; and Strack and Billerbeck, *Komm. z. N.T.*, iii. 818 sq.

[4] Vincent, *Rev. Bib.*, 1919, pp. 532–63; 1921, pp. 442 sqq.; Clermont-Ganneau, *C.R.*, 1919, pp. 91 sqq., 300 sqq.; *Q.S.*, 1920, pp. 82 sqq., 139 sqq., 1921, p. 189. I am indebted to Father Vincent for information by letter and for the photographs here reproduced.

the Jewish inscriptions *in situ* as a 'holy place', it is remarkable for its mosaic designs: a fragment of the story of
Daniel in the lion's den, plants, animals, fantastic decora-
tions, and, especially, a circle containing the Hebrew names
of the signs of the zodiac, more or less intact. In the middle
is a solar quadriga, and outside are the four *teḳūphōth* or seasons symbolized by four female figures (Pl. xxxvii).[1] But the
place where we should expect the month Tammuz (July)
is badly mutilated—is it because of the name? Ṭebeth
(January) is in position, but Nisan (April) stands where
the autumnal Tishri should be, its place being taken by the
entirely obscure letters L—y. The date is perhaps the fifth
century A.D., or even earlier.[2] This zodiac is not unique.[3]
Indeed, although astrological speculation was frowned upon
by Jewish orthodoxy, it was keenly pursued, and there are
many traces of it in the pseudepigraphical literature and
popular sources.[4] Josephus knows of the zodiacal interpretations of the twelve loaves of shewbread, and Philo has a
zodiacal interpretation of the high priest's breastplate. Of
special importance for our purpose is the view (found

[1] Cancer (*sarṭān*), Virgo (*bethūlah*), and portions of Pisces (*dāgīm*)
and Aries (*ṭāleh*) are visible on our illustration. The bird is noteworthy.

[2] See *Z.D.P.V.*, li. 136.

[3] One at Beth Alpha (foot of Mt. Gilboa) is very similar; it is dated
in the reign of King Justinus and is therefore of the sixth century A.D.
(see Sukenik, *Ency. Judaica*, iv. 390; Barrois, *Rev. Bib.*, 1930, pp. 265 sqq.).
The Twins are said to occur in the Synagogue at Chorazin (*Bulletin
Amer. Schools of Or. Res.*, Feb. 1928, p. 6).

[4] Pirke Aboth, iii. 18 (astrology [*teḳūphah*] is merely a 'luxury', not
necessary for wisdom). Enoch sees the zodiacal signs revolving in
celestial chariots (Enoch lxxii. 3 sqq., see Charles, *Secrets of Enoch*,
xxx. 3). Cf. the old astrological text edited by Gaster in *P.S.B.A.*, xxii.
329 sqq. On the persisting interest in the zodiac and in seasonal changes,
see Feuchtwang, *M.G.W.J.*, lix. 241–67. The 'zodiacal' figures found
below the Muristan are too dubious (*Q.S.*, 1903, pp. 77 sqq.); but an
interesting example of astronomical activity is to be seen in the late
Byzantine circle from el-Ḥuṣn near Jerash (Séjourné, *Rev. Bib.*,
1900, p. 119; R. Brown, *P.S.B.A.*, 1901, p. 255). See in general Strack
and Billerbeck, ii. 402 sqq.

already in the Targum Pseudo-Jonathan) associating the Twelve Tribes with the twelve signs.[1] Ain Dūk, the Maccabaean Docus, has preserved legends of Joshua, in the shape of the Imam Ali who rode round Jericho and overthrew its walls.[2] Moreover, close at hand is the place where the Twelve Tribes crossed the Jordan; while at Gilgal the twelve stones commemorating the passage long continued to be shown. It is possible, therefore, that this particular mosaic may have been interpreted other than as a zodiac.

The best known and most important of Palestinian mosaics is the map found at Medeba.[3] Dating towards the end of the sixth century A.D., it gives a view of the land from Phoenicia to the south of Beersheba and the border of Egypt. Together with place-names, there are outline representations of distinctive buildings, especially churches. At Gilgal is shown a building with two rows of six stones. Since Medeba was near Mount Nebo it is possible that the mosaic was supposed to suggest the view from Mount Pisgah; although, as Dr. Peter Thomsen points out, Jerusalem and its buildings are depicted as seen by a pilgrim approaching from the west. The geography of the map is based upon the Onomasticon of Eusebius, but there is some knowledge of Jewish tradition. Ebal and Gerizim are located near Jericho, and there is some confusion as to the site of Gilgal, due to rival claims.[4] One of the most curious of the names on the map is Βητομαρσεα η και Μαιουμας, where, following Clermont-Ganneau, we recog-

---

[1] See Skinner, *Genesis*, p. 534 sq. (and Index); Benzinger, *Hebr. Arch.*, p. 257; A. Jeremias, *Babylonisches i. N. T.* (1905), pp. 87 sqq. Cf. also the animal signs as the patrons of the Legions (Domaszewski, *Abhandl. z. Röm. Rel.*, pp. 3 sqq.); and as worshipped by Arab tribes (Abulfaraj, *Hist. Dynast.* [ed. Pococke], p. 101).

[2] See *P.E.F. Archaeol. Res.*, ii. 26; *Q.S.*, 1874, p. 87.

[3] See *Q.S.*, 1897, pp. 167, 213 sqq., 239, 1901, pp. 235 sqq., and for the literature, P. Thomsen, *Z.D.P.V.*, lii (1929), pp. 151 sqq., 156 (p. 161 sq. general remarks, p. 170 sq., the date, p. 172 the maker, p. 173, the source; also *Byzant. Zeitschr.* xxx. 597 sqq.).

[4] See *Rev. Bib.*, 1919, pp. 550, 562; *Reallex. Vorg.*, 'Gilgal', § 2.

nize a locality where communal rites were performed (*Beth-Marzēaḥ*), the scene not only of a fair (*māyūma*), but doubtless also of orgiastic gatherings after the manner of the cult of the not far distant Baal Peor.[1]

Although it may be possible to 'explain away' the zodiac at the synagogue of Ain Dūk—that at Beth Alpha would still remain—the unorthodox character of the Galilaean synagogues has long been the subject of comment.[2] The buildings that have been examined prove to be of one general type and are probably of one period, viz. about second to fourth century A.D., all traces of any of earlier date having disappeared.[3] They are usually oriented towards the north, the entrance being in the south; the Rabbinical tradition which places the entrance in the east may refer to local usage west of Jerusalem.[4] The decoration—particularly at Chorazin (Kerazeh)—goes beyond the bounds of what was considered legitimate, and it has been inferred that the synagogues were founded by rich non-Jewish patrons (cf. Luke vii. 5) who employed their own workmen, and that the Jews—who, it is supposed, could hardly have been responsible for it themselves—were unable or unwilling to protest. On this view it is possible to explain why the decoration seems in some cases to have suffered from later Jewish reaction rather than from anti-Jewish fanaticism, which would presumably have destroyed more, and

---

[1] *Q.S.*, 1901, pp. 239, 369 sqq.; Büchler, *R.E.J.*, 1901, pp. 125 sqq.; see further *Rel. Sem.*, p. 627. For the fair, cf. p. 181 and n. 1.

[2] Edward Robinson (1852), Wilson, Kitchener, &c. See *P.E.F. Survey of Western Palestine* (1881), pp. 294 sqq., 299 sqq.; cf. E. W. G. Masterman, *Studies in Galilee*, pp. 209 sqq.

[3] See Kohl and Watzinger, *Antike Synagogen* (1916); Orfali, *Capharnaüm et ses ruines* (1922); Krauss, *Synagogale Altertümer* (1922), p. 213 sq. (the literature); *M.G.W.J.*, lxv, articles by Grotte (pp. 16–31) and others; Galling, *Z.D.P.V.*, l. 310 sqq. (useful summary); see also Power, *Biblica*, 1925, pp. 100 sqq. (cf. *Q.S.*, 1925, p. 159). Also S. Klein, *Jüdisch-Paläst. Corpus Inscriptionum* (1920).

[4] On the orientation see Krauss, *M.G.W.J.*, lxv. 213 sqq.

especially the distinctively Jewish emblems. On the alternative view, however, the decoration represents an extremely free tendency—possibly at the time when the Jews received favour under Severus and Caracalla (A.D. 193–217) and Galilaean Rabbis were accused of an unpatriotic loyalty to Rome. In agreement with this it can be urged (1) that it is unlikely that all the synagogues were built by non-Jewish friends, (2) that the decoration is Graeco-Oriental and not wholly foreign, and (3) that sometimes (as in the case of the eagles at Yafa near Nazareth) the clumsy carving looks like native work rather than that of skilled workmen from outside.[1]

Needless to say, in the matter of symbols and emblems all Jews were not equally strict. The Zealots—who were Galilaeans—would not carry coins or look at them because of the human figures they bore, and pious Jews would not pass under a gate where there were statues.[2] There was no absolute prohibition of the representation of human figures; and a *stoa* might have figures on it, provided men did not pray to them.[3] But Jewish suspicions were easily aroused, when, for example, Herod was believed to be introducing images in the theatre; and when effigies or images were carried on the ensigns.[4] The Galilaean synagogues go further.[5] We meet with centaurs and hippocamps (especially at Chorazin), sphinxes, half-a-dozen winged genii bearing garlands, and the like. Lions are

[1] See *Q.S.*, 1921, p. 183.

[2] Büchler, *J.Q.R.*, xvii. 67 sqq., 76, 78.

[3] See Krauss, *M.G.W.J.*, lxv. 218 (on the Targum Ps.-Jon., on Lev. xxvi. 1); also Elmslie, *Ab. Zar.*, pp. 74 sq., 190 sq.; Büchler, *Q.S.*, 1923, p. 154; Strack and Billerbeck, iv. 384–414, on the attitude of the synagogue to the non-Jewish world. The seals of the old Rabbis included designs of fish, ship's mast, branch of date-palm, human head, &c.; and medieval writers, at all events, laboured in vain to find a meaning in them (*Jewish Ency.*, 'Seal', vol. xi. 136).

[4] Josephus, *Antiquities*, xv. viii. 1; xviii. iii. 1, v. 3.

[5] Kohl and Watzinger, p. 12, fig. 16, p. 114 sq., fig. 223, p. 199; Orfali, pp. 42 sq., 98.

familiar. A lion and vase *motif* has Mithraic associations, and the fragmentary lion in relief at en-Nebratēn is note-worthy for the curious circles on it.[1] The lion was a per-missible emblem, and appears on the Jewish glasses from Rome. In the Middle Ages it is an ornament on the cupboards containing the Law; and it is interesting to observe that it is explained as a symbol of the strength and power of the Law. Late tradition even averred that the lion appeared on the escutcheons and banners of the kings of Israel.[2] Remains of a striking lion-frieze are still to be seen on the front of the castle of Hyrcanus at ʿAraḳ el-ʿEmīr near Heshbon, the home of the family of Tobiah, famous in Nehemiah's time and later.[3] There was a frieze of animals on the palace of Herod the Tetrarch in Tiberias, and its destruction by iconoclasts, as recorded by Josephus, is a fair illustration of the temper that could be aroused from time to time by departures from strict usage.[4]

Representations of the eagle, common enough outside the Jewish frontier (e.g. Marissa, Petra, Heliopolis), recur in the synagogues (Meiron, el-Jīz, &c.). They are to be seen mutilated at Tell Ḥum (Capernaum), see Pl. xxxviii.[5] The eagle is depicted on a Jerusalem mosaic,[6] and one with out-stretched wings is on a Samarian seal.[7] The eagle was the

[1] For the former, see Orfali, p. 97, fig. 67, and for the latter Kohl and Watzinger, fig. 201.

[2] *Jewish Encyc.*, l.c. For the lion in early Palestine, see above, p. 60.

[3] A descendant is named in the Zeno papyri. See Sir G. A. Smith, *Jerusalem*, ii. pl. xii; Vincent, *J.P.O.S.*, 1923, p. 66 sq.; Driver, *Samuel*, p. xx, and the *Princeton Archaeol. Expedition*, Div. II. § A i. 1 sqq.; Div. III, § A, 1–7. [4] Josephus, *Life*, § 12.

[5] See J. Garrow Duncan, *Q.S.*, 1926, p. 16 sq. and fig. 2 of Plate xxxviii (the two eagles on the keystone of the arch of the central door have been shattered almost beyond recognition). Fig. 1 gives a general view, fig. 5 may be a laver.

[6] Vincent and Abel, *Jerusalem*, ii. 512; also ii. 794 sq., 802, and Taf. lxxix. 5, 6.

[7] *Samaria*, i. 377, pl. lvii, *a* 5. Thureau-Dangin (*Rev. d'Assyr.*, 1927, p. 199) points out how faithfully even the first Sumerian artists repro-duce the wings.

bird of the sun, the symbol of Zeus and of the supreme gods; it was the eagle that bore the souls of the dead to the celestial regions, and on the Arch of Titus the emperor is being taken up to heaven by an eagle.[1] It can be traced back to the Hittites and Babylonia.[2] But it does not seem to occur as an emblem in Carthage, and there are gaps between the old Oriental period and that of Greek influence. None the less, it may well be through the influence of the Syro-Hittite region that the eagle travelled westwards towards Greece, and also was freely accepted again, in the Greek age, in the Syrian lands where the old culture had not died out. When Herod aroused opposition by placing the golden eagle over the Great Gate of the temple it is probable that his act was primarily one of deference to Rome—he also put the eagle on his copper coins; but the eagle was also the symbol of Zeus, and the act served therefore to identify Zeus and Yahweh.[3]

Among the ordinary Jewish objects are rosettes, stars, amphoras, and especially palms (notably at Capernaum).[4] Pomegranates are not necessarily Dionysiac; but at Chorazin, where the ornamentation is especially luxuriant, the friezes depict vintage, wine-press, bunches of grapes, &c.[5] Grape and vine *motifs* are very common in Palestine and Syria;[6] and on the façades of the Tomb of the Kings outside

[1] The eagle in Graeco-Oriental art is discussed by Dussaud, *Mythol. Syr.*, pp. 15 sqq.; Cumont, *Études Syr.*, p. 58 sq., and *Syria*, viii. 164 sq.; Ronzevalle, *Mélanges*, v. ii. 39* sqq.

[2] Garstang, *Hittite Empire*, p. 123. See especially Bacon, *Annual of Amer. Schools*, v. 5, 19, and Dougherty, ib., 37 sqq. (eagle-emblems at Marissa, Petra, and Medain Salih, south of Tēma).

[3] *Ant.*, xvii. vi. 2 sq.; *B.J.*, i. xxxiii. 2 sq.

[4] Kohl and Watzinger, p. 186; Orfali, p. 89 sq. In Christian art the palm becomes a symbol of eternal life (cf. *Z.D.P.V.*, xlii. 179). Old Assyrian usage is preserved in the late Jewish notion that palm-trees have to be married (*hirkīb*), and that they possess a *lēb* or sap-cell (properly 'heart'), Grünbaum, 'Beiträge z. vergleich. Myth. aus d. Hagada', *Z.D.M.G.*, 1877, p. 330 sq., n. 60.

[5] K.-W., p. 200.

[6] *Eph.*, iii. 161, 182, K.-W., p. 186 sq. The Midrash associates the

Jerusalem are garlands, bunches of grapes, sprays of olives, and circles which, it has been suggested, represent flat cakes.[1] Garlands are familiar in non-Jewish art, and recur in Christian art; but the Mishnah tractate on Idolatry looks upon them as heathenish.[2] The knots which are depicted have no doubt lost the apotropaic value which they primarily seem to have had.[3] Distinctively Jewish are the seven-branched candlestick—a symbol of the congregation of Israel;[4] also a pitcher of oil, a pot of manna, trumpet, and *lūlāb*.[5] Still more so are the Pentagram or Seal of Solomon ⛤ and the Hexagram or Shield of David ✡. Like the Heptagram found upon a Babylonian astronomical tablet (? from Nippur) they may be of astral origin.[6] The Pentagram is the more common. It is found at (*a*) Nerab, (*b*) Gerar, (*c*) a jar-handle from Ophel, and a curious type with Hebrew letters in the angles found at (*d*) Tell Zakariya, (*e*) Gezer, and (*f*) Ophel.[7] The legend has been acutely taken to be Shelemau, and identified with

Messiah and the Vine, the latter being a symbol of Israel; cf. Apoc. Baruch, xxxvii, xxxix. 7 (Scheftelowitz, *M.G.W.J.*, lxv. 116).

[1] P. J. O. Minos, *P.S.B.A.*, xxxiii. 19–25.

[2] K.-W., p. 188 sq., *Ab. Zar.*, i. 4; see Elmslie, pp. 7, 92 (Tertullian, *De Idolatria*, ch. xv).

[3] K.-W., p. 190, Orfali, p. 92.

[4] Klein, *M.G.W.J.*, 1921, p. 277.

[5] Orfali, p. 93 sq., cf. also *Rev. Bib.*, 1922, p. 120. The decoration of a fragment of the capital of a pillar at Umm el-Kanātir has suggested that of the pillars of Jachin and Boaz—did the resemblance go further? (Grotte, *M.G.W.J.*, 1921, p. 29 sq.)

[6] Hilprecht, *Explorations in Bible Lands*, p. 529 sq.; for the interpretation, see A. Jeremias, *Old Test. and Ancient East*, i. 37; Benzinger, *Hebr. Arch.*, 3rd ed., p. 162. For the literature, see Kohl and Watzinger, p. 185; Orfali, p. 88; Grotte, p. 27 sq.; *Jew. Encyc.*, i. 546; ii. 251 sq. For the Pentagram, see also Nock's references in *J.E.A.*, xv. 229 n. 2.

[7] (*a*) *Syria*, ix. 306; (*b*) Petrie, p. 19, pl. xliii. no. 10; (*c*) *P.E.F. Annual*, iv. fig. 202, no. 5; (*d*) Bliss and Macalister, pl. lvi, no. 44; (*e*) *Q.S.*, 1904, p. 211 sq., Macalister, *Gezer*, ii. 209, fig. 359, and (*f*) *Annual*, iv. p. 191, fig. 203, no. 7. Cf. also the late inscribed (Arabic) stone from Latron (*Q.S.*, 1919, p. 174).

the Shelemiah of Neh. xiii. 13.[1] The Pentagram is also
used as a potter's mark.[2] At Marissa various pentagrams
and hexagrams were said to be found on the jamb of a door
in one of the tombs, but the latter are very rare.[3] It is the
more remarkable, therefore, that there should be one on
the archaic seal of Joshua son of Asaiah, perhaps as old
as the seventh century B.C.[4]

The most interesting of all the objects depicted in the
synagogues is undoubtedly the coffer or ark on wheels at
Tell Ḥum. It is a structure resembling a temple, with five
Ionic pillars, standing on a base provided with six-spoked
wheels (Pl. xxxviii, figs. 4, 6).[5] It is evident that this is not
'the car of the Patriarch'. There are no traces of horses, no
place for the driver; it is therefore impossible to think of the
vehicle, the *carruca*, used, e.g., by the famous Judah I han-
Nasi (A.D. 135–220), and reserved for conveying princes and
other dignitaries.[6] On the other hand, it is akin to the cupboards and boxes in which the scrolls of the Law were preserved in the synagogues.[7] This, then, is a portable Torah
shrine, the so-called 'Ark' (*tēbhāh*), which, as a matter of
fact, was sometimes taken out of doors, e.g. when there was

---

[1] So Albright, *J.P.O.S.*, vi. 100 sq.

[2] Bliss and Macalister, pl. xxix. no. 42; cf. pl. lvi. no. 53 (from Tell
Sandaḥannah, ib., p. 122 sq.), *Gezer*, pl. cxc. no. 59.

[3] Peters and Thiersch, *Tombs of Marissa*, p. 60. (Opposite is a baetyl
being anointed, ib., fig. 20, see Vincent, *Rev. Bib.*, 1906, p. 319, n. 2
[end].) For the pentagram in the synagogues see K.-W. figs. 54,
59; Orfali, fig. 40; for the hexagram, K.-W., p. 30, figs. 55–57.

[4] Lidzbarski, *Eph.*, ii. 145; Torrey, *J.A.O.S.*, xxiv. 205 (seal of יהושע
בן עשיהו), see p. 46 above.

[5] See K.-W., p. 193 sq., fig. 68; Orfali, pp. 76 sq., 94 sq.; Grotte,
M.G.W.J., 1921, p. 29; Klein, ib., p. 136; Krauss, ib., p. 213; Galling,
Z.D.P.V., l. 313.

[6] See Büchler, *J.Q.R.*, xvi. 100 sq.; *M.G.W.J.*, xlviii. 193 sqq.

[7] Notably at Tell Ḥum, see K.-W., p. 142, and p. 40, fig. 73. Illustrations on glasses from the catacombs show the rolls most clearly, see K.-W.,
fig. 280 sqq., Gressmann, no. 511, and *Jewish Studies ... I. Abrahams* (New
York, 1927) pp. 177 sqq. There is a fine representation of the Ark on
the mosaic of the synagogue at Beth Alpha (*Encyc. Jud.*, iv. 391).

a fast in consequence of drought. Men were said to 'go down' to pray before it for rain.[1] The unique object is the Jewish equivalent of the portable shrines which we have already seen on the coins;[2] and when we consider how familiar the Jews would be with them, or with the cars upon which deities or baetyls were conveyed, we may ask whether they really ceased to have any sacred Ark of their own after the fall of Jerusalem and the exile in the sixth century B. C.[3]

As we move away from the centre of Judaism the influence of other religions upon the Jews is more marked. Among the Jews of Palmyra, the ancient Tadmor, known to history as early as the twelfth century B. C., there occur such names as Levi, Samuel, and Jacob. But in one family, together with Simeon and Marthi (Martha)—whose husband has not a Jewish name—there is a Wahb-allath, i.e. 'gift of Allath', the goddess who in Greek dress becomes Athene;[4] and on a Palmyrene tessara the name Simeon is accompanied with a crescent and star.[5] Various phrases in the Palmyrene inscriptions might suggest Jewish influence, e.g. the close of an inscription upon an altar runs: 'who called upon them in affliction and he answered

[1] See Krauss, *Synagogale Altertümer*, pp. 324, 371 sq.; Strack and Billerbeck, iv. 137; and cf. Oesterley and Box, *Religion and Worship of the Synagogue*, p. 310.

[2] pp. 164 sqq. In general appearance it more closely resembles the covered wagon from Tepe Gawra (near Khorsabad), *Annual of Amer. Schools of Or. Res.*, ix. 34 sq., 53 and fig. 97.

[3] G. H. Box, *Church Quarterly Review*, July, 1925, p. 321, in reference to the Psalms of Ascents to celebrate the accession or procession of the Ark (*arōn*) into the sanctuary, raises the question whether the Ark was merely a memory of the past: the Mishnah *Yōmā* (after A. D. 70) speaks as though there were still an Ark.

[4] Cooke, no. 120. On Jews in Palmyra, see C. Moss, *Q.S.*, 1928, pp. 103 sqq. There was probably a synagogue there, note the Jewish inscriptions, Mittwoch, *Beit. z. Ass.*, iv. 203 sqq.

[5] Lidzbarski, *Ephemeris*, iii. 34.

them [setting them] in a wide place'.[1] The words find an echo in Psalm cxviii. 5. There is a well-known Palmyrene formula: 'to him whose name is blessed for ever, the good and compassionate one.'[2] Although it recalls Psalm lxxii. 19, Daniel ii. 20, a comparison of the inscriptions of Moab, Phoenicia, and North Syria proves that words or phrases which resemble or are identical with those familiar in the Old Testament are not necessarily derived from Hebrews or Israelites. The formula is an interesting one, and if the god is left unnamed it is because he is ineffable, or one that cannot be defined.

It was an age of monotheizing tendencies, and the God of Israel had powerful rivals in the great Baals of Syria. A very important title in the Palmyrene inscriptions is 'lord of the world (*or* of eternity)'. This, too, has a familiar Jewish sound: the 'everlasting El' of Genesis xxi. 33, and the Rabbinic 'lord of the world (or worlds)'.[3] The meaning of these, however, is clear, whereas the Palmyrene title is ambiguous, and there is a good deal to be said for either of the possible interpretations, e.g. a god is sometimes shown holding a globe. But ideas of universality and of eternity readily exchanged or blended in this age of Greek-Oriental speculation, and we may suppose that both interpretations were often combined into one.[4] The title recalls the *Deus aeternus*, applied in Latin inscriptions to the Zeus of Doliche,

[1] Moss, l.c., citing Chabot, *Inscriptions de Palmyre* (1922), p. 80: די קרו לה בעקא וענגן ברוחא. The last word is not clear.

[2] See Cooke, no. 135, לבריך שמה לעלמא טבא ורחמנא. 'Blessed be his name' occurs in a Samaritan bilingual, where the Greek has εἷς θεός (Lidzbarski, *Handbuch*, p. 440 [2]). On 'compassionate', see Lagrange, p. 134; Baudissin, *Kyrios*, iii. 342 sq. For the Palmyrene תירא, 'merciful' (*Z.D.M.G.*, xlviii. 340 n.), Lidzbarski (*Eph.*, i. 79 sq.) reads תיבא, which is found also in Mandaean texts together with 'compassionate'.

[3] *Mārē ʿālmā* in Palm., Rab., רבונו של עולם or העולמים /ר; see Lidzbarski, *Eph.*, i. 257 sq.; Baudissin, op. cit., i. 459 n., iii. 679, 684 sq.; and cf. Zeus Aldemios of Gaza, p. 181 above.

[4] See Cumont, *Comptes Rendus, Acad. d. Inscr.*, 1919, p. 320 sq.; *Rel. Orient*, 2nd ed., p. 203 sq.

but in so far as a *mārē ʿālmā* was a *cosmokrator* it was applicable to any of the supreme gods.

The great anonymous god of the Palmyrene inscriptions is the Sky-Baal, Baal-Shamin. This title was widespread; on the one side it is the Jewish 'god of heaven' (e.g. at Elephantine, p. 143), and on the other, Ioshamin, the demiurge of Mandaean doctrine, replaces Baal by the more specific Io (Iao, Yahweh). It is to be observed that the Sky-god is sometimes conspicuously absent from the national gods.[1] This is because he stands in a class by himself, apart from and over the rest. In the much-travelled story of Achiacharus (named in Tobit i. 21 sq., xiv. 10), Baal-Shamin thunders and stops the sun from rising, he restrains Bel and hinders the moon and stars from appearing. Here he is distinct from Bel, the supreme god of Palmyra whose name comes from Babylonia. The Sky-god as 'lord of the world' is identified on a bilingual with Zeus Megistos Keraunios.[2] On Palmyrene tessarae Bel is accompanied by a sign representing the sun with its beams; yet Bel and Shamash are otherwise named as separate gods.[3] Yet again, in a dedication 'to Bel the god' at Killiz, near Aleppo, there are two large bulls, thus associating Bel with Hadad. As of old, the attributes of Shamash (sun) and Hadad (bull, storm, &c.) were readily combined.[4] The vicissitudes of the Sky-god, too, are of interest for the history of religion, in that the name is sometimes an entirely non-distinctive one for 'deity', just as Zeus, Juno, and other names were wont to be;[5] or he is the supreme god, in which case he is either given a supreme

---

[1] Cooke, no. 112; cf. *Eph.*, i. 255 sq. (See i. 242–60, ii. 122, for Lidzbarski's important article on the Sky Baal.)

[2] Cooke, p. 296. Chabot (op. cit., p. 74) is rather sceptical as to the value of this evidence. At his fine temple at Sī of 33/2 B.C. the god is radiate (*Princeton Expedition*, Div. II, Sect. A, part vi, pp. 374 sqq.; see p. 383 sq.).

[3] Together with the goddess Nanai; Chabot, p. 136, Euting, *Florilegium Vogüé*, p. 238 sq.

[4] Cf. *Syria*, viii. 164, 167 sq.; see p. 131, n. 1. [5] Cf. above, p. 189, n. 4.

position in the physical universe (in the uppermost heaven), or he is entirely incorporeal, outside and independent of the world.[1]

Bel, the pre-eminent god of Palmyra, had his own temple, and an inscription of A.D. 175 refers to the gates which, as befitted a solar god, were of bronze.[2] His consort was the Syrian goddess Atargatis. Similarly at Damascus the chief deities were Hadad and Atargatis: the latter known also as Hera of Damascus, while at Puteoli (Pouzzoles) there was a temple of Jupiter Optimus Maximus Damascenus.[3] Artaxerxes II introduced into Damascus and other important centres of the Persian Empire the cult of Anaitis, a goddess of the Astarte type who is the Nanai of Palmyrene and Greek inscriptions.[4] Neither name can be connected with that of the goddess Anath, in spite of the similarity of their functions.

A far more important centre of religion was Baalbek, whose Greek name Heliopolis designates it the seat of a

[1] See Cumont, *A.f.R.*, ix. 329 sqq. (especially p. 332), on the theologies of the period. The current spiritual teaching of *Ouranos*, as taught by the 'Chaldaean' priests, reminds us of the lofty ethical god Varuna (= οὐρανός), who was known to the Anatolian Hittites and to the Mitannians of N. Syria, *c.* 1400 B.C. This is not the only case where, at the death of the last old Oriental religions, we are reminded of some of the distinctive features of the Amarna Age.

[2] Lidzbarski, *Eph.*, i. 256, 276 sqq. (who identifies Bel with the younger Bel [Marduk] of Babylonia). On the temple see S. B. Murray, jun., *Journ. of Amer. Arch.*, xix. 268–76, and compare the glistening bronze eastern gate of the temple of Jerusalem (Strack and Billerbeck, ii. 623; Morgenstern, *Hebrew Union Coll. Ann.* vi. 1–37).

[3] See Dussaud, *Syria*, iii. 219 sqq. Cf. *C.I.S.*, ii. no. 157 sq., where a Nabataean colony at Puteoli maintains the cult of Dushara (a couple of camels are offered). On Damascus, see Watzinger and Wulzinger, *Damaskus die Antike Stadt* (1921, 1924), and Dussaud, loc. cit.

[4] See *Ency. Bib.*, 'Nanea', and G. Hoffmann, *Auszüge aus syrischen Akten persischer Märtyrer* (1880), pp. 130 sqq. Of two Palmyrene tessarae one reads 'Protect! O Bel, Shamash, Nanai', the other replaces Shamash by *Ḥ-r-th-a* (חרתא—one might expect Hera!), see Euting, *Florilegium Vogüé*, p. 238 sq.

sun-cult.[1] It was the great battle-ground of paganism and Christianity, and old cults of ceremonial prostitution were fanatically maintained to the middle of the fourth century A.D.[2] The double temple, one of the wonders of the world, has been carefully studied.[3] While the larger of the two was presumably dedicated to Hadad or Zeus, it is not easy to decide whether the smaller, on the south, was in honour of Dionysus-Bacchus (so most probably), or of Atargatis, or of a son-god Hermes-Mercury-Adonis (?).[4] We know also that there was a triad Jupiter, Venus, and Mercurius. The Semitic equivalent of the third may be Nebo, or Seimios the male form of Simē (p. 151), or the Palmyrene Malakbel, whose name designates him the angel or messenger of Bel.[5]

[1] The Talmudic and Arab spellings are against any connexion with the Beḳaʿ or valley; although an altar in Rome mentions the god Adados of Libanos and the god Adados of the mountain-top (Zeus, i. 551). I. Lévy (R.E.J., xliii. 192 sqq.) identifies B. with the Talmudic ʿēn Bakī, where there was a ritual 'descent' (yĕrīd; cf. p. 172). If the god was a Baal of Weeping, some have thought of the counterpart Baal Marḳod, the B. of Dancing, at Deir el-Ḳala (p. 151), or of Adonis rites. That Baalbek was renowned for its garlic (Neubauer, Géogr. Talm., p. 298) is doubtful (Levy, Neuheb. Wörterb., iv. 229 b, 521 b).

[2] Cook, Zeus, i. 550 sqq.; Frazer, Adonis, i. 37.

[3] The excavations of the Germans in 1898–1905 are edited by Th. Wiegand; on the cults see especially Winnefeld, ii. 110–28. Haas, Bilderatlas, Urchristentum, nos. 85–8 and p. xi, includes representations of city-goddesses with mural crowns and veils (no. 88 = Wiegand, ii. pl. 40).

[4] See, for the second, Macrobius (cited in Zeus, i. 553), and for discussions of the Heliopolitan temples and cults, Thiersch, Nachrichten of the Göttingen Univ., 1925, pp. 1–24; Ronzevalle, C.R., 1901, pp. 437–82; Seyrig, Litteris, v. 165 sqq., Syria, x. 314 sqq.; Parrot, Syria, x. 120 sqq.

[5] מלכבל, see Cooke, pp. 104, 268 sq. There was a separate temple to Hermes at Baalbek (Winnefeld, p. 124); but when a Latin inscription (C.I.L., xiv. 24) speaks of Jupiter angelus Heliopolitanus 'we can understand how Shamash, Bel, Malakbel, are all really the same chief deity, under various aspects' (Cooke, p. 269). A Latin inscription (from Hungary) commemorates Malacbel, Bebellahamon (B. Hamman?

Malakbel is mentioned along with Aglibol on an important bilingual from Rome; and while the latter (? 'wagon of Bōl'),[1] as a moon-god, has the priority, his associate Malakbel is solar; moreover a third Palmyrene god Yariḥbol, so far from being lunar, as the first part of his name would suggest, was also a sun-god.[2]

The cult of the god of Baalbek spread to Delos by the latter part of the second century B.C., later to Rome and Gaul, finally reaching Magna Carvoran near Greenhead.[3] It is not unlikely that the peculiar sanctity of Thors-day in central Europe may have been facilitated by the god's prominence.[4] He is represented standing between two bulls, and his sheath-like body is panelled with various deities. The complete symbolism is extremely elaborate[5] and has

---

B. of Lebanon?), Benefal (Phanebal?), and Manavat (i.e. the Nabataean Manāt [Manawāt] or 'fate').

[1] Cf. the old Syrian R-k-b-el ('chariot of El'), Cooke, p. 165, Lagrange, p. 509.

[2] *C.I.L.*, iii. 1108: *Deo soli Hierobolo* (Cooke, p. 280). The change from moon to sun might be connected with a change in the calendar (Lagrange, p. 415, n. 8); or is another illustration of the increasing prominence of the solar monotheism of the day.

[3] *Zeus*, i. 551 sq. From Carvoran comes the altar to the Syrian Goddess (Atargatis) erected by men of Hama(th), archers whom Hadrian employed in building the Roman wall. For the cult at Rome see in particular Gauckler, *Le Sanctuaire Syrien du Janicule* (1912), pp. 139 sqq. See pp. 209 sqq. and pl. xxxiv for the snake-encircled deity (?Kronos), cf. Haas, *Urchristentum*, no. 109 (and Atargatis, no. 110).

[4] F. H. Colson, *The Week*, p. 114.

[5] See, further, *Zeus*, i. 552 sqq. Typical is the raised whip (as charioteer of the sun), see *C.R.*, 1902, p. 195. The thunderbolts which Macrobius ascribes to the god are wanting. Dussaud (*Myth. Syr.*, p. 50, n. 1) understands the typical statuette to be the enigmatical 'Balanion' of Heliopolis, as though the word were from ba'lan, 'our Baal' (cf. Marna[s]—Marneion); it is otherwise supposed to be the Greek βαλανεῖον, 'bath' (see *Zeus*, i. 555, n. 3), or it may be derived from a place-name (Baudissin, *Kryios*, ii. 42 n). Between the bulls is to be found a female figure (at Nīḥa), or immediately in front is a herm (*Zeus*, p. 570 and n. 2), this associates Hermes with the god, cf. the messenger-god above, p. 193. The lion-*gennaios* at Heliopolis

the effect of combining in one object, under one Zeus or Jupiter, all the significant gods and goddesses.[1] One of the best examples is remarkable for its novel symbolism (Pl. xxxix, fig. 1).[2] As explained by Cumont, the panels are—reading right to left and downward—(1) Selene-Luna and (2) Helios-Sol, (3) Hermes-Mercury and (4) Athena or rather Ares-Mars, (5) Hera-Juno-Venus and (6) Zeus-Jupiter, and (7) Kronos-Saturn. Now the names read downwards (1, 3, 5, 2, 4, 6, 7) are those of the seven planets in the order of their distance from the earth, while, read across (2, 1, 4, 3, 6, 5, 7), they are the presiding deities of the week. The scheme reflects Pythagorean speculations on astronomy and the gods of the week; and this interest in the planetary week at Baalbek is an illustration of Oriental astral lore, which, indeed, long persisted at Harrān, and has left some traces among the Nosairis. Naturally, it is not an *old* type (this is dated to about A.D. 150); for a more ancient form of Hadad of Baalbek we may probably look at the strange syncretistic figure, perhaps of the Persian age, which includes an Egyptian *uraeus* in the front, two bull's horns, a solar disk, the Egyptian ostrich plumes, and traces of an eagle (Pl. xxxi. 1).[3] If it justifies the tradition (in Macrobius) that the Jupiter Heliopolitanus came from Egypt, it is necessary to remember that interrelations between Egypt and North Syria prevailed intermittently at very much earlier times (cf. p. 93).

(also on the sheath, *Zeus*, i, pl. xxxiii) has the epithet 'protector' (cf. the appeal 'protect' [*aggēn*] on Palmyrene tessarae); in the Arabic form it becomes the familiar *jinn*.

[1] Macrobius (*c.* A.D. 400) preserves the belief that Hadad meant 'one, one', as though it were a reduplicated form of *ḥad* (cf. Syriac *ḥĕdādē*, 'one another'); but the derivation of this very ancient name (with *h* not *ḥ*) is obscure.

[2] See Dussaud, *Syria*, i (1920), 3 sqq.; Cumont, ib. ii. 40 sqq.; also Gressmann, no. 357.

[3] See Dussaud, *Syria*, i. 12, fig. 3. There is a trace of the 'Adam's apple' on both figures; it is the natural sign of an oracle god, and not (as ordinarily interpreted) the Egyptian 'false beard' (Dussaud).

Baalbek, like Damascus, lay near enough to Palestine for its typical Zeus to appear on coins of Neapolis and Eleutheropolis; but another great Baal, that of the old Hittite site of Doliche, between Hieropolis and Marash, is better known outside the land of his birth.[1] Descended from the old Hittite god of storm and war, he is best seen on a monument at Rome where, with double axe in his right hand and a thunderbolt in the left, and wearing the Hittite pointed cap, he faces his consort Atargatis.[2] As is to be seen on another and more complete monument, they stand on their respective animals; and the whole is an instructive illustration of the vitality of old Hittite tradition. Usually Jupiter Dolichenus stands on a bull, he is clad as a Roman soldier, fully armed, with double axe and thunderbolt; he is often accompanied by an eagle and is sometimes beardless (Pl. xxxix, fig. 2).[3] Syrian traders, slaves, and especially soldiers carried his cult as far west as Great Britain (c. A.D. 150–300), and one very striking though much mutilated monument comes from Cilurnum (Chesters).[4] The god is often joined with the Jupiter of Heliopolis, and sometimes with the healing-god Asklepios—there is a curative spring hard by Doliche. Of especial interest is his association with Mithras: his temples are sometimes found close to Mithraic caves. The Dioscuri also appear to be associated with him, and not only can their cult be directly or indirectly traced in the Near East, but it recalls the Nāsatya twins who are named with Mitra and Varuna in a treaty between the Anatolian Hittites and the Mitanni of Syria, c. 1400 B.C.[5] It is possible that the association of the god

[1] *Zeus*, i. 604 sqq.; Cumont, *Études*, pp. 173 sqq.; Gressmann, no. 355 sq.; cf. Frazer, *Adonis*, i. 136. The modern Tell Dülük still has a Mohammedan shrine.

[2] Haas, *Urchrist.*, p. xvi, no. 116 (cf. no. 117, with Helios and Selene).

[3] See Cumont, *Syria*, i. 183 sqq., one of the few examples from the Near East.

[4] The god has also been found once (in or near Marash) in Persian garb (*Zeus*, i. fig. 478).

[5] See above, p. 170. The *Castores Conservatores* are mentioned with

with Mithras, and the eminence of the god of heaven
Ahura-mazda, may have helped to spread his cult.[1] Certainly, like their predecessors of old, these Baals of the opening centuries of the Christian era were no mean gods.
While the priests of Heliopolis hailed their god as Ἥλιε,
παντοκράτορ, κόσμου πνεῦμα, κόσμου δύναμις, κόσμου φῶς,[2] the
god of Doliche is *Deus aeternus*, 'preserver of the whole sky,
a godhead pre-eminent, provider invincible'.[3]

The Roman dress of Jupiter Dolichenus is a familiar
feature and is well illustrated in the wall-paintings discovered in 1920 to the east of Palmyra at Dura-Europos on
the Euphrates.[4] The earlier paintings (about the close of
the 1st cent. A.D.) represent a family sacrificial scene, the
central figure of which is the richly attired Bith-nania,
whose name connects her with the goddess Nanaia-
Artemis who, we know, was worshipped here. A wealth of
detail (conical head-dress, white clothes, bare feet, palm-
branch thrust into the water,[5] &c.) furnish a unique illustration of Palmyrene ritual, and the skill of the artist
(Ilasamsos) testifies to an artistic tradition which (after

Jupiter Dolichenus and Juno; see Cumont, *Études*, p. 353 (who notes
the Anatolian ancestry), and cf. *A.f.R.*, ix. 328.

[1] The Persian god is found on coins of Cilicia, &c., in the 4th cent.
B.C.; Mazdaean inscriptions in Aramaic from Cappadocia of *c.* 2nd
cent. B.C. (Lidz., *Eph.*, i. 69, 73). Evidence for Mithraism in Palestine
is scanty, but a fine typical sculpture of Mithras and the bull was found
in front of the temple of Dushara at Sī in Transjordania (*Princeton Expedition*, Div. II, Sect. A, part vi, p. 398 sq.).

[2] Macrobius I. xxiii. 31. See on this, Cumont, *C.R.*, 1919, p. 322.

[3] *Zeus*, i. 608 sq.: 'The title "Provider Invincible" suggests that he
was, on the one hand, a god who fertilized the earth for the benefit
of men, on the other hand, a being comparable with various semi-
barbaric deities described by the Greeks as "Zeus the Unconquered
Sun".'

[4] Breasted, *Oriental Forerunners of Byzantine Painting*, &c. (Chicago
1924). See now the fine account by Cumont, *Fouilles de Doura-Europos*,
1922–3 (1926). Cf. also Haas, *Urchristentum*, nos. 113 sqq.

[5] Diez (*Archiv f. Orientforsch.*, iii. 126 sq.) interprets this last as the
Babylonian ritual of the water of life.

Breasted) we may regard as the forerunner of Byzantine painting, and whose influence can be traced in the sixth-century mosaics of San Vitale in Ravenna. The later paintings (about A.D. 200) represent an elaborate Roman scene. The Roman tribune, with a liturgical roll in his left hand, is at the head of his troops; an altar stands between him and the Roman standard, and three Roman figures, each with a nimbus, receive the veneration of the soldiers. But though the troops might appear to be paying homage to their lords the triad is a native one. The figure in the middle holds a celestial globe, and reminds us of the Palmyrene 'lord of the world'; he is the Sky Baal, to be identified with the *Zeus Megistos* of the Greek inscriptions found here, and his attendants are presumably Malakbel and Aglibol.[1] In this way Roman loyalty was satisfied and Palmyrene susceptibilities were untouched.

The emperor-cult is an outstanding feature of the age. It has already been illustrated when, as at Aelia Capitolina, the city-goddess holds his bust in her hand.[2] The emperor is the patron of the cult of the Supreme God, the Summus Deus, or Sky Baal; he is the earthly representative of the Sun—indeed, he is on the verge of being the very god himself.[3] Conversely, the great god is *imperator*; the monarchical hierarchy and the divine hierarchy run parallel, and the worshippers are the servants or slaves of their god.[4] The

---

[1] Cf. the military standards on the coin of Septimius Severus (Hill, *Arabia*, pl. xii. 4); at Hieropolis the dove set upon a single standard combines native and Roman use. Among other details to be noticed are the Tyche of Palmyra on her lion (i.e. Atargatis) and the Tyche of Dura: each with nimbus and mural crown. The Euphrates is personified as a young child. At Rome Aglibol is represented as a young Roman warrior; see Clermont-Ganneau, *Rec.*, iii. 270 sqq.

[2] p. 191. See Hill, *Proc. of British Academy*, v. 414.

[3] Cumont, *C.R.*, ix. 323, observes that *c.* A.D. 409 Nectarius writes to St. Augustine: *Deus Summus te custodiat*; the Syrian Baal-Jupiter, once adopted by Commodus, the patron of the cult of Jupiter Summus Exsuperantissimus, has almost become Christian.

[4] Cumont, *Syria*, i. 85; *Doura*, p. 109, n. 6.

emperor cult is quite intelligible. The old gods were losing caste, and the visible emperor of the day was clearly the most tangible power. With the solar monotheism of the age we cannot but compare one of the most striking characteristics of the religion of the Amarna Age (p. 149). Even the decadent femininity of Amenhotep IV Ikhnaton finds its last parallel in Elagabalus of Emesa.[1] Among the 'gods manifest' of the age one will notice how, e.g., to a Demetrius Poliorcetes there will be ascribed all the attributes of the Dionysus incarnate in him, and how the many-sidedness of this man-god—to which Plutarch testifies—answers to the needs of the many who found in him a sufficient ideal.[2] These and many other characteristics of the Graeco-Roman age, the age of the twilight of the old gods, deserve attention if we are to understand the opposition between the old orientalism and paganism and, on the one side, Jewish monotheism, and, on the other, militant Christianity.

Christianity inherited the archaeological characteristics of Judaism as regards the symbols and *motifs* which it accepted or rejected. Yet in several respects it was naturally much freer, in that it grew up in districts where Judaism was weak or non-existent, and where there was already an art tradition ready at hand. And the literary and archaeological phenomena are similar in that when two religions come together there may be (*a*) interchange, or (*b*) repudiation, or (*c*) modification, adaptation, and reinterpretation.[3] We note the retention of Jewish burial lamps (but

[1] Cf. J. S. Hay, *Heliogabalus*, pp. 116, 230, 242, 271.

[2] For the ruler as the visible solar god, cf. W. Weber, *A.f.R.*, xix. 329 n., and for the solar religion of Emesa, Domaszewski, *Abhand. z. Röm. Rel.* (1909), pp. 197 sqq. On Demetrius Poliorcetes, see Kenneth Scott, *Amer. Journ. of Phil.*, xlix (1928), 137–66, 217–39; his dress was astral, it was the world-mantle, as befitted a divine incarnation (pp. 231, 237; Plut. *Dem.*, xli. 4).

[3] For the third, cf. Hill's apt quotation from the advice of Gregory I to the Abbot Mellitus (*Church Quart. Rev.*, lxvi. 119).

with Christian mottoes), eyes, the dove, eagle, crown and garland, nimbus, the *criophorus*.[1] The vine, in particular, readily admitted of a new application.[2] Christianity so frequently presupposes Oriental astral and other lore that it is possible that the idea of Lazarus in the bosom of Abraham goes back, not to Jewish ideas of the heavenly feast, but to more realistic ideas of rebirth through contact with a warm body.[3] In Palestine the Christian antiquities begin in Byzantine times—the most notable being a 'pyx' for the reception of a crumb of Eucharistic bread, given to the dying or deposited with the dead.[4] At the interesting ruins of el-Ḥammam there is adaptation, and a Christian cross takes the place of the *menōrah* or candlestick of the synagogue.[5] Many ancient churches in Hauran reproduce the plan and superstructure of the previous sanctuary or Tycheion.[6] The Marneion of Gaza was turned into a

[1] For the lamps, see Macalister, *Gezer*, i. 366 and p. 87 above; for eyes, ib., pl. cxi. no. 15; cxii. no. 12; and for dove, p. 173 above; for the *archaeological* prototype of the Good Shepherd, see Dussaud, *Myth. Syr.*, pp. 60 sq., 182. Doves, fish, ship, lyre, and anchor were orthodox devices on Christian signet rings (Clement Alex., *Paedog.*, iii. 11 sq.).

[2] Cf. the *Didache*, § 9 (the Eucharistic thanks to the Father 'for the holy vine of thy son David' made known in Jesus), and p. 212 sq. above.

[3] So Baudissin, *Z̧.D.M.G.*, lxvi. 187 sq. (Adonis in Aphrodite's bosom). For the ordinary views see Strack and Billerbeck, ii. 225 sq.

[4] Macalister, *Gezer*, i. 387 sq., and for other examples, ii. 454 sq. Among the more than doubtful cases are Virgin and child in a cave at Beit Leyi (Bliss-Macalister, p. 212); a Palmyrene adoration of the Magi (Chabot, op. cit., p. 68, pl. xxii), also at Dura (Cumont, *Doura*, p. 88); part of a head of the figure of Christ, Jericho (Sellin, pp. 163, 190); a crucifixion scene, Saris (*Q.S.*, 1902, p. 128; cf. 1890, p. 71). The cross in Palmyrene inscriptions seems meaningless (Cooke, no. 137, l. 3, *Eph.*, ii. 294, l. 1; Chabot, p. 81, pl. xxvi. 5).

[5] *Rev. Bib.*, xxx. 438 sqq. (see p. 439), xxxi. 115 sqq. An old pre-Christian cave at Sandaḥannah seems to have been consecrated by the addition of crosses cut on the walls (Bliss-Macalister, p. 263 sq.).

[6] e.g. at eṣ-Ṣanamēn, see H. C. Butler, *Rev. Arch.*, viii (1906), 413 sqq. Cf. Jacob of Serugh (*Z̧.D.M.G.*, xxix. 138): 'henceforth on the summit of mountains they build monasteries in place of the Tycheia

church, and at Baalbek the Christian basilica occupied the site of the old rock-altar. At Caesarea, a Greek inscription commemorates both the basilica of a Christian church and the steps of a Hadrianeion,[1] and compromises of various kinds are equally common in literature and art.

With the Odes of Solomon in literature—to mention only one example of the early varieties of Christianity—we may cite a couple of interesting works of art. One is the fine 'Antioch chalice' containing symbols and emblems which blend old and new tradition, e.g. vine, eagle, basket, hare, butterfly, grasshopper, and the youthful Orpheus-like Christ.[2] The details have been closely studied, and it is instructive to note two opinions. Dr. A. B. Cook, who argues, from the classical side, for a date not far removed from the year A.D. 100, holds that the chalice, 'though essentially Christian, owes certain of its features to pagan antecedents, in particular to Anatolian representations of Zeus and Dionysos'. Prof. B. W. Bacon, on the other hand, pointing out the Oriental analogies, gives weight to the primitive Christian literature of North Syria, the 'Orphic' Christ, the composite religion of Syria in the first centuries of our era, and the sun-temples: 'The symbolism of the chalice is the symbolism of the Syrian sun temples of the Antonines adapted to a Christian sense.' The two opinions

(*bēth gaddē*), on the hills they construct sanctuaries instead of temples to the gods'.

[1] Moulton, *Annual of American Schools*, i. 87 sqq. Also at Gerasa a Christian paves with mosaics 'the propylaea of the Lady Artemis', and the Christian church lies close to the temple and the Nymphaeum (Crowfoot, *Q.S.*, 1929, pp. 20, 36).

[2] Eisen, *The Great Chalice of Antioch* (New York, 1923); B. W. Bacon, *Annual of the American Schools of Oriental Research*, v (1923-4), 1-22; A. B. Cook, *Zeus*, ii (1925), 1197-1210. F. C. Burkitt dates it not before A.D. 200 or rather A.D. 230 (*Cambridge Review*, 1924, pp. 253 sqq., and private information); W. F. Lethaby suggests 4th or 5th cent. (ib., p. 271). Dougherty, *Annual of Amer. Schools*, v. 33 sqq. discusses the symbolism of the basket on the Chalice and on Oriental seals (cf. our Pl. ix, fig. 2).

agree in testifying to the persistence of the old 'Syro-Hittite' cultural interrelations and to the diverse factors concentrating upon an area the importance of which has been frequently exemplified in these pages.

It is, again, an 'Orphic' Christ who should perhaps be recognized on a mosaic dated about the fifth century A.D., and found in 1901, north-west of the Damascus gate of Jerusalem (Pl. xxxix).[1] It represents a very well-known type —Orpheus and his lute; but whereas the Orpheus mosaics usually belong to the western Roman Empire, this was the first to be found in the east, and on what was apparently part of an old Christian burial-ground. There is a complete absence of specific Christian emblems; but the myth of Orpheus charming the wild animals was eagerly accepted by Christianity, and 'the fathers of the Church have frequently been inspired by that graceful allegory to celebrate the happy influence of Christian doctrine on humanity; and the painters of the catacombs have told it many times in their frescoes'.[2] With David as the shepherd and musician, and Christ as the Good Shepherd, reinterpretation was easy, and it was even said that Moses was the teacher of Orpheus, for was he not Musaeus?

[1] Schick and Dickson, Q.S., 1901, p. 233 sq., Vincent, ib., pp. 423 sqq. (from Rev. Bib., x. 436–44). The photograph is from a water-colouring by the Dominican Fathers. Another reproduction (with full discussion) is given by Strzygowski, Z.D.P.V., xxiv. 139 sqq. Below Orpheus are two ladies, Theodosia (holding a lotus) and Georgia: they have nimbus, white crown, and red shoes (a colour reserved for the Virgin and angels). Their identity (? saints, local heroines) is unknown.

[2] Vincent, Q.S., 1901, p. 427 sq. Strzygowski (p. 147) would explain the Orpheus-motif as a guarantee of life beyond the grave. Similarly Bacon (op. cit., p. 11) explains the symbolism of the 'Antioch chalice' as 'the quest of life, appropriate indeed for a vessel meant to contain what Ignatius calls the "medicine of immortality" '. Orpheus, he suggests, has inherited the emblems of Etana of Babylonian myth, who flew to heaven on the eagle, whence the eagle was so favourite a symbol (op. cit., p. 5, n. 4, Etana as Ganymede on an eagle with thunderbolt at Baalbek; p. 10, at Antioch Orpheus, the Good Shepherd of the Etana myth, is borne aloft on eagle's wings).

By the fourth century A.D. the old positive religions of the Near East had almost disappeared.[1] Indeed, it is astonishing that so many archaic beliefs and practices should have survived so long, and that they were especially persistent at such places as Gaza, Baalbek, Antioch, and Harran. Yet, even when one comes down to medieval and modern times, much of the old seems to remain unaltered; the old background can be recognized, 'and the old canvas still shows through the coatings it has received'.[2] Unfortunately, the difficulty of dating so much of the archaeological and other evidence aggravates the attempt to form a clear-cut estimate of the actual stages in the development of religion, whether within the borders of Israel or outside. How tenaciously the genius of Israel held itself aloof—at least in later times—from the surrounding religions can, it is true, be seen more clearly than ever. But it is not easy to determine when the separation began. The archaeological material is miscellaneous and incomplete; relatively little has been done in the way of systematic excavation, especially in the land of Israel itself. Moreover, the interpretation of the archaeological, epigraphical, and biblical evidence involves many delicate questions of the origins and evolution of religion and religious movements.

Yet there are two conclusions which can safely be drawn. (1) The land of Israel—Palestine itself—is in completest touch—archaeologically—with the larger area of which it is an organic part; but (2) it has an individuality of its own. There is, in fact, a certain protest or reaction against other religions, even those which best enable us to understand Israel. In close contact with Egypt but un-Egyptian, lying at the tail end of states which were bound up with Mesopotamia and Anatolia, and, throughout, exposed to the incursions of desert tribes, the small land must hammer

---

[1] A. B. Cook (*Zeus*, i. 167) observes that at that time 'a momentous transformation was already in progress by which Christian saints gradually usurped the position of pagan gods and demi-gods'.

[2] S. A. Cook, *Religion of Ancient Palestine* (1908), p. 114; cf. above, p. 7 sq.

out its own career or be swallowed up. The evidence seems to show that the exclusiveness and creativeness, the self-consciousness, one might say, which characterize the religion of Israel date from an early if not pre-Israelite period.[1] The early religion was certainly not that of the prophets, nor was it merely one with the surrounding religions. It had distinctive features of its own, but it was not the religion which has given the Old Testament its worth. In other words, non-Israelite and pre-Israelite conditions of life and thought supplied the material which the great reforming minds of Israel, at certain epochs, reshaped and invested with a fuller content, thereby giving the religion, or rather, the thread of the religious development, a permanent value.[2]

All this, however, involves questions outside the scope of these pages; the present task has been confined to the endeavour to show what archaeological research is contributing to our knowledge of Palestine, and how profoundly it is affecting our Biblical and other problems, cutting across, as it does, many old-time divisions. The archaeological argument is admittedly incomplete; and there is need of further research, and further investigation freed of all efforts to prove *this* or disprove *that*, 'for there remaineth yet very much land to be possessed'.

[1] See Index, *s.v.* 'Hebrew: Individuality'.

[2] It must suffice to draw attention, in a footnote, to some of the more noteworthy results of the preceding survey: the marked practical aspects of the old religions (see Index, *s.v.* 'Fertility'); the significant Dionysian and Apolline traits; the evidence for 'son' and young deities (Index, *s.v.* Young gods'), and the 'Intermediaries' and 'Triads' (Index, *svv.*). The religion of Israel developed in the very midst of a world wherein there were implicit and explicit ideas of no little wealth and complexity.

BIBLIOGRAPHY AND ABBREVIATIONS

THE list includes useful literature and works cited in a more or less abbreviated form. English and French works, unless otherwise specified, are published in London and Paris respectively. Students will easily understand the method employed in referring to the most frequently used sources: the splendid collection of illustrations in Gressmann's *Altorientalische Bilder* (cited as Gressmann, no.—); the seals published by Contenau, Ward, and Weber; the coins, mostly of the British Museum and edited by G. F. Hill; the epigraphical and archaeological material published by Clermont-Ganneau, G. A. Cooke, and Lidzbarski (in particular the *Ephemeris* of the last mentioned); the works on Palestinian excavations in general, by Handcock, and in particular by Hugues Vincent; the references made, in the case of individual sites, either to the name of the site or to that of the excavator (e. g. Gezer *or* Macalister; Beth-Shan *or* Rowe). Some account of the progress in excavation is given periodically in the *Revue Biblique*, *Quarterly Statements* of the Palestine Exploration Fund, *Syria*, *American Journal for Archaeology*, *Archiv für Orientforschung*, *O.L.Z.*, and *Z.D.P.V.* There is a good bibliography in Gressmann's book (cited above); see also Peter Thomsen (below).

Abodah Zarah. See Elmslie.
Abrahams, I. *Schweich Lectures*, 1922; *Campaigns in Palestine from Alexander the Great*, 1927.
Académie des Inscriptions.
Aeg. Z. Zeitschrift für ägyptische Sprache.
Aimé-Giron, *Bulletin de l'Institut Français d'Archéologie*, xxv (1925), 191–211. (See above, p. 108, n. 1.)
Ain Shemesh, excavation of. See Mackenzie and Grant.
A.J.S.L. American Journal of Semitic Languages.
Alte Orient, Der. Series of useful popularizing studies on Oriental subjects. Leipzig, 1899–.
Amarna Letters or Tablets. See Knudtzon.
American Journal of Philology.
American Schools of Oriental Research. See *Annual*, *Bulletin*.
Ancient Egypt.
Angelos.
Annual of the American Schools of Oriental Research.
Annual of the Palestine Exploration Fund.
Antike, Die.
Arch. Anz. Archäologischer Anzeiger.

A.f.R.; Arch. f. Rel.   Archiv für Religionswissenschaft.

Archiv für Orientforschung.

Askalon, excavation of. See p. 172, n. 2.

Baalbek. See p. 15, n. 5, and p. 219, n. 3.

Bāb ed-Drā', excavation of. See p. 92, n. 1.

Badé, W. F. Excavation of Tell en-Nasbeh. See p. 96, n. 3.

Baikie, James. *The Amarna Age: A study of the crisis of the ancient world.* 1926.

Ball, C. J. *Light from the East, or the Witness of the Monuments.* 1899.

Barton, G. A. *Archaeology and the Bible* (Philadelphia, U.S.A., 4th ed., 1925). Profusely illustrated.

Baudissin. *Adonis und Esmun: eine Untersuchung zur Geschichte des Glaubens an Auferstehungsgötter und an Heilgötter.* Leipzig, 1911.

Kyrios als Gottesname im Judentum und seine Stelle in der Religionsgeschichte, ed. by O. Eissfeldt. Giessen, 1926–9.

Baudissin Festschrift. Beiheft zur Z.A.T.W., xxxiii. Giessen, 1918.

Beisān. See Beth-Shan.

Benzinger, I. *Hebräische Archäologie.* Leipzig, 1927, 3rd ed. (431 illustrations).

Beth-Shan. Reports by Alan Rowe in *Museum Journal* and *Q.S.* See p. 94, n. 2.

Beth-Shemesh. Excavations by Mackenzie and Grant (qq. v.).

Bevan, E. R. *Ptolemaic Egypt. A History of Egypt under the Ptolemaic dynasty.* 1927.

The House of Seleucus. 1902.

'Syria and the Jews', *C.A.H.,* viii. ch. xvi.

Bliss, F. J. *A Mound of Many Cities, or, Tell el-Hesy excavated.* 1894.

Bliss, F. J., and R. A. S. Macalister. *Excavations in Palestine during the years 1898–1900. With a chapter by Dr. Wünsch.* 1902.

Bonnet, H. *Die Waffen der Völker des Alten Orients.* Leipzig, 1926.

Bouchier, E. S. *Syria as a Roman Province.* Oxford, 1916.

Breasted, J. *Ancient Records of Egypt: Historical Documents.* 5 vols. Chicago, 1906. (References are made to the sections.)

Brünnow, R. E., and A. von Domaszewski. *Die Provincia Arabia.* Strassburg, 1904.

B.S.A.J. British School of Archaeology in Jerusalem.

Bulletin of the B.S.A.J.

Bulletin of the American Schools of Oriental Research.

Burkitt, F. C. *Schweich Lectures,* 1913; *Jewish and Christian Apocalypses,* 1914.

Schweich Lectures, 1926; III, *Petra and Palmyra,* 1929.

Byblus, excavations of. See p. 93, n. 1.

C.A.H. The Cambridge Ancient History.

C.A.H., Pl. The Cambridge Ancient History, Plates (two volumes).

Chabot, J. B. *Choix d'Inscriptions de Palmyre traduites et commentées.* 1922.

C.I.S. Corpus Inscriptionum Semiticarum. Paris, 1885–.

    i. *Phoenician inscriptions.*

    ii. *Aramaic inscriptions.*

Clermont-Ganneau. For seals referred to under his name, see *Journal Asiatique*, 1883, i. 123 sqq., 506 sqq.; ii. 304 sq.

Les Fraudes Archéologiques en Palestine. 1885.

Album d'Antiquités Orientales. 1897.

Recueil d'Archéologie Orientale. 1888–1907. (A number of the studies appear in English in the *Q.S.*)

Études d'Archéologie Orientale. 1890, 1897.

Contenau, G. *La Glyptique Syro-Hittite.* 1922. (262 seals, here referred to under his name.)

La Civilisation phénicienne. 1926.

Les Tablettes de Kerkouk. 1926.

Manuel d'Archéologie Orientale, depuis les origines jusqu'à l'époque d'Alexandre, i. 1927.

Cook, Arthur Bernard (Queens' College, Cambridge). *Zeus: A Study in Ancient Religion*, i. 1914; ii. 1 and 2, Cambridge, 1925. (Frequently cited as *Zeus*.)

Cook, Stanley Arthur (Gonville and Caius College, Cambridge). *The Religion of Ancient Palestine in the Second Millennium B.C., in the light of Archaeology and the Inscriptions.* 1908.

Cooke, George Albert (Christ Church, Oxford). *A Text-Book of North-Semitic Inscriptions*, Oxford, 1903. (Frequently cited as Cooke, with references to the page or the number of the inscription.)

Cowley, A. E. *Schweich Lectures*, 1918: *The Hittites*, 1920.

Aramaic Papyri of the fifth century B.C. Oxford, 1923. (Referred to as Elephantine Papyri.)

Crowfoot, J. W., and G. M. FitzGerald. 'Excavations in the Tyropoeon Valley, Jerusalem', *P.E.F. Annual*, v (1927). 1929.

Cumont, F. *Études Syriennes.* 1917.

Fouilles de Doura-Europos. 1926.

Les Religions Orientales dans le Paganisme Romain. 3rd ed., 1929. (Numerous articles in *Syria*, &c.)

C.R. Comptes Rendus (de l'Académie des Inscriptions).

Dalman, G. H. 'The Khazneh at Petra', *Annual of the P.E.F.*, i. 95–107. 1911.

Petra und seine Felsheiligtümer. Leipzig, 1908.

Neue Petra-Forschungen und der heilige Felsen von Jerusalem. Leipzig, 1912. (Numerous articles in the *Palästina-Jahrbuch*.)

Damascus. See p. 218, n. 3.

Deissmann, Festgabe für. Tübingen, 1927.

Driver, S. R. *Schweich Lectures*, 1908: *Modern Research as illustrating the Bible*, 1909.

Duncan, J. Garrow and R. A. S. Macalister. 'Excavations on the Hill of Ophel, Jerusalem, 1923–5', *P.E.F. Annual*, iv. 1926.

Dura, paintings at. See p. 223, n. 4.

Dussaud, R. *Notes de mythologie Syrienne.* 1903–5.

Les Monuments palestiniens et judaïques. (*Musée du Louvre*.) 1912.

Les Origines Cananéennes du Sacrifice Israélite. 1921.

Dussaud, R. (*cont.*) (Numerous articles in *Syria*, including vi. 334 sqq. on the dates of Hebrew seals.)

E(ncy.) Bib. Encyclopaedia Biblica. 1899–1903.

Ebert, Max. *Reallexikon der Vorgeschichte.* Berlin, 1924–9.
Vorgeschichtliche Forschungen. Berlin, 1924–.

Eckenstein, Lina. *A History of Sinai.* 1921.

Eiselen, F. C. *Sidon: a study in Oriental history.* New York, 1907.

Elephantine papyri. See Cowley.

Elmslie, W. A. L. *Mishnah, 'Abodah Zarah, The Mishna on Idolatry.* With translation, notes, &c. Cambridge, 1911.

Eph(emeris). See Lidzbarski, *Ephemeris für Semitische Epigraphik.*

Euting, J. *Nabatäische Inschriften aus Arabien.* Berlin, 1885.
Sinäitische Inschriften. Berlin, 1891.
(Also contributor to *Florilegium Vogüé.*)

Fleming, W. B. *The History of Tyre.* New York, 1915.

Florilegium Melchior Vogüé. See Vogüé.

Frank, K. *Bilder und Symbole babylonischer Götter.* Leipzig, 1906.

Frankfort, H. *Studies in the Early Pottery of the Near East.* (Occasional Papers, No. 6, of the Royal Anthropological Institute. 1924–7.)

Frazer, Sir James George. *The Golden Bough: A Study in Magic and Religion,* 3rd ed., 1911–20. References are made to the twelve volumes, numbered consecutively (i and ii = *The Magic Art and the Evolution of Kings,* vols. i and ii; vol. iii, *Taboo*; vol. v sq., *Adonis, Attis, Osiris*; vol. vii sq., *Spirits of the Corn and of the Wild*).
Folk-lore in the Old Testament, 3 vols. 1918.

Galling, K. *Der Altar in den Kulturen des Alten Orients.* Berlin, 1925. (Also articles and summaries in *Z.D.P.V.*)

Garstang, J. *The Land of the Hittites.* 1910.
The Hittite Empire: a survey of the history, geography and monuments of Hittite Asia Minor and Syria. 1929.
The Syrian Goddess; being a translation of Lucian's 'De Dea Syria', with notes and introduction. 1913.

Gauckler, *Le Sanctuaire Syrien du Janicule.* 1912.

G.B. See Frazer, *Golden Bough.*

Gerar (Tell Jemmeh). See Petrie.

Gezer. See R. A. S. Macalister, *The Excavation of Gezer,* vols. i and ii text, vol. iii plates.

Grant, Elihu, Excavations at Beth-Shemesh. *Quart. Statement of the P.E.F.* 1929, Oct., pp. 201 sqq.; *Annual of the American Schools of Oriental Research,* ix (1929), 1–16.

Gray, G. B. *Sacrifice in the Old Testament: its Theory and Practice.* (Posthumous.) Oxford, 1925.

Gressmann, Hugo. References are made by number alone to his *Altorientalische Bilder zum Alten Testament,* 2nd ed., Leipzig, 1927 (678 illustrations, with descriptions, extensive bibliography, indexes and map).
Altorientalische Texte zum Alten Testament. 2nd ed., Leipzig, 1926.

Gressman, Hugo (*cont.*). *Die Lade Jahves und das Allerheiligste des Salomonischen Tempels.* Berlin, 1920.

Die hellenistische Gestirnreligion. Leipzig, 1925.

'Die Sage von der Taufe Jesu und die vorderorientalische Taubengöttin', *Archiv für Religionswissenschaft*, xx. 323–359.

'Dolmen, Masseben und Napflöcher', in *Zeit. f. Alttest. Wissenschaft*, xxix (1909), 113–28.

Orient. Rel. im hellenist. röm. Zeitalter, Berlin, 1930.

Grohmann, A. 'Göttersymbole' (*Denkschriften d. Wiener Akad., Phil. hist.*, lviii. 1). Vienna, 1914.

Groot, J. de. *Die Altäre des Salomonischen Tempelhofes.* Stuttgart, 1924.

Haas, Hans. *Bilderatlas zur Religionsgeschichte.* Leipzig, 1924–6.

Ägyptische Rel. (H. Bonnet); *Rel. d. Hethiter* (Zimmern); *Bab.-Ass. Rel.* (Landsberger); *Umwelt des Urchristentums* (Joh. Leipoldt).

Handcock, P. S. P. *The Archaeology of the Holy Land.* 1916.

Haupt, Paul, *Oriental Studies in Commemoration of.* Baltimore, Leipzig, 1926.

Hay, J. S. *The Amazing Emperor Heliogabalus.* 1911.

Head, B. W. *Historia Numorum: A manual of Greek numismatics.* Oxford, 1911.

Hehn, J. *Die biblische und die babylonische Gottesidee.* Leipzig, 1913.

Hempel, J. 'Westliche Kultureinflüsse auf das älteste Palästina', *Palästina-Jahrbuch*, xxiii (1927), 52–92.

Hill, G. F., *Catalogue of the Greek Coins of Palestine (Galilee, Samaria and Judaea)* (British Museum). 1914.

Catalogue of the Greek Coins of Phoenicia (British Museum). 1910.

Catalogue of the Greek Coins of Lycaonia, Isauria and Cilicia (British Museum). 1910.

Catalogue of the Greek Coins of Arabia, Mesopotamia (British Museum). 1922.

'Adonis, Baal and Astarte', *Church Quarterly Review*, lxvi (1908), 118–41.

'Some Graeco-Phoenician Shrines', *Journal of Hellenic Studies*, xxxi (1911), 56–64.

'Some Palestinian Cults in the Graeco-Roman Age', *Proceedings of the British Academy*, 1911–12, pp. 411–27.

See Mark the Deacon.

How to Observe in Archaeology. (Trustees of the British Museum, 2nd ed.)

Hogarth, D. G. *Carchemish.* 1914.

Hittite Seals, with particular reference to the Ashmolean collection. Oxford, 1920.

Schweich Lectures, 1924: *Kings of the Hittites.* 1926.

Hommel, F. *Ethnologie und Geographie des Alten Orients.* Munich, 1904, 1926.

Hoonacker, A. van. *Schweich Lectures*, 1914: *Une communauté Judéo-Araméenne à Éléphantine, en Égypte, aux vi^e et ve siècles av. J.C.* 1915.

Hunkin, J. W. *Schweich Lectures*, 1926: *II. From the Fall of Nineveh to Titus.* 1929.

Jastrow, Marcus. *Dictionary of the Targumim*, &c.

Jastrow, Morris. *Aspects of Religious Belief and Practice in Babylonia and Assyria.* New York, 1911.

The Civilization of Babylonia and Assyria. Philadelphia, 1915.

Bildermappe zur Religion Babyloniens und Assyriens. Giessen, 1913.

Jeremias, A. *The Old Testament in the light of the Ancient East: manual of Biblical Archaeology.* 1911.

Handbuch der altorientalischen Geisteskultur. Leipzig, 1928.

Jeremias, J. *Golgotha.* Leipzig, 1926.

Der Gottesberg. Gütersloh, 1919.

Jericho. See Sellin, and p. 92, n. 3.

Jerusalem (Ophel). See Crowfoot and Duncan.

J.A. Journal Asiatique.

J.A.O.S. Journal of the American Oriental Society.

J.B.L. Journal of Biblical Literature.

J.E.A. Journal of Egyptian Archaeology.

J.P.O.S. Journal of the Palestine Oriental Society.

J.Q.R. Jewish Quarterly Review.

J.R.A.S. Journal of the Royal Asiatic Society.

J.S.O.R. Journal of the Society of Oriental Research.

J.T.S. Journal of Theological Studies.

K.A.T. Die Keilinschriften und das Alte Testament. 3rd ed., by H. Zimmern and Hugo Winckler. Berlin, 1903.

Karge, P., *Rephaim: die vorgeschichtliche Kultur Palästinas und Phöniziens.* Paderborn, 1918, 1925.

Kerkuk, Kerkouk. See Contenau.

Kittel, R. *Studien zur hebräischen Archäologie und Religionsgeschichte.* Leipzig, 1908.

Geschichte des Volkes Israels. 1923. (Vol. i. valuable summary of archaeological results).

Knudtzon; *Die El-Amarna Tafeln mit Einleitung und Erläuterungen.* With notes, &c., by O. Weber and E. Ebeling. 2 vols. Leipzig, 1915.

Kohl, H. and C. Watzinger. *Antike Synagogen in Galiläa.* Leipzig, 1916.

Kohn. *Mitteilungen d. Anthropol. Gesellschaft,* xxxiv (1919), 81–135. (Early Palestinian culture in its relation to the Levant.)

Krauss, S. *Synagogale Altertümer.* Vienna, 1922.

K.-W. See Kohl and Watzinger.

Lagrange, P. M.-J. *Études sur les Religions Sémitiques.* 2nd ed., Paris, 1905.

Lammens, 'Les Sanctuaires Préislamites', *Mélanges de l'Université.* Beirut, xi (1926), 37–173.

'Le culte des Bétyles', *Bulletin de l'Institut franç. d'Archéologie Orientale,* xvii (1920), 39–101.

(Numerous archaeological notes in the *Mélanges . . . Beirut.*)

Legrain, Leon. *The Culture of the Babylonians from their seals in the collection of the University Museum, Philadelphia.* 2 vols., 1925. (Numerous seals, a number of which are said to have come from Gezer, p. 75).

Leipoldt, J. *Die Religionen in der Umwelt des Urchristentums;* in Haas, *Bilderatlas zur Religionsgeschichte.* Leipzig, 1926.

Lévy, Isidore. 'Cultes et rites Syriens dans le Talmud', *Revue des Études Juives,* xliii. 183–205.

Levy, J. *Chaldäisches Wörterbuch über die Targumim.* Leipzig, 1867.
Neuhebräisches und Chaldäisches Wörterbuch. Leipzig, 1876–89, 1924.

Levy, M. A. *Siegel und Gemmen.* Breslau, 1869.

Lidzbarski. *Handbuch der nordsemitischen Epigraphik nebst ausgewählten Inschriften. i. Text, ii. Tafeln.* Vienna, 1898.
Ephemeris für semitische Epigraphik (frequently referred to as *Eph.*). 3 vols. Giessen, 1900–15.

Littmann, E. *Semitic Inscriptions.* Part iv of the publications of an American Expedition to Syria in 1899–1900. New York, 1904.
Nabataean Inscriptions. Publications of the Princeton Expeditions to Syria. Division iv, Section A. Leyden, 1914.

Liv. A.A.A. Liverpool Annals of Archaeology and Anthropology.

(Pseudo-) Lucian. 'The Syrian Goddess.' An abstract is given in A. B. Cook, *Zeus,* i. 582–4. Translation with notes by J. Garstang (see above).

Macalister, R. A. S. *The Excavation of Gezer, 1902–5 and 1907–9.* Vols. i and ii letterpress, vol. iii plates. 1912.
Schweich Lectures, 1911 : *The Philistines, their History and Civilization.* 1913.
A Century of Excavation in Palestine. 1925.
and Bliss. *Excavations in Palestine, 1898–1900.* 1902.
and T. G. Duncan. *Excavations on the hill of Ophel, Jerusalem, 1923–5.* 1926.

Mackenzie, Duncan. 'The Megalithic Monuments of Rabbath Ammon at Ammān', *P.E.F. Annual,* i. 1911, 1–40.
'Excavations at Ain Shemesh (Beth-Shemesh)', i. 1911 (pp. 41–94), and ii. 1912–13.

Madden, F. M. *History of Jewish Coinage and Money in the Old Testament.* 1864.
Coins of the Jews. 1881.

Mallon, Alexis. *Les Hébreux en Égypte.* Rome, 1921.

Mareshah, Marissa. See p. 202, n. 1.

Mark the Deacon, *Life of Porphyry, Bishop of Gaza.* Translated with notes, &c., by G. F. Hill. Oxford, 1913.

Megiddo (Tell el-Mutesellim). See Steuernagel, Watzinger.

Meissner, B. *Babylonien und Assyrien.* Heidelberg, 1920.

Mélanges de la Faculté Orientale. Beirut.

Meyer, Eduard. *Geschichte des Altertums.* 2nd ed., i (1907–9), ii. 1 (1928).
Die Israeliten und ihre Nachbarstämme; mit Beiträgen von B. Luther, Halle a.S., 1906.
Reich und Kultur der Hethiter. Berlin, 1914.

Meyer, M. A. *Gaza.* New York, 1927.

Müller, W. Max. *Asien und Europa nach altägyptischen Denkmälern.* Leipzig, 1893.

Egyptological Researches, 1904–6. Washington, 1906.

Egyptian Mythology. 1924.

Museum Journal. (The references are to Alan Rowe's reports on Beth-Shan.)

Mutesellim, Tell el-. 1. *Fundbericht, erstattet von G. Schumacher, herausgegeben von C. Steuernagel. A. Text, B. Tafel.* Leipzig, 1908.
2. *Die Funde, bearbeitet von C. Watzinger.* 1929.

M.D.O.G. Mitteilungen der Deutschen Orient-Gesellschaft zu Berlin.

M.G.W.J. Monatsschrift für Geschichte des Judentums.

M.V.A.G. Mitteilungen der Vorderasiatischen Gesellschaft.

en-Nasbeh, excavation of. See Badé.

Nielsen, Ditlef. *Der dreieinige Gott in religionshistorischer Beleuchtung.* Copenhagen, 1922.

Handbuch der altarabischen Altertumskunde, i. Copenhagen, 1927.

Ohnefalsch-Richter. *Kypros, the Bible and Homer.* 1893.

Ophel. See Jerusalem.

Orfali. *Capharnaüm et ses ruines.* 1922.

O.L.Z. Orientalistische Literaturzeitung.

Pal. Jahrb. Palästina-Jahrbuch.

P.E.F. Palestine Exploration Fund.

P.E.F., Annual. Annual of the P.E.F.

P.E.F., Q.S. Quarterly Statement of the P.E.F.

Pennsylvania Museum, Journal. Cited as *Museum Journal.*

Perrot and Chipiez. *History of Ancient Art: Phoenicia and Cyprus (1885); Sardinia, Judaea, &c. (1890).*

Peters, J. R. and H. Thiersch. *Painted Tombs in the necropolis of Marissa (Mareshah).* 1905.

Petra, excavation of. Bachmann, Watzinger, and Wiegand. Leipzig, 1921. See also Brünnow, Dalman, and p. 15, n. 5.

Petrie, Sir Flinders, *Gerar.* 1928.

Hyksos and Israelite cities. 1906.

Researches in Sinai. 1906.

Tell el-Hesy (Lachish). 1891.

Philo Byblius, or P. of Byblus. See Baudissin, *Studien zur semit. Religionsgeschichte* i. 1–46, Leipzig, 1876, and art. 'Sanchuniathon', *Real-Encyklopädie f. prot. Theologie und Kirche.* (Leipzig, 1906–.)
Lagrange, *Études des Religions Sémitiques,* pp. 396–437.
Paton, *Encycl. of Religion and Ethics,* 'Sanchuniathon'.

Phythian-Adams, W. J. *Guide-book to the Palestine Museum of Antiquities.* Jerusalem, 1924.

Piana, George La. 'Foreign Groups in Rome during the First Centuries of the Empire', *Harvard Theological Review,* 1927, pp. 183–403.

Pietschmann, R. *Geschichte der Phönizier.* Berlin, 1889.

Princeton. Publications of the Princeton University Archaeological Expeditions to Syria in 1904–5 and 1909.

Prinz. *Altorientalische Symbolik*. Berlin, 1915.

P.S.B.A. Proceedings of the Society of Biblical Archaeology.

P.W. Pauly-Wissowa, Real-Encyclopädie der classischen Altertumswissenschaft.

Q.S. Quarterly Statements (of the Palestine Exploration Fund).

Reallexikon der Assyriologie, ed. Ebeling and Meissner.

Reallexikon der Vorgeschichte. See Ebert.

Rec. See Clermont-Ganneau, *Recueil d'Archéologie Orientale*.

Reifenberg, A. *Palästinensische Kleinkunst* (1927). 157 illustrations.

Reisner, Fisher, and Lyon. *Harvard Excavations at Samaria*, 1908–10. 2 vols, Cambridge, U.S.A., 1924.

Rel. Sem. Religion of the Semites, by W. Robertson Smith, 3rd ed. 1927.

Renan. *Mission de Phénicie.* 1864–74.

Répertoire d'Épigraphie sémitique. 1900–.

Rev. d'Ass. Revue d'Assyriologie.

Rev. Arch. Revue Archéologique.

Rev. Bib. Revue Biblique.

Rev. Hist. Rel. Revue de l'Histoire des Religions.

Reinach, T. *Jewish Coins.* 1903.

Rhein. Mus. Rheinisches Museum für Philologie.

Ridgeway, W., Essays and Studies presented to. Cambridge, 1913.

Robertson, D. S. *Handbook of Greek and Roman Architecture* (pp. 220 sqq.; bibliography, pp. 374 sqq.). Cambridge, 1929.

Roeder, Günther. *Ägypter und Hethiter.* (*Der Alte Orient*, xx.) Leipzig, 1919.

Röscher. Lexicon d. griech. u. röm. Mythologie.

Ronzevalle. Many articles in the *Mélanges de la Faculté Orientale*. Beirut.

R.E.J. Revue des Études Juives.

R.E.S. Répertoire d'Épigraphie sémitique.

Samaria, excavation of. See Reisner.

Sanchuniathon. See Philo Byblius.

Saulcy, F. de. *Numismatique de la Terre Sainte.* 1874.

Schürer, E. *Geschichte des jüdischen Volkes im Zeitalter Jesu Christi.* 3rd ed. Leipzig, 1898.

Sellin, E. *Tell Ta'annek.* Vienna, 1904.
 Eine Nachlese auf dem Tell Ta'annek in Palästina. Vienna, 1905.
 Reports on excavation of Shechem. See p. 92, n. 3.

Sellin, E. and C. Watzinger. *Jericho.* Leipzig, 1913.

Sellin. *Festschrift.* Leipzig, 1927.

Serabiṭ (el-Khādim) excavation of. See p. 91, n. 2.

Seyrig. 'La triade héliopolitaine et les temples de Baalbek'. *Syria*, x. 314–56.

Shechem, excavation of. See p. 97, n. 1.

Shiloh, excavation of, See p. 96, n. 2.

Smith, Sidney. *Babylonian Historical Texts relating to the capture and downfall of Babylon.* 1924.
 Early History of Assyria to 1000 B.C. 1928.

Smith, William Robertson. *Religion of the Semites.* 3rd ed., with introduction and notes by S. A. Cook. 1927.

Steuernagel. *Tell el-Mutesellim*, i. Leipzig, 1908.

Strack and Billerbeck. *Kommentar zum Neuen Testament aus Talmud und Midrasch.* Munich, 1922–8.

Syria: Revue d'Art Oriental et d'Archéologie, 1920–.

S.B. Sitzungsberichte (of the Universities of Berlin, &c.).

S.B.A. Society of Biblical Archaeology.

Taanach, Tell Ta'annck, excavation of. See Sellin.

Thiersch, H. Articles in the *Archäologische Anzeiger* of the *Jahrbuch des kaiserlichen deutschen Archäologischen Instituts.* 1907, cols. 275 sqq.; 1908, cols. 3 sqq., 343 sqq., and elsewhere. See Peters.

Thomsen, Peter. *Kompendium der Palästin. Altertumskunde.* Tübingen, 1913.
Die neueren Forschungen in Palästina-Syrien. Tübingen, 1925.
Die Palästina-Literatur: eine internationale Bibliographie in systematischer Ordnung mit Autoren- und Sachregister. Leipzig, 1908–.
(Numerous articles in Ebert's *Reallex. Vorgesch.*, and summaries in *Z.D.P.V.*)

T.S.B.A. Transactions of the Society of Biblical Archaeology.

Vincent, H. *Canaan d'après l'Exploration Récente.* 1907.
Jerusalem sous Terre. 1911.
La Peinture Céramique Palestinienne. (From *Syria* v. 1924.)
(Numerous reports and reviews in the *Revue Biblique*: see pp. 53, n. 5; 128, n. 4).

Vogüé. *Mélanges d'archéologie Orientale.* 1868.
Inscriptions Sémitiques: Syrie centrale. 1868–77.
Florilegium Melchior de Vogüé. 1909.

Vorgeschichtliches Jahrbuch. Edited by Max Ebert, i. 1926 (Berlin and Leipzig). Bibliography and summaries.

Waddington and Le Bas. *Voyage Archéologique.* (The proper names in the Greek and Latin inscriptions are indexed by Chabot in the *Revue Archéologique*, 1896.)

Ward, William Hayes. *The Seal Cylinders of Western Asia.* Washington, 1910. (1315 are illustrated, described, and classified.)

Watzinger. *Tell el-Mutesellim.* ii. *Die Funde.* Leipzig, 1929.
and Kohl. *Antike Synagogen in Galilaea.* Leipzig, 1916.
and Sellin. *Jericho.* Leipzig, 1913.
and Wulzinger. *Damaskus, die antike Stadt.* Leipzig, 1921.

Weber, Otto. *Altorientalische Siegelbilder;* i. *text,* ii. *abbildungen* (*Der Alte Orient*, xvii–xviii. Leipzig, 1920. (596 seals, reference is made to them by the name alone.)
Die Kunst der Hethiter (*Orbis Pictus*, no. 9).
Altorientalische Kultgeräte. M.V.A.G., xxii. 370 sqq.

Wiegand, T. *Baalbek.* Berlin, 1921.
(with Bachmann and Watzinger). *Petra.* Leipzig, 1921.

Wiener, H. *The Altars of the Old Testament. Beigabe z. Orientalistischen Literaturzeitung*, 1927.

Wijngaarden, W. D. van. 'Karacter . . . van den God Resjef. *Mede-deelingen, Rijksmuseum van Oudheden te Leiden*, x (1929).

Wood, W. C. 'The Religion of Canaan.' *Journal of Biblical Literature*, xxxv (1916), 1–121, 163–279.

Wroth, W. *Catalogue of the Greek Coins of Galatia, Cappadocia and Syria.* 1899.

Zeno Papyri. See p. 202, n. 4.

Zeus. See Cook, Arthur Bernard.

Z.A. Zeitschrift für Assyriologie.

Z.A.T.W. Zeitschrift für die Alttestamentliche Wissenschaft.

Z.D.M.G. Zeitschrift der deutschen morgenländischen Gesellschaft.

Z.D.P V. Zeitschrift des deutschen Palästina-Vereins.

CHRONOLOGICAL TABLE.[1]

B.C.   PRE-HISTORIC. The 'Galilee skull' (p. 73).

4000–3000 Egypt and SW. Asia in contact (cf. *Camb. Anc. Hist.* i. 258, 274 sq., 580 sq.). Transition from stone to

3000–2500 EARLY BRONZE. Royal tombs of Ur. Fourth Egyptian Dynasty: Egypt and Byblus already in close touch. Palestine already 'Semitic'.

2770–2670 Syro-Phoenician coastlands reached by the Sumerian Lugal-zaggisi of Erech (2776), and the Semites Sargon (2750), and Narām-Sin (2670).

2600   Gudea of Lagash.

2500–2000 ANCIENT CANAANITE BRONZE AGE. Macalister's *Pre-Semitic Gezer.*

2300–2200 Amorite phase begins. *Middle Egyptian Empire (c. 2400–2000). Middle Minoan I.*

2169–   *First Babylonian (or Amorite) Dynasty.* Period of Cappadocian tablets.

2067–25 Hammurabi. *Golden Age of Babylonia and Egypt. Presumed age of Abraham.*

2000–1600 MIDDLE CANAANITE BRONZE AGE. Macalister's *Gezer, Semitic I.*

1926   Raid of Anatolian Hatti on Babylonia.

1800–1700 Hyksos invasion of Egypt. Non-Semitic Kassite Dynasty in Babylon (1746). *Gezer, Semitic II.*

1600 (or 1550)–1200 LATE CANAANITE BRONZE AGE. *New Egyptian Empire* (XVIIIth Dynasty 1580–1346). Egypt in Asia. 'Golden age of Palestinian pottery'. Strong Aegean influence. *Late Minoan I.*

1500   Thutmose III (1501–1447); battle of Megiddo, 1479. Kerkuk seals.

1400   Amenhotep III (1412–1376). *Gezer, Semitic III* (? 1600–1350).

1375   Amenhotep IV (Ikhnaton). Amarna period (p. 5, n. 1). Akkadian the *lingua franca.* Decline of semi-Iranian Mitanni. Strength of Anatolian Hatti. Anti-Egyptian movements (Hatti Amorites, the Habiru). Disorder in Palestine.

1360   Tutankhamen.   *The Mosaic Age. Entry and* ↑

1350   Egyptian XIXth Dynasty (1346–1210). *settlement of Israelites.* ↓

1321   Seti I (1321–1300) re-establishes power of Egypt in Palestine. Egypt *versus* Hatti.

1288   Battle of Kadesh (on the Orontes). Ramses II (1300–1233), treaty with Hatti (1272). *Middle Assyrian Period.*

1225   Merneptah (first mention of Israel, 1221). Movements in the Levant against Egypt and Hatti.

1200–600 IRON AGE. RECENT CANAANITE (or EARLY PALESTINIAN PERIOD). *Sub-Minoan Age.* Egyptian Twentieth Dynasty (1205–1100), after a brief anarchy. Ramses III (1204–1172). Cultural continuity along Palestinian coast ('Philistine' phase of earlier ware); decline in the interior. Weakening of Egyptian authority in Palestine, Phoenicia, and Sinai. Independence of Delta states. Post-Hatti

---

[1] This list is compiled for working purposes only. See further the synchronistic tables in the *Cambridge Ancient History*, the classification of pottery by Vincent and others (*Union Académique Internationale; Revue Biblique*, 1923, pp. 272–5; *Q.S.*, 1923, pp. 54 sq., 201; Dussaud, *Syria*, ix. 139).

B.C.

culture in north (Carchemish, &c.). Assyria striking westwards; Tiglath-Pileser I reaches Phoenicia (1115).

1000 Macalister's *Gezer, Semitic IV.* 'Philistine' age followed by the Israelite. Independent states (Israel, Edom, Damascus). North Semitic alphabet in use. Israel (Saul, David, and especially Solomon) closely involved in surrounding political events.

930 Egypt (Shishak) invades Palestine.

860 Israel, Phoenicia, Damascus, &c., combine against Assyrian encroachment. (Foundation of Samaria, *c.* 880.)

850–840 Disturbances in S. Palestine; Moab (Chemosh) revolts. Break-up of the Anti-Assyrian league. Israel (under Jehu Dynasty, 842–841) renounces Phoenicia (Baal of Tyre) and Damascus (Hadad). Rivalry of Assyria and Urarṭu (Armenia) affects Syria. Israel nearly overwhelmed by Damascus.

750 Strength of Israel (Jeroboam II) and Judah (Uzziah). Rise of Hebrew prophecy (Amos). Aramaean states (Sam'āl, &c.), Damascus (fall 732), and Samaria (fall 722) controlled by Assyria. Egypt *versus* Assyria conditions the internal history.

701–700 Defeat of Egypt, &c., at Eltekeh; siege of Lachish and of Jerusalem; Judah despoiled. Activity of northern hordes. Revival of Urarṭu. Rise of Medes. Increase of intercourse with the west.

675–650 Assyria in Egypt. Cuneiform tablets of Gezer (650).

630–625 Scythian and nomad movements. Decline and fall of Assyria (Nineveh 612). Egypt *versus* Neo-Babylonia; victory of the latter at Carchemish (605).

600–300 MIDDLE PALESTINIAN AGE. *Neo-Babylonian period* (612–539). Archaistic revival. Decline in pottery. Fall of Jerusalem (586). Effect of the 'exile' upon internal conditions obscure. Paucity of historical data.

539 *Persian Period* (to 332). Persian empire includes Babylonia (Egypt and SW. Asia) and Media.

500–400 Period of the Elephantine papyri. Jews enjoy Persian favour. Period of restoration and reconstruction. Egypt *versus* Persia. Persia looking to Ionia and Greece. Greek influence spreading east.

333–332 *Alexander the Great.*

312, Oct. Seleucidan era begins. Ptolemies *versus* Seleucids. Ptolemy seizes Palestine and Phoenicia.

300–50 RECENT PALESTINIAN PERIOD. Deep Hellenistic influence. Revival of Babylonia.

276 Intermittent Egypto-Syrian wars. (217, battle of Raphia, peace between Ptolemy IV and Antiochus III).

247 *Parthian (Arsacid) era begins.*

200 Seleucid control of Coele-Syria.

175 Hellenization of Jerusalem (under Jason). *Antiochus the Great.* Invasion of Egypt (169), sweeping religious standardization (167).

167 Persecution of the Jews. *The Maccabees.*

164, Dec. 25. Rededication of the altar at Jerusalem.

B.C.

160   Parthian conquests (Mithridates I, Philhellene).

145–140   Jewish expansion (Joppa, Samaria, &c.). Native Jewish coinage. Hasmonaean independence.

142–141   Babylonia becomes Parthian. Fresh spread of Persian religion and of 'Chaldaean' lore.

135–104   John Hyrcanus I. Growth of Judaean state (Samaria, Beth-Shan, &c.).

92   Parthia and Rome in contact.

69   Aristobulus.

65   Pompey annexes Syria.

50 B.C.–A.D. 300 (or 350) ROMAN PERIOD.

40   Antigonus Mattathias.

37 B.C.–A.D. 4 Herod the Great.

A.D.

6–   Roman Procurators. *Nabataean and Palmyrene inscriptions.*

30   *Rise of Christianity.*

66   *First Revolt of the Jews.*

70   Capture of Jerusalem by Titus.

106   Trajan controls Palmyra and the Arabian desert. *Sinaitic inscriptions.*

132–5   *The Second Revolt (Bar Cocheba).*

135   AELIA CAPITOLINA. Hadrian (A.D. 117–38).

138–61   Antoninus Pius, emperor.

173–217   Julia Domna of Emesa.

193–211   Septimius Severus, emperor. *Period of Dura-Europos* (p. 223).

218–22   Elagabalus. Archaic coin-types, &c.

253–60   *Sasanian period.*

260   Persian movement westwards. Palmyra temporarily controls eastern Roman empire.

323–36   Constantine the Great. Recognition of Christianity.

331–63   Julian. Brief revival of old Oriental cults. Period of transformation (p. 229 and n. 1).

350–640   BYZANTINE PERIOD.

400   Destruction of the Serapeum (391) and of the Marneion (401).

616   Persian conquest of Syria and Palestine.

622   Islam (the Hegira).

640   ARABIAN PERIOD.

GENERAL INDEX

The arrangement ignores the geographical prefixes Tell (mound), Jebel (mountain), &c., and the Arabic article (el-).

The following letters are used after the entries to indicate the nature of the reference: *c* (cult scene), *d* (name of a deity), *i* (inscription), *m* (monument), *s* (the owner of an inscribed seal), *sym* (symbol).

PLATE I

1. DOLMEN AT EL-MAREIGHĀT, WADY ZERKA MA'IN

2. SARĪR NEBI SHEM'A

PLATE II

THE 'ROCK', JERUSALEM. LOOKING DOWN FROM THE GALLERY
TOWARDS THE SOUTHERN GATE

Photo by the American Colony, Jerusalem

PLATE III

1. OLD ROCK-ALTAR, JERUSALEM

2. CUP-MARKED SURFACE OF OLD ROCK-ALTAR,
JERUSALEM

PLATE IV

1. ROCK-CARVING NEAR
DAHARIYEH

2. ALTAR WITH 'HORNS' (?), GEZER

PLATE V

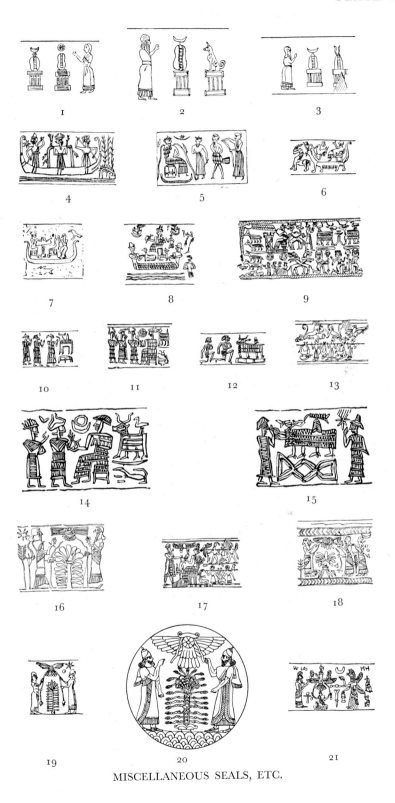

MISCELLANEOUS SEALS, ETC.

PLATE VI

1. SARCOPHAGUS OF AḤIRAM, BYBLUS

2. TRIADS OF PILLARS
AT PETRA

3. SEAL FROM THE
SHEPHELAH

PLATE VII

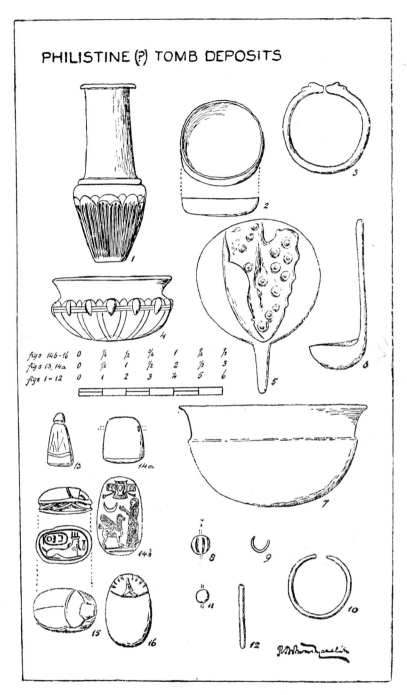

PHILISTINE (?) TOMB DEPOSITS

'PHILISTINE' TOMB IV, GEZER

PLATE VIII

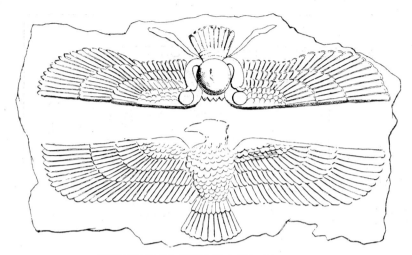

1. PHOENICIAN WINGED DISK AND EAGLE

2

3

4

SEALS FROM GEZER

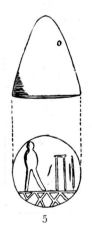

5

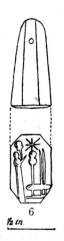

6

½ in.

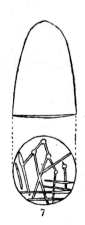

7

SEALS FROM TELL EṢ-ṢĀFI

PLATE IX

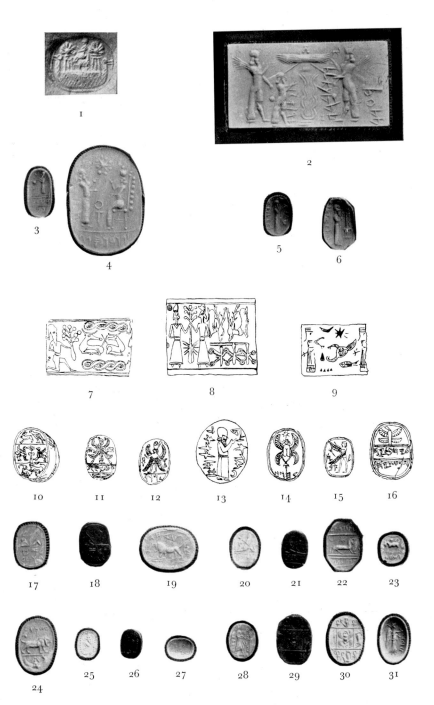

MISCELLANEOUS SEALS

PLATE X

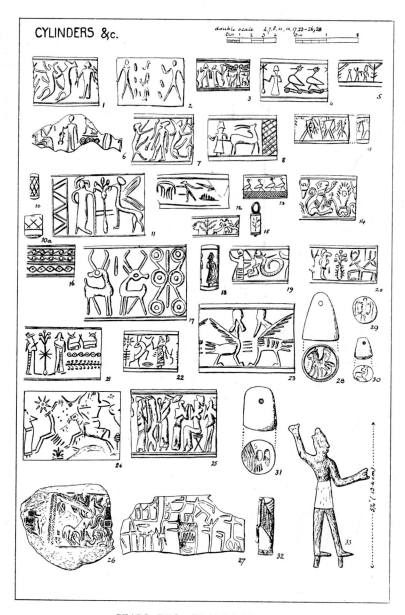

SEALS, ETC., FROM GEZER

PLATE XI

INCENSE-BURNER(?), TAANACH

PLATE XII

1. CUNEIFORM TABLET WITH SEALS, GEZER

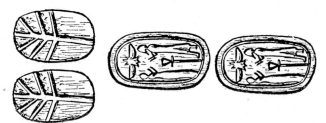

2. THE SEALINGS ON THE GEZER CUNEIFORM TABLET

3. SECOND CUNEIFORM TABLET WITH SEALS, GEZER

PLATE XIII

1. SEAL, TELL EṢ-ṢĀFI

2. SEAL, TELL ESH-SHIHĀB

3

4

5

6

MISCELLANEOUS SEALS

PLATE XIV

1. CARVED LIMESTONE OBJECT, JERUSALEM

2. CARVED LIMESTONE OBJECT, JERUSALEM

PLATE XV

1. SEAL, BETH-SHAN

2. SEAL, GEZER

3. SEAL, OPHEL

4. SEAL, GEZER

5. SEAL WITH CONFLICT SCENE,
TELL ZAKARIYA

PLATE XVI

ROCK SCRIBINGS IN A GEZER CAVE

PLATE XVII

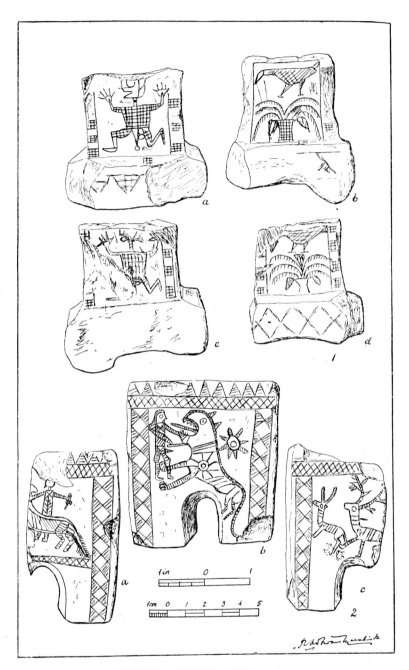

'VOTIVE ALTARS', GEZER

PLATE XVIII

1. 'VOTIVE ALTAR', GEZER

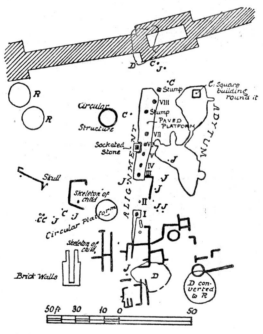

C = Cup-mark in the Rock   D = Troglodyte Dwelling

J = Jar-buried Infant   R = Reservoir for Water

2. GROUND-PLAN OF THE ALINEMENT, ETC.,
GEZER

PLATE XIX

PART OF ALINEMENT OF STONES, GEZER

PLATE XX

REMAINS OF TEMPLE OF MEKAL, LOOKING SOUTH-EAST, BETH-SHAN

PLATE XXI

MAṢṢEBAH IN TEMPLE OF BETH-SHAN

PLATE XXII

PLATE XXIII

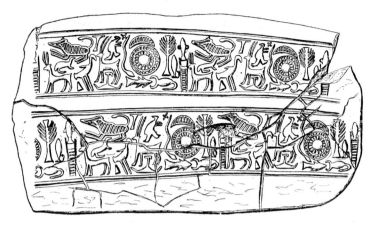

1. DRAWING OF THE GEZER TABLET

2. LIVER TABLET, GEZER

PLATE XXIV

1. GODDESS ANATH, BETH-SHAN

2. KADESH BETWEEN MIN AND
RESHEPH, ANATH BENEATH
(*British Museum*)

3. KADESH WITH MIN AND RESHEPH
(*Louvre*)

4. ASI THE WAR-GODDESS
(*Berlin*)

PLATE XXV

1. AMON AND MUT. PTAH,
KHNUM AND SETEKH
(*Berlin*)

2. RESHEPH, 'GREAT GOD
HEARING PRAYER'
(*Berlin*)

3. RAMESES II AND SETEKH, BETH-SHAN

PLATE XXVI

1. COMMON TYPE
OF WAR-GOD
(? RESHEPH)

2   3

'PILLAR' TYPE OF IDOL, GEZER

PLATE XXVII

1. GODDESS, BETH-SHAN

2. ASTARTE, BETH-SHAN

3. VEILED GODDESS, GEZER

PLATE XXVIII

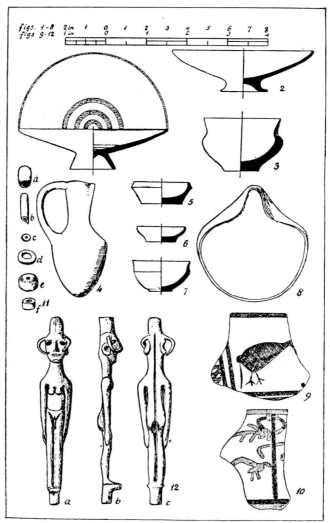

1. GEZER TOMB-DEPOSIT INCLUDING 'HORNED' GODDESS

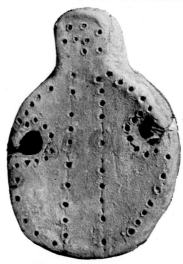

2. CONVENTIONAL ASTARTE-PLAQUE, GEZER

PLATE XXIX

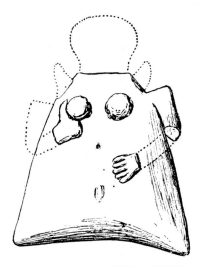

1. 'ASTARTOID' VASE, GEZER

2. PHOTOGRAPH OF POTTERY SHRINE, GEZER

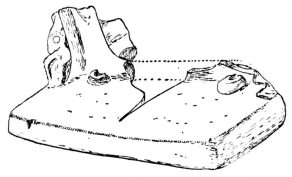

3. DIAGRAM OF POTTERY SHRINE

PLATE XXX

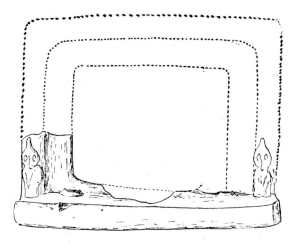

1. DIAGRAM OF POTTERY SHRINE, GEZER

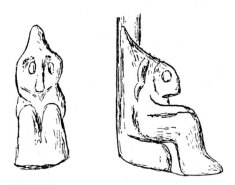

2. FIGURE ON THE POTTERY SHRINE

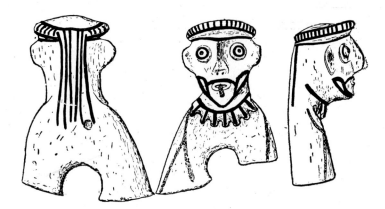

3. POTTERY FIGURE, GEZER

PLATE XXXI

1. LATE SYNCRETISTIC HADAD-TYPE   2. THE GOD OF TAHPANHES

3. TRIPTOLEMUS IN HIS CAR (FROM NEAR BYBLUS)

PLATE XXXII

'YAHU' AS A SOLAR ZEUS

PLATE XXXIII

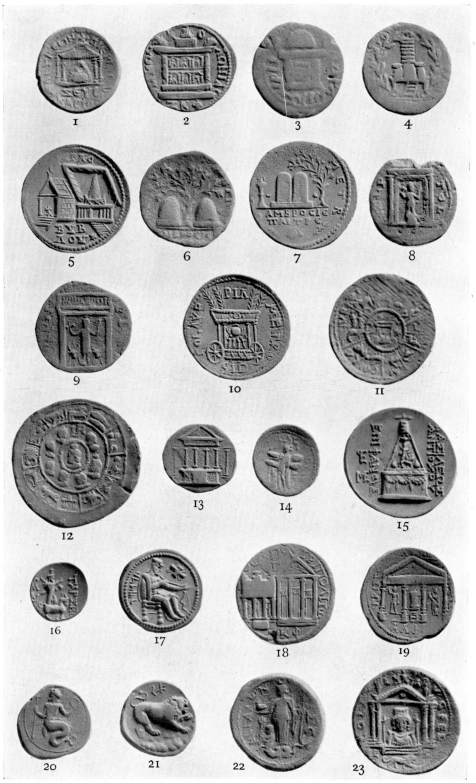

MISCELLANEOUS COINS

PLATE XXXIV

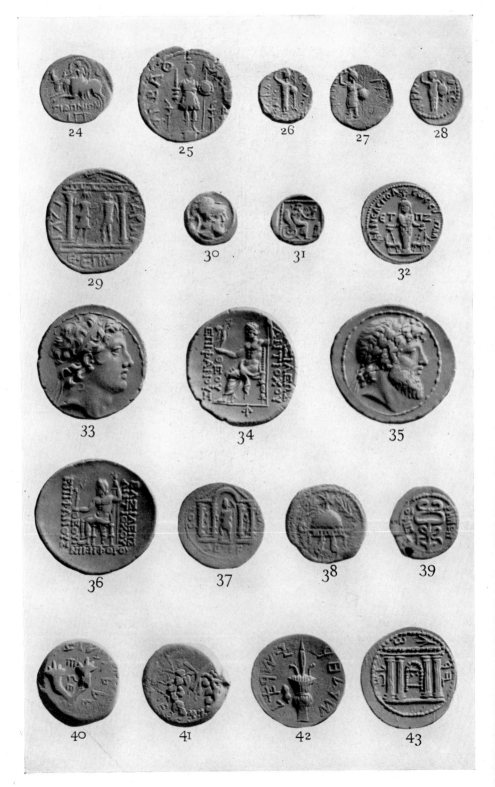

PLATE XXXV

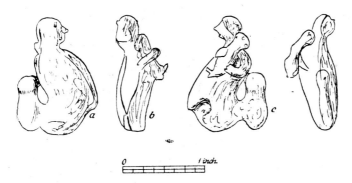

1. FISH-GODDESS (?), TELL ZAKARIYA

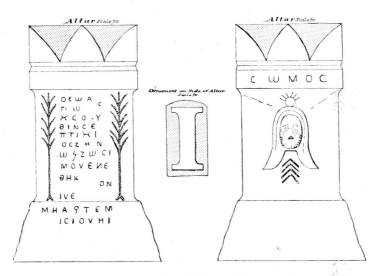

2. ALTAR FROM KADESH-NAPHTALI

PLATE XXXVI

2. THE GODDESS OF TELL
SANDAḤANNAH

1. GREEK INSCRIPTION FROM
MT. HERMON

PLATE XXXVII

PORTIONS OF A SYNAGOGUE MOSAIC AT AIN DŪK

PLATE XXXVIII

1–5. SYNAGOGUE REMAINS, TELL ḤŪM (CAPERNAUM)

6. THE WHEELED COFFER, CAPERNAUM

PLATE XXXIX

1. JUPITER
HELIOPOLITANUS

2. JUPITER OF DOLICHE

3. 'ORPHEUS MOSAIC', JERUSALEM

PRINTED IN GREAT BRITAIN AT THE UNIVERSITY PRESS, OXFORD
BY JOHN JOHNSON, PRINTER TO THE UNIVERSITY